Dr Royston Lambert studied history at Cambridge and Oxford and was a Nuffield Scholar at the LSE. He was a Fellow of King's College, Cambridge for eight years and later Principal of Dartington Hall, Devon. He published extensively on historical, sociological and educational matters. For the last few years he lived in Greece where *Beloved and God* was conceived and written. Dr Lambert died shortly after completing this book.

BELOVED AND GOD

THE STORY OF HADRIAN AND ANTINOUS

ROYSTON LAMBERT

A PHOENIX GIANT PAPERBACK

First published in Great Britain
by George Weidenfeld & Nicolson Limited in 1984
This paperback edition published in 1997
by Phoenix, a division of Orion Books Ltd,
Orion House, 5 Upper St Martin's Lane,
London WC2H 9EA

A CIP catalogue record for this book is available
from the British Library.

ISBN: 1 85799 944 4

Printed and bound in Great Britain by
Butler & Tanner Ltd, Frome and London

FOR
BARBARA AND MAURICE

CONTENTS

ILLUSTRATIONS

41 Hadrian (a) pursues (b) confronts the lion of Libya, bronze medallions

42 'Antinous the god', a final pagan challenge to Christianity? Contorniate of *c.* 384

43 The infamous ephebe-god of Antinoopolis reconciled with Christianity? Stele from Antinoopolis, Staatliche Museen, Berlin

44a Entrance gate of Antinoopolis as seen by Jomard in 1789–1800

44b The entrance to the theatre

45a 'A perpetual peristyle', the ruins of Antinoopolis, looking east from the river, as seen by Jomard

45b All that was left of the main street in 1913

46 Medallions and coins of Antinous: from Arcadia (a) (b) (c); from Chalcedon (d); from Alexandria (e) (f)

47 Medallions and coins of Antinous: from Bithynion (a) (b) (c) (d); from Tion (e); from Corinth (f)

48 Medallions and coins of Antinous: from Tarsos (a) (b); from Smyrna (c) (d); from Adramyttion (e); from Stratoniceia (f)

49 Early bust from Patras by a Greek artist, from Athens National Museum (*Photo Museum*)

50 Early bust from Patras by a Roman artist, Athens National Museum (*Alinari*)

51 Portrait or caricature? The bust now at Kansas City (*Photo Museum*)

52 A fifth-century BC inspiration: the Apollo of the Tiber, Roman copy now in Museo delle Terme, Rome (*Alinari*)

53 Statue of Antinous now in the Bank of Italy, Rome (*German Archaeological Institute, Rome*)

54 Another fifth-century BC inspiration: the Doryphoros of Polycleitos, Roman copy, Naples National Museum (*Alinari*)

55 Statue of Antinous in the Naples National Museum, 'the Farnese' (*Alinari*)

56 Antinous as an Egyptian god, from the Museo Gregoriana-Egizio, Vatican, Rome (*Alinari*)

57 Head of Antinous as Egyptian god from Dresden

58 The serene and compassionate god-man; cool and smooth workmanship from Rome: detail of the Sala Rotonda Dionysos (*Alinari*)

59 The innocent and divine adolescent: crisp and lively workmanship from Greece: detail of the Delphi statue (*Ecole Française d'Archéologie, Athens*)

60 Antinous the god: the colossal statue of Antinous-Dionysos in the Sala Rotonda of the Vatican, 'the Braschi' (*Alinari*)

Acknowledgement is gratefully made to the above copyright owners for permission to reproduce the pictures.

EMPERORS OF ROME

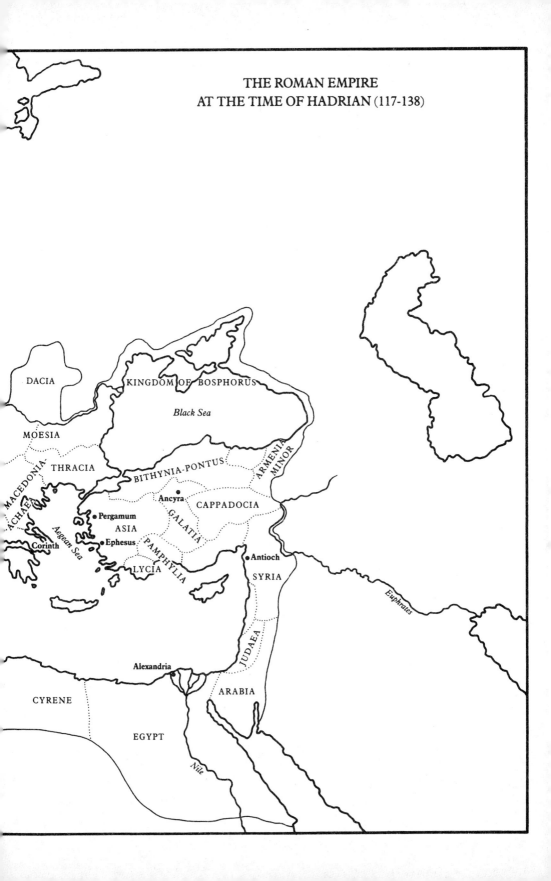

THE ROMAN EMPIRE
AT THE TIME OF HADRIAN (117-138)

DACIA

KINGDOM OF BOSPHORUS

Black Sea

MOESIA

MACEDONIA

THRACIA

BITHYNIA-PONTUS

ARMENIA MINOR

ACHAEA

Ancyra

CAPPADOCIA

Pergamum

ASIA

GALATIA

Aegean Sea

Corinth

Ephesus

PAMPHYLIA

LYCIA

Antioch

SYRIA

Euphrates

JUDAEA

Alexandria

ARABIA

CYRENE

EGYPT

Nile

FOREWORD

Like most people who visit the great collections of Europe, I had long been
familiar with the distinctive face of Antinous. I had also learnt something about
his relationship with Hadrian and its amazing aftermath from the discreet
notes of museum catalogues spiced with the sniggering anecdotes of their
guides. From time to time I read various accounts, moving or lurid, of the
affair in which fact and fiction always seemed to be inextricably woven. All the
while I had naturally assumed that, somewhere, this notorious, bizarre and
artistically creative episode of ancient history had been thoroughly written up.
When, however, I came to search out such a comprehensive book about it, I
had to go back a century to that written in German by an industrious
Norwegian professor, Lorentz Dietrichson, in 1884. Though, I found, there
had been plenty of scholarly treatises since then covering aspects of the
posthumous cult and art of Antinous and many novelistic, poetical and
dramatic interpretations of the relationship between him and Hadrian, no one
for a hundred years had attempted factually to reconstruct the extraordinary
story as a whole or to explain fully and frankly the issues it raises.

Boldly then I decided that I would repair this strange deficiency – only to
discover very rapidly why it existed. He who dares to piece together this story
not only has to be master of the two ancient languages and the five principal
ones of modern Europe (leaving aside exotic excursions into modern Greek,
Serbo-Croat and Polish) but has omnisciently to grapple with the findings and
techniques of specialised fields of knowledge: of the political, religious and
sexual history of Greece and Rome, of archaeology and Egyptology, epi-
graphy, textual analysis, numismatics, iconography and art history. With
help, I could just about cope with the languages, but for the substance I have
often had to draw on the primary labours of others. Indeed, I have had to stride
through vast fields of scholarship, leaping the hedges which divide them,
picking other men's flowers while trying to recognise their weeds and avoid
their stinging nettles. Even after this exertion, the results woven together soon
wither from a triumphant garland of knowledge into a lopsided crown of

xvii

thorns. What little can be gathered about the unusual life and mysterious death of Antinous as an enigmatic human being compares painfully with the relative abundance of information about his subsequent career as the last god of the ancient world. Even then, around virtually every point of the story which seems to have been established, doubt and controversy begin to swirl. No wonder writers have been daunted by the prospect of vast labour for such apparently meagre and disputatious results and have turned to imaginative fiction as the best way to fill the gaps and solve the riddles found in the history.

More extraordinary still, the same is broadly true for the other protagonist, Hadrian. Every schoolboy knows the name and some of the achievements of one of the greatest emperors of Rome. But no thorough biography, based on scholarship, has appeared in English since Henderson's of 1923 and that is neither comprehensive nor penetrating. In any language, the basic study is still the German one of Weber published in 1907. Of course, there is a huge and steadily increasing body of academic monographs and articles about aspects of his life, reign and work: but the very scale and complexity of it all seems to defy ready synthesis. It is as if the more we discover the less we know. Even what we do know is frequently the subject of irreconcilable controversy: from the place of Hadrian's birth to the poem which he wrote or did not write on his deathbed. In his case the fertile and unending prairies of learning turn into explosive minefields of contention through which the researcher has warily to thread his way.

Hadrian's private and sexual life has been generally ignored or treated laconically or wrapped up in sanitary euphemisms. Such intimate matters, some historians loftily assert, have no impact on the general trend of policy, the development of peoples and of the Empire as a whole. This may well be true of many Roman Emperors but not of Hadrian, whose personal and emotional predilections certainly did impinge at times on his public actions with far-reaching effects. In view of these omissions and uncertainties in the literature, I have thought it wise for Hadrian as for Antinous to go back to the diverse ancient sources as much as possible, interpreting them in the light of modern specialist scholarship.

This book is intended for the general reader and it presupposes no prior detailed knowledge of the period or of the characters involved in this story. All quotations are in translation and the few technical terms are explained. However, in view of the absence of any authoritative study, of the doubts, controversies and difficulties of the evidence, I have felt bound to indicate the sources for what I say. These references and some notes of elucidation or discussion are put at the back of the book so as not to distract the ordinary reader who will have no need to consult them. For the irritation caused to those who wish to do so I apologise. I have tried to read and to digest everything written on the matter from the days of Hadrian to the present and, before my publishers advised a drastic condensation, the references were three times their present extent. Nevertheless, my debts to the innumerable scholars on whose work I have drawn are fully acknowledged in the notes and bibliography. Here I wish to express my gratitude to them all and to exonerate them from blame for my errors.

My other principal debts are to Günter Kowa of the University of Bonn who diligently provided me with several crucial texts not available in London; to Dr Robert Howes who fluently translated de la Maza's rare book, a copy of which was generously sent by the Director of the Instituto de Investigaciones Esteticas of the City University of Mexico; to Ugo and Anna-Maria Pampallona for invaluable help with photographs from Rome; to Giorgos Kontogiorgas for photographs from Greece; to Maurice Stephenson for helping with the typing; to the staff of the Joint Library of the Hellenic and Roman Societies of London for ungrudging help; and to Graeme Steel who coped with unfailing cheerfulness, patience and resource not only with my endless demands for material and photographs but with the intricacies and frustrations presented by numerous libraries, museums, officials and foreign travel.

SCANDAL OF THE CENTURIES

One day in the slanting sunlight of late October in the year 130 AD a body was found in the murky receding floodwaters of the river Nile. It was that of a young man, aged between eighteen and twenty, athletic in build, with a massive chest, hair clustered over the brow and down the neck in thick curls and a broad face of such unusual and poignant beauty that it was to haunt the imagination and the conscience of civilised men for nearly two thousand years.

There were no signs of violence on the body: not a clue why such a vigorous and healthy young man had met so premature and isolated a death: only that he had drowned. The scrawny boatmen of Hir-wer, the miserable little town of mud brick cringing under the stumpy columns and haughty pylons of the ancient temple of Rameses II on the east bank of the river, must have jabbered in wonder as they saw the corpse dragged out of the brown silt and carried over to the lush new grass beneath the palm trees of their plain. Who was he? What had he been in life? How did he die – was it accident, suicide or even murder? Their questions have been repeated and debated ever since.

The onlookers – and indeed the whole world – were soon to learn that this was not just another anonymous corpse cast up by the sullen river to be hastily buried in the nearby desert before it turned green and putrid. After his two brief decades of human life, this young man had just attained immortality and, with it, at least another two millennia of posthumous and turbulent notoriety.

His name must have been whispered from mouth to mouth with that mixture of avid curiosity and malicious speculation which probably had always been and certainly was ever after to be his lot. The name was Antinous. And he was the Greek boy, the beloved, if nothing more, of the fifty-four-year-old ruler of the Roman Empire, Hadrian.

All those who gathered to watch the body borne away, the courtiers, scholars and sailors from the flotilla of imperial barges moored nearby, perhaps some of the immaculate linen-clad priests from the sacred city of Hermopolis on the opposite bank, the grimy folk of Hir-wer, would have been amazed if they could have foreseen the extraordinary consequences of that day's event.

As we, so many generations later, are still.

Within less than four years squalid Hir-wer was no more. It had been replaced by the city of Antinous. Greek in plan and Greek in its specially recruited population, endowed with privileges and new trade routes, it boasted temples, monumental gates, splendid civic buildings, a theatre and a hippodrome. Its exceptionally broad main streets were lined by Doric colonnades so endless that as late as 1715 an amazed visitor declared the ruins to be 'a perpetual peristyle',[1] and eighty years after that Napoleon's surveyors diligently calculated that there must have been at least 1,344 columns in the two main streets alone. Innumerable images of Antinous adorned them. For the whole city was his memorial and his shrine, though not, perhaps, his burial place. People were soon flocking to his temples to hear the oracles pronounced by his newly established priesthood, to invoke his aid, his healing, his miracles and to participate in his 'sacred nights', those ecstatic, uninhibited mysteries which were later to be castigated by pagans and Christians alike as disgraceful homosexual orgies. From far and near countless pilgrims came bearing offerings to Antinous: half a million jars containing them are said to have been discovered. The unknown young man had suddenly become world-famous, the inert corpse possessed of an immortal power.

Antinous had become a god, the last of the ancient world. His apotheosis startled those people used to the routine and tepid deifications of the imperial family. The necessary solemn sanction of the Senate in Rome does not seem to have been obtained for this swift ascent to Olympus. Unlike other mortals so elevated in the past, Antinous had a puzzling lack of qualifications for his promotion: no divine ancestry, no noble blood and, on the face of it, no heroic deeds. The informality was suspicious, and vicious Alexandria soon whispered that the apotheosis was no more than the whim of the boy's distraught and unbalanced imperial lover.

Nevertheless the deification proved remarkably popular and proceeded apace. In Egypt Antinous was automatically identified with that other young god of myth who had died in the Nile and been resurrected, conquering death and bringing fertility to the earth – Osiris. In the Greco-Roman world he was sometimes venerated as a god in his own right or as a 'hero', that is a divinised mortal. He was frequently assimilated to the Hellenic equivalent of Osiris, the god Dionysos, who had also suffered, died, been reborn and brought fecundity to the soil. At other times he was identified with Hermes, to whose pleadings the older gods lent an ear and who had the power to rescue mortals from the eternal shades. Antinous also had a vogue as a god of the fields and flocks, like Hermes Nomios, Sylvanus or Vertumnus. Whatever the strange official silence, the syncretic nature of this divinity, the sneers of some cynical pagans, the gathering chorus of disgust from the Christian sect, there was evidently some ingredient in Antinous' life or death which stirred and satisfied the religious feelings and needs of many people of all ranks of society. He was venerated as a holy being with saintly powers of intercession for human folk with the greater deities, a former mortal whose death and resurrection promised salvation to others and who, in his new divine status, would care for the repose of the dead, the well-being of the living, the renewal and prosperity of the earth. Soon to be derided by his detractors as little more than a trumped-up male whore, to his devotees he remained, as coins and inscriptions proudly proclaim, 'Antinous the good'.[2]

Four years after the drowning in the Nile a cult of Antinous had extended throughout the Mediterranean world and penetrated to the very frontiers of the Empire. The earliest Christian commentators sneered that it had been forced on people by the dictates of the autocratic Hadrian and there can be no doubt that he had ardently promoted its spread. But in the peculiar ecstatic atmosphere and religious climate of the 130s, particularly in the Greek-speaking world, the advent of the god Antinous was greeted with a spontaneous enthusiasm which must have surprised even the Emperor himself.

A new star in the heavens was proclaimed as the eternally luminous soul of divine Antinous. Poets immediately rushed in to elaborate and perpetuate the myth of the new god. A literature of Antinous grew up of which traces have recently come to light in Cyprus and Tebtynis.

In Egypt the cult spread from Antinoopolis, propagating temples, priests and festivals in several major cities. In the Greek world from which he came, the chief cult centres, with temples, priests, mysteries and initiations, were his birthplace, Bithynion, near the coast of Asia Minor, and its own mother city, Mantineia in the Peloponnese. We know of at least forty cities in the Hellenic east where there was some form of veneration of him, a dozen where there were specific cults and seven which held regular festivals or games in his honour. In an astonishing outburst of enthusiasm in the years 133–7 over thirty Greek cities which possessed the right of minting issued commemorative coins or medallions of great variety and sometimes consummate beauty, bearing the image of Antinous and his titles, and linking him to their own local gods or heroes.

Meanwhile the sculptors of Greece, Asia Minor, Italy and Egypt had been hard at work creating those images of the new hero-god in marble or bronze of which the ample remnants are still to be seen all over Europe. Perhaps never in antiquity had so many and so varied images been produced of one individual in so short a time, for most of them were made before Hadrian died in 138. A recent authority has calculated that, including all those in Antinoopolis, about 2,000 sculptures were produced in these eight years.[3] Exaggerated as this estimate may seem, there can be no doubt of the unusual quantity produced to meet an enormous demand. There is still less doubt about the quality. Inspired by the story, the character and the strange physical beauty of Antinous, the sculptors of the imperial world evolved the last of the great types of ancient art, works which, though original in spirit and technically very much of their time, were imbued with the elevated nobility of classical art, the sensitivity and expressiveness of that of the Hellenistic age and the incisive grasp of character of Roman portraiture. In spite of the profusion and diversity of these images, they all present, however idealised, the immediately recognisable features of a distinctive individual, the youth Antinous, 'of unsurpassed beauty', as one of the most vehement critics of his deification and morals, Clement of Alexandria, warmly admitted.[4] Circulating the civilised world in the shape of statues, reliefs, busts, paintings, coins, cameos and gems, the image of Antinous established a new canon of adolescent perfection for generations to come, so that it is now difficult for art historians to tell whether some works are actual portraits of him or approximations to his ideal.

It is sometimes said that Italy itself was lukewarm to the new cult because its cities produced no coins. As they did not have the same freedom to mint as did those of the east, the absence of coins proves nothing. On the contrary, there is evidence of a substantial veneration of Antinous in the peninsula, and this is apart from the official monuments in Rome and Hadrian's obsessive glorification of his dead favourite in the sumptuous villa at Tivoli. Nearly four times the number of sculptures, the origins of which we know, have been found in Italy (44) than in Greece and Asia Minor (12). Of those from Italy, half were found away from the imperial villa, and the colossal size of several indicates some religious or public function. There are surviving traces of the veneration of Antinous from ten cities, from the far north to the extreme south of the peninsula. The response of the Italians may have been less ostentatious, less collective (there seem to have been no games), more private and purely aesthetic than that of the Greek cities, but its intense domesticity ensured its duration to the end of antiquity itself and the careful preservation then of the threatened images of the god.

In ten years the face of Antinous had spanned the western world: from the statue in the temple on the rock promontory of Trapezus under the beetling Caucasus in the far east, to the coin found by a startled Edwardian gentleman in the winter mud of Godmanchester in Britain in the far west. Along the coast of North Africa – in modern Algeria, Tunisia and Libya – his statues have been discovered, though only one definitely in the Levant. Sporadic finds of images or inscriptions elsewhere – in Malta, Lyons in France, in Holland, Spain, Cyprus, Yugoslavia – attest the pervasiveness of his worship. Finally his likeness in the debased form of small bronze incense jars penetrated to the very frontiers of the Empire – they have been found in a great arc from Holland, along the Rhine, through central Germany, down the Danube to the Black Sea.

The new young god attracted in various ways all social groups. At the apex there was the sick and embittered Emperor, surrounding himself in his last years at Tivoli with endless images of his greatest and probably his only real love. Wealthy notables in the Greek cities hastened to commission public sculptures or medallions of Antinous – though piety may not have been their sole motive. In Italy more genuine devotees of means acquired images for their homes or private cults. Other well-off folk had small collapsible busts made so that their beloved Antinous could even accompany them on their travels. Many preferred to carry his features in miniature on their bodies in the shape of exquisite cut gems or cameos. Middling groups such as the Dionysian actors of Athens and Rome subscribed through their associations to sculptures and priesthoods. Still lower down the social scale, the burly miners of Socanica, in modern Yugoslavia, were provided with their own temple to Antinous, while the humble artisans and slaves of Lanuvium, south of Rome, set up their burial club only two years after the events on the Nile in the joint names of Diana and of this newest god, Antinous, conqueror of death. More joyfully, the townsfolk of Curium, in southern Cyprus, gathered in their theatre near the glittering sea for a festival to Antinous replete with choirs, hymns and elaborate solos sung or twanged by the resplendent gold and purple clad citharode.

Everywhere the coins and medallions were worn as ornaments or pierced and worn round the neck as talismans against evil or as tokens of salvation. The demand was so great in Alexandria, the second largest city in the world, that several official issues had to be made in good metal, then afterwards in much cheaper lead, and even then were so eagerly wanted that they were worth illicitly counterfeiting. The dead in Luxor in southern Egypt bore on their mummies the redeeming name of Antinous and those in Aquileia in north Italy had terracotta plaques bearing his image nailed to their sarcophagi: *he* would guide and protect them in the dark realm beyond the grave. For those still living and who could perhaps afford no such material emblems, there was still one gift that could be bestowed freely on their children, that of Antinous' beneficent name.

Such in outline was the immediate sequel to the death in the Nile of the obscure boy from Bithynia. And there were to be yet other, more gradual and serious consequences: upon Hadrian himself and his actions and policy as Emperor.

Simultaneously with the homage, the scandal began: that posthumous babble of adulation, denigration, speculation, fabrication and concealment which has reverberated stridently and confusedly around the affair of Antinous and Hadrian down to our own day. It sprouted on the Nile, flowered in Alexandria, spread its seed more quickly around the world than the cult itself and reached such over-ripe proportions that Hadrian himself had to intervene.

Not that the pagan people were gossiping and laughing so much about the alleged sexual nature of the affair: they accepted that as natural. At first it was the deification and elements like the miraculous new star and the Emperor's whole exaggerated response which provoked wonder and sniggers in sceptical circles. Soon, however, rumours concentrated on the death. That, it was widely reported and readily believed, had not been such a simple affair after all. Antinous had either committed suicide out of despair of his difficult relationship with Hadrian or, more sinisterly still, had, on the advice of magicians, sacrificed himself or even been sacrificed to save the Emperor from some hideous fate. That became the standard view which the ancient historians peddled down to posterity. Hadrian himself felt obliged to issue a curt denial of the last allegation, but the ambiguous brevity of his words provoked only further suspicion and surmise.

After his death in 138 there was always a thin stream of pagan criticism of the apotheosis. But it was the Christians who kept the scandal burning, stoking the flames with new explosive ingredients. Timidly under Hadrian himself and his adoptive successors, but boldly for centuries thereafter, they lambasted this most recent spurious man-made divinity and the cheap deceptions of his cult, as a means of attacking the credentials of the whole pagan pantheon. It was they who, obliquely at first and then frontally in a shrill and outraged chorus, raised that other and, for them, ugly and sinful issue: sex. This so-called god Antinous, they asserted, had been nothing more than the depraved and willing object of Hadrian's perverted passion and this consecration of a lust demonstrated the ultimate profanity and worthlessness of the old religion. The stress on the sexual depravity of the relationship was a response to some practices in the cult itself, flourishing uncomfortably close to some of the Fathers, but was also an indignant counter-attack on those who dared seriously to publish comparisons between Antinous, the young, sacrificial and resurrected god from Bithynion, and Christ, the young, sacrificial and resurrected god from Nazareth.

We do not know the effects of all this scandal on the cult itself in the two and a half centuries in which Christianity conquered the Roman Empire. Its prosperity in Egypt about 250 AD provoked the fury of Origen and aroused the scorn of Prudentius and St Athanasius in 350–400 AD. The games of Athens and Eleusis continued at least until the records stop in 266–7 and those of Argos, it is said,[5] for another hundred years. The colossal bronze statue of Antinous erected in Antinoopolis in 134 was torn down only after 375 AD. But, surprisingly, as late as that date a series of crude medallions (or contorniates) was issued of Antinous, one showing him as a sturdy warrior, identified with notorious pagan Pan and boldly proclaiming him as 'God'. Could Antinous have thus been used as a last, aggressive, pagan challenge to the sensibilities of Christianity in its decade of final triumph?

Devotion to Antinous persisted in places to the very end. When the Delphi statue (figs 1–2) was toppled in a barbarian incursion into the sanctuary, it was afterwards lovingly raised again, minus its broken lower arms, in the place where it was to be found, still standing, under the debris of centuries, in 1893. In Italy, as the Christian iconoclasts or rampaging barbarians smashed the images of the pagan gods, the devotees of Antinous or of the old religion and its artefacts took evasive action. The Sylvanus relief (fig. 5) was carried out into the fields from its villa, laid down carefully on a bed of specially sifted soil and then buried. The huge Antinous-Dionysos, now in the Vatican (fig. 60), was gently laid down and covered so that when it was found in 1795 scarcely any of its vulnerable extremities was damaged. The Mondragone head (fig. 8), severed from the colossal body which was abandoned to the destroyers, had been so delicately interred at Frascati that fragments of the rare marble infill and silver sheathing of the eyes were still intact in the 1760s.

At the end of antiquity, the memory of Antinous might also have been buried for ever. Ironically, it was the very scandal which kept it alive.

But in the thousand years after the end of paganism, it was the writings of those early Fathers or Christian apologists of the years 150–400, widely read, copied and circulated, which perpetuated vividly the memory of Antinous and indeed crystallised his character and that of his apotheosis for long to come. There was a perplexing and memorable mixture of praise, blame and pity for him: praise of his beauty, blame for his morals and pity for his fate. Though St Jerome compares him to a public male concubine, he also declares him 'a boy of uncommonly outstanding beauty'.[6] One minute the violent Tertullian denounces him as a 'bugger', the next he almost pityingly depicts this new boy-god as 'unhappy' and later rapturously asks 'What Ganymede was more fair?'[7] No wonder the memory of Antinous survived.

Who would not be struck by Prudentius' scathing image of Antinous nestling in Hadrian's 'purple clad bosom' and being 'robbed of his manhood' or lolling on a couch 'listening to the prayers in the temples with his husband'?[8] Who could not be moved by Clement's profound sorrow at this boy 'of unsurpassed beauty . . . blighted by outrage . . . in the flower of his youth'?[9] Who would not thrill to the thunderous fulminations of St Athanasius, vented in about 350 AD but extracted here from a free and robust translation of 1713:

> And such a one is the new God Antinous, that was the Emperor Hadrian's minion and the slave of his unlawful pleasures; a wretch, whom those that worshipped in obedience to the Emperor's command, and for fear of his vengeance, knew and confessed to be a man, and not a good or deserving man neither, but a sordid and loathsome instrument of his master's lust. This shameless and scandalous boy died in Egypt when the court was there; and forthwith his Imperial Majesty issued out an order or edict strictly requiring and commanding his loving subjects to acknowledge his departed page a deity and to pay him his quota of divine reverences and honours as such: a resolution and act which did more effectually publish and testify to the world how entirely the Emperor's unnatural passion survived the foul object of it; and how much his master was devoted to his memory, than it recorded his own crime and condemnation, immortalised his infamy and shame, and bequeathed to mankind a lasting and notorious specimen of the true origin and extraction of all idolatry . . .[10]

How could anyone ever forget Antinous and Hadrian after reading that? In such ways the characters and the whole affair were fixed and stigmatised. By about 1000 AD when Suidas came to compose his lexicon and sought a personification for the Greek word *paidika*, defined by him as 'an agreeable boy but usually of lascivious and foul affections', there was but one obvious candidate: Antinous.[11]

In the centuries 1500–1850, while the images of Antinous were undergoing a physical and aesthetic resurrection, the attitudes to his history and deification remained unaltered from that of Athanasius. Whether it is Casaubon in 1603, Nicosias in 1689, Weber in 1707 or Levezow in 1808, Antinous is always Hadrian's 'catamite', branded as 'infamous', 'nefarious', 'this boy of shame'.[12] Morally delicate souls like M. Dupaty, promenading the Uffizi gallery in 1785, cast their eyes down apprehensively as they approached his bust. Gibbon, who praised the political wisdom and virtue of the Emperor, declared that his response to Antinous 'still dishonours the memory of Hadrian'.[13] Others castigated him as prey to 'criminal weakness'. 'Never was seen a passion more unbridled and more extravagant'.[14] The deification was denounced as late as 1851 by Hadrian's first modern biographer, Gregorovius, in words which might have been borrowed from Tertullian of 200 AD, as 'a moral enormity when we consider what this deified youth was in his lifetime', the product of 'profane caprice . . . insane desire'.[15] Usually, in these years, the death was accepted as a form of sacrifice, but in the seventeenth century a macabre new twist was given to the theory. Hadrian had perpetrated the foul deed himself on his beloved and searched for omens among the reeking entrails of Antinous with his own blood-stained hands. The subsequent apotheosis was therefore explained as no more than an act of remorse for this 'barbaric curiosity', to expiate a crime 'the most horrible of which an Emperor was capable'.[16] Such a view was solemnly put forward as late as 1846.[17]

While the moral scandal simmered and the brew grew more salacious, the aesthetic appreciation of Antinous in art grew ever more laudatory. As yet the moral response and the aesthetic one did not much impinge on each other. From the early 1500s numerous busts and works of art of Antinous began to appear as prized items in the collections of princes and artists. There was soon a lucrative industry making copies of them. Raphael himself drew and Lorenzetto sculpted in 1522–7 a head of Antinous for a figure of Jonah in the Chigi Chapel of the church of Sta Maria del Popolo in Rome (fig. 4) – an ironic circumstance which a school of agonised Victorian writers pounced upon as profoundly symbolic of the belated recognition by Christians of the purity of Antinous and the nobility of his sacrifice. In fact it was probably a purely aesthetic gesture. So was that of Cardinal Leopold de Medici who led a procession to the Roman Gate of Florence in about 1680 to greet the newly discovered bust of Antinous now in the Uffizi (the very one which later gave M. Dupaty such intimations of sin) as 'a miracle of art'.[18]

As the primitive archaeology of the eighteenth century unearthed in Italy, mainly from the Villa Adriana, a profusion of sculptures of Antinous, the courts and nobility of Europe vied to acquire them. The Pope, eminent cardinals, Frederick the Great, English peers, all intrigued, bribed and even smuggled to get new works of Antinous for their palaces. Lesser mortals had to be content with copies, like the one of the Ildefonso group which Goethe had on his staircase at Weimar. The face of Antinous, or that version of it based on a group of works of Italian provenance, had become more fashionable with cultivated people in Europe by 1800, when Napoleon displayed no less than thirteen major works looted for his Paris museum, than it had been at the height of the religious cult in antiquity. The high priest of this new aesthetic cult was the German, Winckelmann, the first serious historian of Greek art. It was he who popularised in the 1750s and 60s the character of Antinous as displayed in the celebrated groups of sculptures of Italian origin as 'brooding' and 'melancholy'.[19] Elaborated by later northern writers into cosmic theories of *Weltschmerz* and *Sehnsucht* and linked with the alleged self-sacrifice, this view of Antinous has persisted down to our own times – despite the evidence to the contrary which has steadily accumulated since. It was Winckelmann too who passed those rapturous judgements which, widely accepted, constituted a second, aesthetic apotheosis for the boy from Bithynia. The Mondragone head, he enthused (1767), was 'one of the most beautiful things in the world' and it and the Albani relief (fig. 9) were (1769) 'the glory and crown of art in this age as well as in all others . . .'[20]

Antinous' aesthetic resurrection was followed by an even more surprising one. By the mid-nineteenth century, in which the first serious studies of the Antinous affair appeared, the scandal surrounding it was no longer tolerable. To some it was so obscene that Antinous had better be eliminated completely: an attitude of which M. Dupaty's remark, 'Eyes down, here comes Antinous', in front of the Uffizi bust was an early symptom. Thus Bishop Kaye, in editing the *Apologies of Justin the Martyr*, still the only translation in English, cut out all references to Antinous without mentioning the fact. And when John Addington Symonds, gathering material for his penetrating essay on Antinous in 1878, innocuously applied to the leading authority in the British Museum for help with the coins, he received the chillingly unhelpful reply that 'it is very courageous to ask even artistic questions about him'.[21] Symonds himself, ardent rehabilitator of Antinous and semi-concealed champion of 'Greek Love' as he was, felt obliged to tone down his sultry poem on the sacrifice so as not to offend British sentiment.

Such was the public repugnance to homosexual love and hostility to pagan religion in mid-Victorian times that serious scholars now studying the story of Antinous and Hadrian, of the apotheosis and cult, and responding to the superb works of art which they produced, simply could not accept that they all derived from origins so profane and disgusting. 'One would wish,' sighed the French archaeologist Solomon Reinach, 'to efface his [Antinous'] name from

9

the history of Hadrian as personifying the shameful weakness of a great man.'[22] Art historians now developed painfully acute moral qualms in front of inanimate marbles. If the apotheosis and all that it produced derived from no more than carnal love, wailed Symonds in his essay of 1879, 'we leave the worship of Antinous as an almost inexplicable scandal, an almost unintelligible blot on human nature'.[23] Dietrichson, the Norwegian professor who published in 1884 the first comprehensive study of Antinous, set out deliberately to clear his name, 'to cleanse a noble and pure form from dirt', confessing ingeniously that had he not felt sure of removing 'the horrible slanders' and 'dark shadows' which smirched his subject he would never have undertaken his vast labours in the first place.[24]

Laundered and disinfected by the ingenious arguments and earnest eloquence of Dietrichson, Symonds and others, the reputation of Antinous emerged 'spotless and pure',[25] with a gleaming moral respectability acceptable to late Victorian prudery and even to partisan Christianity. Sex? There had been nothing so vile between boy and man, they concluded: the relationship had been aesthetic and Platonic and incorruptible like that of the noble, self-restrained Socrates with Alcibiades. Sacrifice? This there certainly had been – but it was the sublime voluntary self-sacrifice of Antinous to save the ruler of the world (and thereby the civilised world itself) from some malevolent fate. An effeminate voluptuary, as Antinous had earlier been described, would, they declared, have been incapable of such an heroic deed. Only this noble and free self-sacrifice could adequately explain the response of the apotheosis, the genuine religious enthusiasm Antinous inspired and the way he took 'such a notable place in the imaginative life of mankind'.[26] Into the brooding melancholy of his statues they read not just 'the innocence of youth touched and saddened by a calm resolve or accepted doom', but the whole tortured spirit of late antiquity, its nobility, its self-doubt, its yearnings, its present-iment of imminent destruction.[27] These themes of self-sacrifice and suffering for others enabled such authors to sweep away the millennia-old calumnies of the early Fathers of the Church and to reconcile the pagan cult of this dead boy with their own burning Christianity. 'The youthful, beautiful Antinous with the melancholy expression of resigned suffering', declared Stahr, 'is the Christ of the Roman Imperial age.'[28] 'Antinous', concluded Dietrichson happily, the moral and spiritual rehabilitation complete, 'is the reflection which awakening Christianity throws back upon dying antiquity.'[29] What would Origen or St Athanasius have made of that?

At the beginning of our own century enthusiasm for the now purified Antinous reached another culmination. Indeed, on one memorable occasion, by another ironic twist of history, Antinous was reinvested by popular will in Italy with some of his ancient spiritual power as a god of fertility. It was in 1907 when the lovely relief of a languorous Antinous as Sylvanus, preparing to harvest the vine, was discovered at Torre del Padiglione in the desolate

Campagna south of Rome (fig. 5).

On the day that workmen began digging up the Campagna to clear it in preparation for planting vines – an experiment in the hope of turning unhealthy malarial marshland into fertile soil – excavators chanced to dig deep enough at this particular spot to strike something hard. At once they threw away their spades and began anew with the little tools made specially for such discoveries. The hard object was cleared off; it was the smooth base of a slab of pentelic marble . . . They lifted it out, whole; they cleared off some of the caking soil. There were raptures of rejoicing! The excavators were stirred to the heart by the beauty of the carving. From other farms and labourers' houses nearby came farmers with their children and diggers with their spades, all happy and laughing. 'It is an omen. An omen of success in our work . . . Antinous will bless the Campagna, our vines will flourish.'[30]

The learned archaeologist Lanciani echoed their faith. 'Surely,' he urged, 'it cannot be a trick of fate that on the day when workmen had been directed to that knoll to try an experiment in vine growing, Antinous should appear in the guise of a sylvan god, attending to the vintage with bunches of luscious grapes hanging in profusion from his own vines.'[31]

Dietrichson's exhaustive catalogue of 399 old and modern works of art of Antinous, followed by the discoveries of two masterpieces of the genre, the statue of Delphi and the relief of Torre del Padiglione, and other notable works (the statue of the Bank of Italy in 1886, that of Aidepsos in 1907), and the first public exhibition of the magnificent Marlborough sardonyx of Antinous in 1904 (fig. 7), sustained aesthetic interest. The museums of Europe continued to give Antinous' sculptures pride of place and they were earnestly appraised and interpreted by the public. 'Ah!' said Tennyson, somewhat earlier, stopping before a bust of Antinous in the British Museum, 'the inscrutable Bithynian! If we knew what he knew we should understand the ancient world.'[32] Though art-historical scholarship was more informed and discriminating than in the days of Winckelmann, the tone was scarcely less fulsome. Eugenie Strong, the leading authority of the time on Roman sculpture, in 1907 declared the works of Antinous to be 'one of the most powerful presentiments created by the sculptor's genius. . . As the Antinous is the last of the great classic types given to the world by the antique, so also it is among the most powerful and majestic.'

In our own hypercritical times, Antinous and his history have been toppled from this pinnacle of adulation and smashed into fragments of specialised learning. Several valuable monographs have appeared, but all of detailed aspects of the affair – the coins, the cult and the sculptures. Rarely has a general survey of the story and its evidence been attempted and then only as an incidental part of something bigger. It seems as though the accumulation of minute knowledge, much of it marginal, not only inhibits the moral fervour, indiscriminate enthusiasm and sweeping generalisation aroused in the past but any conclusions at all in the present. The same is true of Hadrian. Though his stature has risen in Roman history under a mountain of particular studies, there has been no comprehensive biography of him for sixty years and none to surpass that of Weber published in 1907. It is symptomatic of the constricting specialisms and the oppressive burden of fact of our time that it has been left to the imagination of a novelist, Marguerite Yourcenar, to create the broadest, the most balanced and in many ways the most authentic interpretation of the affair.

Nowadays historians attempt a scrupulous objectivity on the matter and repudiate partisan or moralistic attitudes. Nevertheless, it is remarkable how some who admire Hadrian cannot bring themselves to consider any serious homosexual streak in his nature. The sexual innuendoes of the past are either dismissed in favour of Platonic interpretations or quietly accepted and quickly passed over. Mystic or elevated explanations of a sacrificial death tend these days to be discounted in favour of that of a prosaic, if unexplained, accident. Only rarely now is the apotheosis accounted for solely in terms of Hadrian's personal loss. Instead, it is interpreted more in the light of Egyptian tradition, deliberate policy, the heady religious and political atmosphere of the Greek world and even as an affirmation of western unity and values against the subversive doctrines of the orient. Antinous himself is no longer the object of delirious adulation nor is he acclaimed as the personification of the best qualities of his age: indeed, he has even been dismissed as 'a useless thing' and 'a brainless beauty'.[33] Though critical opinion continues to regard the coins and sculptures as 'among the last great creative expressions of classic art', 'a great and original achievement',[34] they cease to evoke rapture. When the most recent discovery, an attractive statuette of Antinous, appeared in 1960 from a cistern in Athens, it was not greeted with ecstasy but promptly locked up in a shed where it still languishes. If the ghost of Tennyson came back to the British Museum to wrest the secret of the ancient world from the bust of the inscrutable Bithynian, it would be disappointed, for not a single sculpture of Antinous is on show there or indeed anywhere in London. The fashion for archaic or early classical art has swept Antinous out of the display rooms of the museums and down into the basements. Not one sculpture of him is on view in the museum of Athens and some of the most interesting of the Louvre and the Vatican have been consigned to the impenetrable eternal shades below. It is all as if, in the effort to put the whole matter into a thoroughly informed and shrewdly judicious perspective, the ancient scandal and with it the history of Antinous himself has dwindled in the distance to nothing.

Like the people on the banks of the Nile in October 130 we are left with a host of insistent questions. Unlike them, however, we have to contend with two millennia of clamorous and conflicting answers.

Who was this Antinous in the first place? Was he, as has variously been claimed, a slave, a shepherd, a page, a hostage prince or Hadrian's own illegitimate son? When did they meet and how did their relationship develop? Was it really a tragedy 'in which a healthy nature [Antinous'] was pushed into intercourse with a diseased one'?[35]

What did the favourite look like? Is the image of him derived from a group of Italian variants of the basic model and worked up by Nordic romanticism into the famous stereotype of bowed head and doomed innocence, consumed with brooding melancholy, true of what other sculptures and evidence tell us of a youth varied and vital enough to captivate the many-sided and fickle ruler of the world?

What of his character? Was Antinous 'a creature of the senses', so that 'conscience or discriminating activity did not exist for him'?[36] Or was he a handsome nonentity 'more than anything else empty; you could take him for a young Armenian rug salesman'?[37] Was he lacking in 'spiritual depth'[38] or did he have to have outstanding gifts to satisfy the mind and sensibilities as well as the carnal appetites of the Emperor?

And sex? Was Antinous simply a catamite? Do his images 'announce and glorify sex' or do they look 'as serene and pure as if no shadow could ever have been cast upon his memory and it is with the halo of innocence that he takes the heart captive'?[39] Was that innocence but a mask for a 'deep impotence'?[40] Was Hadrian's relationship to him based on lust, or was it purely ideal love, in the Platonic sense, or something else, father to son, or avuncular, as has recently been proposed? Are these categories in real life so exclusive anyway?

Then that death: an accident, a suicide of despair, an enforced ritual immolation, a voluntary sacrifice to save Hadrian or, as a modern historian luridly proposes, pure murder – 'death carried by an unknown hand'?[41]

Where is Antinous buried – in Antinoopolis, in the mountains nearby where his tomb and effigy still await discovery, in Hadrian's mausoleum in Rome or in the Temple of Fortune there, in that lavish underground chamber discovered near the Porta Maggiore in 1917 or in the Villa Adriana?

Must we regard the apotheosis as an impulsive and vulgar freak of megalomaniac grief or remorse on the part of a demented Hadrian and the subsequent cult as his autocratic imposition, or was his mind more calculating and were there other forces at work at the time which helped suggest, initiate, spread and then sustain the veneration of the new young god of the Nile? May this apparently unique and arbitrary event be part of a bigger pattern which, in the middle of the second century AD, brought Rome to its apogee and Greece to its final efflorescence?

And there is Hadrian himself. What impact had this whole affair on him, on that breakdown to 'madness', which his most notable modern historian diagnoses,[42] on that bizarre sequence of arbitrary and violent acts which led one of the most constructive, pacific and tolerant of absolute rulers the world has seen to die in misery, 'hated by all'?[43]

Antinous has left us the splendid legacy of his art which, besides its intrinsic value, illustrates enigmatically the whole of his story and raises issues of its own. But could this tiny, remote and indistinct explosion of energy on the Nile have contributed its momentum to other cosmic events – the triumph of Christianity, the final expulsion of the Jews from Judea – which affect us all even to this day?

Immanuel Weber published the first study of Antinous in Latin in 1707. Since then our knowledge has been vastly increased by archaeological, epigraphical, numismatic and papyrological discoveries and by the meticulous scholarship of devoted historians. We know a great deal more about the background and the consequences of the affair. But as far as the central issues go – the history of Antinous, his relationship with Hadrian and the death – we have precious little more first-hand information than the earliest writers.

To begin to understand what happened we have to approach the story not just as a fraught and hideously conspicuous love affair which ended in personal disaster but as a drama shaped by some of the central forces of Greco-Roman society, religion and politics. To this end recent evidence and analysis do provide a coherent framework within which to interpret these apparently isolated, capricious and inexplicable events. The terrain which we do know thereby becomes more intelligible and that which we do not know can at least be penetrated by fragile bridgeheads of rational guesswork linked to solid facts. Even so, at every step we meet fresh doubt and unexpected contradictions and plunge suddenly into total darkness.

Clinical historical explanation may remove the stale savour of scandal which the Antinous–Hadrian affair has generated. But, fortunately perhaps, it can never quite dispel the wonder which those events still evoke. And it will never resolve the mystery which Antinous was to his own time, has been since and must be always.

ANTINOUS, THE YOUNG GREEK
c. 110–23

Antinous was Greek. Such an origin might imply a liability, even an indelible stigma of inferiority, for any young man living under the Empire of Rome. It was Antinous' fate, however, to be born in a place and at a time when his very Greekness was to become his greatest asset, propelling him from obscurity to fame. Because he was Greek, he found himself elevated to his temporary pinnacle of imperial adulation. Because he was Greek, he was posthumously proclaimed a hero or divinity by his enthusiastic compatriots. Because he was Greek, he was immortalised so uniquely and so profusely in marble.

He came from Bithynia, itself in history, geography and culture a bridge between Rome and Greece, west and east, temperate Europe and the broiling orient. Situated on the north-west coast of Asia Minor, its major cities facing the vital Propontis, its lesser ones the Black Sea, the province was about the size of modern Denmark and at the end of the first century AD contained about one million people. On the south it was fringed by the mountain ranges framing the great central plateau of Anatolia. To the west of the Sangarius river, which winds its way laterally across central Bithynia before breaking northwards through the mountain gorges to the sea, lay the fertile plains of the Propontis on which stood the most important cities: Nikomedia, Nicea, Chalcedon, Cius and Apameia. To the east, smaller plains and lush valleys unfolded between high mountains and were watered by small tributaries. In one of these verdant, mountain-girt plains, about thirty miles from the sea, lay the modest city of Bithynion-Claudiopolis where Antinous was born. Its climate and vegetation were strangely un-oriental or even un-Mediterranean. No gnarled olive trees were to be seen, but, instead, vast forests of firs and deciduous oaks and beeches clad the mountain slopes and supplied successive navies with timber. The temperate, moist climate nurtured succulent grasses on which the cattle grew fat, producing superlative milk and cheeses.

The coastal fringe and the western plains had long ago been colonised by settlers from the mainland of Greece: fierce Thracians and more pastoral folk from Arcadia in the central Peloponnese who, it was said, established themselves at Bithynion. The Greeks set up their separate city-states as enclaves of intense and jealous civilisation in a wilderness of barbarism. By 297 BC they had been welded together into a Hellenistic kingdom ruled from Nikomedia, a city of sumptuous buildings and shady gardens. The kings gradually pushed the frontier of civilisation eastward by founding cities, and the ancient pastoral settlement at Bithynion may have been remodelled and renamed as a military bastion to control territories nearby conquered from the Paphlagonians.

When, in the first century BC, the Roman Republic extended its control over the Hellenistic world, Bithynia became more of a client kingdom and a battlefield, devastated like much of Greece in the wars between Sulla and Mithridates of Pontus (the neighbouring kingdom) to which Pompey mercifully put an end. Already in 74 BC the last king, Nikomedes IV of Bithynia, had bequeathed his state to Rome, which promptly made it a province governed by a proconsul appointed by the Senate. In 64 BC, Pompey, with typical Roman adaptability to viable circumstances, reorganised the Greek system of local government and established twelve city-states. Further development was checked here, as all over the Greek world, by the civil wars of the late Republic, fought mainly on Greek soil and financed by Greek resources, which culminated finally in the victory of the Roman west and Octavian over the Hellenistic-Egyptian east and Mark Antony at Actium in 31 BC.

Under the early Empire in the first century AD recovery was steady, aided by the Emperors themselves who founded cities, donated buildings and, especially in the case of Vespasian, built or improved the great trunk roads to the east. Bithynion now dubbed itself 'Claudiopolis' as a tribute for some benefaction, now forgotten, from that philhellene Emperor in distant Rome.

What attracted the interest of successive Emperors to Bithynia was not its cheeses or timber, or even its military resources, but its strategic position and its roads. The province lay like a hinge equidistant between the two most active and vulnerable frontiers of the Empire in the late first century – that of the Danube in the north and the Euphrates in the south-east. The great roads linking the two divided after Nikomedia, the northernmost ones ranging eastwards across Pontus to Cappadocia and Armenia, the others crossing the plateau south-eastwards to the passes of the Cilician gates and thence Syria or the Euphrates. Troops changing frontiers or hastening to war had to use these Bithynian roads. And whoever held or lost the Cilician gates and the approaches to the Propontis held or lost the world. Many later Emperors lingered and wintered with their troops at Nikomedia, not so much for its balmy air and civic luxuries, but because from this focal point they could swiftly control both the western and eastern divisions of their vast realm.

By the days of Antinous the people of his province had acquired a mixed reputation. Personally they were genial and, as a whole, so peaceable that the Emperor Trajan refused appeals to increase the few troops stationed among

16

them. But in civic and political affairs they were impossibly contumacious. Not only did the cities squabble endlessly among themselves and before the jaded Emperor, but within them the large poor populace was always prone to riot against the wealthy civic elders supported by Rome: phenomena common enough throughout the Greek world. The Bithynians, however, loved agitation, so much so that the usually tolerant Trajan banned even the formation of a fire brigade in Nikomedia in case it became a centre of sedition. Nor were the civic leaders any more complaisant. On no less than five occasions they remorselessly prosecuted their proconsuls for corruption and malad-ministration. Little wonder that Trajan took control out of the hands of the Senate's nominee and appointed Pliny the Younger as his direct representative in the province *c*. 111 AD. Maladministration and corruption had not been confined to the proconsuls. The cities, in their new-found prosperity and ancient megalomaniac rivalry, had expended vast sums on public works which, through incompetence or peculation, had often come to nothing. Pliny found that Nikomedia alone had spent three and a third million sesterces on an aqueduct so unsound that it had to be destroyed and Nicea ten million on a theatre left unfinished and falling to pieces.

The culture of Bithynia which Antinous imbibed was equally varied. The cities produced some notable contributors to the classical civilisation of the day: Dio, the rhetor of Prusa; Arrian the historian and Quirinus the sophist of Nikomedia: and later Dio Cassius the historian of Nicea. Outside the cities, however, the rural folk retained ancient dialects and traditions and were never fully integrated into Hellenic city culture. There was a marked blending of the different racial types which had settled or passed over the land. Above all, the ancient eastern beliefs persisted, even if respectably disguised in the shape of orthodox Olympian deities, and grew ever more powerful in the second century as the old pantheon succumbed before the eastern gods of mystery, salvation and ecstasy: Cybele, Men and Attis among them. Dionysos, who was locally reported to have been born on the Sangarius river, and Demeter, both deities of fertility and renewal, were here invested with the dark, compelling force of primitive folklore. Both were to have their role to play in the destiny of Antinous. Everywhere, mountains, trees and streams were venerated as gods to be placated, and legends of local heroes and mythical founders proliferated and were credulously believed.

It was in this atmosphere of reverence for natural forces, the practice of secret mysteries and ecstatic participation that Antinous may have been reared rather than in lukewarm observance of the cults of the anthropomorphic deities of Olympus.

Claudiopolis, which was so proudly to announce itself the birthplace of Antinous, is at present called Bolu or Boli, after 'polis' in the classical name. Like all the cities of Bithynia, it has never been excavated, and it is now partly sealed under the main road to Ankara though some tantalising fragments of it were unearthed in the 1940s. Its acropolis rose near a river in the midst of a beautiful plain which was plentifully settled in ancient times. On these luxuriant pastures and cool mountain slopes browsed cattle which produced the famous Salonian cheese commended by Strabo.[1] The city stood on the great highway, improved substantially in the 70s and 80s of the first century, which ran parallel to the coastal ridge from Nikomedia in the west and, after Claudiopolis, divided to the east and the south-east. The volume of military traffic rumbling along the road was so great that Claudiopolis could boast two special centurions to control it. From this passing trade and its agricultural produce it had already attained a modest prosperity, minting its own bronze change in the period before Hadrian and ranking then about eighth among the cities of Bithynia.[2]

Its council was composed of an oligarchy of the local wealthy who paid fees to be admitted. One leading citizen, a M. Domitius Euphemus, was rich and distinguished enough even to have a seat in the Senate of Rome. Claudiopolis was equipped with the usual buildings which made up a city – administrative offices, markets, gymnasium and palaestra, a theatre – and, to the horror of Pliny c. 111 AD, was busily erecting an enormous baths at the foot of the mountains to the south where there were hot springs. Both the finances and the construction of this enterprise were so dubious to the outraged legate that he scribbled his consternation and requests for help to his imperial master in Rome. Of other buildings and those sumptuous ones erected by Hadrian in the 130s, when the town reverted to the name of Bithynion with the addition of 'Hadriana', only a few impressive pieces have come to light. In the seventeenth century the traveller Tavernier described the little Turkish cemeteries dotted around the plain as full of columns, bases and architraves from the ruined city. But when, in 1948, the Austrian epigrapher Dörner arrived with his camera, most of these had fallen or been used as door jambs, walls or platforms for the muezzins. Even so, the fragments of sarcophagi, columns, entablatures and dedicatory tablets (including a base to Antinous now used as the headstone of a Moslem grave) which his lens recorded bear pathetic witness to a once elegant city.

With its crisp mountain air, green meadows, tall woods and lazy stream outside, with its colonnades, temples, porticoes, markets and bustling streets inside, its fresh produce and passing commerce, Claudiopolis must have been a wholesome enough place for any lad to have grown up in. It had balance: it was neither frenziedly metropolitan nor sluggishly remote, neither overwhelmingly grand nor claustrophobically minute, at once urban and rural. And there was always the incessant life of that great road – flowing faster than the river with a stream of people, commercial and military, eastern and western, magnificent and humdrum – to excite and intrigue. Indeed, that road was an ever-inviting open question: who knew who might pass this way next?

★   ★   ★

Antinous was born in November, the month of Metes or Cybele, the earth mother, in the calendar of Bithynia, probably on the 27th. The inscription of the burial club at Lanuvium, south of Rome, of 136 AD confidently gives this birthday as one of the feast days and for this reason it has been dismissed as a convenient fiction.[3] Recently, however, a papyrus dug up at Oxyrhynchus in Egypt and of about a hundred years later than the inscription, records part of a calendar of festivals, listing events chronologically, starting with the deification of Antinous (which is known to have been on or about 30 October) and ending with the birthday of the Emperor Lucius Verus (which was on 15 December).[4] The fourth entry in the sequence of cult days is the birthday of Antinous, which therefore must have been in November, though there is no proof in this document that it was on the 27th. Perhaps the poor club-members of Lanuvium, a place full of senatorial and imperial villas, had taken advice and were better informed than later historians thought. Evidently, the date was widely known anyway.

For the year of his birth we have not a scrap of evidence. It can only be conjectured from the sculptures done of him after his death in 130 and from the terminology used about him. In the ancient Greek texts he is frequently called *meirakion* and sometimes *ephebe*, terms for late adolescents which imply that he cannot have been more than twenty, if as old as that, at his death. The sculptures support this. Even the gravest of them show him as a very young man and the last depiction of him as a human being (accepting that it *is* him), on the lion tondo of the Arch of Constantine, with shorn hair and incipient whiskers, would suggest an age of between eighteen and twenty at his death. Thus we can be fairly sure that Antinous was born between 110 and 112, while Pliny was busy in Bithynia and at the very zenith of victorious Rome under the Emperor Trajan.

His name is not without its significance. Just possibly, it may derive from that Antinous who was the most beautiful of the doomed suitors of Penelope in Homer's *Odyssey*. On the other hand, the people of Bithynion claimed to be a colony founded by Arcadian settlers from the faraway city of Mantineia, a walled city on a plain among the humpy blue hills of the central Peloponnese and distinguished for its connection with the warrior-hero Epaminondas buried nearby. The second founder of this city was a woman, Antinoë. It may well be that this name was common in the daughter city of Bithynion and that its masculine variant was given to Antinous. Some historians are sceptical about any such Arcadian settlement there,[5] but Mantineia certainly became later, with Hadrian's support, the chief centre of the cult of the deified Antinous on the mainland of Greece and seems to have maintained close relations with Bithynion.[6] Perhaps, therefore, the legendary colonisation may have been more than an opportunistic fabrication by a city anxious to possess or to cash in on the new god or, by Hadrian's mythologers, claiming the purest Hellenic roots for his Antinous.

19

The boy's ancestry is also unknown but there is general agreement that in his blood flowed strains other than the purely Hellenic. This admixture has led to some ridiculous speculation. Kenneth Clark talks of his 'dark Arabian beauty'. Salmon calls him 'Asiatic'. Laban even sees Jewish characteristics in him.[7] Others speak of his 'sultry oriental' qualities, somewhat heavy, intense and very physical.[8] And indeed his features have elements which are obviously unclassical: the angle and bluntness of his nose, the breadth at its roots, the width of the face, the squatness of the neck, the thickness of the eyebrows and the indefinable curvature and protrusion of that 'pomegranate mouth' which many see as voluptuous.[9] But no clear racial signs can be identified. All we can say is that his name may have been purely Arcadian but that in his body and perhaps in his nature mingled those diverse contributions of the west and the east which made up his homeland.

About his more immediate family the epitaph on the obelisk on the Pincio Hill in Rome provides us with only the tiniest clue. Erman thinks that a badly mutilated phrase could refer to him as 'the first-born of his mother'.[10] Certainly his mother's womb is praised and there seems to have been more about his family and birthplace where the granite is now irretrievably damaged. Perhaps the drafter of these lines, Hadrian, had got to know and to like the family or the mother enough to give them a favourable mention in the epitaph. For what it is worth, this doubtful phrase might imply that Antinous came from a settled and respectable family (otherwise Hadrian would scarcely have mentioned it) and was the first of perhaps several children, not an orphan or an abandoned waif as has sometimes been supposed.

Was he then free or a slave? The question is important as it involves not only Antinous' autonomy but also Hadrian's own consistency and daring. Even some of the most careful of modern scholars refer to him consistently as a slave[11] and claim (not quite accurately) that 'the divinisation of a slave was a unique fact among the annals of antiquity'.[12] The tradition of automatically calling him a slave goes back, as part of the general denigration of his and Hadrian's characters, to the Renaissance. But not beyond that. If the whole of the ancient references to him are examined, he is described as a slave by only one of about fifty different authors. This occurs in a quotation which the ecclesiastical historian Eusebius, writing about 310 AD, gives from an earlier Christian polemicist Hegesippos who, angrily inveighing against pagan idolatry, refers to 'Antinous the slave [doulos] of Hadrian Caesar'.[13] Now Hegesippos had been in Rome in about 155–65 and compiled his five volumes of memoirs in about 175–80. He could well have been a contemporary of Antinous and, if this quotation some 150 years after the original can be relied upon, was one of the earliest writers about him. What he says – though Henderson calls his testimony 'valueless'[14] – must therefore be taken seriously, despite its obvious denigratory bias.

What makes Hegesippos' evidence so extremely doubtful is its embalmed uniqueness. If Antinous had actually been a slave and raised to godhead this would have constituted a scandal in the social system of the ancient world far more reprehensible than the elevation of even a catamite. A slave was a chattel and as such did not even qualify for Hades, let alone Olympus. There was a widespread fear of slaves who jumped out of their place: they threatened the whole settled fabric of society. It would, therefore, have been an outrage for such a divinised slave to claim the veneration of respectable free folk. Those, pagan and Christian alike, who, for other reasons, were anxious to denounce this apotheosis or Hadrian, would surely have seized upon this extra enormity and trumpeted its brazen horror to all posterity. Instead we have absolute silence. Not even a faint echo of such a charge. In all the various references to Antinous by ancient writers he is called a 'slave' only in the one extract given by Eusebius which was quoted by Jerome, though when Jerome provides his own three independent descriptions of Antinous he is never in them mentioned again as a slave.[15] Either the ancient critics did not know of the allegation (incredible if Antinous had been of servile status) or chose deliberately to ignore it because it was so obviously false that it was scarcely profitable to repeat it.

Other evidence points to the same conclusion. For example, slavery was relatively uncommon in Bithynia and it would have been a strange chance for Hadrian to have become enamoured of one of the few slaves of the province.[16] And such a choice would have been even stranger still given what we know of Hadrian's own attitudes. Though he, as Emperor, legislated humanely to improve the treatment and rights of slaves in general, he had little time for them personally, as his 'violent diatribe' against those causing trouble earlier in his reign shows.[17] Nor could he abide slaves who did not keep to their subordinate place. Once when he saw one of his slaves walking away from him familiarly between two Senators he had him boxed soundly on the ears and reprimanded for daring to be so presumptuous. Is it likely that such a punctilious stickler for the social order would have flaunted a slave as his intimate companion and violated all the conventions of society and religion by making him a god? Of course, Antinous could have been like Hadrian's secretary, Phlegon, and other close assistants, a freedman, but there is not a hint that he was. We shall never know for sure. Hegesippos' single insidious word, his 'subtle lie' as one historian calls it,[18] must always raise a doubt, but the chances are that, whatever else he may have been, Antinous was not a slave.

What then *was* he, and his family? In the void of information, the myth-makers have busily spun their webs made of no more than gossamer. According to the seventeenth-century antiquarian Hardouin, anxious to absolve the affair of at least perverted immorality, Antinous was Hadrian's illegitimate son by a concubine and he became governor of Bithynia. According to the Spanish historian Pijoan, he was the son of an eastern prince and was taken hostage in Trajan's wars against Parthia. For such a high-ranking background there is not the slightest probability. Much more pervasive has been the low-ranking one. Tristan, an antiquarian of the 1640s, noted that the coins of Antinous from Bithynion showed him with a staff and leading an ox (fig. 47b). From this he deduced that the boy had been a shepherd and the idea was enthusiastically taken up by the romantic historians of the nineteenth century to whom the tale of a beautiful, innocent shepherd boy whisked from a simple bed of fresh green grass to a seductive one of imperial purple silk had an irresistible appeal. However, Wilhelm Weber long ago showed that on those coins Antinous appears as the gods Hermes-Pan or Hermes-Nomios, and that his role as a god of nature had a lot to do with the religious outcome of his death and the local assimilations to divinities which followed but nothing necessarily to do with his life.[19] It is also unlikely that Hadrian, one of the most accomplished and sophisticated men of his time, would have sustained an intimate relationship of at least three years with an unlettered and crude cattle-tender.

Nevertheless the fact that we hear nothing at all about the family is in itself eloquent. We can be fairly sure that they did not come from the upper crust of Bithynian society. Justin, the earliest of all writers about Antinous, is scornful, if discreet, about his origins.[20] Much later, Lucian, writing of Ganymede in a passage which many think refers to Antinous, has Zeus forbid 'causing the boy any pain by reproaching him with his birth and family'.[21] Again we have nothing concrete. We can only guess that Antinous' family came from lower down the social scale of Claudiopolis – perhaps peasant farmers or small business men, free and respectable enough, owning slaves of their own perhaps, but socially undistinguished.

We can, however, reasonably assume, from what the Pincio obelisk explicitly tells us about his intelligence and early wisdom, and from what we know of Hadrian's taste in companions, that Antinous was educated. As we shall later show that he probably remained in Claudiopolis until he was about eleven to thirteen, he most likely attended classes there and exercised in the palaestra, like all the free-born boys of the town. The following description, glowingly idealised, of a fairly well-off Greek boy's day in the provinces of the late Empire may give at least some savour of Antinous' own regular experience: we shall see later that Hadrian considered him a skilled rider and marksman with the spear. It comes from the dialogue *Affairs of the Heart* by a late imitator of Lucian and from a speech by Callicratidas, an ardent advocate of pederastic love.[22]

He rises at dawn from his single bed and washes the sleep from his eyes with pure water and fastens his shirt and mantle at the shoulder. He leaves his father's home with eyes down and does not look at anyone he meets . . . He is followed by his slaves and tutors who carry . . . many-leaved writing tablets or books that relate the virtues of ancient deeds, or a tuneful lyre if he is going to his music master.

After he has fortified his spirit zealously with the precepts of philosophy and nourished his mind with diverse knowledge, he perfects his body with noble exercise.

He loves the horses of Thessaly and, after his own youth has been broken in like a colt's, he practises in peace the arts of war, throwing javelins and hurling spears with unerring aim. Next come the games of the palaestra, all glistening with oil, where under the heat of the midday sun his developing body is covered in dust and sweat which pours from his toils in the contests. Next a quick bath and a meal the frugality of which allows, shortly after, work to be resumed. For again his masters appear to expound the facts of history and to help him engrave on his memory which heroes distinguished themselves by courage, which by prudence and which by temperance and justice. When he has soaked his growing young soul in the dew of such virtues, he gives his appetite the reward of nature and thereafter he sleeps soundly amid dreams all the sweeter for the exertions of the day.

'Who' [asks Callicratidas, anticipating Hadrian's response to Antinous] 'would not fall in love with such a youth?'

What did Antinous look like in these early days at Claudiopolis? A small group of sculptures which seem to show him as a boy-god of this age may derive from lost early portraits or later retrospective ones or may be just artistic imaginings, though the uniformities among them seem to exclude the latter. At least, they enable us to guess at his appearance (fig. 16). The features we shall come to recognise as those of the older youth are obviously here; but this boy is plumper in the face, wider in the eyes, more pouting in the lips, with an expression of alert or amazed innocence or solemnity, tinged, in the heads of Tunis and Munich, with sensuality. There is little here of that 'fragrance of dreaming melancholy' which Dietrichson thought had been nurtured in the young Antinous by his solitary sojourns as a shepherd 'in forest glades and forest lonelinesses' of the mountain slopes of Bithynia.[23] Instead, the feeling of this lad is of bright and wondering ingenuousness, a little self-consciously serious, as though the youngster from the palaestra of Claudiopolis had just arrived at the overwhelming imperial court of Rome.

Assuming (as we shall argue in Chapter 5) that Antinous grew up in Claudiopolis until the year 123 AD, a whiff of the great events outside his little schoolboy life must have been carried to him along the great road. He would have been too young to have seen Pliny, accompanied by his master of the works, the biographer Suetonius, bustling about the province in 111–12, interrogating, expostulating and annotating. He would only have been a toddler when in 113, the whole Greek world was electrified and elated as the Emperor of Rome, like Alexander the Great, set out for war on behalf of Hellas and its civilisation against the traditional foe, Parthia. The wide- eyed little boy might well have gaped at the legionaries striding along the road late in 114 to their winter quarters in Ancyra some eighty-five miles away whence rumours of their royal entertainment by the local grandee C. Julius Severus must have filtered back to curious Claudiopolis.

It was only when the war came to its equivocal conclusion and Trajan had died suddenly in 117 that the young Antinous might first have glimpsed an Emperor. The successor, Hadrian, marched to claim his inheritance, not at once to Rome but to Nikomedia, that fulcrum city from which he could direct affairs in both the west and the east of his restless new domains. It is thought that he spent the whole winter there and passed on his way through Ancyra in November 117. He might have travelled on from there via Claudiopolis – though there is no surviving evidence – in which case the young boy might have caught his first sight of the piercing grey-blue eyes, tense lips, trim beard and fastidiously curled fringe of the man who was later to shape his destiny. Or perhaps he saw him on a visit to Nikomedia. It is unlikely that Antinous joined the entourage at this time.

Some years later, between 120 and 122, the Propontis was shaken by a massive earthquake which destroyed much of both Nikomedia and Nicea and must have been at least felt at Claudiopolis. There is a theory that Antinous lost his family in the devastation but we simply do not know. At the same time there were ugly signs of another war with Parthia. The roads around Ancyra were hastily renovated for the crisis and troops marched again towards the eastern frontier. Meanwhile, however, Hadrian himself had hastily scudded by ship right across the Mediterranean from Spain to resolve the crisis personally by firm diplomacy. With more leisure, he now turned again north-west towards Asia Minor and his beloved Greece, but paused on the way to inspect and help restore the earthquake damage in Bithynia – he long retained a special regard for Nikomedia. At length he arrived at Ancyra where he presided at a new mystic festival of the arts in the name of Dionysos, the god of renewal and abundance with whom the Greeks were already identifying him. And then, after a detour, in June 123, Hadrian and his entourage moved down the great road into the valley where lay Claudiopolis. This time Antinous was surely waiting.

Greek was the native tongue of well over half of the inhabitants of this Empire of Rome. Though the takeover of the Hellenic world by the Roman one had been substantially completed by 30 BC and its once fiercely independent territories had been ruled as mere provinces from Rome, Greek civilisation had continued, remarkably uninfluenced by its political subjugation. The Greek way of life, crystallised in the separate city with its council and assembly, its stoa, agora, games, gymnasium, palaestra, theatre and stadium, persisted over the mainland of Greece and Macedonia and the islands, round the shores and within the hinterland of Asia Minor, in parts of the Levant, in the great city of Alexandria and Ptolemais in Egypt, in Cyrene in Libya and sporadically along the coast of Africa. Greek was even spoken in Mauretania, while Naples and other former colonies in South Italy never completely lost their Hellenic character. One of the most astonishing features of Roman history is not just this resilient survival of Greek civilisation but its brilliant resurgence, its cultural conquest of Rome, its rapid attainment of political parity and then, as the Latin Empire dwindled, the emergence of a powerful Greek Empire in

Byzantium. In this process the first half of the second century marks a major turning point in which Antinous had his contribution to make.

Part of the Roman genius lay in its pragmatism. When Rome conquered the eastern Hellenic kingdoms it did not (as with the barbarian west) seek to impose the Latin way of life or even Roman institutions but to adapt those already working. The army, always Latin-speaking, which in Europe had been such an agency of Romanisation, was here in the east, as in Bithynia, not even garrisoned in the conquered territories but kept near the frontiers. Already deeply impressed by ancient Greek civilisation, Rome preferred to work through its characteristic unit of the city and its leading citizens. Rome tinkered with the cities' constitutions to establish oligarchy and to eliminate democracy, reformed their laws, established a provincial administration to harmonise the cities one with another and offered higher legal tribunals to solve their endless disputes. But the cities were left substantially intact to continue their own intense life and even to mint their coins.

Under the Republic, the Greeks had been plundered and drained by exactions and civil wars. The cities of the mainland had withered and those of Asia Minor failed to develop: everywhere the economy had declined. Little wonder then that the Greeks acclaimed the settlement after Actium, nominally a defeat for the east, and the establishment of the Principate under Augustus, with relief. The Empire brought order, internal stability of institutions, better supervision, more honest administration and an intelligible single leader to the world.

From the start the Emperors had recognised the importance of their Greek possessions and heritage, though they varied in their enthusiasm. Augustus, who was never fluent in Greek, had won the devotion of his eastern subjects without forfeiting that of the Romans who were suspicious of the glib, ingratiating and corrupt Greeks. In reaction, Tiberius banned the use of Greek in the Senate. Claudius, who spoke and wrote Greek ('the finest language of all') voluminously, who had influential Greeks in his household and who granted benefactions to many cities besides that of Antinous, even wished to introduce the great mysteries of Eleusis to Rome.[24] Nero was for his time impossibly, even grotesquely, philhellene. He appointed the first Greek Prefect of Egypt – one Balbillus, a female descendant of whom had a part to play in the final moments of Antinous. Nero, to the sneers of Latin stalwarts, impetuously introduced Greek festivals, dances and gymnasia to Rome itself, conducted himself in public spectacles like a Greek actor and, in 66 AD, at the Isthmus of Corinth, issued a declaration making the mainland of Greece free of senatorial rule and taxation. His successor Vespasian (AD 69–79) very soon rescinded this, commenting acidly that 'the Greeks have forgotten how to be free'.[25] A strong but historically obscure reaction of hostility to Rome stirred among the Greeks. In Alexandria, always the disgruntled focus of Hellenic opposition to Rome, there were the inevitable disturbances.

Nevertheless, under the Flavians the loyal Greek establishment began to be promoted to the very centre of power. Vespasian himself appointed the first two Greek Senators and his son Domitian promoted them to the highest office of Consul in 92 and 94 AD. Indeed, Domitian accepted the archonship (chief magistracy) of Athens, rebuilt the temple of Apollo at Delphi, wore Greek dress and tried to introduce a Hellenistic style of theocratic monarchy. Trajan created other Greek Consuls in 108 and 109 and elevated Greeks to governorships and even coveted second consulates. His reign saw the most spectacular increase of Greek influence in Rome. In the Senate the proportion of Italian-bred magnates began to dwindle. At the time of Antinous' birth, provincial Senators of distant Italian origins (like Trajan and Hadrian themselves) came to the forefront if not to a majority. The Greeks were at first insignificant among them – under Vespasian they constituted 16.7 per cent of the provincials in the Senate, but under Trajan's patronage their share leapt to 34.8 per cent; it rose slightly under Hadrian to 36.8 per cent, jumped again under Antoninus Pius to 46.5 per cent and reached 60.8 per cent in the times of Commodus in the 180s.[26] In the lifetime of Antinous, Greeks were busy in the Senate, governing provinces, commanding armies, running the imperial secretariat. It as as though the political disaster of Actium and the reversal of Nero's policy of freedom only sixty years before had not happened.

There had never been a cultural setback. From the start, with their dazzling inheritance in art, philosophy, literature and science, the Greeks had influenced Rome rather than the opposite. In vain under the Republic did Cato the Censor and Cicero denounce the insidious corruption of wholesome Latin virtues by Greek morals and character. The language, education, philosophy, the artists and fashions of Greece (though never its mode of athleticism), invaded Italy to such an extent that under Augustus the poet Horace could declare: 'Captive Greece has in its turn conquered its savage vanquisher and carried civilisation to barbarous Latium.'[27]

Despite the reaction against Nero's premature philhellenism and the ferocious criticism of Roman traditionalists like Pliny the Elder, Tacitus and Juvenal, castigating the 'scented sons of Corinth' and their values until well into the reign of Hadrian, there was no stopping the triumph of Greek culture over that of Rome.[28] Men of a later generation like Pliny the Younger paid automatic and sincere homage to it. Eastern religions, the eastern cult of the Emperor, Greek rhetoric, Hellenistic styles of sculpture and literature all flourished in Rome, blending more or less with indigenous kinds. By the death of Hadrian, creative Latin literature was dead too, its last great exponents being Juvenal and Suetonius. That of Greece was in full spate and Greek was to be the language of the new religions of mystery and salvation. Even the Emperor of Rome, Marcus Aurelius, published his *Meditations* in Greek.

Hellenes of the second century had a healthy respect and a thinly veiled contempt for Rome. They welcomed the new partnership as one by which Rome provided the political institutions, external defence and internal peace under which the superior culture of Hellas could flower untroubled. Plutarch, whose career as a priest of Apollo and a friend of Rome and whose 'Parallel Lives' between Rome and Greek heroes celebrated the new partnership, sincerely welcomed 'this tranquillity which is ours, for there reigns everywhere a great peace and a great calm; all wars have stopped; one sees no more emigrations or rebellions, no more tyrannies, no more of those other endemic sicknesses and scourges of Greece'.[29] Aristeides, in his oration a generation later, saw in the 'beautiful order' harmonised by the Emperor at the centre with his fair administrators and his disciplined armies, and in the distribution of Roman citizenship among 'the better part of the world's talent', the means by which 'all the Greek cities rise up' from arbitrary government to freedom. The whole world was unified into 'a single harmonious, all-embracing union' of self-governing cities under the protection and hegemony of Rome.[30] But though both Plutarch and Aristeides admired Roman organisation, justice and disciplined might, they still referred to its culture, if at all, as alien. The only culture was that of Hellas and the role of Rome was to provide the material support for its splendid renaissance.[31]

Antinous came into his Greek inheritance at a peculiar moment of balance and self-consciousness. The spiritual glories and discoveries of ancient Greece, which partly derived from experimental and ultimately self-destructive freedom, were not to be rivalled. The turbulent city-state had now degenerated to a municipality, governed by an oligarchy, its popular assembly an empty ritual. This Hellenic revival was to be one of material display and verbal fireworks rather than one of creative profundity.

Everywhere the prosperous cities of the east grew more resplendent as their wealthy citizens and indulgent Emperors endowed them with sumptuous new libraries, temples, gymnasia, baths, markets and aqueducts, and countless jostling statues. Education had never been more abundantly available. The old feverish rivalry between the cities issued now not in wars but in competition for honorific titles and precedence, for the most lavish buildings, festivals, prizes to visiting artists and athletes. The rich, loyal to Rome and actual citizens of Rome (for all magistrates received its citizenship), nevertheless still remained proudly based in their provincial native cities for which they provided bread and charity as well as less basic fare. The gap between the few rich and the many poor was widening and the latter preferred bread to buildings, races to rhetoric, frequently demonstrating their preferences by riots and stonings. Though the gap between the two classes was not yet unbridgeable there was little scope for the really poor to rise. Aristeides' tempting prospect of 'paths open to all' was no more than a mirage, as the low-born and highly-talented writer Lucian found when he struggled as a clerk to make his way in the world. However talented a boy like Antinous may have been, without the inherited wealth which Aristeides and most of the other sophists had, it is unlikely he would have risen to eminence.

There were plenty of writers in Greek from all over the provinces – Lucian, Arrian, Appian, Herodian, Philostratus, the two Dios, Mesomedes and Strato, to name only a few. The quality of their output seldom matched the quantity. More typical of this age of words rather than thought were the sophists, those rhetors who had attained such an enormous following that cities vied to house them, men of staggering influence, rank and wealth. As they frequented Hadrian's circle, Antinous must have got to know – or to endure – many of them. Polemo, for example, of Smyrna, who was a travelling companion of Hadrian in 123, had his own vast entourage and was powerful enough to extract huge sums from the Emperor for Smyrna and to evict without a qualm the proconsul of Asia, the later Emperor Antoninus Pius, who had been lodging in his house during an absence. Of him it was said, 'he talked with cities as his inferiors, with Emperors as not his superiors and with the gods as equals'.[32] Herodes Atticus was the unlikeable son of a father who left twenty-four million drachmas to the people of Athens rather than to him. Besides serving as ambassador, and endowing Athens, Corinth and Delphi and other places with splendid buildings or aqueducts, he became tutor to the young Caesar, Marcus Aurelius, a *corrector* of cities, and rose to be Consul in 143. There were countless others of whom Favorinus the Hermaphrodite from Gaul, Aristeides, and Dio of Prusa were among the better-known. In their artificial volubility, their ostentatious wealth and aristocratic backgrounds, their versatility in the affairs of the world and their devotion and generosity to their cities, in the ubiquity of their travels and their supreme self-confidence, they are the ripest fruits of this final efflorescence of Greek civilisation.

Yet the lifetime of Antinous was still an age of balance between east and west. When the heirs of Celsus, the first Greek Senator of Rome, built the enormous library to his memory at Ephesos, the record of his career was inscribed on one side in Latin and on the other in Greek. The old Olympian gods, too, still held their own against the religions of salvation, rebirth and mystery of the east. The great sanctuaries of Hellas – the Asclepieion at Pergamon, the Artemiseion of Ephesos, the shrine of Demeter at Eleusis, even the rather faded oracle of Apollo at Delphi – were magnificently renovated and thronged with pilgrims.

Helping create this new harmony between east and west was the ease and security of travel in the second century either on the great roads or the safe seas with their rebuilt havens. As the journeys of St Paul earlier in Asia Minor, those of Polemo, those of Pausanias or Arrian reveal, never before and never – to our own day – since had travel all over east and west been so secure, so unimpeded by bandits, by pirates, by customs or national barriers. As Aristeides, gratefully put it: 'neither Cilician gates nor narrow sandy approaches to Egypt through Arab country, nor inaccessible mountains, nor immense stretches of rivers, nor inhospitable tribes of barbarians cause terror, because for security it suffices to be a Roman citizen or rather one of those united under your hegemony'.[33] And the greatest traveller of all, one who more than any other knit the whole Greco-Roman polity together by his endless, vigilant peregrinations over the whole of the Empire, was the new Emperor, Hadrian.

Yet there was a ferment. The Greeks, though generally content with their partnership with Rome, were aware of their differences and convinced of their superiority. The wars of Trajan against Parthia had kindled memories of a noble, stirring antiquity and revived a proud identity in being Greek. Architectural display and elaborate rhetoric, refurbishment of the old gods, were not enough. In the days of Antinous there was a yearning for new symbols, refashioned political means by which to focus and animate this heady consciousness of a common heritage and a shared renewal, the achievements and aspirations of which were sadly frittered over a thousand separate cities. There was, for the first time for centuries among the fractious peoples of Hellas, a feeling of unity and a desire to embody it.[34]

The best hope of this, paradoxically, came not from Greece but from Rome and not originally from Rome but from Spain. For the tastes and policy of the man travelling down the road into the valley of Claudiopolis and towards Antinous in the summer of 123 had long been known. The Greeks had found 'their restorer', 'their saviour', the 'new Dionysos', to use their own ecstatic terms.[35]

HADRIAN, THE ROMAN EMPEROR
76–123

'Among all the sovereigns, the Emperor Hadrian has done most for the happiness of each of his subjects.'[1] Thus wrote the shrewd topographer Pausanias, with evident sincerity, a generation after the death of the Emperor when empty flattery had no purpose to serve.

His judgement has been echoed by historians down the centuries. Hadrian is regarded as one of the greatest of the Emperors, the true founder of the so-called 'Golden Age of the Antonines' in which the world-empire of Rome reached a culmination of peace, harmony and prosperity. Yet he remains a strange, enigmatic, even forbidding man. We know a great deal about the grand strategy, the complex politics, the subtle propaganda and the strenuous labours by which he strove to attain 'tranquillity', 'times of felicity', 'a stable world', to quote some of his own slogans,[2] but when we search for the man himself, his sources and motivations, we are presented with a mass of contradictions, the brilliant diverse facets of an external self which designedly dazzle and confuse us, leaving the human being within concealed from vision. This is not another fluke of historiography. Even contemporaries who knew him well found the same. Perceptive men like Cornelius Fronto, the effusive sophist who respected Hadrian, or Marcus Aurelius the prim Emperor who despised him, could easily enumerate his public virtues and vices, but to them, as to us, the inner man remained elusive, too remote to be approached, too complicated to be summed up.[3] Little wonder, then, that the ancient historians took refuge for their depictions of him in strings of puzzling paradoxes.[4] Few great men have been so much admired, so seldom comprehended and so little loved.

Antinous was to be the one person who seems to have connected most profoundly with Hadrian. Something in the youth from Bithynia satisfied, for a time at least, deep needs in the nature of the man. Hadrian's tortuous personality seems to have attained a fleeting serenity at the same moment as his policies reached an acclaimed fulfilment. But not for long. Perhaps the man needed far more than the lad could give, saw more in him than was there or offered nothing nourishing or durable in return. In any case Hadrian was never to establish another human relationship – even that with Aelius Caesar – of such obsessive intensity and rich meaning.

But Antinous after death was to do more than sustain his morbid lover personally. Hadrian, the cunning and vulgar politician, knew how to exploit publicly his own genuine and private grief. Just as the images and memory of the beautiful boy remained an intimate necessity for himself, so the resurrected hero could be used to serve larger political designs for others. Thus Antinous in life was desperately entangled in the devious web of Hadrian's personality and in death was elevated into the lucid mainstream of his policy. That personality and that policy now claim our attention.

Hadrian had obviously been fashioned by forces in his earliest years, long before he attained the throne in 117 at the age of forty-one. Some German historians stress his Spanish origins as powerfully formative. Although his ancestors were of Italian stock from Hadria on the coast of north-east Italy, they had been settled in south-west Spain in the town of Italica on the Guadalquivir near Seville since 205 BC. From this and a calculated 510 predecessors of mixed Iberian, Punic and Phoenician blood, these historians discern inherited strains of sombre mysticism, brooding intensity, convoluted energy, provincial assertiveness, hostility to Rome and even a streak of cruelty.[5] Such theories of inheritance have been dismissed as mere 'fancies'.[6] The Aelii, along with their relatives the Ulpii and other connected families from the district of Baetica, had for some generations been among those provincial families from Spain and Mediterranean Gaul who were rising to prominence in the Senate in Rome under the Flavians.

Publius Aelius Hadrianus was born in Rome itself on 24 January 76 AD. He may have been in Italica as a child and definitely went back there for a couple of years of military preparation when he was fifteen, spending his time hunting enthusiastically.[7] But his education was in refined Hellenistic circles in the Rome of Domitian (with even perhaps a spell in Athens), where his devotion to all things Greek earned him the nickname *Graeculus*. He never visited Italica again, even when wintering in Spain, and later took pains to mock and upbraid deputations of its citizens. Perhaps, characteristically, he bore the place some grudge, never avowed. Equally characteristically, he later rebuilt the town he so disliked on a megalomaniac scale, making it, though only a summer resort, the fourth largest in the whole peninsula.

His mother, Domitia Paulina, came from Cadiz and lived into her sixties and into her son's reign. His father died in his forties in 85 AD. His elder sister, Paulina, married Julius Servianus, a distinguished Senator, thirty years Hadrian's senior, with whom there was to be a lifetime of concealed or open enmity ending in bloodshed. Their daughter's husband, Pedanius Fuscus, who as Hadrian's nephew was his nearest male relative and prospective heir, figured with him as Consul in 118 but then disappears from history, leaving a son of the same name and aspirations who was also to die violently at his great-uncle's command. Paulina, the sister, was commemorated after her death in about 130 among the tribe-names of Antinoopolis and by funeral games. But that is all. Hadrian bestowed no other honours on his family by blood as Trajan had done for his natural parents and sister. Was this over-refined Greekling in some way ashamed of his provincial background, as he was ashamed of and later worked hard to eradicate his provincial Latin accent at which the Senate laughed?[8] In any case there seems to have been coolness, distance, jealousy and concealment in those fundamental family relationships where warmth, intimacy and trust make for healthy growth. One suspects that Hadrian never received much love at home and thereafter had precious little to bestow.

Left fatherless at ten, Hadrian became the ward of two other men from Italica now prominent in Rome. Acilius Attianus was a knight who later, as Prefect of the Guard, was to play a crucial part in securing the throne for Hadrian. Far more important as an influence on Hadrian's character and whole life was the other guardian, the cousin of his father, more than twenty-two years older than himself: Trajan. *Praetor* in 85 AD, married to a distant relative Plotina the next year, commander of a legion in 89, *consul ordinarius* in 91, this bold general, sagacious and temperate politician, survived the persecutions and profited by the downfall of the tyrannical Domitian in 96. The next Emperor, the ageing and weak Nerva, felt compelled to adopt this strong military man as his heir in October 97 and Trajan succeeded to the *imperium* three months later, the first provincial to sit on the throne of Rome.

His reign – to the ancients – was one of the most spectacular and successful of Roman history, marked by political harmony, economic prosperity, the advent of the provincials in government, sumptuous rebuilding of the capital and a policy of expansion abroad – the peaceful annexation of Arabia, the conquest of rich Dacia beyond the Danube in 106, and the crushing of the Parthian Empire and its satellites in 113–17. The fact that the latter adventure ended in disastrous retreat and rebellions was glossed over by the euphoric Romans, obscured by the sudden death of Trajan in 117 and blamed on his successor. Trajan ever after remained in history as he had been officially acclaimed in his lifetime, *Optimus Princeps*, 'the best of Emperors'.

Nowadays historians see many continuities in the developments and even the policies of the reigns of Trajan and Hadrian. But the two men themselves were vastly different. Trajan, with his big round face and prosaic fringe, appeared bluff, direct and open. As Syme puts it, 'he looked stupid and was believed honest' (fig. 17).[9] (Hadrian's curse was to appear and be considered the opposite.) Indeed he has sometimes been depicted as a brilliant soldier and ruler, but otherwise a barrack-room boor of sparse cultivation, swilling his wine copiously, fawning over bawdy pantomime actors and his favourite boys. But if the replies to Pliny's endless requests from Bithynia are his, or even reflect his opinions, he is revealed as a man of considerable wisdom, patience and sensitivity, scrupulous of the rights of individuals and localities, though with perhaps an amused contempt for 'those poor Greeks' and lacking in curiosity.[10] His close friends included some of the most civilised men of the day, his wife with whom he was on good terms was philosophically inclined and he endowed Rome with a splendid library. Nevertheless he was obviously no intellectual, still less an aesthete. Though Hadrian on his part was certainly not lacking in physical courage or military capacity and 'was a right good eater of rich food',[11] he shared only one taste thoroughly with Trajan: a love of boys and beautiful young men, and that may have brought them sometimes into conflict. In his complicated and devious nature, his bruised and thrusting ego, his fastidious, dandy-like appearance, his brightly polished versatility, his precious language, the mature Hadrian was in nature, presence and interests far apart from the *Optimus Princeps*. He had much more in common with Plotina, so much that hostile contemporaries assumed they were lovers. Hadrian's bottled-up inner feelings of hostility to Trajan leaked out only after his own succession.[12]

The years between the recall of the avid young hunter from Italica in 91 and his unorthodox and suspicious accession in 117, can only have strengthened in Hadrian qualities of deep insecurity, concealment of feelings, solitariness, and capacity to harbour grudges, just as they trained and broadened his political and military skills and his sure grasp of the diversity, needs and limitations of the Empire. Trajan was childless and Hadrian was his nearest male relative, married in 100 AD to Sabina (then aged 12–14), the Emperor's great-niece and hitherto his nearest unmarried female relative. The marriage was an evident dynastic contrivance and never became anything more. Hadrian was thus doubly confirmed as the obvious heir. His problem was that Trajan would never openly acknowledge him as such. The young man was not advanced through the usual official career more quickly than any other of his rank and ability. He held the usual minor magistracies in Rome, military tribunates in Germany and on the Danube in 95–6, was the Emperor's *quaestor* to the Senate in 101, tribune of the plebs in 105, commander of a legion in the Dacian war of 105–6, a vigorous and strict governor of Pannonia in 107 and Consul in 108. Such a career was distinguished but not spectacular. Sometimes, tantalisingly, Trajan seems to have singled him out, giving him two million sesterces for his praetorian games and even, more significantly, rewarding his military feats with the same diamond ring which he, Trajan, had received from Nerva. The influential Sura even confided to Hadrian in 108 that he was to be officially adopted as heir. Others also saw him as the rising star: the citizens of Athens, sensing like a weather-vane the way the wind was blowing, elected the Senator as their archon or chief magistrate in 112. But, despite all these hints, and the fact that he wrote the Emperor's speeches and served virtually all of his offices in Trajan's vicinity, his adoption as heir never came.

It is clear that the relationship between them varied from hot to cold. Indeed in the earlier days until they fell out in an intrigue, it seems, over some boys, their friendship was so hot (*in amore*) that their connection has even been claimed as sexual in overtone.[13] But at other times there was open hostility, fomented by the jealous Servianus. Hadrian grew worried enough to consult the Virgilian oracle. Plotina had to persuade her reluctant husband to agree to the vital marriage with Sabina. It was Plotina again who got Hadrian the crucial legateship of Syria in the Parthian war. Hadrian was forced to fall in with Trajan's drinking habits, to bribe his freedmen and boy favourites to curry favour. He was treated with 'contempt and neglect' by the Emperor's friends. Even towards the end it was rumoured that Trajan was thinking of naming as heir an elderly lawyer. Whatever Trajan's motives – personal antipathy, vain refusal to accept the inevitability of a successor, need to conceal his dynastic aims – Hadrian was kept on tenterhooks, denied formal recognition, but, in the strength of his dynastic claim and marriage, and in the vast power of the army of the east consigned to him at the end in 117 by the sick Emperor, given the effective means to claim the principate.[14]

Trajan had a stroke in Syria on returning from his disastrous campaign in Parthia to confront revolts within the Empire. He died in Selinus in Cilicia while hastening back to Rome. Hadrian, who had been left in Antioch, in charge of the army of the east, received letters of adoption as heir on 9 August 117 and news of Trajan's death on the 11th. But even then his insecurity was not removed. It was rumoured for centuries afterwards that Plotina had forged the adoption letters and suppressed the news of Trajan's death for some days so that they could be delivered, and even poisoned her husband's valet who knew too much. No doubt the resourceful woman did her best for her protégé in this crisis, but whatever action she took probably confirmed her paralysed husband's intentions. Hadrian, however, felt uneasy enough to stress the legitimacy of his adoption and of his links with the Ulpian house on his coins for some years afterwards. He also apologised to the Senate for accepting the army's acclamation and not its selection as the basis of his power. Whatever the doubts, there was no organised opposition to his accession.

Secure in the support of the army on which he had lavished a double donation of money and of friends controlling twenty-one of the Roman legions, Hadrian showed at once his mettle and decisiveness. Following decisions already taken by Trajan, he immediately relinquished what little remained of the conquests east of the Tigris and Euphrates. Within hours of taking power he boldly dismissed his formidable enemy in the army, the Moorish general Lusius Quietus. Using Marcius Turbo, an able soldier but only of equestrian rank, and others, he acted vigorously to suppress the Jewish revolts in Palestine, Egypt, Cyprus, Libya and Mauretania. Meanwhile, Attianus and Plotina had hastened to Rome with Trajan's ashes. There the former guardian, now Prefect of the Guard, bullied the Senate into executing four of the most distinguished generals and statesmen of Trajan's reign, including Quietus, all undoubtedly opposed to Hadrian but unlikely to be, as Attianus alleged, actually plotting together his assassination. Though Hadrian always denied his complicity in the deaths of these four consulars, their removal undoubtedly relieved his position. The Senate, underneath its meek compliance for much of his reign, never forgot or forgave him.

Wintering with his legions in Nikomedia in 117–18, from which point he could help quieten unrest in east and west, he moved up to the disturbed Danube frontier next year, settling the disaffected tribes by a mixture of military action and monied diplomacy. He felt sure enough of his position to delay entering Rome until 9 July 118. To win over the sullen Senate, he promised never again to punish any of its members without its consent. To placate the seething population, he distributed a double largesse of gold and remitted debts to the Treasury amounting to 900 million sesterces, the tax returns being burnt in a huge bonfire in Trajan's forum.

It was a strange and disconcerting beginning for one who had waited so long and detrimentally to himself for his inheritance. Bloodshed, tax bonfires and massive bribery ushered in the 'times of felicity', advertised so proudly on the first coins of the reign bearing the slogans 'concord', 'peace', 'justice' and 'piety'.[15]

Hadrian was fair-skinned, taller than average and of stalwart build (fig. 19). Like many who seek to hide their real selves, he took great care about his external appearance, wearing the toga in Italy, an elegant, informal travelling outfit on his journeys and Greek dress for the festivals of Athens. His hair was carefully combed forward in waves, in his early forties, and fell over his brow in dainty little curls produced by tongs. He sported a short, well-barbered beard – the first Emperor to do so – and all his successors were to follow suit. Some claim that the beard was to proclaim his philosophic pretensions or his identification with the heroes of ancient Greece, others that it simply hid acne or wounds on his face. The most memorable features, apart from the strong nose, rather puffy high cheeks and puckered brow, were the eyes and mouth. The grey-blue eyes were set close, with thin lids, and pushed up into their sockets. They had an air of incessant scrutiny, flickering with suspicion and doubt: 'weaselish' they have been called.[16] The lower lip was more prominent than the upper, and both were clamped together, tensely compressed. It was a face full of will-power, energy and inquiry but just a little shifty and untrustful in the expression and strained and joyless in the lines.

Of his powers of moral and physical courage and endurance, there was no doubt. He was never afraid to take and stand by unpopular decisions. He survived two assassination attempts, compassionately handing over the mad slave who attacked him in Spain for treatment by doctors. In winter snow and desert heat he marched hatless and fully armed with his troops, sharing their simple camp fare. He remained an intrepid hunter – despite a broken collar bone and rib – still chasing the lion at the age of fifty-four. At the same age he was prepared to clamber up the sheer slopes of Mount Casius in Syria to see the sun rise. Fastidious, dandified and *soigné* as he looked, there was nothing flabby or soft about Hadrian. His mind was swift and sure, capable of conceiving grand designs, of concentrating on the details to see them through and equipped with the patience and enthusiasm to win the willing co-operation of others in their execution. So capable was Hadrian that it was said he could dictate, write, listen and converse with friends all at the same time and that his prodigious memory enabled him to recall the names of countless veterans and to repeat verbatim obscure books which he had read.[17] His energy was unbounded, sustaining him in all the manifold duties of the ruler of the world, fuelling his incessantly curious mind and propelling his body, restlessly travelling the lands and seas of his vast Empire. His ego was vast. He saw himself as Herakles, Dionysos or Theseus, the bringers of civilisation and renewal of life and, later, even as Zeus, the supreme god himself. Megalomania was never far away: colossal size, as in his rebuilding of Athens, his gifts to Smyrna, the scale of his buildings, seemed to him a virtue in itself. His self-consciousness too was so overwhelming that, at times, he seemed to be watching himself acting out the various roles of god, hero, soldier, lover, mourner, common man, patron of the arts, architect, with a theatrical affectation, recording his most trivial sentiments in imperishable or grandiose forms.

If anything, he was over-educated to the point of decadence or pedantry. His style was precious and artificial, concerned more with verbal effects or learned allusions than original meaning. Bored with the obvious, he affected to prefer obscure authors to the established classics: Cato to Cicero, Ennius to Virgil, Coelius to Sallust and Antimachus to Homer. He supported the retrospective trend of the sculpture of his time to early classical models, though his villa was eclectically full of works of all periods and in his architectural designs and constructions he was daringly advanced. His enthusiasm for the past was not just retrospectively antiquarian: it fired his imagination with ideas and schemes for the present.

Hadrian was an outright lover of all things Greek. On the first monument of his reign, the arch of Beneventum, he appears as a demure Greek scholar alongside the tough Roman general Trajan. Hadrian cared little for Latin letters, dismissing Suetonius and antagonising Juvenal, the two greatest Latin authors of his day. But he was surrounded by Greek sophists and scribblers, promoted their academics and artists, and even, at the end of his reign, introduced a Greek-style university into Rome. When it was unfashionable, even dangerous, he had identified himself as a citizen of Athens, enrolling in a district with a name which was later to have a sinister connotation in his life: Besa. He was to visit that city three times as Emperor in the course of the eight or more happy years he was to spend in his Greek domains. And when, in soured old age, he retired to his vast villa outside Rome, he gave its various parts names to remind him of the Greek places he had loved. Ever mindful of the political, military and religious strengths of Rome, Hadrian had filled himself with Roman determination, practicality and shrewdness; but the thrust of his mind, imagination and spirit was towards the artistic inventiveness and heroising mythology, the profound mysteries of Hellas.

Deep forces of insecurity and a nagging sense of inferiority drove him not only to excel but to be jealous of excellence in others. We are told that he wrote, painted and sculpted, was skilled in astrology and architecture, expert in arithmetic and geometry. He was a renowned huntsman, practised in military tactics and gladiatorial combat, but was equally able to hold his own with scholars and philosophers and became legendary as a musician, especially as a flute player. It was all too much: the strain always to excel was intense and showed. He had to do better and to know more than anyone else and to make his superiority crushingly clear to all: rivalry could not be tolerated. No one was more generous to artists, academics and his friends. But there came a point with the able or aspiring men around him when he had to squash them. Always humane in his public actions and in his private relations, he used to say that he could not bear to hurt anyone's feelings; but his caustic tongue, tormenting questions, carefully prepared barbs and jibes did just that.[18] He singled out for his conspicuous favour Favorinus the sophist from Gaul, only later to exile him. Others – Suetonius, Dionysos of Miletus the sophist, Apollodorus the architect, Heliodorus the rhetor, secretary and Prefect of Egypt – were all taken up and later humiliated, if not disgraced. There was a cruel streak in him. Always suspicious, he employed spies to report on his political and military friends.

Those who possessed imperial capacity or dynastic lineage, or anyone who had exposed Hadrian's weaknesses by helping him politically, aroused a festering animosity in him which he knew how to dissimulate for years. Thus Attianus his guardian who had done more than anyone to secure the throne was, by 119, swiftly promoted to senatorial rank as a way to political extinction. Later Turbo, the brilliant soldier, was curtly dismissed and Arrian, the versatile all-rounder, found it prudent to retire to the provinces from the ageing Hadrian's suspicions. There may even have been, at the end, coolness from Hadrian towards Plotina.[19] His friendships never lasted because he was too reticent and withdrawn ever to bestow unstinting trust or ultimate confidence on any human being. No wonder people never knew exactly where they stood with him. His contradictions baffled them: 'austere and genial, affable and harsh, hesitant and impetuous, mean and generous, deceitful and straightforward, cruel and merciful, and always in all things changeable'.[20]

Hadrian was more at ease with his social inferiors. He cultivated the common touch, liked to appear as a private citizen, a man among men, joking naked with the scrawny veterans at the public baths, quaffing sour wine with the troopers, bantering familiarly with petitioners, presiding over gory spectacles in the arena. There can be no doubt of the genuineness of his concern for the humble, whether slaves, tenants or common soldiers. His attendants loved him if no one else did – as the obelisk on the Pincio boasts and Marcus Aurelius sourly had to admit – though Hadrian never allowed them any influence over himself. It was a tragic pose. Hadrian was secure only in relationships in which his superiority of rank – though elaborately masked by egalitarian *bonhomie* and genuine concern – was apparent to all. It was as much a sham as his self-effacement on those buildings which he sumptuously rebuilt, preserving the original donor's name, and ostentatiously omitting his own: though everyone knew his role.

Hadrian's most intimate concerns were so deeply concealed beneath his public persona that they have to be guessed at. The occult and religion always fascinated him. He never lost an opportunity to dabble in mysteries, to explore or rebuild temples, to consult priests, oracles and magicians. His devotion to the gods of Greece and Rome was consistent and manifold in its expression. How deep all this went is a matter of dispute. To some historians, especially of the German school,[21] Hadrian was a profound, indeed agonised, mystic, seeking all his life for some communion with the absolute, some anticipation of the felicity beyond death which would resolve his tormenting doubts and engender a state of inner peace. To other historians,[22] his religious pre-occupations were a mere reflection of his antiquarian enthusiasms, his insatiable curiosity, his aesthetic sensibility, his restless desire for new experiences. Certainly, as we shall see, he knew how coldly and objectively to manipulate religious feeling for political ends. And the famous poem to his soul written on his death-bed reveals not serene faith but a jaded and wanly amused scepticism. Perhaps such corrosive doubt and acid cynicism prevented him from attaining for long the transcendent assurance of the true mystic. Nevertheless, for one period at least, that between his higher initiation at Eleusis in 128 and the apotheosis of Antinous, he does seem to have been swept up with a genuine fervour, a sense of mystic exaltation, even of spiritual rebirth, which clearly shaped the events and the imagery of those years. Even towards the end of his life his devotion to Demeter, the earth mother of Eleusis, was such that he is said to have introduced her mysteries to Rome.

His emotional life was meagre and tortured. We shall dwell more fully on his sexual nature and activities in Chapter 7 in connection with his relationship to Antinous. Only that boy seems to have aroused in him the overpowering and ungrudging response of love, though how giving, uncalculating and un-complicated even that was remains to be seen. For Lucius Ceionius Commodus (Aelius Caesar) the only other known object of his affection (apart from his dogs and horses), his feeling was altogether more qualified. With women he seemed most at ease with mother-figures. Plotina, his adoptive mother, who may have been only 4–14 years older than him and may have genuinely regarded him as a lover, evidently was nothing more than a warm maternal force for him (fig. 18). His actual mother-in-law, Matidia, his link with the Ulpian dynasty, received lavish honours from him in life and death, including the first temple ever erected in Rome expressly for a woman. He called her 'helpful to all, troublesome to no one, ill-humoured with nobody'. These fulsome and strange compliments seem almost deliberately designed to contrast with the one minimal reference in the same speech to his wife, 'my Sabina', whose qualities were almost exactly the opposite of those of her mother.[23] Some years later, after an obscure intrigue or indiscretion involving Sabina with Suetonius and Septicius Clarus, he was less glumly reticent about his wife. He declared that she was 'moody and difficult' (*morosa et aspera*) and if he had been a private citizen he would have divorced her.[24]

At what might have been the calm, warm, emotional centre of his life, his marriage, there was a canker of mutual distaste. Though their relations varied from frigid tolerance to bitter detestation, as we shall see, Sabina and Hadrian kept them going for decorum's sake, even officially projecting themselves as models of nuptial fidelity and bliss as in the grotesquely misconceived sculpture of them as Mars and Venus in the Louvre. Sabina was at least ten years younger than Hadrian and, even had his sexual appetites been towards women, she would never have suited him. Though she clearly tried to adapt herself to her husband's intellectual tastes and grew in later years more into an imperial stature, even receiving late and minimal honours, she was no Plotina. She had not the resources to sublimate her sexual rejection by her husband into unstinting personal companionship, political and cultural activity, gaining a reputation for the incorruptible matronly virtue of ancient Rome. As Sabina's portraits progressively show, especially the tight button of a mouth under the long nose, her lot was festering frustration and unconcealed bitterness (fig. 20).

Isolated already by his position, Hadrian, by his inner nature and his inability to create durable relationships of trust, must have been the loneliest man in his Empire.

We can still study the full enigma and contradictions of his personality in the ruins of the villa, designed by himself, which he began to build seventeen miles from Rome at Tibur in 118 and which had its part to play in the tale of Antinous. Set below the mountains and with a grand, calm view across the Campagna towards the capital and the sea, the enormous (1,000 × 500 yards) sequence of buildings and courtyards was still being added to when Hadrian returned there from his last journey in 134. Its size and elaboration defied its function as one man's rural retreat: there were innumerable reception halls, nymphea, dining rooms, libraries, guest rooms, baths, theatres, a praetorium, a stadium and palaestra and huge underground corridors, functional, for entertaining, or, like their name, Hades, symbolic. The scale was stupendous, megalomaniac: it could never have been comfortable, still less homely. In its construction, Hadrian made full use of new materials of brick and poured concrete to create fluid forms and dynamic spaces. The plans were ingenious combinations of squares and circles, geometrically inventive but lacking repose or the resolution of a central focus. Despite its size and profusion, the whole was extraordinarily public, very few private spaces existed. Water was everywhere – supplied by a brilliant hydraulic system – in lakes, canals and huge fountains which refreshingly sprayed in the exedrae of the summer dining rooms. The materials were of the most sumptuous – varied marbles and coloured stones from all over the world, mosaics, moulded and gilded stucco. The place was crammed with works of art – paintings and mosaics either elegantly abstract or full of joyous animal life, splendid bronze and gilt furnishings, and sculptures, both originals and copies of the masterpieces of Greek art of all periods.

The Villa Adriana has been called the first museum and the first work of architecture which subjectively portrays its creator's entire personality.[25] Here indeed is Hadrian: theatrical, almost vulgar, in the vast scale and bold, even strained, in the use of materials; coldly abstract and infinitely complex in the forms; full of fancies, recollections and abrupt changes of mood; restless, never relaxed, finite or direct in the interplay of space, rhythm or light and shade; contemptuous of cosy domesticities or humdrum functions; using the architectural vocabulary of the past to create something unprecedented in the present; never private yet always isolated.

Hadrian told the Senate that he would never mix public matters with private affairs. It was a promise he was not to keep, as the story of Antinous alone shows. It is, however, emphatically true that, however tortuous, complex and restless his private nature, his public policies were lucidly conceived, consistently pursued, adequately serviced and wholly matched to the needs of his peoples and the times. Only rarely, and then mainly at the end of his life, did the flaws in his personality, 'the crack in soul',[26] endanger his public achievement.

The new Emperor had a clear grasp of what he intended to achieve. Steeped in the cultures of Greece and Rome and aware of their continuities and interdependence, he saw no reason for the Empire to expand into lands with religions and values which he considered barbarous, which would be expensive to conquer, difficult to control and impossible to absorb. The Empire should stop, as Augustus had decreed, at its natural boundaries – the Rhine, Danube and Euphrates – though Hadrian did not abandon Trajan's lucrative annexations of Dacia and Arabia Nabatea. So diverse had the Greco-Roman world become that its parts needed now to be drawn together, to be made aware of their common unifying inheritance as opposed to the barbarians outside. He did not wish to obtain such unity by imposing a crushing uniformity of creed or culture. Every part of the Empire, he believed, had its distinctive part to play and should be encouraged to develop its identity provided this contributed to the Greco-Roman tradition common to them all. Italy – so Hadrian the man with the Spanish background and provincial Latin clearly saw – was but one part and by no means the most thriving or creative part of his domains: it should be no more than one among an equal fraternity of provinces and nations harmoniously linked by tradition and administration around the person of the Emperor.

Such a policy of containment, unity and equality was dangerously radical. The Italians were never fully to appreciate it. It could only be made palatable if served up as something else. Hence Hadrian, antiquarian by taste, took up with relish the imperial role of Augustus, parading his policies as a continuation of those of the early Empire and always stressing their traditional elements. With time the emphasis changed. His ecstatic journeys in the east undoubtedly gave the preservation and renewal of Hellenic culture greater prominence in his mind and, while always stressing the common links between east and west, himself chief among them, he encouraged the growth of a Hellenic identity focused on Athens and Zeus, as he did a Latin one focused on Rome and Jupiter. More and more, he came to believe that the chief task of Roman power was to safeguard and enrich the classical culture of Greece. Always the ideal remained unchanged: local prosperity and universal peace, the flourishing of individual cultures, awareness of a great common heritage: the regaining of the mystical age of bliss.

To attain this Hadrian sought peace through strength. He avoided wars but fought the few which were necessary ruthlessly, notably those against the rebellious Britons in 119–21 and the Jews in 132–5. The frontier defences were everywhere strengthened and the client kingdoms beyond were kept obedient by fear and bribery. The army was maintained at war standard. New armour, equipment and tactics were introduced and discipline and promotion by merit rigidly enforced. On his extensive travels all over the Empire, Hadrian strenuously inspected his troops, marched and exercised with them, harangued them, weeded out abuses, decided promotions, conferred honours, granted privileges, visited the sick, getting to know as many personally as he could. The armies of Rome had never been in better shape, their reputation never more formidable. These 400,000 men strung along the frontier camps allowed the 60 million folk snug within the Empire to flourish in peace. As Aristeides, the sophist, exclaimed, 'an encamped army encloses the civilised world in a ring like a rampart'.[27] The troops adored the man who plodded and munched and bathed alongside them. There was to be not a whiff of military revolt against this Emperor throughout his reign.

In Rome Hadrian worked to conciliate and unify. He scrupulously attended the Senate and showed every deference to its members, though its power had long been waning. His letters show similar tactful respect for civic bodies and traditions all over the world. Following the trend of his predecessor, he recruited the equestrian order into the civil service, downgrading freedmen, thereby powerfully improving its effectiveness, though here unification was later to mean centralisation and ultimately petrifaction.

A spate of legislation helped improve the lot of the lower classes and vulnerable groups, thereby reducing social friction to a minimum. Administration, Hadrian stressed, should always 'combine justice with human kindness'.[28] A great series of legal reforms, which spanned his whole reign, provided the first coherent foundations for the uniform system of Roman law later transmitted to posterity by Justinian. Even in religious matters the stress was towards unity: strengthening the cult of the Emperor, bringing together all the gods in an amazing new Pantheon built to symbolise the community of heaven under its prodigious and daring dome. In all these activities, Hadrian, whatever the brittleness of his relationships, knew how to choose the ablest agents, not the aristocrats and dynasts favoured by Trajan but new and able men of senatorial rank, frequently provincials on the make.

With his theatrical flair and spiritual insight, Hadrian realised that all this dry machinery of unification was not enough. Something deeper and more stirring was needed to pull the loyalties of his subjects towards Rome. He recollected how the city of Athens had immemorially been personified and venerated in the goddess Athena. In 121 therefore he founded a cult of the goddess Roma (along with that of Venus, the patroness of the imperial family) and himself designed a huge temple, the largest in Rome, which was dedicated in 128 but not finally consecrated until 136–7. Veneration of the goddess Roma and celebration of the foundation of the city on 21 April thereafter became one of the common denominators of citizenship all over the Empire. The cult proved extraordinarily popular and enduring. And the haunting phrase with which he propagated this unifying cult, *Romae aeternae*, persisted long into the Christian era – for Rome is still 'eternal'.

By 121 Hadrian felt his position in Italy completely secure. He had removed the opposition (and his overweening supporters), conciliated the Senate, placated the people, set on foot his measures of administrative, legal and social reform. The villa was rising at Tibur. Already in 119–20 he had travelled around the peninsula inspecting and improving the cities of Italy. But Italy was too confining for this ecumenical Emperor. The moment had come to inspect the Empire itself. Sometime after the founding of the cult of Roma on 21 April 121, leaving Sabina at home to brood by herself, Hadrian set out on his first great journey. The coins blared forth his mission as 'the restorer', 'the enricher of the world'.[29]

For well over half of his reign, at least twelve and a half years out of twenty-one, Hadrian was travelling outside Italy. Of the forty-four provinces of which the Empire was composed, we can be sure that he visited thirty-eight and the few which he may not have seen were hardly significant.[30] No Emperor before, except for the pathetic Nero, had journeyed across the eastern Mediterranean on errands of peace, none had felt so secure – or so out of place – at home to be away for such continuous stretches of time: 117–18, from 121 to 125, from 128 to 134 and possibly again in 135. Hadrian's journeys were partly a product of his incurable restlessness, his insatiable desire to explore lands, cities and cultures, mountains, rivers and monuments, and to experience everything at first hand for himself. No doubt, too, especially on his three visits to Athens and Asia Minor, he simply enjoyed himself and indulged his antiquarian and aesthetic tastes.

But all such personal motives were subordinate to the pursuit of his public policies. The Emperor, dispensing with pomp and even official dress, travelled with a functional retinue of engineers, architects and builders to survey, help and knit together his Empire. Wherever he went, frontiers were studied, defences improved, roads built, legions exercised, client kings and vassals impressed and kept loyal. The cities through which he passed found themselves equipped with new harbours, markets, aqueducts, revised laws, with gymnasia and libraries, games and festivals, stadia and theatres. Many new cities bearing his name rose from the virgin soil. The cults and temples of the gods (and the shrines of past heroes) which he never failed to examine and to venerate, flourished again, adorned with magnificent buildings, sculptures and dedications, equipped with new priesthoods and endowments, animated with new vigour and confidence. Even now, after almost two thousand years, it is impossible not to be amazed at the extent and diversity of Hadrian's benefactions, at the inexhaustibility of his activity and at the speed and comprehensiveness of his travels. No wonder his grateful subjects in the east responded to him as a god come down to earth, lavishing extravagant titles on him like those from the league of Platea: 'saviour, protector, nourisher of his very own Hellas', which made even the title *Optimus Princeps* look pale and tame.[31]

The first great journey which brought him to Claudiopolis sums up the man, his interests and his policy.[32]

From Rome in 121 he passed up through Gaul to Germany where he inspected the Rhine army (the coins stressing 'Discipline'),[33] afterwards moving eastwards through the central European provinces, examining and restoring the whole Rhine–Danube defensive system. He then turned back to Holland (Batavia) crossing the sea to Britain where he was in the spring of 122. There he inaugurated the magnificent defensive works still known as Hadrian's Wall. Back in Gaul in the autumn of 122, he headed swiftly south (Narbonensis) to deal with the ominous riots raging in Egypt, the vital granary of Rome, which he settled by vigorous missives. In Nimes (Nemausus) he erected a basilica to Plotina who was born there and may have died recently. Nearby in Apt he erected a tomb and a poetical inscription to his favourite hunting horse Borysthenes which also had died: like Sabina, Hadrian had learned to love animals with their dumb unchanging faithfulness, perhaps more than fickle human beings.[34] The winter of 122–3 was spent at Tarragona in Spain and then early in 123 he crossed over to North Africa and there personally conducted military operations against rebel forces in Mauretania. Suddenly, in the spring of 123, alarmed at problems with the Parthian empire on the Euphrates frontier, he sailed from the western to the eastern extremity of the Mediterranean. At some point, Polemo the wealthy sophist from Smyrna joined the party, gaining tax exemptions for himself and his posterity as a reward. Hadrian was never to return to his Empire north and west of Italy, then slumbering in deep peace, and, perhaps, dazzled by the east, he failed to realise its gathering potential for good or ill.

From Ephesos he crossed rapidly to the Syrian border and there on the Euphrates, amid ostentatious preparations for war, he delicately negotiated with Osroes the Parthian king, finally reaching an agreement for peace which was to hold unbroken throughout the rest of his reign. With relief, he then turned north-westwards up through Galatia to Bithynia where we first met him in the summer of 123. Apart from Claudiopolis, he visited the cities along the coast before devoting his attentions and resources to the devastated cities of Nikomedia and Nicea and to finishing the monumental temple at Cyzicus. He passed down through the Troad, restoring the tomb of Ajax. In under-developed Mysia, he founded three cities, one called Hadrianotherai, ostensibly to commemorate a famous hunt for a bear, but all in fact shrewdly designed to boost the settlement and economy of such a backward region. A bewildering number of the cities of Asia Minor were then inspected, improved or endowed. At Smyrna the persuasive Polemo extracted a cool ten million drachmas from his friend for markets and other buildings. The jealous Ephesos nearby received comparable benefactions. From this port, Hadrian set out by ship for Rhodes and the Aegean islands. Late in September 123 he stopped off at Samothrace where, ever keen to probe to the frontiers of spiritual experience, he was probably initiated into the mysteries of the Cabiri.

His movements in late 123 and early 124 are not clear. According to Weber, he came down through Macedonia and Thessaly into central Greece in the summer of 124. At Thespiae, near Mount Helikon of the Muses, he dedicated along with the spoil of a bear he had slain an elegant poem of his own in Greek to the local god Eros – the poem, as we shall see, provides a rare clue to his emotional state at the time of the beginning of his association with Antinous. By September 124, all historians agree, he had reached his spiritual home, Athens, which was to be his base until the following March.

The visit to Athens was brilliant. It started with Hadrian's inauguration into the lower category of *mystes* at the great festival of Demeter at Eleusis in the autumn and ended with him presiding in Greek dress as agonothete at the festival of Dionysos in the spring. He saw himself as another Theseus, the founder of the famous city now seedy and second-rate with decay. In a few hectic creative months, the spirit and the appearance of Athens were revived. Hadrian revised its laws and constitution, made concessions to invigorate its economy and started work on a spacious new residential district near the Ilisos river, 'the city of Hadrian and not of Theseus' as the elegant new gateway joining the two, somewhat arrogantly, proclaimed (fig. 21). Seeing the projected temple of Zeus Olympios, the head of the whole Greek pantheon, still hardly started after the sporadic efforts and vain promises of three centuries, Hadrian decided to complete the edifice on a gargantuan scale and in a lavish style. Around this great task, Olympian in its superhuman scale and demands, the whole Greek world could be drawn together. Athens, Hadrian determined, should become again the spiritual centre of reviving Hellas, if not of all civilisation. He did not disguise his preference for this city of the spirit above all others. Athens accorded him an equally unique honour – placing his statue in the sacred Parthenon of the goddess Athena.

In spite of his manifold activity, Hadrian found time in the winter of 124–5 for a tour in the Peloponnese, restoring the great gold and ivory statue of Zeus by Phidias at Olympia. His efforts to revive and embellish this great national sanctuary of all the Greeks perhaps kindled ideas of strengthening still further such cultural bonds between them. At Mantineia, the city of Antinous' forbears, he restored the ancient name, provided a teacher of grammar and sensitively preserved and restored the ancient sanctuary of Poseidon. Nearby he visited the grave of the hero Epaminondas, who had fallen between two beloved comrades, and composed an epitaph for it.

After the splendid concluding ceremonies of Dionysos, held in the ancient theatre below the Acropolis, in which each of the thirteen districts of the grateful city had erected a statue of Hadrian, he headed westward. He tarried in Delphi, with its famous oracle of Apollo, a city he had long been helping restore and enlarge like Athens and which he may earlier have had in mind as the focus of Greek unity. There he may have met the aged Plutarch, the apostle of Greco-Roman reconciliation, who applauded the Emperor as 'our guide in the conduct of these affairs'.[35] Passing via Nikopolis, where he talked with the stoic philosopher, Epictetus, he crossed to Sicily, ascended Mount Etna and reached Rome by the autumn of 125.

His head was full of the creative and spiritual wonders of Greece and the echoes of the wild acclamations of its people. He had begun to conceive the idea of bringing them all together not just in diffuse veneration around the Olympian Zeus or in national athletic competitions but in some form of concrete organisation. Impressed by Delphi as the spiritual *omphalos* (navel) of the earth, perhaps influenced by the advice of Plutarch whose life of Pericles had stressed his panhellenic schemes and by the precedent of Augustus, Hadrian wrote enthusiastically from the villa at Tibur in September 125 suggesting the widening of the Delphic League of cities into 'a commonwealth of all the Hellenes'.[36] This was to be another great theme of unity which he would develop on his next tour and with which the posthumous fate of Antinous was to be closely bound.

Such then, in brief, was the extraordinary man whom the young boy from Bithynion was to see and possibly to meet in 123. He must already have heard and understood why his fellow Greeks were hailing this bringer of new life, splendour and civilisation as the 'New Dionysos' and the 'New Herakles'. Hadrian himself doubtless relished these titles but he preferred for the moment one other. In that same year 123, to commemorate the 150th anniversary of the founding of the Empire, the imperial coinage underwent a major change. The old, somewhat stodgy portrait of Hadrian was simplified into one of gracious classical nobility. In this new self-confident austerity the old clutter of titles and insignia was also swept away in favour of two words. Thenceforward the Emperor was designated simply and grandly as 'Hadrian Augustus': the revered founder of the Empire was thus identified with the man who was in a sense refounding it. The legend on the coins proclaimed the same mixture of roseate retrospect and sublime prospect: it announced the advent of the *saeculum aureum*.[37] 'The age of gold' had at last come back to mankind.

TRACES IN TIME

On the hill of the Pincio in Rome rises an obelisk reconstructed from three pieces of scarred and damaged granite. In 1824, Champollion, who first deciphered hieroglyphs, noticed the name of Antinous among those on its surfaces. Down to our own day scholars are still attempting to wrest its secrets. This strange and puzzling object is fundamental to the story of Antinous: for the words scratched on to it are nothing less than Hadrian's own epitaph for his beloved. In the same city, rears the Triumphal Arch of Constantine. On either side are four medallions sculpted with figures. They are not of the same date as the arch, for the style of the reliefs is obviously that of an earlier period. One surviving head, of a young rider galloping furiously in pursuit of a wild boar, has long been recognised. It is Antinous. And these eight mutilated and displaced medallions offer another unique testimony. Of the many sculptures we have of him, only here can we be sure that he is shown as a human being. Far away at Oxyrhynchus near the Nile in the year 1910 a bottle was dug up, its mouth stuffed with a screwed up papyrus. On it was written part of a poem. It is none other than the remains of that epic written by Pancrates describing the celebrated lion hunt in which the friendship of Hadrian and Antinous reached a climax and perhaps a fatal turning point. Of the forty lines retrieved only about twenty-five are decipherable. In 1719, de Montfaucon, a French antiquarian, published an illustration of an engraved gem, belonging then to a Mr Masson. It was said to show Antinous and Hadrian in a grouping which explains the death in the Nile. If it is genuine, its witness could be crucial. But we shall never know. For the cornaline has long since disappeared.

Such is the kind and such the lamentable state of the evidence which we have to use before we can start to trace the relationship of Hadrian and Antinous. We know much more about what happened to Antinous after his death than in his life, for it is only with his apotheosis that his recorded history begins. We do not have a single word about him or a single image of him which can indubitably be dated to his own lifetime. From the mass of art and literature, coins, memorials and inscriptions created in his honour in the years immediately after 130 AD we can glean scraps of information about those before, but that evidence is fragmentary and sometimes tantalisingly ambiguous and is often still the subject of scholarly debate. When, well after the death of Hadrian, ancient historical writers launch upon this subject, yet further information is proffered but that is tainted always by distance, sometimes by prejudice and by the alarming and bizarre ways in which the principal sources have been transmitted to us.

About Hadrian himself we are naturally much better informed from his own writings and speeches, from more objective material of all kinds, from the comments of his contemporaries and successors, and the much fuller accounts of the ancient historians. Though some aspects of his reign (e.g. his whereabouts in the years 131–4) are an almost total blank, we have enough knowledge of it to set the Antinous affair firmly in a sequence of developments, personal, political and religious.

From this jumble of fragments, we have – like an archaeologist reconstructing a Roman mosaic – to assemble a coherent picture of their friendship. For some scenes – the sojourn in Egypt in 130, for example – there remain an unexpected number of pieces of the mosaic, colourful and detailed, but for others – like the early years of the relationship with Hadrian – nothing but the merest scraps of background material from which to determine events in the foreground. Between the surviving clusters of authentic tesserae we have to paint in conjectural links; but in devising these, different restorers might opt for various of the several possibilities which suggest themselves.

One of Hadrian's idiosyncrasies was the need he often felt to give his private sentiments public, indeed grandiose, expression. That Hadrian sought to commemorate his beloved in images and words, written or expressly commissioned by himself, we know; and what remains of these contributes some of the basic material to our story.

We have plenty of Hadrian's own words in official letters and documents, funerary and military orations, speeches to the Senate, poems, satiric verses, inscribed epithets, even a few personal letters which may be genuine. Of those that concerned Antinous hardly anything survives. We know that the Emperor wrote erotic poems about his boy favourites but none of these still exists. To answer critics, he even composed an autobiography in the last years of his reign. It too has perished. We have only half a dozen, mainly trivial, extracts from these memoirs incorporated in the writings of much later historians. We know that the Emperor had something to say about the death of Antinous: exactly what, however, eludes us, for, as we shall find, the two surviving colourless words are open to many interpretations. He may have written letters concerning the affair or the scandal which it aroused, if the one to his brother-in-law, Servianus, which is given in the *Historia Augusta*, is in the least bit genuine.

Certainly Antinous figures in the genuine and extraordinary group of names from the ten main districts (phyles) and fifty sub-districts (demes) of the new city of Antinoopolis which Hadrian must have drawn up shortly after its foundation. But though this fascinating array of names reveals much about the Emperor's dynastic, familial and historical preoccupations and the elevated atmosphere in which the whole apotheosis was conceived, it tells us nothing new about Antinous himself nor of their relationship, except that the Emperor felt that the dead Osiris-Antinous was worthy enough to be placed alongside his imperial predecessors, his wife, sister and mother-in-law and the goddess Athena.

It is from two visual monuments in Rome with which the Emperor was personally concerned that we learn much more: the obelisk and the sculpted medallions.

The obelisk, of moderate height (9.25 metres), has stood on the Pincio only since 1822 (fig. 10). As it claims to mark the actual burial place (not just the empty cenotaph) of Antinous, its original position in antiquity is of considerable importance to us.

Its faces are decorated with reliefs of Hadrian and Antinous in the hieratic Egyptian manner, but this Egyptian character of the obelisk, which led earlier antiquarians to assume that it originally came from the tomb in Antinoopolis itself, is spurious: it is no more authentically Egyptian than the statues and busts of Antinous in the same style found in such quantity in the Villa Adriana. The strange, barbarically shaped hieroglyphs were evidently incised by Roman workmen ignorant of the true Egyptian canons. The text itself, perhaps composed by a sacred scribe from one of the temples of Egyptian cults in Rome, is couched in grandiloquent archaising phrases. Modern scholars who have wrestled with this text have concluded that the scribe was himself translating into stilted Egyptian a text, possibly even a poem, drafted in Greek and, therefore, found it difficult to give precise equivalents for some specifically Greek or Roman words and concepts. As the inscription mentions that Sabina is still living, it must be dated before her death in late 136 or 137.[1]

The author of the original Greek draft is not in doubt. It is Hadrian himself, composing an epitaph to his beloved, now called 'Antinous the just', whose 'salvation has been accomplished . . . after he has again been raised to life'.[2] What Hadrian wanted to say is of supreme interest – if only we could understand it. Unfortunately, the damage to the surface of the obelisk leaves several critical gaps in the text and the vague, circumlocutory Egyptian leaves the Emperor's original words or precise ideas distant from us, usually obscure and sometimes downright unintelligible. To the generation of Dietrichson, before Erman's fundamental translations in 1896 and 1917, the words on the obelisk were no more than 'empty rhetoric'.[3] To us, however, aided by recent scholarship, they provide some vital clues. No other source offers so much, if so cryptically, and no other source stems so directly from the stylus of the grief-stricken Hadrian himself.

The eight sculpted medallions on the Arch of Constantine are equally suggestive and baffling. About 2.3 metres in diameter, they present a coherent series of scenes linked around the theme of the imperial hunts. Hadrian originally appeared on them all. The generally accepted sequence starts with the departure of the hunting party from Rome, followed by the vigorous chase of a bear which is linked thematically to the next medallion of the consecration of the bear's skin to the Italian god Sylvanus. Then comes the hunt of the wild boar and the offering of its spoil to Artemis or Diana. There follows a unique scene of Hadrian and his companions animatedly discussing the corpse of an enormous lion lying dead at their feet, the pelt of which appears in the next medallion as an offering to Herakles. The series ends with a final sacrifice to Apollo for the safety he has offered to those surviving such perils.

Few works of art of the period have provoked such a prolific debate as these. Some conclusions, however, now seem agreed. The tondi are from very late in the reign of Hadrian, not much before 136, and they may well have been finished in the reign of his successor Antoninus Pius who appears on three of them. Hadrian himself must have devised the subjects and chosen which of his followers to include.

On other matters there is still disagreement. For example, do these scenes illustrate precise historical events or are they just of general significance?

We can be certain that the singular scene with the dead lion (fig. 13) commemorates the famous hunt for a ferocious marauding lion in the Libyan desert undertaken by Hadrian and Antinous from Egypt, probably in the September of 130. The fact that the handsome young man Lucius Ceionius Commodus, adopted by Hadrian as his heir with the name of Aelius Caesar in late 136, appears on this medallion in no way invalidates the identification with the lion hunt in Libya.[4] He may have been introduced into the relief anachronistically in 136–7 as Caesar for dynastic publicity or he may have actually been, as the rising 'western favourite' (as he has been called), among the imperial party in Egypt in 130 as some other evidence suggests.[5]

It is about Antinous that there has been the widest disagreement. How often does he appear on these reliefs? And why? There is now general agreement that he appears at least once, as one of the riders pursuing the boar (fig. 12). Some historians claim that this is his only appearance, whilst others see him in at least six other figures on the tondi, including even that of the god Apollo. Indeed, it has recently been claimed that, apart from Hadrian, Antinous is the only person who continuously appears in the series.[6]

The whole issue has been raised to the first magnitude for us by Heinz Kähler who, supported by a later scholar, claims that Antinous appears in six of the eight scenes, that they are as much a memorial of his relationship to Hadrian as of anything else, that they deliberately set out to depict his growth from a graceful boy to a virile young man of around twenty and to chart his vertiginous social ascent from a mere lowly page to the intimate and proudly displayed comrade of the Emperor. If all this is true then these reliefs must become one of our richest sources for the actual life of Antinous.

Of the identifications Kähler makes to support his case, besides the accepted one of the boar hunt, easily the most significant is that of Antinous on the lion medallion. Only two of the five figures there have one of their feet triumphantly planted on the mane of the dead beast, as tokens of conquest: Hadrian and the young man on his right. From the details given of the hazardous slaying of that lion in the poem of Pancrates, this young man must be none other than Antinous. In any case his facial features are consistent with some surviving sculptured heads of him.[7] What is different is the hair-style (fig. 14). Gone are the luxuriant curls of the beautiful adolescent and instead we see close-cropped locks, developed side whiskers and even the downy growth of a beard. Such a cropping of the hair was a sign of attaining manhood and Kähler contends that this had happened before Antinous' death. Certain similar images of a virile, short-haired Antinous on coins, apparently unknown to the scholar, support his case.[8] As, however, most of the posthumous sculptures of Antinous display him with his full mass of hair, then, Kähler contends, they must have been based on his actual appearance some time before his death, perhaps as he looked on the splendid imperial visits to Athens and the cities of the east in the years 128 and 129. It is not at all implausible that the sculptors of the new god (and Hadrian approving their models) preferred the ancient Greek ideal of the ephebe, as Antinous had appeared in the resplendent fullness of his adolescent bloom, to the shorn, whiskery and stubbly reality of Antinous just before his end. This matter of the hair is not trivial. It has direct bearings, as we shall find, on the mysterious happening near Hir-wer.

The other identifications made by Kähler and other scholars are more problematic.[9] The most we can claim is that two of the series probably show Antinous at different stages of his bodily development and of his relationship with Hadrian. But the whole group, supported by literary and other visual evidence, does powerfully suggest the context in which that relationship ignited and does illustrate, if only by analogy from its youthful figures and their functions, the sort of rapid physical growth and dazzling advancement in status which Antinous may well have experienced in his short, meteoric life at court.

The other sources from Hadrian's remaining years, 130–38, are other writings, inscriptions, coins and sculptures.

Some papyri found recently in Egypt provide realistic and even culinary details about the fateful trip on the Nile, but most illuminate the cult and the life and the long history of Antinoopolis. Of other writings, that found in Tebtynis once again refers mainly to the new god, and only the inflated homerics of Pancrates, fragmentary as they are, vividly recapture a climactic moment and perhaps some significant strains in the actual relationship of youth and man.

A paragraph in another contemporary work early roused the attention of posterity interested in Antinous. It occurs in a report of about 135 AD by Flavius Arrianus. An almost exact contemporary of Antinous, also born in Bithynia, Arrian exemplifies the prominence that cultivated and versatile Greeks attained in the Empire under Hadrian and later: philosophic author, politician in Rome, the first Bithynian to be a Consul (c. 129), explorer, governor of a key province, successful military commander, author of a life of Alexander the Great. His account of his investigative journey round the shores of the Black Sea, composed for his friend the Emperor Hadrian, suddenly launches into an encomium of the hero Achilles and his virtues, praising 'his untimely death in the flower of his youth . . . the force of his love and constancy of his friendship, in so much that he would even die for his friends'.[10] Some have seen in this passage destined for the ageing Emperor's eyes not just a flattering consolation for the loss of Antinous by comparison with that of the ancient hero, but an indication of the lost beloved's own qualities and especially of the actual nature of his death.[11] Whether this passage, with its analogies far from unambiguous, bears such an interpretation, we shall have to consider later.

Incised inscriptions are a major source for Roman history. For the period of Hadrian they not only give us fragments of his speeches and actions, the outline of his early career and his poetry, but also provide mundane, though not always clear, evidence of his passage through parts of the Empire on his lengthy journeys. Some inscriptions are more precise. Those, for example, placed by an imperial guest on the left foot of the colossal statue of Memnon at Thebes in Upper Egypt, only three or four weeks after the death of Antinous, provide a unique insight into the company, the preoccupations and even the atmosphere of his tragic voyage up the Nile. There are inscriptions directly about Antinous too – but all deriving posthumously from the cult for which they are a prime source. Only meagre clues emerge from them about his life and death, such as the contradictory context for his alleged suicide from those of Naples and Lanuvium. The latter inscription, giving the constitution of a burial club set up in his name and that of Diana in January of 133, and placed in the portico of his temple there on 9 June 136, has, however, given us one precious item: the day and month of his birth.

The imperial coinage of Hadrian, deliberately used by him as by his predecessors as a medium of mass communication, provides one of the richest sources for his reign. From its legends, its portraits, its extraordinarily diverse images, we can learn where he went (though not always when), what he and his family looked like at different times, what were the policies and slogans he wished to project and even more intimate details: for example, when he was seriously ill or when he was publicly on good terms with his shrew of a wife.

The coins of Antinous are, alas, less informative. Although over 140 different kinds are known, all are posthumous and, as usual, they tell us far more of his divinity and cult than of his life. We even learn from them about works of art of him which no longer exist. But of Antinous himself, except for one or two hints about his appearance, birthplace, character and interests, we glean virtually nothing.

The same is true of his gems, though these have not yet been collected and studied as a whole and we remain, therefore, in lamentable ignorance. Two only need detain us. The famous Marlborough sardonyx (fig. 7), now in Italy, presents a masterly executed, obviously early and very realistic likeness. As Marguerite Yourcenar says: 'Of all the objects still present today on the surface of the earth, this is the only one of which we may assume with some certitude that it has often been held in the hands of Hadrian.'[12]

The Masson cornaline (and its replica the Fauvel gem) described by Tournemine in 1713 and de Montfaucon in 1719, remains an enigma (fig. 11). Dietrichson claims that it definitely shows Antinous sitting contemplating his doom and holding a lyre, while a sick Hadrian and Aelius Caesar (less definitely portrayed) gaze at the goddess Hygeia and the snake of Asclepeios, both divinities of healing. There is indeed a remarkable similarity between the Antinous shown here and on a coin from Tion (though in reverse).[13] Certainly the haggard Emperor given in the engraving could be Hadrian but the third male figure is nothing like Aelius Caesar. If the gem was authentically Hadrianic and if the goddess, snake, Antinous and Hadrian were identifiable on it, then it would point to a contemporary belief, if nothing more, that Antinous sacrificed himself for the health of the ailing Emperor. Even Dietrichson is forced into doubt and so, pending the rediscovery of these gems, are we.

For the years immediately after the death of Antinous we are left with his sculptures. Out of all those created then, there remain now about 115 (listed in Appendix 1) for which there is a scholarly basis to assume they are of Antinous himself, but there is a host of other Antinous-like candidates clamouring for inclusion in this privileged circle. As cult objects they obviously are one of the best sources for the divinity and worship of Antinous the god or hero. But what do they tell us about the human being and his life? Are any of them pure portraits in the sense in which the numerous realistic sculptures of Hadrian at various ages and of Sabina so evidently are? Do any come from the lifetime of Antinous?

We know for certain that Hadrian, who is said to have sculpted and painted himself, had statues made of his friends in their lifetime.[14] We can assume that the vast Villa Adriana, nearing completion by 130, was not empty of such: it was certainly replete with images of Antinous eight years later. It is very likely that Hadrian could have had sculptures made of his beloved either in Rome (if Antinous was there before 128) or in Athens and the Greek cities, including

Alexandria, where they definitely were together between September 128 and October 130.[15] As Hadrian's entourage included artists[16] and wherever he went he met them, Antinous, the reigning favourite, must have been intently studied or even sketched by those at the time or later to reproduce his features.[17] It is fair then to conclude that there must have been portraits of Antinous carved in his lifetime and some of those made after his death may have been based on such earlier works or were by artists who recollected his strikingly distinctive looks.

Do any of these exist now? None of those we possess is dated, only one is signed and (apart from those on the tondi) only one seems to refer back to an incident in his life – the statue at Eleusis. The many which indicate him as a god or hero are obviously posthumous, though they may, of course, derive from earlier models. Even the famous series of busts of Antinous without divine attributes relate so closely to statues with them that they clearly derive from the same prototype. That group of seven or so sculptures which seem to show Antinous as a child or boy between ten and fifteen years of age seem all to be later than 130 AD in date, though why they should have been produced and whether they represent lost originals created when he was so young or artistic memories of him at that age, must remain a mystery.[18]

There are virtually no heads of Antinous which do not to some degree idealise his features just as there are none which do not at the same time reproduce all or most of his distinctive features. The most apparently realistic is the bust in the Sala Rotonda (fig. 6), which has been dubbed 'angry and cruel', 'lascivious and malicious', 'a somewhat fat gourmet who needs exercise'.[19] One critic has singled out this work as the only portrait surviving from life. Indeed, some features – the spiral ringlets of boyhood, the puppy fat, the air of a spoilt, sullen and bored favourite and the origin in the Villa Adriana – all support such a view. It also seems to belong more to the Roman portrait tradition than to the Greek idealising one. But stylistic and iconographical analysis soon confirm that it is both posthumous and intended to be heroic.[20] Thus the living Antinous eludes us again. We have come full circle: there ought to be works of him direct from the life but, as far as we know, none have yet been found.

This does not mean that the sculptures tell us nothing about their subject. On the contrary, seldom in antiquity do images of an individual transmit a more distinct physical presence and a more unforgettable personality. However great the idealisation, however diverse the artists' interpretations, certain physical features of Antinous come through consistently, in the hair, in the shape and detailed features of the face, in the neck and even in the body. It is rare indeed in this – or any – period for the body to be so strongly characterised, but so recognisable is that of Antinous that art historians readily identify headless torsos or decapitated bodies in stone as those of him. The most hideously mutilated heads (those of Athens, Cherchel or Amsterdam, for example) are also confidently catalogued as him on the basis of a few surviving features.

But the identity is not only physical. There is an unmistakable Antinous personality. Though it is clear that many of his sculptures derive from one basic – now lost – model, at least a third of the whole deviate widely from that. A close analysis of them all reveals an Antinous much more varied and dynamic than the passive, bowed and brooding youth publicised by Winckelmann and Dietrichson. To appreciate this, we should remember that most of these sculptures were made *immediately* after Antinous' death – we know from the surviving coins alone that at least eighteen sculptures, and numerous reliefs and paintings (all except for one now disappeared), were in existence by 134 at the latest. We know that Antinous had been prominently displayed all over the Greek world in the years 128–30 in the presence of the Emperor. Little wonder then that the artists who saw him and remembered him or heard about him chose, even if following a basic prototype, to stress different aspects of him as they remembered or conceived him to have been. Antinous emerges from their art as a real adolescent, one of many moods and surprising shifts of personality. Nevertheless, there persists once more a distinctive core of individuality which, however enigmatic, elusive and difficult to express in words, pervades them all. Whatever they may tell us about the god, the sculptures of Antinous certainly confront us in all his opaque complexity with the human being.

We are left with the later writers on whom we have to depend for other information: the Christian Fathers and the principal historians of Hadrian's reign. Each source, as always seems to be the case with Antinous, presents us with more conundrums about itself than about him.

Indeed, are any fragments of fact embedded in the lava of invective from the Fathers? Though not all erupted so scaldingly as Athanasius, all were hostile and anything gathered therefrom has to be very gingerly examined for prejudice. Nevertheless, we can learn much about the cult of Antinous and are offered a few unique details about his life, the truth or falsehood of which has to be assayed against other evidence. The comments and terminology of the Christians (and of less biased pagan writers like the topographer Pausanias) are also very explicit in their description of the emotional and sexual relations of Hadrian and Antinous, though it is suspicious that distance from the events discussed seems to increase knowledge about them. It is also clear that the Fathers borrow and embroider from one to another. We must beware in case this volcano of indignation has unjustly buried two reputations in sooty infamy.

The ancient historians present us with unexpected and weird problems of their own.

The main source for the reign of Hadrian is the 'Life' contained among thirty biographies of Emperors, their heirs and imperial claimants, known as the *Scriptores Historiae Augustae*. This work purports to be by six different authors writing in the times of Diocletian and Constantine (i.e. about 290–320 AD). In recent years, scholarly opinion has tended to agree that the whole work is by one man (and the latest computer analysis of the words confirms this),[21] writing almost a century afterwards in the reign of Theodosius, in about 392–5. The whole compilation is seen as an elaborate and erudite parody of the precious and pompous learning of its time. As his writing proceeded, this rogue scholiast warmed to his agreeable task, his imagination caught fire as his supply of solid information ran out and he invented progressively more false names, unsubstantiated facts, fictitious authorities and faked documents. 'The *Historia Augusta*', declares Sir Ronald Syme, 'is a fraud.'[22]

Fortunately for us, in his first nine lives of the Emperors this unscrupulous author drew heavily on a collection of imperial biographies, long ago lost, by a writer neatly given the convenient nickname of 'Ignotus' ('The Unknown') and datable to about 210 AD. Now Ignotus was 'sober, precise and addicted to the facts'.[23] To enliven Ignotus' too serious tale, the plagiarist drew on another author, Marius Maximus, who, in about 219, published a set of twelve imperial biographies in the manner of Suetonius a century before, full of juicy scandal, gossip, omens, food and sex. The biography of Hadrian with which the *Historia Augusta* opens is evidently drawn mainly from Ignotus, spiced with sections from Marius Maximus. The facts contained in this 'Life' have been shown over the years by much corroborative evidence to be basically sound: 'the information', continues Syme, 'is proved excellent'.[24]

For Hadrian it remains the fundamental source, describing with a wealth of capricious detail his career, his policies, travels, actions and tortuous character – all without untoward political bias. It also provides a whole series of clues about his emotional nature and sexual tastes, in phrases which historians either ignore or dismiss as scandal but which are remarkably consistent in themselves, and tally with his undoubted actions and with external evidence. It briefly treats the death of Antinous, Hadrian's reactions and the founding of the cult. Its tone here is slightly derogatory but what it says, representing the facts or the opinions of about eighty years after the event on the Nile, has to be taken very seriously.

Less serious perhaps for us today is the famous letter of Hadrian to his brother-in-law, Servianus.[25] This is quoted much later in the *Historia Augusta*, when the inventive author really gets into his stride. If it was authentic, it would provide us with confirmatory evidence about the scandal caused by the deification and further clues about Lucius' presence in Egypt in 130 and his close relationship then to Hadrian. Unfortunately, it is riddled with anachronisms so gross that most historians dismiss it as an outright fake – 'sheer delight', chortles Syme, 'for it is all fiction'.[26] However, a group of historians dispute this view.

Mercifully, the other main historian of Hadrian's reign is not a fraud. But we encounter another appalling snag. The eighty voluminous books in which he compiled his history of Rome no longer exist – at least, as he wrote them. Dio Cassius was another Bithynian, born at Nicea, not far from the birthplace of Antinous but about thirty-four years after his death. Like that of Arrian, his career, uniting loyal and proud Hellenic culture with a Roman political outlook, typifies the well-born and cultivated Greeks of his time. In the years 197–207, he gathered material for his vast history of Rome which he wrote in Greek between 207 and 219. The sixty-ninth book, on Hadrian, was probably written about 217–18, ninety years after the death of Antinous. Unfortunately, Dio's original work has been lost. All that we have is an epitome compiled by Xiphilinus of Trapezus in the first half of the eleventh century and another by Zonaras a century later. Xiphilinus' epitome of book 69 is thought to be not so much a precis of Dio as a selection of his material, chiefly in its original order and close to his words.

Dio represents a senatorial tradition hostile to Hadrian and is more of a chronicler than a biographer, but his work contains a mass of authentic information about the reign and valuable contemporary criticism of the ruler. It is a prime source for Antinous, for it not only gives Hadrian's brief and neutral account (or is it Xiphilinus' precis?) of the death in the Nile but promptly contradicts it with 'the truth', that is what Dio thought really happened, which is decidedly less favourable to the Emperor. Dio's bias necessitates caution, but his testimony is of the greatest importance.

Our final historian is too late in time to be more than repeating views of earlier writers and his work also seems to have come down to us in epitome. Sextus Aurelius Victor was a notable politician in the Rome of 360–90 and his *Caesares*, sketches of the lives of the Emperors, dates from then. His brief account of Hadrian does contain some details and facts not given anywhere else and is more forthright than any of the others about his sexual proclivities. He elaborates more than other historians on the reasons for the alleged sacrifice of Antinous and the way it was accomplished. We simply do not know where he or another elegant Epitomator of Hadrian's character of the same date went to for their information.

Each of our sources is defective and each problematic. The words – even Hadrian's own – come down to us at second or third hand. The images, at first so lucid, become the more obscure the more we look at them: they seem to evade definitive focus. Tiny details wink like lonely stars in the encompassing void. Our knowledge of Antinous' divine existence looms like a mountain of fact over the grains of doubt left to us from his temporal life.

Put together, however, isolated, incomplete or flimsy items frequently strengthen and elucidate each other and a frail, interlocking structure of probability, nailed together with fact, in the end emerges. This is further reinforced if embedded in the concrete context of the times. On this slender footbridge we must venture forth.

RISE TO IMPERIAL FAVOURITE, 123–8

How did the obscure lad from Bithynia become so recognised and so intimate as the favourite of the Emperor Hadrian that the relationship between them could be simply and knowingly summed up for posterity in the words: '*his* Antinous'?[1] Did it happen suddenly, perhaps at their first meeting, or more gradually? And what was there in this one boy to arouse the fascinated and passionate interest of the master of millions?

There has been much imaginative speculation about the meeting. Dietrichson puts it as late as 129–30 when a group of slaves from Cappadocia, supposedly including Antinous, were sent to Hadrian's camp – though this date is now generally considered far too late. He also denies that Antinous was ever in Rome.[2] Rydberg has Antinous as an earnest and brilliant student of philosophy meeting Hadrian in Athens at some unspecified time.[3] Marguerite Yourcenar depicts the Emperor's eyes first resting on the form of a youth lolling, half-abstracted, next to a pool in the palace of Nikomedia in 123.[4] Carandini suggests that Hadrian encountered the boy on his first great journey and then met him again by appointment in Athens in 128 at the start of his second.[5] Several recent historians assume that Hadrian and Antinous were already close enough to take part together in the mysteries of Eleusis in the September of 128, only a few days after the Emperor had arrived from Rome; a reasonable enough assumption though still begging the question of when they first met.[6] Some others place this much earlier. Thus Perowne contends that they were 'inseparable' for nine years, which would place their meeting in 121. Indeed the biographer Suetonius is said to be vindictively attacking Hadrian's already notorious love-affair with the boy in his obsessive linking of Bithynia with homosexual scandal in his *Lives of the Caesars*, possibly published in 120 when Antinous would have been a child of no more than eight to ten years.[7]

The absence of concrete proof may seem to give any or all of these suggestions plausibility. In fact, however, if we piece together the surviving clues, we shall find that, together, they tend to indicate consistently one point in time.

The most important is furnished by a mutilated phrase from the epitaph on the obelisk, where the author is talking about Antinous' home and family. It says: Antinous 'was already from his birthplace by the . . . raised up by . . .' (or 'taken away by').[8] Infuriating in its gaps and ambiguity, this does explicitly tell us that it was from Claudiopolis that the boy was removed to greater things, presumably by the Emperor himself. References to the boy's mother on the obelisk and the possessive claims of the later coins of Bithynion support the idea of him being well settled in his home town before leaving, though there is nothing to endorse the view that he was wrenched away from his family as forcibly as Zeus snatched Ganymede from Mount Ida. On the contrary, the respectful references to his parent and siblings and Hadrian's later devotion to Bithynion-Claudiopolis suggest an amicable and enduring relationship between the Emperor and his beloved's family and birthplace.

Now the only time that we can be fairly sure – given again the absence of dated proof for so much of the imperial itineraries – that Hadrian was in Claudiopolis during Antinous' lifetime was, as we have seen, June 123. This, then, is the most likely date for the lad's 'raising up' or 'taking away', if it were done by the Emperor or his courtiers.[9]

More circumstantial evidence supports the probability that Antinous was a boy of about eleven or twelve rather than an adolescent of sixteen or seventeen or more when he entered the service of the Emperor and also that he spent some time in the Latin west, including Rome itself, before returning to the east on his fateful voyage. That curious small group of sculptures representing him as a boy may well reflect some memory of him as belonging to Hadrian's circle at a young age, while the juvenile head of Antinous from Ostia, wearing a diadem embossed with imperial cameos, betrays some specific role of dependence on his part within the imperial family. Tertullian, the Christian polemicist from Carthage, writing about 197 AD, clarifies the chronology and career of Antinous still further when, in one of his violent outbursts, generally accepted as referring to the favourite, he describes this odious catamite-cum-god as coming from the school for pages of the imperial court (*de paedagogiis aulicis*), almost certainly the well-known one in Rome.[10]

Other inferences – much more tenuous and oblique – support these suggestions. If the reliefs on the Arch of Constantine do illustrate the life of Antinous, then he must have been in the west as a page, especially if he figures on the bear hunt and the related sacrifice to Silvanus, a Latin god with whom he was also to be significantly associated in Italy after his death. Moreover, the fact that the villa at Tibur became a sort of shrine to Antinous has led to the supposition that this commemorates the happy times spent by the couple there, embodied in a joyous extension begun at the time[11] and marked by a specific monument to Antinous erected in the small summer triclinium later.[12] In that room, it has even been luridly proposed, they sexually consummated their affair, laughing behind 'a mosquito net all of gold thread with a blue serpent embroidered on one side'.[13] More prosaically the finding of a sculpted head of Antinous at Cherchel (Caesarea) in Algeria has prompted the claim that he was visibly and memorably with Hadrian on his visit to North Africa in the summer of 128.[14] It has also been deduced that Juvenal's denunciation of Nero and his male concubine in the tenth *Satire* is a scarcely disguised attack on Hadrian and Antinous and that this must have been written before 128.[15]

None of this constitutes proof. Even the weightier and acceptable items of evidence are vague and the others flimsy and disputable. Nevertheless, when put together, the individual scraps do form a coherent pattern, more convincing than for any other solution. They suggest that Antinous left his home town directly into the service of Hadrian possibly in 123, was trained in Italy and grew to prominence as the companion of the Emperor by the mid-summer of 128 when he was noticed at remote Caesarea. Already established as the imperial favourite, he travelled with Hadrian over to the Greek mainland where, as is widely agreed, they both participated in the mysteries of Eleusis in the September of that year.

Accepting some such tentative chronology, we can begin to explore how and why Antinous grew in Hadrian's favour.

It is far from likely that Hadrian was enamoured of the boy on first sight. We know that his friendships, even the closest, lasted for relatively short spans of time and evidently that with Antinous was at its climax – or ominously starting on the downward slope – at the time of the Nile journey in 130. It is scarcely possible that it had been pulsing at that intensity for seven years or more beforehand. Moreover, the poem which Hadrian dedicated with the spoil of a bear at Thespiae, on his way through central Greece in the summer of 124, invoking the help of the wise god Eros with the heavenly Aphrodite, contains a plaintive and puzzling request for grace, a hint of emotional longing, as if Hadrian was searching for a love which had not yet been bestowed on him.[16] Far from being already 'part of the cycle of Antinous', as has been claimed,[17] the poem reveals a rare, instantaneous glimpse of the aching emotional void within Hadrian which Antinous had obviously not yet begun to fill. Indeed Hadrian may not even have set eyes on the boy the year before at Claudiopolis. As a handsome, robust and intelligent lad, he may have been recruited into the royal service by some official who anticipated the Emperor's taste in retainers. Even if Hadrian did select him, it is unlikely that the untrained and provincial boy would have been added to the deliberately lightweight entourage which travelled over Asia Minor, the Danube and Greece in 123–5. It is much more probable that he was packed off to Italy and arrived, a bewildered and awestruck bumpkin, in the great bustling metropolis of Rome to be groomed for his tasks ahead.

The imperial paedagogium where, as Tertullian implies, Antinous found himself, was not just another of those seraglios of seductive and willing boys collected by the wealthy debauchees of the day, though, as the obscure conflicts in the past between Trajan and Hadrian over some of its more delectable inmates show, it may have functioned partly as such. It was a formidable institution, separately housed, under the control of a master, usually a freedman, for the training of pages for the court. It was as one of these, we can presume, that Antinous started his career. These boys, often from well-to-do backgrounds and, as the graffiti scratched onto the surviving walls vividly tell us, from all over the Greco-Roman world, were being schooled not only to perform domestic duties in the household while young but to graduate into civil servants when older. As such they were highly prized and cared for. In Nero's extravagant days they travelled in special carriages, their delicate complexions protected from the climate by masks of ointment and breadcrumbs, their bodies provocatively clad in tucked-up tunics and adorned by silver rings. In later, more discreet, times they wore gold tunics and purple boots. The school was originally housed on the Palatine hill in part of the Domus Gelotiana, but by Hadrian's day another had been opened on the Caelian Hill, in the street called Caput Africanae, though some of the rooms in the old one may still have been used, if only for punishment purposes.

However pampered they appeared to others, the boys, like those of any epoch, inevitably found school onerous. The graffiti low down on the walls of the small rooms on the Palatine, incised by lads from Asia, North Africa, Greece, Gaul and even perhaps Bithynia (but *not* by Antinous), chorus immemorial schoolboy grouses. One shows a donkey toiling at the mill and bears the legend: 'work, work, little donkey as I have done and you will be rewarded for it'. Most of the two hundred inscriptions are gleeful exclamations of release either at leaving the school altogether or at least the cramped and dark punishment quarter: 'Corinthus is leaving the paedagogium!' 'Narbonensis is leaving the paedagogium!' etc. Sometimes, hinting at the protective mutual affections which helped these homeless youngsters survive the strange and brutal world of Rome, two friends or brothers write their names together and one inscription refers to 'lovers'. Only rarely is there a boast of contentment: 'Epitynchanus from Asia is the happiest of boys'. Juvenile cruelty and mockery reach deeper issues. Thus there is a caricature of young Alexamenos, a boy with short cropped hair, standing, hands raised, in front of a cross on which hangs a Christ with a donkey's head, inscribed with the jibe: 'Alexamenos worships his god' (fig. 15). Evidently this particular lad was resilient and undeterred in his beliefs, for elsewhere we find the proud and simple affirmation: 'Alexamenos the faithful'.[18] We even know the names of some of the freedmen who ruled over this polyglot and boisterous mob, doubtless with a rod of iron.

From this experience the young Bithynian must have emerged polished in manners, broadened in morals, toughened in body and responses, though not, it would seem, coarsened in quality. He must have picked up a little learning too, even Latin, since all the graffiti are in that language.

There is a long tradition, going back to the Renaissance and disseminated widely by Winckelmann, who used it to champion Antinous' sexual impeccability, that the boy's job in the court was that of *atriensis*, the privileged and responsible page who looked after the valuable secular and sacred sculptures and paintings in the *atrium*.[19] This legend derives from a passage in the Augustan poet Phaedrus who describes an *atriensis* dressed and coiffured like the Antinous shown on the Albani relief. The resemblance is surely nothing but a coincidence. Wherever in the palace Antinous started, he was soon involved in pursuits less sedate and more demanding than dusting the ancestral busts.

Hadrian, returned from the east, had installed himself in the ever-growing villa at Tibur by September 125. When he left for Greece again three years later, Antinous had become his favourite and the focus of his emotional, even spiritual life. For the process by which this happened we have no explicit evidence, but clearly the rise of Antinous was gradual. No doubt he started off, like the attractive young page in the departure tondo, doing menial jobs, acting as groom, tending the hounds, still one of the *famuli*, the most inferior of the Emperor's retainers. Within a couple of years, however, he had not only grown in size and in length of hair but, as indicated by the parallel of the bear hunt relief, had been promoted in rank, being one of the select group of *amici* or imperial friends, closer in status and contact with the Emperor and riding near to him. By the time Antinous indubitably makes his appearance chasing the boar – which may refer to a hunt in Asia Minor in 129 – he has moved immediately behind the Emperor, hobnobbing in rank with the much older marshal of the court and obviously next in intimacy with Hadrian. On the lion relief, commemorating the hunt of 130, the shorn and manly Antinous is Hadrian's right-hand man, the only person standing on the conquered beast's mane with him, evidently again, as Pancrates' poem confirms, a very special bosom companion, separated from the respectful officials and dynastic followers and remote in status from the busy groom which he had himself once been. From all this and from the clue provided by the Cherchel head, we can guess that it was only fairly late in Hadrian's sojourn in the west, perhaps in the winter of 127–8, that he began to be gripped by an obsessive love for the adolescent and only then that Antinous found himself propelled into the exciting but conspicuous and invidious role of imperial paramour.

What qualities attracted the middle-aged Emperor to the youth?

There is a complete divergence of opinion about Antinous' mental capacity. To some modern authors he had a 'dull oriental mind', was 'a stupid person', 'lacking in spiritual depth', a mere 'creature of the senses', only 'partly lettered' and so vapid as to be 'more a state of [Hadrian's] mind than a flesh and blood person'.[20] Others virtually attribute him with genius, as one 'endowed with something of Phoebean inspiration', or talk of 'his fine intellectual gifts', or imagine him plunged avidly in philosophy and extol his marvellous facility for apprehension, his 'extraordinarily deep spiritual life' and 'glowing intellectual beauty'.[21]

Fortunately we have some contemporary evidence to decide the issue. Hadrian himself in the epitaph on the obelisk says categorically and authoritatively that Antinous' 'heart was wise, his intelligence was that of a grown man'.[22] Arrian in his analogy which seems to refer to Antinous also speaks of the 'strength of his mind and understanding'.[23] In other words, the lad was not stupid but sage, not retarded but precocious. And one has only to look at some of the sculpted heads – that in the Museo delle Terme (no. 200) or that in Copenhagen (no. 685) (figs 23–4) for example – to confront a face of penetrating, acute intelligence. This is no more than one would expect. However 'bewitched' Hadrian may have been, or drawn to the boy by carnal or emotional impulses, there must have been enough intelligence in the lad to satisfy and sustain his own exacting brain in a relationship over several years. No doubt, though, Antinous' cast of mind was very different from that of his master. The obelisk's references to wisdom and early maturity and the contemplative serenity found in so many of Antinous' images imply that his mind was of a placid, balanced, ruminative kind: far from the restless, dissatisfied and tortuous one of the Emperor. This calm sagacity may have provided the soothing complementarity Hadrian's mind ached for: hence one aspect of the youth's hold over the man.

What Antinous' attainments and interests were we cannot tell. Again, however, they must have been rich enough to fertilise his relationship with the voracious, varied and demanding intellectual he served. There is not the faintest evidence that he was inclined to philosophical study: nor was Hadrian. But some other broken phrases on the obelisk, facets of his cult and his posthumous reputation for oracles do hint at some expository or literary gifts. Perhaps he shared and even shone in the poetical activities of the court.[24]

Many writers have seized on a shared mysticism as the strongest bond between the two. Antinous, it is claimed, was a 'musing mystic' of enthusiasm and religious profundity. Such traits are deduced from that group of his posthumous images in which the quality of brooding introspection is paramount. The oriental streak in his blood and the eastern and primitive religions of Bithynia may well have fostered a tendency to rapt contemplation and a preference for cults of ecstasy and participation. Certainly with Hadrian at Eleusis and later travelling up the haunted valley of the Nile, Antinous was readily open to mystic exaltation, occult experiences and profound spiritual responses. But it may be doubted if he stayed at such an ethereal level for very long. On the contrary, he was just as often indulging in more earthy pursuits as an intrepid sportsman. This mixture – it was not a contradiction – again matched Hadrian's own.

However much we shall stress that Antinous appears the normal variable adolescent, there clearly was a magnetic, positive quality about him which drew Hadrian, impressed contemporaries and still pervades his cold marble images. There is about him an air of innocence surviving experience, of serenity overriding anxiety, devotion overcoming doubt. Not without justice has it been said that in him Hadrian's quest for the absolute was at last fulfilled. He seemed to embody the old Greek ideal of divine virtue embodied in a beautiful adolescent in his fleeting prime. Certainly there must have been some moral nobility about him for people who knew him like the priests of Eleusis, Polemo and the magistrates of eastern cities so enthusiastically to promote his divinity as 'the good', as one 'worthy in the hearts of men', and for more humble folk who only heard tales about him to warm so readily and so persistently to his cult.[25] It is remarkable that we do not find a word of criticism about him in antiquity, except from the biased Christian sect, and even that is sometimes muted or apologetic.

All of Antinous' qualities came together in that pursuit which may have drawn him and Hadrian together in the first place: hunting. Ever since Hadrian as a boy had been recalled from Italica by an irate Trajan for over-indulgence in the sport, he had been a passionate huntsman. In an age of peace, the chase was the one way in which the Emperor could test and demonstrate his courage and endurance. And there can be no question of his skill and bravery: surviving injuries, despatching a huge boar with a single blow, coolly confronting the enraged lion of Libya. With his theatrical flair, Hadrian made sure that his contemporaries and posterity were kept aware of his triumphs. Inscribed poems, foundations of cities, visual memorials, the issue of coins devoted to the gods of the chase and the splendid medallions of Hadrian spearing boar and lion all advertised the almost superhuman prowess of the Emperor (*Virtus Augusti*).[26]

But, for Hadrian, hunting was not just a matter of personal vanity, physical courage, the close and exhilarating interdependence of men, horses, hounds and the prey. The chase had a moral, mystic and religious significance, a cosmic symbolism. Hadrian ardently shared the views of his admired Xenophon and his friend Arrian in their treatises on cynegetics. Hunting was an invention of Artemis and Apollo. It made men morally better, wiser, braver, more patriotic and reverent. Those who hunted were therefore specially dear to the gods; they should sacrifice to them before setting out and dedicate the first fruits of the chase to them on return.

Now Antinous was a bold huntsman too. This has been overlooked by those who, on the basis of false assumptions about the inevitable effeminacy of a royal favourite, and reliance solely on one group of images, dismiss him as a flaccid and spineless dreamer. On the coins of Corinth, Ephesos and Tion, he is shown as a hunter and there may have been sculptures of him in such a role in these places. The one now in the museum of Izmir has been proposed as

Antinous-Androcles, on foot, vigorously hurling his spear at a charging boar (fig. 12).[27] The superb Marlborough sardonyx shows the energetic huntsman Antinous bearing such a spear. Other gems repeat this theme. The burial club at Lanuvium linked the new god with Diana, the patroness of hunters. On the Arch of Constantine we recognise him again in close pursuit of the wild boar which, according to Xenophon, was the most dangerous of beasts with its red-hot tusks, exacting 'high courage' from those who dared to confront it.[28] Pancrates in his poem flatters Antinous with divine hunting associations, calling him 'son of the Argos-slayer' (i.e. Hermes who slew that fearsome monster) and tells us that in facing the equally fearsome lion, Hadrian had sufficient confidence in the youth's nerve and skill to leave him to administer the *coup de grâce* alone – 'wishing to test to the full how straight the other aimed'.[29] If, in the outcome, his skill did not match that of the more experienced man, Antinous' vigour and courage cannot be doubted.

It is scarcely over-imaginative to propose that the relationship between Hadrian and Antinous ripened in this atmosphere of shared danger and excitement, of equality of prowess and endurance, of mutual aid and dependence, of masculine *bonhomie*, of heroic retrospect and mystical sublimation. Perhaps, as one interpreter of the tondi would have us believe, it was on a hunt that their intimacy began, just as, we shall suggest, it was a hunt which precipitated its end.

There are plenty of other characteristics of Antinous at the advent of his fame at the age of sixteen to eighteen, besides those which immediately stirred Hadrian. They speak to us from behind the dignified and frigid veil of divinity enveloping the numerous images of him created shortly after his death, which, we have contended, may derive from portrait models, actual observations or accumulated reports of him in life. So varied have been the interpretations of his character from these images that Antinous has been called 'the chameleon of ancient art'.[30] One suspects that the extraordinary contradictions so discerned – innocence and viciousness, naivety and coquetry, reticence and candour, effeminacy and toughness, alertness and dreaminess, to list just a few – must be more than merely the subjective responses of historians. No doubt Antinous was, like all adolescents, perplexingly variable in the diverse facets of self he displayed to others and beneath them all remained somehow inscrutable.

The most common and the oldest interpretation of Antinous, based principally on the statues of Naples, the Vatican and Delphi, the Albani and Lanuvium reliefs (figs 55, 60, 2, 9, 5) and the series of busts (all of which works derive from the same lost model), is that of a bowed youth of aloof and dreamy melancholy, of brooding sorrow tinged with bitterness of resignation. Some of these qualities may be no more than the artists' attempts to invest their subject with divine mystery and Olympian detachment as well as to suggest the tragedy of his unfulfilled and perhaps deliberately sacrificed life. Nevertheless, it is likely that the real Antinous did have a capacity suddenly to withdraw into intense introspection, a serene self-absorption which isolated him from his surroundings, investing him, as the poignant heads from Berlin (fig. 25) and Leningrad demonstrate, with an enigmatic wistfulness in the memories of his contemporaries.

With this alleged melancholy, critics often discern a languorous ease in his body, an athletic structure clad in soft, supple, unmuscular flesh which, in the long, elastically modelled thighs of the Naples statue, the imperceptible abdominals of that at Delphi and the succulence of flesh at the armpits and breasts of the Albani relief, for instance, are pronounced 'feminine'.[31] Effeminate qualities have also been discovered in the smoothness and hairlessness of his skin, in his rounded cheeks, in the curve of his upper lip, even postulated in Venus-like mistiness of the eyes. Once again one suspects that some of these qualities derive more from the artists and the sculptural models they used than the living body of Antinous. The supple languor or world-weary lassitude, when it exists, as on the Lanuvium relief or in the Naples statue, may come from an effort to invest the dynamic, rugged prototypes of Polycleitos with a Praxitelean subtlety of mood and modelling or to evoke the morbid sentiment of grave reliefs of the fifth and fourth centuries BC. The soft, feminine bodily grace may also arise from the assimilation of the new god in many of his sculptures to Dionysos, who was conventionally displayed with such features.

But some of these so-called 'feminine' characteristics are obviously only described as such because of the preconceived and erroneous notion on the part of modern critics that the youthful partner in a pederastic love-affair in antiquity must have been passive and girlish if not impotent and a sexual invert. Indeed it has been suggested that Antinous may have been, like Domitian's boy favourite from Pergamon, Earinus, a eunuch.[32] The only evidence for this is a phrase in Prudentius' poem of about 384 AD, referring to Antinous being 'robbed of his manhood' in the imperial embrace, which seems to be more a euphemism for seduction than castration.[33] None of the sculptures hint at mutilated genitalia. And, as Hadrian himself sternly re-enacted earlier laws banning castration and we have evidence of Antinous' virility and hirsuteness, we can dismiss this suggestion as improbable. But this is not to say that Antinous – like most adolescent boys – may not have been capable of drooping lethargy, a floppy relaxation and drained bodily ease; that in periods of inaction or over-indulgence his muscles wilted and the puppy-fat thickened and that some of his peculiar features – the prominent breasts and nipples, the round cheeks, the silky texture of the flesh – may not have recalled aspects of the other sex.

A diametrically opposite Antinous leaps at us from another group of works: one in which writers discern 'unbroken power', a 'healthy nature', even 'supreme kingly youthfulness'.[34] In the head of Copenhagen (no. 685) (fig. 24) we see not languorous, passive effeminacy but a fierce, incisive and dominant virility: no image could be more charged with potency. That of the Museo delle Terme (fig. 23) is not limp with brooding and resigned melancholy but erect, tingling with vital intelligence, tense with challenging scorn. The Marlborough sardonyx exudes an optimistic energy. And there are other surviving sculpted heads and busts not downcast with sadness but ahead-looking, confident and occasionally even with the trace of a smile. Nothing could be further from the soft, sinuous body and wilting stance of the Naples type of statue than that now in the Bank of Italy (fig. 53). Here an alert and extrovert head is poised above a sturdy body, standing four-square and rippling with the hard muscularity of a trained athlete. In the small marble of Berlin this stocky athleticism of Antinous reaches an extreme of sinewy strength and manly sternness which banishes all notions of his effeminacy, sensuality and even tenderness (fig. 27). His body reappears as sturdily powerful in the Athens frieze or as fluidly energetic in the statue of Aidepsos (fig. 28) and in several others seemingly developed by training in the palaestra.[35]

As with the alternative soft version, this harder conception of Antinous obviously reflects stylistic or iconographic models affecting the sculptors: the proud, erect heads refer back to those ruler or hero images created in the Hellenistic period in Asia Minor, and the muscular bodies may be attributes of one or two of the gods with whom Antinous is here identified or may simply be an aesthetic preference for the monumental, full-square and simplified virility of late archaic and early classical models (e.g. Hegias or early Phidias) over the more complex and elaborated ones of the later Polycleitos. But, even if we may doubt that in life Antinous ever approximated to the leathery gladiator of Berlin or the hefty club-wielder of the Athens frieze, this view of him as a virile youth rings true. It fits what we know of his exploits in the chase and in accompanying the indefatigable Hadrian across burning deserts and up sheer mountain sides. It is much easier to conceive the aggressive hero of Copenhagen, the stalwart athlete of the Bank of Italy or the lithe stripling of Aidepsos crouching, poised to meet the charging boar or pouncing lion than the delicate ephebe of Delphi, the spoiled and plump aesthete of the Villa Albani or the weary and effete vine-cutter of Lanuvium.

In the end there is no irreconcilable contradiction between these two main contemporary views of Antinous. We see them repeated in coins issued by civic notabilities like Polemo of Smyrna who we can be sure met the lad himself: Delphi and Alexandria purveying the softer image, Bithynion and Smyrna the harder one, Corinth and Mantineia both of them. Antinous may have changed bodily, like other lads of his age, very fast. And like adolescents of any epoch he was capable of abrupt and extreme changes of mood. The artists could only record one of his facets or phases. Hence the mystery of the whole person and hence perhaps another reason for the fascination of Hadrian.

The other qualities seen in him are much more subjective. 'Sensuality' is the most common. It is difficult to pinpoint where it resides. Is it in the arch of the upper lip, in the liquid protrusion of the lower one, in the fullness of the cheeks, the ambiguous longing of the eyes, the tousled luxuriance of the hair or the voluptuous surface of the skin? There is no gainsaying that Antinous does exert a physical magnetism even from the marble and must have kindled sensual appetites in the flesh.

Some authors go much further, basing themselves on the exceptional bust of the Sala Rotonda and the relief of the Villa Albani. Now, it is not just sensuality but 'nauseating satiety',[36] lasciviousness and vice; not melancholy but sulkiness, not energy but cruelty, not reticence but emptiness, not resignation but impotence. Perhaps these and a few other eccentric images do hint at such extremes: but an Antinous composed of them is surely a caricature. It is difficult to accept that a sensitive and exacting man such as Hadrian would sustain an intense love for someone so difficult, depraved or vapid, still less that other people who knew the boy or his reputation would genuinely adore such a capricious young monster as a god.

What, then, did Antinous look like as he emerged into the harsh scrutiny of history? Even his severest Christian critics readily admitted that 'his beauty was unequalled'.[37] But it was of a novel kind, with distinctive features which pervade all of his images, however varied (including those in the Egyptian mode), and which established a new fashion of male perfection for decades thereafter.

The head is not big, but the cranium is nobly arched and the face is exceptionally broad with widely set eyes, the whole sometimes more square than oval. The rich hair-style was unique and a joy to the sculptors with their new techniques of boring and undercutting. It soon became world-famous, prompting the lyre-player at the festival of Antinous at Curium in Cyprus to sing rapturously of the 'violet-curled, beautiful-haired, blessed Bithynian'.[38] It was considered so indispensably part of the Antinous image that, violating the archaic precedents of Egyptian iconography, it is allowed to coil out from under the calantica head-dress and frame the face in the bust of Antinous as Osiris now in the Louvre. It is a principal and uniformly recognisable feature of all his sculptures and of his coins, especially those of Arcadia and Alexandria which delight in its luxuriance (figs 46–7). Combed out radially, the hair falls in thick locks which curl at the tips, usually cover the ears and hang in longer hanks at the neck. In the sculptures the inclination of the head, the high cranium arch and the deep undercutting of the locks one above another all stress the impact of this rich mass of hair.

The curls cluster so thickly down the brow that the forehead becomes a low and very broad band of flesh between the fringe above and the emphatic line of the eyebrows beneath. These eyebrows are a major feature, exquisitely chiselled into a peculiar shape, very long, slanting downwards to the root of the nose and so delicately curved that at first sight they seem straight. Below them the eyes, heavy lidded, smallish and almond-shaped, are deep-set. The horizontal shadows cast by the fringe of curls and the heavy brows contribute much to the alleged mystery, melancholy or sultriness of Antinous, that mix of 'pain and joy, darkness and light, death and youth' which Dietrichson eloquently discerns in his face.[39]

The nose is thick at the roots, fleshy, blunt at its tip and unclassical in its angle. Between the nostrils and the upper lip the gap is unusually short. The mouth, 'one of the loveliest ever carved',[40] projects notably, the top lip arching sharply upwards, the lower one protruding fully so that sometimes it seems a trifle open and the moist inner flesh of the mouth extends outwards. Here, if anywhere, is the sensual or expressively oriental element in Antinous. (Indeed, from a surviving ancient fragment of marble showing this 'sensual and lascivious' mouth, recognisable as Antinous', a whole modern head of him has been reconstructed.)[41] Another deep horizontal shadow divides the mouth from the chin, strong in projection and firm in line, sometimes rounded, sometimes square. The cheekbones are high but the cheeks remain always full, curved or straight in contour. It is the interplay of broad horizontal shadows, vertical lines, firm volumes and sharp or delicate curves which give this face its unforgettable combination of power and subtlety. 'You', chanted the citharode of Curium to Antinous, 'with the face that is full of grace.'[42]

The neck is abnormally thick and rises from a chest also exceptional in breadth and which swells forward from the set-back shoulders in a massive arch on which the pectorals and nipples are pronounced. Sometimes, indeed, this great chest seems a little ungainly and disproportionate to the rest of the body below, as in the statue of Delphi. The left shoulder is frequently higher than the other, not, as earlier authors believed, because Antinous was deformed but because in the model from which one series of sculptures derive the left hand was raised up. He may indeed have been left-handed. The thighs are generally long and usually smoothly rounded. Sometimes the muscles of the abdomen, thighs and legs are firmly defined and athletic, at others they are yielding and elastic.

These distinctive features of Antinous are not always perfect in themselves but the face and body as a whole have a unique blend of strength and grace, of clarity and mystery, energy and repose. The very imperfections give the reality of Antinous a memorable individuality compared to many of the impeccable confections of the ideal. So Hadrian obviously thought when he launched all the subsequent encomia of his beloved with the words of the obelisk: 'Osiris Antinous, the just, grew to a youth with a beautiful countenance, on whom the eyes rejoiced . . .'[43]

No doubt Hadrian's own eyes frequently feasted on his young companion in those last months in the west which marked the beginning of the happiest period of his reign. His own features, as on the Baiae bust of 127 (fig. 29), show a lessening of the earlier strain and suspicion, the advent of mildness and benignity as the old insecurity and tensions fell away and as political and emotional fulfilment briefly joined together in his life.

Much of the Emperor's efforts were spent on building. The Pantheon and the temple to Trajan and Plotina were dedicated in splendid ceremonies late in 125. At the sprawling villa at Tibur elegant new suites – the so-called Palazzo D'Oro and the Little Palace among them – were designed and built by Hadrian. Perhaps Antinous while still on the Emperor's periphery slept in one of those rooms in the 'Ospitale', with alcoves for three beds, a window high up and magnificent mosaic floors in taut abstractions of black and white which 'hold the mind like a string quartet'.[44] Later, no doubt, he moved into Hadrian's own ever-changing quarters. So lyrical, feminine and light-hearted are the architectural designs of these years that some art-historians have detected Hadrian's ecstatic love for Antinous as the source of their joyful inspiration.

In March 127 the restless Emperor travelled through the Sabine area of Italy, Picenum and Campania, scattering benefactions, restorations and new buildings in his wake as generously as in the Greek east. About this time he was attacked by a mysterious and grave illness, protracted enough to be publicised on the coinage of the years 127–9 and reflected in the Baiae bust of 127, and to evoke protective prayers in Alexandria.[45] Many doctors were summoned from all over the Empire, but to no avail, receiving from the Emperor a typical reward: an abusive missive denouncing their art as 'devoid of knowledge'.[46] This lingering illness has some significance in our story. It is said to have prompted his recuperative journey to the east in the autumn of 128 and later to Egypt.[47] Indeed he may never have completely recovered, since we are told that the disease which was to kill him in 138 had its origins long before. Perhaps in his debility Hadrian grew closer to the resplendently healthy boy in his entourage from whose blooming presence he gathered consolation and revival.

Hadrian's activities in 128 betray no signs of the incapacity advertised on the coins. On 21 April in a great ceremony in Rome, attended by the priests, Senate and people – and perhaps with Antinous close by – he laid the foundation stone of the vast temple of Venus and Rome which was to focus the loyalties of citizens of the Empire for centuries, becoming the religious centre of the Roman world as the Vatican is of the Catholic one. At this central point in his reign and from this central edifice there emanated a glowing sense of great aims solidly attained and the promise of greater felicity yet to come.

With no time to wallow in such sentiment, Hadrian – ailing or not – whisked away for a strenuous tour of North Africa which lasted until late July. The Cherchel head indicates that Antinous, prominent as favourite, may well have been with him, as we know for sure was that older courtier who rides besides the Bithynian boy on the boar hunt tondo and who joined also the later imperial party to the east: T. Caesernius Macedo Quinctianus. There were two brothers Caesernii, both regular and confidential companions of Hadrian on his travels, and they may have got to know and like Antinous well on their journeys together. Indeed, their patronage may explain the thriving cult of Antinous which grew up afterwards in their home town of Aquileia where they were very powerful.

The western part of North Africa (modern Tunisia, Algeria and Morocco) were then much more lush and fertile than now and provided much of the grain and oil for Italy. Hadrian's visit started auspiciously with a miraculous downpour of rain at Carthage, ending a drought of five years. There followed in coastal cities, hill settlements and remote camps on the plains an endless round of inspections, conferences, judgements, foundations, improvements, restorations and visits to antiquities. However sick the Emperor may have been, he never spared himself, and the locals erected statues and triumphal arches to him in gratitude. The tour reached its climax in early July when, under the scalding sun, Hadrian reviewed the manoeuvres of the cavalry and infantry of the third Legion Augusta which protected the whole region. In five speeches, recorded on stone at Lambaesis, given in clipped, brisk language far from Hadrian's usual artificial prose style, he bestowed praise, advice and a little criticism on his troops. 'Few ancient speeches ring more clearly or decisively down the years.'[48] Indeed this scene in its quiet way is typical of the best of Hadrian's achievement: the bare-headed Emperor, scarcely recovered from illness, standing 'in spite of this heat' (as he put it)[49] at a remote frontier station on the edge of the unknown Sahara, encouraging the small band of soldiers recruited from distant Spain, the Danube and Syria who ensured unbroken peace for the many millions within the vast Empire of Rome. No wonder the troops adored their Emperor. Little wonder too that Antinous, who was probably on the burning, dusty parade ground, grew so devoted to this extraordinary, versatile and indefatigable man.

On 11 August 128, his *dies imperii*, Hadrian at last accepted from the Senate the title of Father of the Country (*Pater Patriae*) offered long ago on his accession and spurned by him until he had proved himself worthy of it. Over the whole Empire lay an unprecedented peace; the administrative, legal and social reforms were under way; and everywhere there were signs of prosperity, confidence and unity. The coins of the year summed up the position in the one noble word: *Tranquillitas*. To Hadrian, this title was no mere empty formula. He truly saw himself as father of his people, individually and collectively, the benevolent and tireless head who drew his huge and heterogeneous family together around his person. He could aspire to no greater honour in the west, though in the lands he was about to visit his pretensions were to be even more exalted. The official bust issued around this time reveals Hadrian at his apogee: grand in its sense of mastery, fulfilled in its message of achievement, majestic in its calm, decisive assurance.

In the general magnanimity of these years even Sabina was not forgotten. From her private status simply as the Emperor's wife she was now raised to the rank of *Augusta*, or official consort, and given the right of coinage. She was even to be taken on the voyage to the east, where she now shared publicly in her husband's official receptions and was included on his private expeditions. The mention of 'concord' and 'harmony' on the coins may have reference to this temporary matrimonial amity.[50]

Did the recent emergence of Antinous have something to do with it? Was Hadrian so sunny with generous love for his favourite that he could beam a little spare affection onto his wife? There is no reason to think that Antinous was a divisive force between them. Roman matrons were well used to their husbands' male paramours, and Sabina may not have harboured any particular resentment against Antinous on that score any more than Domitian's wife was jealous of his favourite, Earinus. Perhaps Antinous played his role so skilfully and discreetly as to spare her any sense of personal and sexual humiliation as a supplanted wife, while Hadrian himself boosted her ego and stature as the new *Augusta*. Indeed Antinous, by playing the role of a son-figure, even brought this childless couple to some reconciliation, enabling them to relate to each other through himself. His name is happily integrated with those of the imperial family, including Sabina's, in the list of district names compiled by Hadrian for Antinoopolis. Moreover, while composing that list in the emotional aftermath of the boy's loss, Hadrian's first generous impulse was to associate his wife's name with the earlier unwonted attribute of 'harmony'.[51] On the epitaph of Antinous incised on the obelisk, Sabina again appears glowingly characterised by her husband as 'by him beloved'.[52] As the reconciling memory of the boy faded, so did the mutual concord linked with him. Some years after the death in the Nile the old animosity between the imperial couple had evidently crept back with a new and shocking virulence. In his lifetime, far from being a disruptive or abrasive intrusion into the imperial family and court, perhaps Antinous, by his sweetness, sensitivity and skill, may have been a cohesive and emollient focus.

As the imperial galley set out across the misty golden Adriatic of late August for Corinth, Antinous may well have had time to ponder the difficulties of his position as the favourite: so brilliant, so conspicuous, so enviable but also so vulnerable. The pressures on him must already have been mounting. Other imperial favourites in the past had used their privileged position to amass wealth, wield influence, even gain ascendancy and plot assassination. Usually, though, they had tumbled to a squalid and grisly end. One can imagine the scheming manipulators already swarming in on the boy from Bithynia, offering bribes and positions in return for jobs, decisions, grants, dispensations, verdicts and secrets divulged in their favour. Even without such inducements, the temptation to influence Hadrian's detailed decisions or general policies must have been difficult to resist. Fortunately the Emperor himself, ruthlessly egocentric, was determined not to be influenced by any man, even the one he loved as no one else. And Antinous seems to have confined himself entirely to private relations with Hadrian. In contrast to another favourite later from Bithynia, Saoterus of Nikomedia, paramour of the Emperor Commodus, there is no evidence that Antinous used his influence to shower favours on his home town. No hint of manoeuvring, self-advancement, desire for power or money on his part has come down to us.

But the strains within him must have been as intense as those without. Hadrian, even at his most benign, could not have been an easy lover or companion: always demanding consummate excellence and always ready to denigrate what was proffered. We cannot forget that in front of the Libyan lion Hadrian deliberately failed to kill the beast with his first thrust, so as 'to test to the full' his young companion. That phrase crackles with the tensions in his expectations and in their relationship.

Then there were the insidious problems of time. Unless Antinous was completely homosexual – and there are no indications that he was – his ambiguous sexual role must also have been disturbing to him as he grew older, even in the permissive ethos of Rome and the romantic one of Greece. Also, it was all very well to be acclaimed as the beautiful ephebe now, but what would happen when Antinous was no longer an ephebe and no longer glowing with adolescent bloom? In addition, Hadrian had just been seriously ill: how long would he survive? His friendships in the past had been notoriously fickle and short in duration. Maybe this profound love-affair was unique in the man's life. But would it endure? What would happen to himself if Hadrian died, or merely his affection? The fate of fallen favourites in jealous, savage and mocking Rome was not encouraging: the Tiber had borne away many of their mutilated bodies.

VI

PEDERASTY IN
THE IMPERIAL AGE

Sex: from the moment of Antinous' death and apotheosis, this word, sometimes subtly insinuated, at others screamed aloud, has been that basic ingredient in his relationship with Hadrian on which much of the attention of posterity has focused. The Alexandrians maliciously gossiped about it. The Christian Fathers fulminated against it. Antiquarians of the Renaissance and the Enlightenment pragmatically took it for granted. The Victorian apologists for the relationship indignantly cleansed away its foul stain. Modern writers discreetly accept it, embarrassedly ignore it or contrive ingenious theories to circumvent its ugly implications.

Historical opinion, heavily influenced by the lurid accusations of some of the early Fathers, has polarised into extremes. For one school of writers the relationship was conceived in lust, Antinous was no more than a willing catamite and the whole affair is 'dirty', 'shameful', 'improper', 'vile' and 'culpable', to quote only a few modern evaluations.[1] For the opposite school the relationship arose from the generous impulse of a gifted and childless man to cultivate the divine qualities embodied in a talented and beautiful youth and remains 'pure', 'ideal', 'noble' and 'uncorrupted' by physical intercourse.[2] Antinous is thus seen either as a depraved concubine or as an angelic innocent, Hadrian as a perverted monster or as an elevated idealist.

Such exclusive and extreme categories of carnality or spirituality would scarcely contain the complex texture of emotional relationships between sensitive people in any period. And if we wish to understand the morals and customs of the ancient world, particularly with regard to sex, condemnations and defences in terms of later Christian ethics are both irrelevant and obscuring. The relationship between Hadrian and Antinous must be explained in the context of the ethos and mores in which it was nurtured and of the particular psychological and sexual natures involved. The moral responses of our own or any later age have no illumination to offer on the matter.

This is especially true of homosexuality, which in the shape of pederasty, the love of an older man for an adolescent boy, is one of the institutions or practices of ancient society most abhorred by moralists of our own: 'one of the darkest parts of the moral life of the people of antiquity'.[3] Very few historians of later Greek and Roman society seem able to face up unequivocally to its persistence. Fewer imperial biographers or scholars seem even prepared to recognise its practice by their subjects. Information supplied on the sexual deviations of various Emperors by ancient writers, especially biographers such as Suetonius, is usually conveniently dismissed as nothing more substantial than denigratory gossip. It may well be true that in the broad development of Roman political, social and economic history, or in the application of specific policies, the sexual aberrations of individual Emperors – like Caligula or Trajan, for example – have no significance, though this is no reason, in biographical studies, for prudishly avoiding discussion of them.

Sometimes, however, as with Hadrian, private and sexual preoccupations clearly impinged on public, political actions. In spite of this, and in spite of an unusually varied and consistent amount of contemporary information, studies of Hadrian either ignore altogether or skate gingerly round the issue of his putative homosexuality or bisexuality. Wilhelm Weber, whose several works on the Emperor remain fundamental and who attributes such profound significance and devotes much verbose eloquence to an unproven racial mix in his blood, never once considers his sexual nature. The last scholarly biographer in English, Henderson, sums up the tortured and frustrated relationship with Sabina in the fatuous phrase, 'perhaps she objected to his beard'.[4] Even Sir Ronald Syme, not a scholar to avoid an issue, confines himself to the cryptic and headmasterly observation: 'some of his habits are known'.[5]

Rather than confront what they regard as the morally repulsive sexual side of his nature, some biographers of Hadrian resort to special pleadings or elaborate evasions. Dietrichson not only sweeps aside the ancient testimonies as malicious and disgusting fabrications and twists and selects what little dubious evidence he can adduce against them, but then eagerly accepts this same malicious gossip as true when, in suggesting the love of Plotina for Hadrian, it seems to exonerate the Emperor as sexually normal. For the Norwegian Christian scholar, it was somehow morally less reprehensible for Hadrian to have been having an adulterous affair with his aunt and Empress, behind the back of his guardian, than to have been consumed with 'unnatural passion' for a boy.[6] As for Antinous, Dietrichson pleads, he could never have been a 'spoilt voluptuary' or 'a victim of perverted lust' because he was capable of heroic self-sacrifice.[7] More recently, Perowne, writing in 1960, and worried about the 'impropriety' of the relationship, coyly proposes Antinous solely as a son-substitute, snugly integrated into the imperial family in this safe and decent non-sexual role. The obelisk on the Pincio is thus for him not a monument to an extravagant and tragic passion but 'a family memorial', more appropriate, one would surmise from his cosy suburban approach, for a

1 July 1893, the statue at Delphi discovered still standing

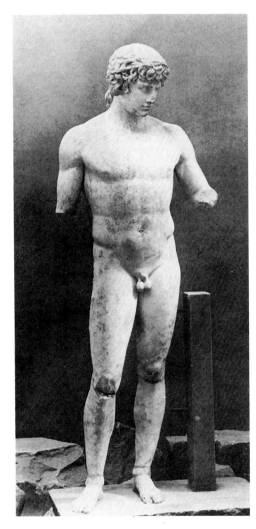

2 The Delphi statue: Antinous as the divine ephebe

3 The notorious pagan god used as the seal of a
Christian bishop, c. 1324

4 Antinous as Jonah, designed by
Raphael and carved by Lorenzetto
1522–27

5 The relief of Antinous as Sylvanus signed by Antoninianus of Aphrodisias

6 The Sala Rotonda bust: 'lascivious and malicious'

7 The intaglio sardonyx gem of Antinous (enlarged)

'The glory and crown of sculpture'
(Winckelmann):
8 The Mondragone head, in the Louvre
9 The relief at the Villa Albani

10 The obelisk on the Pincio, Rome, containing Hadrian's epitaph for Antinous and the secret of his grave

11 The lost Masson gem: does it confirm a sacrificial suicide by Antinous for a sick Hadrian?

12 Hadrian and Antinous hunt the boar: tondo, Arch of Constantine, Rome

13 Hadrian and Antinous stand on the mane of the conquered lion of Libya: tondo, Arch of Constantine, Rome

14 Antinous, shortly before his death, as a shorn and whiskered young man, from a cast of the lion hunt tondo

15 'Alexamenos worships his god'. Graffito from the paedagogium in Rome where Antinous was trained

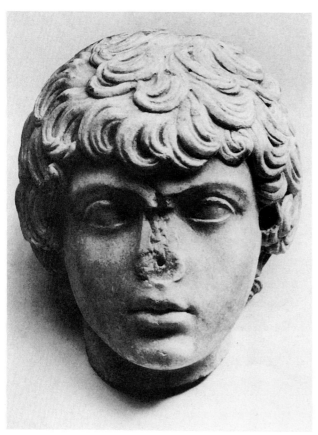

16 One of the boy-like heads of Antinous

17 Trajan: 'he looked stupid and was believed honest' (Syme)

18 Plotina: the aunt, supporter and alleged lover of Hadrian

19 Hadrian, tense and uneasy, shortly after his accession, 117–18

20 Sabina, 'moody and difficult'

21 The Arch of Hadrian, linking the ancient and the new imperial Athens

22 The Temple of the Olympian Zeus, Athens, the focus of the revival and the unity of the Greeks

23 Antinous, penetrating and intelligent: the
Museo delle Terme head

24 Antinous, virile and energetic: the Copenhagen
head

25 The poignant head from Berlin

26 The Antinous-ephebe of Olympia

27 Antinous-Dionysos statuette from Berlin

28 Antinous-Dionysos from Aidepsos, Chalkis Museum

29 Hadrian, 'Father of the Country', serene and
fulfilled in 127-8

30 Antinous confronts the mysteries of Eleusis, as
Dionysos Zagreus

31 An official welcome at Alexandria, from the Nile mosaic at Palestrina

32 Celebrating a good flood of the Nile at Canopus, from Nile mosaic at Palestrina

domestic cemetery.[8]

Indeed the illegitimate son theory has had a venerable and varied run as a proposition which neatly avoids confronting Hadrian's possible homosexuality in his fondness for his two favourites, Antinous and Lucius Ceionius Commodus. We remember that it was first invented around 1700 by the Jesuit, Hardouin, who declared that Antinous was the Emperor's bastard by a concubine. Two hundred and fifty years later, and much more learnedly and ingeniously, the French scholar, Carcopino, has done the same for Commodus. Attempting to explain the arbitrary adoption of this cultivated and profligate young aristocrat 'of kingly beauty' as heir in 136 AD,[9] he, without a scrap of solid evidence, postulates him as an illegitimate son born in 101–2 as the offspring of an adulterous liaison of Hadrian (who had just married Sabina) with a noblewoman whose name and existence is so obscure that it has had to be deduced. He supports this by some elaborate verbal interpretations and heavy reliance on the letter of Hadrian to Servianus which many authorities consider an outright fake. He thereby reconstructs a ripe scandal which eluded the vigilant noses and the fecund imaginations of all the ancient commentators and has taken eighteen hundred years to come to light. At no time does Carcopino, or the various other scholars who have joined in the controversy, take seriously the reports transmitted by the ancient historians that Hadrian's relationship with Commodus was amorous, and then set these reports against what we are told by a variety of sources of Hadrian's earlier sexual inclinations, against the general pattern of his psychological and emotional nature and the whole indisputable and crucially relevant episode of his previous affair with Antinous.[10] No doubt the result might be to make the ancient rumours more credible than the modern 'discovery'. Even a historian who devastatingly demolishes the bastard theory nevertheless congratulates Carcopino for his 'psychological delicacy' in raising the explanation of Hadrian's motives in adopting Commodus from low to honourable status, 'for shaping a repellent chapter' in Roman history 'more bearably'.[11] Better, it is implied again, for Hadrian to have been an adulterer or a dynastic plotter than a homosexual lover.

If we are to try and understand the relationship between Hadrian and Antinous, we must extricate the whole subject from such special pleadings, fabrications, evasions and silences. We must first see how prevalent and permissible were love and sex between men and youths in the Greco-Roman world of the second century AD, and then whether they were acceptable in the imperial house and, if so, on what terms. Hadrian's own emotional and erotic make-up must then be examined along with his relationships with women and his own sex. Then we must try to disentangle exactly what the ancient sources tell us about the specific affair between the fifty-year-old Emperor and the sixteen-year-old Antinous. On that basis, we are entitled to discuss the relationship itself, whether carnal, spiritual or both, and the response of Antinous.

77

Pederasty was not a mere fashion or aberration in ancient Greece. Wherever and for whatever reasons it originated, by classical times it had clearly come to serve certain profound needs existing in society, at least of the leisured or citizen classes. It had matured into an esteemed social institution, fulfilling precise and vital functions, regulated by law and tradition, elaborated into a culture and dignified with a philosophy. So important was its function that it flourished, weakened and adulterated perhaps, all over the Hellenic world under Roman rule and into the times of Antinous, tenaciously surviving even the ineffective edicts of the Christian Emperors of the fourth century AD, which had to be renewed by Justinian two hundred years later.

In the leisured Greek family of classical times, the role of women was strictly limited, children were reared by slaves and the father was absorbed by the affairs of his city. There seems frequently to have been an emotional void in the relations of the conjugal pair and between fathers and sons. Though the boys went to schools, these were despised as mere places for narrow instruction rather than for any broader education.

Here, then, were gaps which the institution of pederasty filled. The older male lover (or *erastes*), aged between twenty and forty, was expected not only to provide his beloved (or *eromenos*), aged between twelve and eighteen, with unstinting affection but to encourage and oversee his development of mind and body and his training in the morals, customs and responsibilities of civic society. In return, the boy was expected to respond by devotion, if not love, and by gratifying the older man's sexual desires, largely by offering anal or intercrural intercourse. Outside rarefied philosophic circles it was accepted that intense spiritual love would seek such sexual expression. The law confined itself to prohibition of prostitution and sexual abuse of free-born and native boys. Men grown beyond the *eromenos* age who still enjoyed the passive role were despised as 'pathics'.

Pederasty thus provided a loving and caring relationship not found within the family and acted as a means of initiation into the male-dominated society of the Greek city. Its foci were the gymnasia and palaestra which every city boasted, where the boys trained and wrestled naked, watched by their admirers, and also the banquet (or symposium) where the youths were encouraged to shine socially and intellectually. The relationship usually ended at around eighteen when the spread of hair on the face and over the body announced the youth's arrival at manhood. The *eromenos* was now of a stature to become an *erastes* in his turn. The man was not expected to be over forty. There was a proverb: 'to be a lover when old is the worst of misfortunes'.[12] One wonders if Hadrian knew it.

This institution fostered a brilliant culture. The boy, beautiful in body and filled with unspoilt promise and unsullied idealism, was conceived as incarnating qualities of the divine. The Greek adolescent, or ephebe, thus became an ideal in himself, invested in art with the attributes of many Olympian gods. A mythology of lovers, some heroic like Orestes and Pylades, Achilles and Patroclus, Herakles and Hylas, Alexander and Hephaestion, some divine like Zeus and Ganymede, Apollo and Hyacinth, and even a god of pederasty in the shape of Eros, endowed the practice with historical and religious sanction. Everywhere in sculpture, fresco and prolific vase painting the relationship was celebrated, sometimes with sublime spiritual idealism and at others with earthy sexual realism. It became a prime inspiration for poetry. Philosophers bestowed on the practice an intellectual and moral nobility: love for a boy, they proclaimed, concerned so much the cultivation of spiritual and divine qualities in him that it far eclipsed love for that inferior being, a woman, which was little more than degrading physical lust, necessary for animal procreation.[13] Plato in his later works went further still and deprecated sexual relations within pederasty itself, erecting an ideal of chastity which suited so much the morality and yearnings of Victorian philhellenes that they gladly assumed that this pure and noble friendship had been the norm in classical times. In fact, such a divorce of the spiritual from the physical was profoundly alien to the whole classical ethos. The Platonic and Socratic ideal of chastity may have set the values of some circles but was widely ignored in actual human relations, as the erotic vase paintings, epigrams and poetry abundantly testify. Indeed it has even been seriously asserted that the young Plato's own physical love for his three *eromenoi* failed to match his later abstract ideals.[14]

Five hundred years later when Hadrian was Emperor and Antinous a lad in Bithynia the position of pederasty, like so many other features of ancient Greek civilisation, had altered remarkably little. The structural features in the family and city which promoted it persisted. The family, for instance, does not figure at all in Plutarch's synopsis of a boy's upbringing written about 120: 'the nurse rules the infant, the teacher the schoolboy, the gymnasiarch the athlete, his lover [*erastes*] the youth, who, in the course of age is then ruled by law and his commanding general'. The gymnasia and the palaestra with their athletic nudity continued as focal points of adolescent training and pederastic attention.[15] It was an institution the Romans never took to. 'Those poor Greeks', condescended Trajan, 'all love a gymnasium.'[16]

Ancient pederastic customs continued. Thus Strabo, writing early in the days of Augustus, describes as still flourishing the primitive and elaborate rituals of pederastic initiation which had been practised immemorially on the island of Crete.[17] Boy-love was still so much venerated in the late second century that Herodes Atticus, the millionaire sophist of Athens, tutor to the young Caesar Marcus Aurelius and a Roman Consul, who had several *eromenoi*, proudly scattered busts around the Greek world of one of them, a mournful, unattractive youth called Polydeukes who had died young and whom the megalomaniac Atticus sought to commemorate in the way Hadrian had recently done Antinous.

Changes there had been. Though the role of married women had not much altered ('love', it was said, 'has no connection whatever with the women's quarters'),[18] *hetairai* or courtesans had become more prominent and open features of society. Feminine forms occurred more often in the visual arts and heterosexual relations had long ago acquired their own culture and philosophic champions. Pederastic love may have lost the austere and heroic idealism of classical times. As Cicero shrewdly asked of the so-called ideal love of the Greeks: 'why is it that no one falls in love with an ugly boy or a beautiful old man?'[19] The tone everywhere became more down-to-earth and often tinged with lasciviousness. It is summed up in a letter from Philostratus, the sophist of the end of the second century AD, to a boy-friend, reprimanding him for his stubborn refusal to indulge in sex: 'whatever the professors may think, yet, while in reputation chastity is noble, in practice it is inhuman. Tell me, what grandeur is there in being, before you depart from life, a chaste corpse?'[20]

The culture of pederasty, particularly of the literary kind, flourished unabated. But much of the high-minded seriousness of earlier times had gone by the second century. Lucian's dialogues take pederastic relationships for granted in a flippant, titillating way in which even Zeus is mocked for his drooling, fleshly desire for the coquettishly naive Ganymede. In the pederastic poems of Strato of Sardis and others collected into the *Greek Anthology* (many from cities which were to the forefront in honouring Antinous), the emotional subtleties of Hellenistic poets like Meleager give way to a franker sexuality in which sodomy, fellatio, masturbation, prostitution and petting figure prominently and frequently with a pornographic relish. Nevertheless, the letters of Philostratus are in the older Hellenistic tradition of courtly love to the boy. And the sculptures of Antinous remain without doubt one of the most elevated and ideal monuments to pederastic love of the whole ancient world.

Even the philosophic argument continued to the end. Such was the prevalence of pederasty about the time of Hadrian's accession in 117, that the happily married Plutarch felt compelled to compose a Socratic dialogue in defence of conjugal love. It was set near Thespiae, a seat of the god Eros, where Hadrian was shortly after to leave behind his enigmatic poem. It is significant that Plutarch does not attack the pederasty of his time: on the contrary, he expounds its moral, self-denying virtues and lists its great heroes. Conjugal love is superior, he contends, for sensible and practical reasons: because it endures and with time deepens into 'an integral union of souls', whereas the love of boys inevitably comes to an end when the 'springtime' of youth turns into the 'autumn' of manhood. Homosexual connections are anyway, he notes, inherently more fragile, being 'parted by a hair as eggs are'.[21] But despite his arguments, the tradition remained so strong that two hundred years later, at the very end of paganism and about the time of the first Christian imperial edicts against sodomy in 342 AD, there issued from Asia Minor the last in the long sequence of dialogues in favour of pederasty.[22] Though bantering in tone and readily accepting of sexual relations as a natural consequence of mutual affection, it contains in the speech of Callicratidas, the lawyer and sophist of Athens, one of the noblest expositions of boy-love in all its burning ideals of spiritual care, mutual devotion and sense of divine presence – a resounding fanfare of farewell to the aspirations of a thousand years.

Such then was the ethos in which the young Antinous was reared. And here was one of those great integrating traditions which the philhellene Hadrian – who specifically honoured Eros, Apollo, Herakles, Alcibiades, Epaminondas and Xenophon, all exemplars of pederastic love – may well have been inclined to preserve.

The conditions which turned pederasty into a vital social institution in Greece did not exist in Rome. There the family constituted the most cohesive and formative unit of upper society. Both inside it and in political and cultural life outside married women played a far more prominent role. The child was reared by his mother throughout infancy and from then onwards his father carefully supervised his training and career. The boy attended schools and on leaving served a period of apprenticeship in minor public duties under the eye of a tutor, usually a family friend. Thereafter, as a junior tribune in the army, he was again subject to the oversight of a superior officer. On leaving and starting his career in public life, he usually gravitated as client to an influential patron, who may also have been connected with his family.

Whatever the emotional and educational deficiencies of the Roman family, there was evidently no need for a system of pederasty to supplement them. Nor did other forces promoting boy-love in Greece generate much power in Rome. Gymnasia and palaestras, which Cicero rightly discerned as the hothouses of pederastic love in Greece, never become the focal points of Latin civic life or education. Indeed participation in athletic or cultural festivals, so essential to the Greek concept of ethical and healthful development, was considered degrading by the Roman upper class who never forgave Nero for his grotesque singing and lyre-playing in the theatres of Greece, or Commodus for sinking so low as to appear as a gladiator. Possessed of a down-to-earth peasant realism, the Romans could seldom discern the divine in the corporeal. Nudity was therefore, in the prim days of the early republic, despised in the Greeks and shunned at home. Ennius said and Cicero agreed that 'the beginning of shameful acts is to strip the body naked amongst other men'.[23] Cato's son, we are told, never bathed alongside his father and never saw him naked, out of shame. Though later attitudes like this were to change, the naked adolescent was not to become a symbolic ideal as in Hellas. In the end, a culture did ultimately grow around pederasty in Rome, but it never developed a philosophy and never found the ultimate sanction of a patron god as in Greece.

Bisexuality, however, seemed inherent in the nature of the Latins and one at least of their stages of socialisation lent itself to some form of pederasty: the system of tutorship and patronage. Many men rose in public life by becoming the private lover of the older man. Thus Catullus tells us that when attached to the entourage of Memmius, governor of Bithynia in 57–56 BC, he allowed himself to be buggered by his patron, as did other aides, hopeful thereby of promoting their careers.[24] Sejanus started his rise to notoriety and power as the boy-friend of Marcus Gavius Apicius. Much later, Theocritus, the influential freedman of Caracalla, owed his fortune to having been the boy-love of Saoterus, in turn the paramour of the Emperor Commodus. In more humdrum circles, Pliny warned Corellia Hispulla that her vulnerably good-looking son needed not a tutor but a protector. Occasionally, perhaps, the attachments so formed possessed something of the loving and cherishing quality of those in Greece, but in the main they seem to have been mercenary, mutually predatory and devoid of the altruism which imbued the Hellenic pederastic ideal.

Homosexuality or pederasty was nevertheless prevalent enough in the days of the early Republic for it to be, at least in the shape of unsolicited assaults resulting in complaints to officials, punished by law. The army, then and later, as in many societies, seems to have been a centre of the practice. Not even distinguished service, as in the case of the brave and much-decorated centurion Cornelius, or officer-rank as in the case of the tribune Laetonius, could save them from the death penalty for seeking sex with unwilling juniors in about 300 BC. A century or so later, as such severe morals relaxed, a lex Scantinia could be invoked in such cases, though the penalty under this was frequently no more than a fine.[25] In later days, as Tacitus tells us of the year 69 AD, the troops' taste in rape covered boys as well as girls and young and good-looking recruits were forced to gratify the lusts of the sergeants.

At the end of the Republic, in the days of Cicero and Julius Caesar, already deeply influenced by the culture of the Greek east, it is clear that homosexuality was common in Rome but still entailed stigma. The alleged affair of Julius Caesar with the last King of the Bithynians, Nikomedes IV, was thus used by his political adversaries to blacken his reputation. Cicero depicted him, lounging on the King's golden couch, arrayed in purple, his virginity lost. Bibulus called him 'the Queen of Bithynia'. Curio denounced him as 'every woman's man and every man's woman'. The troops, however, as one might expect, were much more tolerant. Marching on his triumph through Rome, they sang merrily: 'all the Gauls did Caesar vanquish but Nikomedes vanquished him'.[26] It is clear that it was the passive or 'pathic' role he is said to have played which gave ground for the offence and not a homosexual love-affair itself. The lex Scantinia was now invoked by political enemies to smear each other, often, as in the cases of Drusus and Appius, the very accusers being among the worst offenders.

By the time that Hadrian was a young man in the days of the Emperor

Domitian, bisexuality seemed the norm among the upper classes now steeped in the mores and culture of the east. The fact had reached the ears of the savage enemies of the Empire. Already that fierce female Boadicea had (according to Dio) reviled the Romans as 'men who anoint themselves with myrrh and sleep on soft couches with boys as bedfellows'.[27] Widespread male and boy prostitution and the endless availability of slaves, organised sometimes into seraglios, satisfied carnal homosexual desires. Domitian, something of a puritan, besides banning castration, tried to stop the prostitution of children under the age of seven and attempted to revive the lex Scantinia but mainly as a means of eliminating his political enemies. The atmosphere of unbridled sexual licence depicted in the Satyricon of Nero's day is confirmed in the epigrams of Martial, pervaded by homosexual loves and jealousies and dwelling salaciously on such practices as fellatio and sodomy. The foci of such sexual commerce in Rome were the baths, where the naked men and boys surveyed and tested each other's endowments; the amphitheatre, where homosexual cliques, frequently dressed in green, swooned over the feats and physiques of their favourite *retiarii*; and the theatre, where young actors or dancers had such a delirious and inflammatory impact that they had several times to be expelled from Rome altogether.

In the days of Caesar homosexuality had been a cause for damaging political attack, but by now it could be a ground for political exoneration. Thus a young man, Julius Calvaster, accused of plotting with an older conspirator against Domitian, acquitted himself easily and to applause with the excuse that they had met not to conspire but to make love. 'And', commented the sober Senator Dio Cassius later, revealing in a phrase the whole Greek acceptance of such affairs as natural, 'in fact he was of an appearance to inspire passion'.[28]

Against this background of unrestrained sexual indulgence, there did grow up in cultivated Roman circles a more genuine pederasty with a culture modelled on Greek precedents. Symonds' remark 'that instead of love lust was the deity of the boy-lover on the shores of the Tiber' is by no means always true.[29] Many middle-aged men had their boy-lovers (called *pueri delicati* or *paidika*) whom they nurtured with the same passionate tenderness, no doubt accompanied by physical love, of the ancient *erastes* for his *eromenos*. No couples could have shown more mutual solicitude than the wealthy barrister Flavius Ursus and his fifteen-year-old boy, or Melior and the young lad Glaucias whom he had freed and adopted as his own son. Both these boys died young and their lovers' grief is expressed in poems by Statius which, despite stilted imagery, vibrate with a genuine lamentation which must have been similar to Hadrian's for Antinous.[30] Martial too could refine his coarse interests to exquisiteness when writing of the deaths of boy-lovers.[31] In a tradition more like that of heroic Greece, we find Julius Alexander, being pursued by assassins sent by the Emperor Commodus in 189, opting, instead of an easy escape alone, to stay with his exhausted boy-lover and to die with him.

Even when not accompanied by sex, a mode of courtly love and address could be adopted between man and boy. Thus the sophist Fronto, tutor to the prudish young stoic, Marcus Aurelius (who publicly congratulated himself when Emperor for not falling prey to either hetero- or homo-sexual tempters), skittishly warned his pupil to beware of the attentions of men-lovers who wrote amorous poems, used Thessalian love-charms and called their boys 'darling'. Such advice did not, however, prevent Fronto from describing their own relationship as that of lovers (*amatores*) or from declaring, when Marcus Aurelius was twenty-five: 'What is sweeter to me than your kiss? That sweet fragrance, that delight which dwells for me on your neck and on your lips . . .' Marcus Aurelius in response would assert how 'passionately, by heaven, am I in love with you' and sign off his letters: 'Farewell, my greatest treasure beneath the sky, my glory . . .' etc.[32] No doubt all this was very conventional, innocent and possibly only partly sincere, but it does reveal the acceptable boundaries within which more genuinely passionate relationships could flourish in the highest and most scrupulous society of Rome under the avowed anti-pederastic successor of Hadrian, the Emperor Antoninus Pius.

A genuine or simulated culture of pederasty now flourished in literary and philosophic circles. Most of the great poets of Rome – except Ovid and Propertius – tried their hand at poetry celebrating boy-love. Virgil, in his *Bucolics*, written in the early days of the Empire, exudes a melancholy passion for Alexis which though derived from the Greek model of Theocritus is said to be founded in his own erotic experience.[33] Horace, Catullus and Tibullus all produced verses expressing slighted love for faithless youths. But these works possess a flavour of artificial literary contrivance, based on Hellenistic traditions, when compared with their authors' other poems which clearly reflect more complex and genuine emotions for women. It is, however, significant that these poets, along with Statius and Persius, felt the need to parade openly such homosexual feelings and produce works for the public in the pederastic tradition of literature.

Perhaps the two most profoundly pederastic writers are Martial, whose epigrams, robust or delicate, sensual or ethereal, seem to derive most from authentic feeling when they deal with boys, and Juvenal whose tender and repressed affections peep only briefly and timidly from behind his violent and obsessive hatreds.[34] No philosophic writings in defence of pederasty from Rome survive to us. But Seneca had *paidika* and Juvenal pillories cliques of affected stoic and other philosophers as crypto-homosexuals.

In sum, it seems that though pederasty in Rome frequently arose from sincere and profound relationships and was often fashionable, it never connected deeply enough with the psychology and genius, nor with the social structure of the Latins, to flower into an original and rich culture of its own.

Nevertheless, there was obviously nothing to prevent Hadrian, following perhaps the dictates of his own nature, from indulging in such an acceptable and civilised importation from the Aegean when still only a young 'Greekling' in Rome and a mere private citizen far from any imperial prospects.

Once, however, he had become the unproclaimed heir-apparent, what precedents had he in the history of the Emperors to guide or control any taste for pederasty he may have developed? On what terms, if indeed at all, would the powerful traditional elements in Rome, however broad-minded privately, tolerate in their rulers any pronounced deviation from the heterosexual norms on which their society was officially based and which was symbolised in the protectress and ancestress of the imperial dynasty, the goddess Venus?

In the absence of much evidence on the matter in the earnestly political histories of Tacitus and the tawdry second-hand ragbag of chronicles from Dio Cassius, we have to resort to Suetonius' *Lives of the Caesars*, full of spicy sexual details and obsessive interests. Indeed, it has recently been claimed that Suetonius was yet another repressed homosexual, this time with a penis-fixation.[35] Be that as it may, his sexual anecdotes are often ignored or dismissed by historians as based on rumour or invention, and, as far as homosexuality goes, as being no more than a means of political denigration. The latter is scarcely true as, for example, Suetonius reports more about the pederastic activities of Titus (with his troops of catamites and eunuchs) whom he rapturously admires than about his brother Domitian whom he detests. Even the revered and patently heterosexual Augustus comes in for his meed of homosexual gossip, though it is dismissed as improbable. Only two Emperors seem untouched by homosexual tales in his biographies, neither of whom Suetonius unequivocally admires – the despised Claudius 'who was im-moderate in his passion for women'[36] and Vespasian who, succeeding Nero and the sexually ambivalent group of shortlived Emperors of the year 69, asserted an almost aggressive and primitive normality. He refused a commis-sion to a scented young man with the words, 'I had rather you smelt of garlic', and responded to the criticism of a well-known deviant with the riposte: 'I, at least, am a man'.[37]

Down to the end of the reign of Domitian none of the Emperors seem to have been mainly of a homosexual orientation, with possibly the exception of the elderly Galba, the brief successor to Nero, whose taste in sex was for strong and mature men and who offended conventions by kissing his favourites in public. The rest seem to have been variously bisexual: including the otherwise heterosexual Tiberius, if the antics reported by Suetonius with little boys and girls on Capri in his last years are to be believed. Some sovereigns, before gaining power, had been the lovers of reigning Emperors: Vitellius had been one of those little *spintriae* of Tiberius on Capri, Otho a beloved of Nero's. Others, though married and evidently sexually active with women, kept a boy-friend or *paidika* in the good Hellenistic tradition. Thus Domitian's passion for his long-haired eunuch from Pergamon, Earinus, was celebrated in fawning poetry by Martial and Statius and is recalled by Dio Cassius. Vitellius was completely unable to free himself of his attachment to Asiaticus. Though Titus thought it prudent to remove his harem of boys on becoming Emperor, it is doubtful if this was mandatory and it is clear that bisexual activity among the Emperors was not in itself considered reprehensible in Rome.

Among the deviant characteristics which certainly did violate opinion was 'effeminacy'. For a man to be the willing passive partner in anal or oral sex, the Greek 'pathic', still offended against the contemporary image of the male and accusations of this continued to be made and still stung. Caligula and Otho, for example, were so disparaged. Imperial associates whose masculinity was so impugned were unrestrained in their response: Cassius Chaerea, taunted as effeminate by Caligula, took revenge later by killing him. Asiaticus, the beloved of Vitellius, diverted his critics to the proof of his own manly sexual activity with the words: 'Ask your sons . . . They will confirm my masculinity.'[38] Among the many outrages of Nero was not so much his castration and conversion of the boy Sporus into a wife, but his own prostration as a simulated wife under the vigorous 'husband' Pythagoras and another freedman, Doryphoros.[39] At the beginning of the third century, it was the marriage of another Emperor, the pure invert Elagabalus ('call me not lord for I am a lady') to the centurion Hierocles which, among many other abuses, swept them both to a miserable doom. Rome expected its bi- or homo-sexual rulers to be virile.

Its other expectations can be most clearly discerned if we examine the case of the first thoroughgoing pederast to ascend the imperial throne who yet attained the pinnacle of unanimous public acclaim as *Optimus Princeps*, none other than Hadrian's great-uncle, the Emperor Trajan.

The sources, all favourably disposed to him, do not disguise his inclinations. There was, for instance, the incident in the *Historia Augusta* between Trajan and Hadrian over some boys in the paedagogium 'whom Trajan loved ardently'. Elsewhere in that source we are told about his boy favourites (*delicati*).[40] Dio, no purveyor of ripe slander, tells us that 'of course he was devoted to boys', but that in his relations with them 'he harmed no one' nor evidently his own reputation.[41] He was, Dio confides, particularly fond of young dancers, one of them called Pylades and another we hear of called Apolaustus – a fact which Fronto confirms.[42] The Emperor even sent for them when at campaign headquarters in Syria. Once he even allowed his attraction to a boy to influence his policy, when the handsome and obviously subtle youth, Arbandes, son of an erring eastern princeling called Abgares, successfully interceded with the entranced Emperor on his father's behalf. The boy was another hypnotic dancer, captivating his imperial admirer by performing a barbaric dance at dinner. Trajan's reputation for pederasty echoed down the ages. Julian, the last pagan Emperor, writing about 360, depicts his arriving on Olympus loaded with the trophies of his great campaigns to the loud warning whisper of Silenus: 'From now on Zeus, our master, had better look out if he wants to keep Ganymede for himself.' Later, though, he condemns Trajan as 'a slave of ignoble passion . . . pleasure of the vilest and most infamous sort'. This is the only surviving criticism of Trajan from ancient times.[43]

Trajan was much shrewder and more tactful than some of the group of pederasts who surrounded him. His fellow Spaniard, the champion and confidant of the young Hadrian, Licinius Sura, so loaded his bed-fellows with wealth that the scandal was recounted by the exiled philosopher Epictetus to Arrian in far-off Nikopolis. More embarrassing and instructive still to Trajan of the limits of tolerable pederastic behaviour in those holding high positions was the fate of his cultivated friend, Vibius Maximus, whom he had appointed prefect of Egypt from 103 to 107. The Prefect was accused by some Alexandrian dignitaries of financial corruption, extortion, interfering with magistracies and bribing the father of a handsome seventeen-year-old, Theon, whom he then proceeded to corrupt in another way.[44] The Prefect's attentions went beyond all acceptable bounds of propriety and had the disastrous effect of turning his beloved's head. The boy not only slept with him in the state bed but emerged from it among the morning suitors in the palace and flagrantly flaunted the signs of the previous night's intercourse. He sat next to the prefect on the magistrate's rostrum, was paraded at official banquets and at prefectorial reviews and inspections. He cheeked the court chamberlain to his face in public, mocked the grovelling clients and gaily missed both his school and training in the palaestra. Ironically, the trial and condemnation of Vibius Maximus (on financial not sexual charges) took place in Rome before his friend, Trajan himself, who must have found the whole episode painfully embarrassing, resolving even more to avoid such appalling and destructive indiscretions himself.

In fact, Trajan's well-known pederasty caused no such scandal nor even blemish on his reputation because he never let it grate on the susceptibilities of Rome. He carefully followed some obvious guidelines. He had hardly any need to stress his virility and valour. He respected and dignified his wife in public, lavishing honours on her, taking her everywhere, consulting her, never, in the total absence of any hint of relations with another woman, once compromising her reputation, indeed boosting her as this 'most hallowed woman' (*sanctissima femina*).[45] He also kept his family, his sister Marciana and her daughter Matidia, about him in the palace and included them in his travelling entourage. They provided Rome with a completely unprecedented example of domestic harmony and purity in the imperial house. He never – apart from his trivial concession to Arbandes – allowed his favourites any influence over his policies or prominence on public occasions. Especially, he never flaunted his affections at state functions as when Commodus later shocked the public by outrageously kissing and fondling Saoterus in the imperial carriage in the course of a triumph through the streets of Rome. Trajan, both in his erotic life and in his addiction to wine, knew how to stop short of excess. In other words, he had an acute perception of the demands of his public office as Emperor and the limits they imposed on his private behaviour as a man and as a lover. The *Optimus* title was not undeserved.

Here, then, was an example for his successor and one which the more complex and perverse nature of Hadrian would find it hard to follow.

HADRIAN AND ANTINOUS

Hadrian's tight-lipped reticence, his inability to trust and brittleness of friendships probably made the rare occasions in his life when he did establish a bond of love all the more intense and overpowering for him. On these occasions – with Antinous and Commodus – the discretion exemplified in Trajan's affairs was swept carelessly away and this most secretive of men and most cautious of Emperors declared and published his love in ways so extravagant and unparalleled (one made a god, the other Caesar) as to astonish the world. Even in his poems and memorials to his favourite horses and dogs, his speeches, temples and flamboyant mournings for the Ulpian women there appears this same exaggerated need to express and embody his feelings in a manner bordering on the histrionic. One senses that, like a true romantic, Hadrian was absorbed more by the phenomenon of his own love than by the recipients of it, that his passion was but 'a version of the glorified self'.[1] Perhaps that is why he reacted with such excessive grief after a death: the complex reciprocal feeling between two people was no more, there was now left only his own passion to indulge and to perpetuate in cults and objects which he was now free to shape artistically as he wished, regardless perhaps of the former reality of the relationship. The flame of love may have ignited but rarely in his closed and convoluted nature, but when it did it was all-consuming and tended also to consume those who lit it.

Several times the ancient sources stress his 'excessive' sensuality, voluptuousness and lasciviousness, usually in vague connection with boys,[2] but these stock phrases do not enable us to know whether his temperament really was physically sensual and there are no incidents reported to bear them out. Certainly the way he surrounded himself with richly varied marbles, gildings, stucco and sumptuous effects, as well as his collection of nude sculptures at the villa, speak of his delight in the tactile senses and in the human body. But how far this aesthetic sensuousness was translated, if at all, into forms and degrees of sexual appetite, we cannot tell. The sources may be deliberately confusing his capacity for excessive displays of feeling, which is proven, with that for excessive indulgence, which remains unknown.

Was that desire, even moderately, for women? Despite the confident claims of the school which sees him as the adulterous father of Commodus, or the shamefaced suggestion that he was the lover of Plotina, there exist in the whole of the extensive ancient literature about him only three meagre references to any erotic or sexual relations with women. The *Historia Augusta* tells us in the same breath that ('it was said') he was addicted to passion for males and to adulteries with married women.[3] Though it provides various confirmatory evidence for the males, it is amazingly silent about the women: not a name, not a rumour, not an anecdote is given. Origen, writing in about 249 AD, and doing his best to make Antinous, recently compared with Jesus, seem an ineffective nullity even in his speciality of perverted sex, sneers that 'he did not even keep the man [Hadrian] from a morbid lust for women'.[4] Dio Cassius twice reports the gossip of his father that Plotina was in love with Hadrian, but *not*, it should be carefully observed, that Hadrian was in love with her.[5]

This then is the extraordinarily scanty basis for depicting Hadrian as a heterosexual athlete.[6] The *Historia* is suspiciously vague, Origen is vehemently trying to denigrate Antinous and Dio says nothing at all about Hadrian's response to Plotina's alleged love. If Hadrian was prone to sexual amours with women, especially adulterous ones with Roman society ladies, one might expect from his prattling and inventive biographers at least as much evidence as they give for his amours with boys. This strange silence must therefore be treated as indicative, especially when put against what we *do* know of his relations with women, with boys and young men. Hadrian may not have been exclusively or congenitally homosexual, perhaps sharing the Latin bisexual nature, but his activity in the bed of adultery seems to have been so weak, inextensive and colourless as to have left no concrete traces or even randy stories behind it, still less the extravagant actions and monuments which were inspired by his other emotional ventures. As the sole products of his heterosexual activity, we have only those bastards invented in 1700 and 1949: a frail and insubstantial progeny indeed. We are entitled therefore to examine the hypothesis that the balance of his emotions and sexual nature was in another direction.

His relations with the women about whom we do know confirm this. That Plotina, the adoptive mother, loved Hadrian erotically may well be true. She may not have been much older than him and told him that he was 'most dear to me in all respects'. And there are enough incidents in his rise to power to confirm this solicitous affection.[7] But for the suggestion that her love took a sexual form or was sexually reciprocated there is not the slightest evidence. The recent proposal by an Italian historian that she was Hadrian's concubine is a travesty of the sparse phrases of Dio Cassius and is contradicted by what we are explicitly told by Pliny of her moral qualities and her loyalty to Trajan.[8] The other recent suggestion that Plotina deliberately planted the impossible, shrewish Sabina as Hadrian's wife so that she could keep him as her own beloved, is pure fantasy.[9] Obviously Plotina and Hadrian shared interests, alien to Trajan's, which linked them closely. Clearly, too, there was affection on his part: he was always glad, he said, to grant her tactful requests. But his devotion was obviously more that of a son to a mother figure: 'my dearest and most honoured mother', he calls her in letters, and she responds with 'my own dear son', 'my good son' – not exactly the endearments of a torrid romance and much less passionate than those between Fronto and Marcus Aurelius.[10] And though Hadrian signified his private grief at her death by the singular display of wearing black for nine days and by building her a temple in her home town, his public response was nothing disproportionate like that to the male loves in his life. He did not even issue consecration coins in her memory and in the divisions of Antinoopolis her name ranks only among the demes of the phyle of Matidia. She is subject to a cold protocol and relegated below her niece there and in other honours bestowed, for Matidia was Hadrian's link with the Ulpian house.

With this 'most beloved' mother-in-law Hadrian's relations also seem to have been cordial, more so than with his wife, as the ecstatic and characteristically exaggerated compliments of his funeral oration for her make clear.[11]

Thus the most sympathetic relations with women which we know for certain that Hadrian established were with those who officially and in private fulfilled the role of mother substitute to him, remaining, for all their shrewd practical help at crucial moments, revered and ideal figures to him as his language and actions regarding them suggest. We do not have to be psychological experts to connect this close and idealised mother-relationship with Hadrian's homosexual leanings and with his inability to create a happy and sexually complete partnership with his wife.

The lack of compatibility in temperament, interests and ability between Hadrian and Sabina seems only partly to account for the mutual antipathy which flared between them in the earlier and later days of their marriage. The words Hadrian used about her, *morosa et aspera*, imply a bitterness more deeply grounded in a sense of sexual rejection which she found difficult to bear and which was made all the more frustrating by the way her husband, while busy pursuing his own emotional fancies, dismissed from court any man who showed the least familiarity with her. Only male gods of stone like Memnon or female flatterers like Balbilla were allowed to admire 'the amiable beauty of our queen'.[12] Her own words are full of sexual significance: 'Having experienced all the atrocity of Hadrian's character,' she is reported as saying, 'she had taken steps not to become pregnant by him to the detriment of mankind.'[13] Perhaps Hadrian had wanted sex with her not out of love or desire but simply to father an heir and she had taken a spiteful revenge in preventing this humiliating use of herself, possibly using one of the sterility-inducing drugs mentioned by Juvenal.[14]

Thirty-six years of married life imprisoned in the formality of a strictly enforced etiquette and in a marriage without love or sexual fulfilment would have been enough to wither a woman endowed with greater resources than Sabina. She did not have the reserves of Plotina to sublimate her sexual rejection into cultural and political activities and the cultivation of the grand role of the pure mother of the country. Moreover Sabina had to suffer public humiliations which Plotina was spared. She complained fiercely of the injuries which her husband heaped on her – treating her like a slave, she declared.[15] The customary title of *Augusta* and the right of coinage were long withheld from her. Distinguished friends were publicly banned from her presence. Hadrian's ostentatious affairs with Antinous and Commodus were scarcely the unembarrassing and discreet liaisons with dancers which were all that Plotina had to endure from Trajan. It must have been difficult to bear the cruel irony of being depicted on the coins as equal to the Vestal Virgins, those guardians of chastity, while everyone knew her to be in fact 'the world's greatest sexual supernumerary'.[16] And though Sabina may have got on well with Antinous, who had no imperial pretensions and perhaps a conciliatory nature, the adoption of the ambitious and libertine young aristocrat Commodus is said to have precipitated a final crisis between her and Hadrian. In the end, even the memory of Antinous may have rankled. Visitors to the Villa Adriana would have been confronted by images of him everywhere but would have had to search hard for portraits of her: twenty-two sculptures of the favourite have been unearthed there but only two of the Empress.[17] In such uninhibited ways did Hadrian proclaim his emotional priorities.

What direct evidence is there, then, for Hadrian's pederasty – leaving aside the extensive material about Antinous and the fewer references to Commodus? The sources are varied, independent and mutually supportive.

Perhaps the earliest is a reference in Jerome's *Chronicle* (written in 380–81 AD but relying here on a much earlier source) for the year 118 at the beginning of the reign. Hadrian, we are told, was not only most erudite in foreign languages 'but not restrained enough in the love of boys'.[18] The *Historia Augusta*, apart from references to Trajan's love for Hadrian and the latter's adoption of his uncle's habits, also mentions an obscure but evidently authentic incident in which they clashed because of the intrigues of the pedagogues of those boys whom Trajan loved ardently – a breach between them which that well-known pederast Sura stepped in to heal.[19] Also to be dated before the succession is the story it gives ('generally believed') that Hadrian 'cultivated Trajan's boy favourites and had frequent sexual intercourse with them when an inner member of the court'.[20] Later, when Emperor, his passion ('it is said') for adultery is equated with his passion for adult males, a phrase which may be no more than a pun on the word 'adult' in the Latin.[21] We are told also by the *Historia* that Hadrian wrote many love poems about his boy favourites, a fact which Apuleius who read them a generation later confirms for us independently.[22] Sextus Aurelius Victor refers to 'malevolent rumours' that Hadrian committed sexual violations on youths.[23] Marcus Aurelius, writing in praise of his adoptive father Antoninus Pius in about 170 AD, commends his 'efforts to stop pederasty' in a context which has always been taken to refer adversely to Hadrian.[24] Indeed, it is dubiously claimed that soon after his accession in 138, Antoninus Pius may even have destroyed the recently erected tomb of Antinous as a symbol of his determination to eliminate his predecessor's vice which it so grandiosely commemorated.

There are other, more oblique literary hints on the matter. Both Juvenal and Suetonius are said to be commenting semi-covertly in several passages about Hadrian's pederastic tastes. In this connection, it is surely not without relevance that when that connoisseur of sex, Suetonius, decided to ingratiate himself with Hadrian by giving him a bronze figure of Augustus for his bedroom, he subtly chose one of the first Princeps as a boy.[25] And, turning to visual data, if the attractive youths shown as intimate associates of Hadrian on the tondi of the Arch of Constantine are not Antinous, then they must be, as has been suggested, other favourites like him.[26] He certainly had several youths of seventeen or so around him, besides Antinous, when he set out for the east in 128, as we shall see. Hadrian also took a quite unusual interest in and lavished gifts on the 'boys and youths' of the beloved Athens.[27]

In detail and in isolation some of this evidence is of course dubious: too much of it is self-confessed and second-hand reporting of gossip. But the few direct facts (the love poems, the incident concerning the paedagogium, the figures on the tondi, his interest in the ephebes, the Thespiae poem and Hadrian's attachment to pederastic heroes and gods) do give great support to, if they do not conclusively validate, these reports. The variety and mutual independence of the sources tend to make them mutually confirmatory. At the very least, the evidence for Hadrian's pederastic inclinations is far more abundant, consistent and specific than the meagre references to his heterosexual exploits. It connects too with what we know of his aesthetic and historical tastes, his relations with his wife and with other women, and the sexual mores of his time. And we still have to consider the evidence about the most notorious of alleged pederastic affairs in history: his relationship with Antinous.

The ancient commentators are here far more numerous, about twenty-nine of them.[28] Between them, however, we have to make some distinctions. Many of the later writers, especially Christian ones, are obviously drawing and elaborating on the earlier ones, and much of their testimony is therefore of little value. Some are also biased from the outset, again chiefly the Christian writers, and such partisan approaches should be matched against the more objective ones. We must also bear in mind that the words *eromenos* and *paidika*, so frequently used in these sources, were technical terms for boy-beloved in an established pederastic relationship, the Latin equivalent being usually *puer delicatus*. As we have abundantly shown, in the Greco-Roman world of the second century such a relationship and such terms had come to have definite sexual implications, as did the word *eros* for love.

Among the contemporary pagan writers, Arrian, if his tribute to Achilles and Patroclus in his report of *c.* 134 to Hadrian on the Black Sea voyage is indeed a flattering analogy with the Antinous affair, clearly sets it in the context of pederastic love, as his use of the word *paidikois* shows. He also stresses 'the force of Achilles' love'. This is a theme taken up by Pausanias, writing shortly after Hadrian's death (*c.* 160), telling us that 'he was extraordinarily passionate about Antinous'.[29] Clearly Hadrian's love struck contemporaries as being unusually intense.

Other references are equally explicit. The hymn from Curium of the 130s happily identifies Antinous with Eros himself. Celsus, the solemn defender of paganism, writing about 176, calls Antinous 'Hadrian's *paidika*' and refers to the sexual depravity of his cult.[30] Lucian's dialogue of about 180, in which Zeus dallies amorously and sensually with Ganymede, if it too is another analogy with the affair, places it in the pattern of an easy-going, sexually permissive pederasty.[31]

The major ancient historians wrote later in time but used much earlier sources. Dio, writing in about 217, and never much interested in sexual tittle-tattle, explicitly describes Antinous as Hadrian's *paidika*, a clear enough pederastic term of the day, and talks of Hadrian's *eros* for him as one alternative explanation for the apotheosis.[32] The *Historia Augusta*, composed about 395 but based on a source of about 210, talks simply of 'his Antinous' as if the nature of the intimate relationship was well known or self-evident.[33] Later, it quotes divergent opinions about the death, one knowingly connecting Antinous' beauty with Hadrian's excessive sensuality. The *Historia* also refers to Hadrian's passionate grief, another witness to the strength of his love. Sextus Aurelius Victor, writing about the same date, links the malevolent rumours about Hadrian's sexual violations of boys with the information that 'he burned with passion for Antinous'. Though he declares he kept an open mind on the matter, he finds the relationship between such an immoral man and a boy, of such disproportionate ages, 'very suspicious'.[34]

From the pagan evidence we can conclude that Hadrian's love was generally perceived as of a remarkable and memorable intensity, that the relationship was seen by the Greek writers at least as conforming to the established pattern of pederastic love and that the terms employed, the contexts provided, and the innuendoes and rumours introduced all consistently suggest the possibility that it was sexual.

The Christian Fathers went much further. Though their response to Antinous himself varied, they lambasted the affair as disgustingly sexual. At first, under Hadrian's immediate successors, the descriptions of Justin, Tatian, Theophilos and Athenagoras were tactfully muted, but the affair was set in the context of prostitution, debauchery, incontinence and false and ignoble gods. The interpolation about the affair in the *Book of Wisdom* of about 180 introduces a surprising new image of a father consumed with grief for the premature death of his son, a reference soon taken up by Clement of Alexandria in his rhetorical question about Antinous: 'Why do you order that he be mourned as a son?'[35] This theme in the relationship we shall consider later.

Clement it was who in about 190 released the deluge of sexual criticism on Hadrian and Antinous. His sources we do not know, though as he was born and educated in Athens and wrote in Alexandria, he must have been familiar with the mores of the pederastic relationships of his time and the talk and tales about this particular one. The affair, he declared, was not only that of *erastes–eromenos* but was based on nothing more than unrestrained lust. He even depicts the bedroom scenes with Antinous at night which, he fulminates, were 'really shameful as the lover who kept them with him well knew'.[36] The followers of the cult practised similar orgies, he claims, in commemoration of this god honoured by fornication. Tertullian, about 197, calls Antinous roundly a 'bugger', equates him with Ganymede and sets him among prostitutes and promiscuousness.[37] Origen, also writing from Alexandria in about 249, describes Antinous as *paidikos*, but is generally more restrained, contrasting the licentiousness of Antinous with the purity of Christ.[38]

Later writers essentially embroider these accounts: Athanasius in 350 with outrage, calling Antinous 'the slave of Hadrian's lust'; Prudentius with salaciousness, depicting the couple, Hadrian as Antinous' 'husband',[39] lolling, embracing and quaffing together. The terms used by later and more matter-of-fact writers are again frequently *paidika* and *eromenos*. Among them, Jerome, always more restrained and perhaps in his praise of Antinous' beauty cryptically sympathetic, calls Antinous, in one of his references, simply, 'the love of his heart'.[40]

Obviously the defamatory intentions of the Fathers render their evidence highly suspect. The picture of Hadrian as a monster of lust and of Antinous as a blighted flower or a degraded concubine are pulpit fantasies rather than realistic appreciations. We have even less idea than for the pagan authors on what, if any, sources they based their charges: though both Clement and Origen refer to the practices of the contemporary cult in Antinoopolis and must have had access to much information of varying reliability. It is, however, notable that they all see the relationships as that of *erastes–eromenos* and simply assume that sex will arise within it. In this, at least, their violent diatribes generally tally with the more neutral accounts of the pagan authors.

About the relationship of Hadrian and Antinous, we can be sure that it was not just that of a lustful man using a willing catamite or plaything. All that we can reconstruct of this affair – the shared initiation at Eleusis, mutual reliance in the perils of the desert, the apotheosis, the tender phrases of the obelisk, what we know of Antinous' character and role – all contradict the age-old idea that this relationship was one of mere physical passion, though this is not to exclude that as one of its ingredients.

Hadrian, who equated himself with Herakles and Zeus and sometimes even with Eros the god of pederasty, with the heroes of antiquity and who venerated ancient culture, probably saw himself as re-creating an *erastes–eromenos* relationship in the great classical tradition. As the tribute to Antinous' wisdom and intelligence on the obelisk, the shared experiences of the Eleusinian mysteries, of the great hunts and of Egyptian religion all indicate, Hadrian was concerned to develop not just the body but the mind and spirit of the boy in the true tradition of an elevated *erastes* of antiquity. Here it is significant that, though Hadrian, as we shall see, soon eagerly accepted assimilation to Zeus himself in his eastern domains, only one out of the hundreds of images of Antinous – on coins, gems, and in sculpture – shows him as Ganymede (the 'Hope' Ganymede now at Port Sunlight) and even this attribution is very uncertain. The analogy with the servile and sexually complaisant cupbearer of the chief of gods (as depicted amusingly and popularly by Lucian) was obviously one that Hadrian and those who commemorated the affair excluded or censored as degrading. The relationship was played out and publicised at a much higher level of spirituality and of mutual concern.

There can be no doubt that, like the great lovers of five hundred years before, and in accordance with some mystical yearnings in his nature, Hadrian discerned elements of the divine in his beloved in his lifetime and this was no doubt confirmed by the nature of his death. The combination of sagacity and innocence, of profundity and diversity in Antinous' character can only have aided this. Hadrian, with his love of art, scarcely needed to be convinced that in the enigmatic beauty of this boy were incarnated some deep qualities of the gods. In this sense, the apotheosis was but a public and posthumous announcement of what Hadrian had already privately apprehended in the boy's lifetime.

There must too have been a paternal element, as was inevitable between a fifty-year-old man and a sixteen-year-old boy. Hadrian was childless and, as his earlier rise to power and final dispositions of the Empire show, was not without dynastic hopes. Sabina's virulent remarks reveal that he had wanted a child. No doubt Antinous fulfilled the filial role more admirably than any natural child because, as he was clearly not a candidate for the succession, he never challenged or compromised Hadrian's own power and position or attracted adverse cliques. Because Antinous had no political role but purely an emotional one, his public career could not disappoint or arouse criticism. The strange phrases in the *Book of Wisdom* and Clement of Alexandria about being ordered to mourn the boy as a son, the intrusion of Sabina on the memorial obelisk, the way the adopted Commodus later associated himself with Hadrian in monuments to Antinous, point to a relationship consciously promoted as filial in quality if not in origin. We should not leap to the conclusion that Antinous was, after all, Hadrian's bastard, still less to the supposition that their love was sexless. We see a similar paternal quality in the loves of Flavius Ursus and Melior for their boys which were no doubt also sexual. Here then was a long-felt void in Hadrian's life which Antinous filled.

The love of Hadrian for Antinous went far beyond the convention of an *erastes* or that of a father-substitute. The Thespiae poem hints at some nagging emotional longing in Hadrian in about 125. Once Antinous entered his life that longing turned, as is often the case with those who find emotional relationships difficult to construct, into a voracious love. The sources all stress that his love was passionately intense, extraordinary even for days when such feelings had no need to be demurely restrained. The way that Hadrian took the boy with him on his travels, kept close to him at moments of spiritual, moral or physical exaltation, and, after his death, surrounded himself with his images, shows an obsessive craving for his presence, a mystical-religious need for his companionship. Though there is no ground for the belief that Hadrian neglected the affairs of Rome because of his preoccupation with Antinous, and much evidence that later he shrewdly manipulated his experience, even his grief, to promote his policies, it cannot be denied that this obsession for Antinous consumed him as no other affection in his life, brought him to the brink of credulity if not temporary derangement and may have damaged his political judgement and actions in his last years. Hadrian's almost total disregard, in launching and propagating the apotheosis, for the conservative circles in Rome which he usually so carefully placated, the absence of any of the precedents he loved to parade, demonstrate the overwhelming power of this love which may have become all the more ardent in his romantic mind once the ephemeral and no doubt sometimes difficult adolescent had been transmuted into the immutable perfection of godliness.

Was the relationship sexual? It has been shown that the antithesis erected by later critics between the ideal and the real, the spiritual and the carnal, was alien to the Greco-Roman mind in general and to the *erastes–eromenos* relationship in particular. It was possible, without incompatibility or defilement, for Hadrian to have cultivated the boy's soul, to have venerated the divine element in him, to have abstractly admired the beauty of his form and yet to have consummated his devotion and adoration in physical love-making. There was, as we have shown, nothing in the mores of the time or in the history of the imperial house to inhibit this. Hadrian's own nature, whether or not it was excessively lascivious, was clearly sexually oriented mainly to boys and young men. His love for Antinous was white-hot. There is not the faintest evidence either in his gastronomic or other tastes that Hadrian practised bodily asceticism. Why should he then have withheld himself from sexual expression of his burning feelings for someone whose physical beauty alone, when transmitted to posterity even through the medium of frigid marble, has so often been experienced as sensually moving? The writers of antiquity and not just the biased Christians generally imply a sexual content to the affair. The balance of probabilities therefore tilts heavily in favour of a sexual basis to the relationship. But that is not decisive proof. The secrets of the imperial bedchamber must for ever be denied to us, and, in view of all the hideous and speculative publicity about their love, Hadrian and Antinous are surely entitled to keep this ultimate and intimate secret.

The various depictions of Antinous as a passive invert, a degraded and supine pander, a defiled and dejected instrument of diseased lust do not fit what we know of him or of this relationship.

He was reared in the Greek world where, as we have seen, the tradition of pederastic relations persisted as normal and honourable. There was certainly nothing degrading in the role of *eromenos*: on the contrary, as the dialogues of Plutarch and the followers of Lucian show, to the end of antiquity it conferred prestige and aroused jealousy. Though the anal sexual act it implied was passive, at this adolescent stage (unlike the case of the older and confirmed 'pathics') there were no connotations of effeminacy or inversion in its performance. Antinous probably felt no humiliation, no gnawing guilt, no harrowing ambivalence of gender at the sexual part he may have been called on to play. To be an *eromenos* was still an accepted stage on the way to an uncompromisedly virile manhood. Shortly after Antinous' death the chanting citharode of Curium could publicly and glowingly equate this new god with Eros and thereby stir his audience's approving recollections of the boy's former relationship with Hadrian.

As far as we can see, Antinous responded to Hadrian's affection with loyalty, doing his best to rise to his lover's high expectations, to share his elevated aspirations and perhaps, in the end, repaying his own rescue from death and the whole trust and concern of Hadrian for him, with the ultimate contribution of his life. He seems to have played his difficult role without regard for his own interests and with a discretion and conciliatoriness which may have exceeded Hadrian's own. He certainly seems to have offered back to his lover not just sex and affection but, as the phrases on the obelisk enable us to conjecture, sagacious and selfless counsel.

However, it may well be doubted if the role of the imperial *eromenos* was always easy to bear, not just because of the difficulties of coping with Hadrian's devious, restless character, but because of the very conspicuousness of the position. The Emperor may not have violated the protocol of his public office by flaunting Antinous on inappropriate occasions, as Vibius Maximus did his boy in Egypt, but there can be no doubt that the lad was seen and known by everybody. At first, such notoriety and vicarious power, all the wonder and attention, may have been exciting to Antinous but, with time, both the pressures and the malevolent gossip they generated may have palled and provoked anxiety. It is from the public response to the affair rather than from its intimate nature that the poison of degradation may have spread and festered in Antinous' consciousness. And, in addition, there was always the sense of insecurity, that 'parting by a hair' (as Plutarch put it) of such relationships, doomed to end with youth itself anyway, and doubly under strain from Hadrian's congenital instability in all friendships.

Hadrian's love was not confined to that accepted in the *erastes–eromenos* coupling. It was not normal. It was obsessive, engulfing and it may have been jealously possessive as well, as Hadrian was of Sabina, for whom he cared nothing. At any time – even in classical Greece – it must have been difficult for a growing, unformed lad to cope with the physical and spiritual passion of an older man. But when that man was the all-powerful Emperor of Rome and that passion amounted to an insatiable adoration, Antinous may soon have found it oppressive, constricting and over-exacting. It may not have been easy for a sixteen-year-old to be the lover and possibly the sexual partner of a fifty-year-old. But how much more difficult it was for this boy in addition to have to play the roles of god incarnate, intellectual companion, intrepid huntsman, wise counsellor and domestic diplomat all at once! These expectations may have become too overwhelming, the love suffocating. There is something in the idea that the romantic burden Antinous was made to bear became steadily more intolerable. He may have longed to find some escape from the pressure of this gargantuan affection, from the dilemma of his future and from the conflict between the role of devoted symbolic ideal, which he was expected to live up to, and that image of him as an avid sexual plaything luridly fabricated by malicious claptrap.

The spectacular and exposed visit to the east would put the whole complex relationship between Hadrian and Antinous fully to the test.

'A BRILLIANT LIGHT'
GREECE AND THE EAST, 128–30

The imperial party landed at Corinth in late August or early September in 128 and made their way along the splendid road which Hadrian had built by the wild and beautiful shore to Athens. There they were greeted in solemn processions and state ceremonies by civic worthies, the ephebes and the enthusiastic populace.

No one could then have foreseen how momentous and extraordinary this great second journey was to prove: how it would last at least four and perhaps six years; how the status of Athens in the Greek world would be transformed; how the Greeks themselves would generate a fever-pitch of self-consciousness and exultation resulting in unprecedented unity; how the most bloodthirsty war of the reign would be almost intentionally ignited; how two of the group now entering the Greek east as mortals would soon be elevated among its gods; how all the splendour and elation of this tour would be marred by inexplicable aberrations, tragedy, grief and breakdown and how, throughout, in one way or another, it was to be haunted by the unwelcome spectre or the deliberately provoked challenge of death.

Fortunately we know some of the entourage among whom Antinous now found himself.

Sabina, now publicly paraded as the new *Augusta*, had brought along her younger, unmarried sister, Vibia Matidia, of whose character we know nothing. Among her ladies was the elderly but still spritely Julia Balbilla, an intellectual and poetess with a taste for archaic verse-styles which may well have amused Hadrian. Juvenal summed up her type:

> Worse still is the well-read menace, who's hardly settled for dinner before she starts praising Virgil, making a moral case for Dido (death justifies all), comparing, evaluating rival poets, Virgil and Homer suspended in opposite scales, weighed up one against the other . . . Such a rattle of talk . . . [she] hurls well-rounded syllogisms like slingshots, has all history pat . . . and with antiquarian zeal quotes poets I've never heard of . . .[1]

She was descended from the defunct kings of Commagene, a lineage of which she made sure nobody remained ignorant, and her brother, Philopappos, had been one of the great benefactors of Athens in the previous generation and something of a model for Hadrian. On her Roman side, her maternal grandfather was that Balbillus, an astrologer, equestrian and Prefect of Egypt, who had advised his friend Nero to slaughter some distinguished subjects as a vicarious means of placating omens of death. Perhaps Julia Balbilla may also have dabbled in astrology as well as in poetry and her influence, or the precedents from her family, may have sinisterly affected Hadrian's pre-occupations with the occult and Antinous' own decisions on the fateful trip up the Nile.

Among the male companions whom Antinous certainly knew were the faithful Caesernii brothers, one or both of whom seem to have accompanied Hadrian on this as on earlier journeys. One of them, identified as Macedo, rides behind Antinous on the tondo of the boar hunt which may have taken place in Asia Minor in 129. The other brother, Statianus, was closer to Hadrian personally and, as he carried out confidential missions concerning the young, was probably on good terms with Antinous too. Together the brothers no doubt formed, both in organisation and in wise counsel, the stable core of the intimate group around the Emperor.

The others whom we know are all doomed young men. A few historians place Lucius Ceionius Commodus, the elegant and lively young aristocrat already winning Hadrian's favour, with him in Athens. There is no evidence for this, though Commodus may well have joined the sight-seeing party later in Egypt. Another lad, aged fifteen, and brought up in the imperial household, attracted attention. He was Hadrian's great-nephew, Pedanius Fuscus the younger, the closest male blood-relative of the Emperor, who already participated in his Councils, had been invested with the office of pontifex and was attended by a lictor of his own. People saw him as being groomed for the succession. Hadrian did nothing to keep him in the background. He was noticed alongside the Emperor in philosophic discussions in Athens and was pronounced at the time as 'very modest and of pious aspect'.[2] So prominent was he in the imperial circle that the citizens of Ephesos in 129 thought it expedient to put up a statue to the sixteen-year-old. Flattery of this kind, however, went to the lad's head. As he grew older he was found to be weak-willed, over-ambitious and tactless. It may be unlikely that Fuscus got on well with his almost exact contemporary Antinous whom he must have known and perhaps despised. There may have been rivalry and jealousy for Hadrian's attention between them. And the presence of this young, pushing and impeccably bred heir-presumptive can have done nothing to lessen Antinous' feelings of insecurity and complication of role.

However, there was one other youngster in the group whom Antinous also probably knew and may have got on with better as he had no pretensions to power, only to learn. A funerary inscription sums up his determined character and short life:

> I, Lucius Marius Vitalis, son to Lucius, lived seventeen years and fifty-five days. Being accomplished in book learning, I persuaded my parents to let me learn art. I departed from the city in the suite of Hadrian Augustus Caesar. While I was studying, the Fates became jealous of me. They snatched me away from art to this place.
>
> Maria Malchis, his most unhappy mother, to her most revered son.[3]

He probably died in Athens. The great journey had started with an omen.

In that September of 128 the squalid, narrow streets of ancient Athens were crowded for the annual celebration of the Great Mysteries of Eleusis to which people flocked from all over the world. These mysteries were the immediate destination of the imperial party also, most of whom, including Sabina and her sister, Hadrian and Antinous, were to participate. Hadrian had already been initiated in 125 to the lower grade of *mystes*, the first Emperor since Augustus to have been so. Now, however, fired by a yearning to go to the end of a spiritual experience, he was anxious to proceed to the higher grade of *epoptes* ('one who has seen') which few people and fewer notabilities ever attained.

What happened to him and Antinous and perhaps to the whole imperial entourage in these warm September days of preparation, renunciation and revelation, in Athens and at the sanctuary of Eleusis some fourteen miles away, was to set the tone of the succeeding journey. It was to precipitate in and around the party, and especially within Hadrian himself, a transcendent fervour, a sense of divine purpose and accomplishment, which were to last for some years. The faith and confidence generated by the mysteries, the imagery and deities of the profound myth of Demeter and Persephone, charged Hadrian's actions and imagination not only for the rest of this journey but, to a waning degree, for the rest of his life. Antinous too experienced something powerful and fundamental in and around the sanctuary of Eleusis that autumn, of that we can be sure, something which was in the end to shape and to explain the obscure death in the Nile two years later and all its dramatic consequences.

We shall never know exactly what happened to him. For what did take place within the vast, severe hall of initiation (the *Telesterion*), seating three thousand, at Eleusis, remains one of the best-kept secrets of all time. Though the mysteries were revealed there for nearly two thousand years, were open to anyone regardless of age, sex, rank, free or servile status, and may have been experienced over time by millions of folk, so awe-striking, so deeply moving was the experience, so severe the penalties for betrayal of confidence, that not one of them broke for posterity his vow of secrecy about the proceedings. Alcibiades was sentenced to death just for parodying when drunk some words of the chief priest. And Pausanias, usually so informative, refuses even to describe the outside of the sanctuary for fear of sacrilege.

Eleusis, situated on a rocky outcrop facing a bay of the sea, was the setting for one of the seminal myths of the ancient world. Persephone (or Kore), the daughter of Demeter the goddess of the earth, had been forcibly taken down to Hades, the kingdom of death, as the wife of its ruler, Pluto. Demeter, the archetypal mother, full of love and sorrow, forsook the pleasures of Olympus and of divinity, wandering the earth, grieving and seeking her daughter, bringing an eternal winter. Unrecognised as a goddess, she was succoured by the sympathetic king of Eleusis. In the end, to save the world from eternal sterility, the gods intervened and Persephone was restored to her mother from a cave at Eleusis. Henceforward she would spend two-thirds of the year upon the earth and one-third below in the shades with Pluto, a cycle symbolised in the seasons. Persephone had thus triumphed over death through the renunciation, suffering and devotion of her mother, offering the example of resurrection to mankind, just as she restored the eternal pattern of growth, decay and renewal to nature.

It is not difficult to understand why this myth and the mysteries by which its meaning was revealed gained such a following in the ancient world, never greater than in the second century AD. By then the old pagan gods had lost much of their hold over the spirit of men to those of the east. These oriental divinities were all-powerful, offering to their adherents in return for piety and obedience, explanations of the universe, redemption from evil, and eternal salvation of the soul. Through special rites and initiations, the individual believer established a personal relationship with the godhead which enabled him to transcend his worldly status and problems and to anticipate in life the serenity of paradise.

The mysteries of Eleusis were a bridge between the old and the new religions. Unlike the eastern faiths, this cult was not monotheistic nor totalitarian in its claims. It did not impose control over its initiates by strict codes of morals and practice supervised by a non-secular priesthood organised into an extensive Church. Like them, however, it did provide impressive ceremonies and initiations necessitating total participation of body and soul. It did offer, through a sustained union with the tribulations and triumphs of its goddesses, a transcendence over the pain, problems and status of this world, and sustenance in a common brotherhood of faith. Above all, by a spectacular act of revelation, it confirmed to its initiates salvation, triumph over death and eternal felicity. To many people, like Hadrian, who were repelled by the alien practices, fanatical claims and tight possessiveness of the newer creeds, but found the older ones too limited to meet their yearnings, the mysteries provided much of the powerful and deep inspiration of the more recent faiths but kept it in a proper balance and safely embodied within the most venerable and authentic culture of Greece.

There can be no doubt of the profound and beneficial impact of the mysteries on those, great and small, who went through them. As Cicero, who had been so initiated, put it: 'though Athens brought forth numerous divine things, yet she never created anything nobler than those sublime mysteries through which we have become more gentle and have advanced from a barbarous life to a civilized one, so that we not only live more joyfully but also die with a better hope'.[4]

It is generally agreed that Antinous took part in the mysteries of September 128, though there is no conclusive proof.[5] His initiation must have been one of the supreme moving experiences of his young life.

The first four days were spent in Athens itself, receiving instruction, making offerings, sharing in ceremonies and racing boisterously to the coast to plunge into the sea and be purified along with a small pig which was later sacrificed. Mounting tension and exhaustion, the thrill of venturing towards the great unknown, began to induce a state of ecstatic fervour. On the fifth day all the initiates, crowned with wreaths and carrying branches of myrtle, left on foot in procession for Eleusis, following the image of the god Iacchos and the sacred objects of the revelation sealed in their baskets. As the long procession wound over the pass of Aigaleos, the hills echoed with its cries and chanting. When night fell, torches were lit and on the bridge of the Cephisos (recently rebuilt by Hadrian) masked men hurled insults, symbolically to humble the grander initiates, amid laughter and a growing sense of togetherness. The outer courtyard of the sanctuary was entered in the flickering, unworldly light of torches and the whole night was spent in singing and dancing in honour of the goddess Demeter. The following three days were a whirl of movement, visual and oral dramas, symbolic drinkings and sacrifices, fastings, communal chantings and ritual purifications, interrupted by pauses for rest and quiet instruction: all promoting a state of almost trance-like expectancy, a deep inner receptivity to impressions. With the inmates once more crowned with wreaths and clad in the long himation, the mysteries reached their climax in a mimed passion play, taking place again at night in the eerie light of torches and accompanied by singing, music, the reverberations of gongs and the spoken invocations of the priests. The whole drama of Demeter and Persephone, of love, grief, death and resurrection was re-enacted on the sites of the original happenings by the initiates themselves who thereby inwardly identified themselves with the divinities and their vicissitudes.

The final moment of initiation was reached in the darkness of the great and crowded hall of the *Telesterion*. What exactly happened there, we do not know, except that amid a hubbub of anticipation, the chief priest suddenly appeared in a blinding light before the small shrine (*anaktoron*) in the middle and there exhibited to the dazzled, enthralled, awestruck and abruptly silent throng the sacred objects associated with Demeter. This was the supreme moment of revelation for which they had been so diversely prepared, when, in a state of abject terror and pulsing ecstasy as though they were approaching death, they apprehended the appalling immensity of what lay beyond the grave and experienced the surging, overpowering assurance that there, for them, awaited only eternal happiness. Plutarch described the sensation: 'just before the end, the terror is at its worst, there is shivering, trembling, cold sweat and fear. But the eyes perceive a wonderful light. Purer regions are reached and fields where there is singing and dancing; and sacred words and divine visions inspire a holy awe.'[6]

The sculpture of Antinous erected after his death in the outer courtyard of Eleusis captures this instant in his life, though officially it depicts him as the god Dionysos Zagreus, another divinity of suffering and resurrection associated with Eleusis (fig. 30).[7] Technically, it is not one of the greater of the works. The artist was not interested in capturing an elegant likeness but in evoking a mood and a moment.[8] He clearly envisaged the 16–17-year-old lad, draped in his himation, standing, perhaps close to Hadrian and Sabina, in the darkened and hushed *Telesterion* and confronted for the first time in his existence with the overwhelming, blinding revelation of what lay beyond the tomb. He clutches at the folds of his himation anxiously, frowning, staring wide-eyed into the infinite, his mouth pursed in awe, the whole expression a mix of apprehension, intent rapture, determination and lucid awareness of the tremendous significance of what was being revealed before him. It is the crucial dawning moment when Antinous first experienced both the negative horror of death and, simultaneously, the sublime realisation that, through his mystic identification with the goddesses of Eleusis, he had been allowed remission from its annihilating force and granted instead the prospect of life eternal.

From this moment at Eleusis he must have carried away a deep conviction of the inevitability of his own, like Persephone's, survival beyond the grave. It was this faith now kindled in Antinous which partly explains what happened later on the Nile.

Hadrian too underwent a similar profound experience. After all the *mystai* had trooped out of the *Telesterion*, he went through a second, more intimate and still more profound initiation as *epoptes*. Again we do not know what happened, though there was another act of revelation. The priestess was also deeply impressed and publicly congratulated herself on having initiated not the ancient heroes 'but the master of the vast earth and the sterile sea, the sovereign of innumerable mortals, Hadrian, who has poured out indescribable riches on all the cities and above all on the famous city of Kekrops' (Athens).[9]

The impact of the revelation upon the Emperor, who had recently been seriously ill and was to be preoccupied throughout this journey with the issue of death, was not kept private. So tremendous was the experience that he felt spiritually renewed. This rejuvenation was announced to the public on an official coin issued from Pergamon in 129, on which Hadrian declares himself 'reborn'.[10] For some time thereafter Hadrian, possessed by a fervid exaltation, conceived himself as being invested with a kind of immortality, until later his old dark imaginings and the whispers of Egyptian magicians revived his nagging doubts. Much of the extraordinary behaviour of the next year can be explained by the effect of the mysteries upon him: if he had been assured of immortality in heaven, it was no big step to assume divinity on earth as well. On the shrine of Eleusis he gratefully bestowed gifts and remissions of taxes and wherever he went he promoted these mysteries and those of the associated Dionysos above all others. He seized on those of Demeter as another civilising influence unifying the Greek world. Later the experience at Eleusis was undoubtedly to be linked in his mind with the death and apotheosis of Antinous, and, in composing names for the districts of Antinoopolis, he introduced allusions to the mysteries and their divinities no less than eleven times. He was to found separate mysteries to the risen Antinous and a special cult and festival to him at Eleusis itself. Even at the end of his life we find him fostering the mysteries of Demeter in the city of Rome.

It was in this aura of amity, transcendent conviction and spiritual fervour that Hadrian conceived his next daring gestures to focus the loyalties and imaginations of the Greeks.

The imperial visit to Athens from September 128 to March 129 brought to fulfilment Hadrian's aim of re-establishing that city as the spiritual centre of the Greek world. The weeks passed in an atmosphere of perpetual festival and spectacular events, ancient annual celebrations being supplemented by new ones created by Hadrian and by splendid ceremonies to inaugurate or to conclude his endless projects. The economic plight of the city had been ameliorated by his grants of cash and grain, relieving tension between rich and poor. Already the new city to the south-east, begun on his previous visit, with its arch and baths and grid layout, was substantially complete. Hadrian's generous example was eagerly emulated by other rich citizens. The sophist Lollianus gave a park and Herodes Atticus, jealous and not to be outdone, built a temple and, much later, a great white marble stadium and the impressive Odeion on the slopes of the Acropolis.

The winter was spent in a round of audiences, ceremonies, banquets and philosophic discussions in which the younger members of the suite like Antinous were expected to shine. Hadrian patiently listened to the first of the great series of apologies for Christianity. Never much interested in such an alien creed but always anxious for civil peace and tolerant by nature, the Emperor seems to have stopped the persecution of the sect in Athens. More congenially, expeditions were made to shrines and temples of Demeter and Dionysos in the outlying country and to indulge in some vigorous hunting.

One by one the great public buildings started years ago were reaching completion and new ones being designed. The Pompeion, a centre for oratory, was formally opened, the Pnyx restored, a temple to Hera dedicated. The huge and sumptuous new gymnasium for the ephebes with its hundred columns of Libyan marble was inaugurated with appropriate festivities. The aqueduct, its ample cistern in use by the city to this day, must have been under construction already, while the splendid library, rich with columns of Phrygian marble and alabaster panels, may have been begun on this visit.[11]

One building was to have a much greater impact on Hadrian's pretensions, his policies and the whole Greek world. The huge temple to the chief god of the Greek pantheon, Zeus Olympios, the construction of which Hadrian had resumed four years ago, was still not complete: its staggering dimensions of 135 by 354 feet, its 104 pentelic columns over 56 feet high, required a few more years for their realisation (fig. 22). However, the inner covered shrine or cella was now finished and with it probably the statue of Zeus Olympios, over 11 metres high, covered with gold and ivory. This Hadrian decided to dedicate at the most impressive ceremony of the whole visit, accompanied by festivities and games in which representatives of all the cities of the Greek world took part.

Just as in the previous year he had deliberately drawn the loyalties of all Roman citizens together round the temple and cult of Venus and Rome in the capital city of the west, so now Hadrian decided to gather the loyalties of the scattered and endlessly bickering city-states together at this principal shrine to their commonly acknowledged supreme deity, set in the splendidly re-furbished capital of the east. Hadrian was determined to weld together his pettily divisive Hellenic subjects in preservation of their civilisation. What better start than to make this magnificent temple the focal point of the religion, culture and history they all shared in a city whose past they all revered? Thus the Olympeion took on a major political significance as the centre of a carefully promoted panhellenic unity. Already excited, as we shall see, by the presence of this munificent Emperor in the east, eager to respond to his flattering desires and gripped by a new proud self-consciousness in being Greek in these days of economic and cultural resurgence, the Hellenic subjects responded with a deluge of enthusiasm which may have surprised Hadrian himself and swept him away on his next and still more ambitious venture.

When consecrating the cella in 129, Hadrian had also, we are mysteriously told,[12] dedicated an altar to himself outside. A few months later an official coin, struck to commemorate his arrival at Ephesos, explained the mystery and announced to the world that this living Emperor had himself become a god, or at least had become invested with the powers of a god. None other than Zeus (Jupiter) Olympios himself had now descended to earth in the person of Hadrian, the Emperor.[13]

There was nothing new in the Greek tendency, long ago demonstrated in the days of Alexander and after, to divinise their living rulers – an act which the more sober and suspicious Romans carefully delayed until their Emperors were harmlessly dead. Augustus, hailed as the saviour of the Greek world, had frequently been called and worshipped as god in his lifetime and over sixty-two altars to him have been discovered. By the second century, with the Greek peoples prospering and self-confident as never before, the Emperor was venerated as the source and guarantor of this revival. 'No one', declared Aristeides to Hadrian's successor,[14] 'is so proud that he can fail to be moved upon hearing even the mere mention of the ruler's name but, rising, he praises and worships him . . .' Zeus, he went on, had brought order to a chaotic universe and so, Zeus-like, had the Emperor of Rome to a divided world: 'confusion and strife ceased, and universal order entered as a brillant light over the private and the public affairs of men'.

No Emperor had done more for Hellas than Hadrian and none had been so ubiquitously visible (*epiphanios*), not a remote and incomprehensible abstraction of beneficence and power, but a living being endlessly moving among his peoples, always concerned to do them good, arousing their fervent adulation and scattering his benefactions with superhuman munificence. He had already been showered with exotic titles, of which 'saviour' and 'founder' were the most frequent. It is therefore easy to understand why, in the popular mind, on this second spectacular journey in the east, Hadrian began to take on the surrogate identity, even the reality, of Zeus, the most mighty of the gods, the most bountiful (*Eleutherios*), the Olympian (*Olympios*).

Already, well before 128, Hadrian had sporadically been called a god on the inscriptions of the east. But with strict Roman propriety he had ignored such spontaneous appellations. When he had been formally offered divine honours by the Achaean League in 126, like his predecessor Trajan he had firmly refused. That was in Rome. In the west he was always to remain content with the proud but purely secular title of Father of the Country. Now, however, in the east in the spring of 129 he not only gladly accepted the title of *Olympios* but, by issuing coins, and consecrating altars and temples to himself in Athens and Asia Minor, deliberately propagated the cult of himself as the incarnation, or at least the earthly representative of Zeus. Even the citizens of Athens, enthusiastic as they were to adore him (95 altars and 47 statue bases to him have been found in the city) balked a little at his presumption and could not bring themselves to call him Zeus, preferring to associate him more discreetly with the god in the title *Olympios*.[15] But the Greeks elsewhere and especially in Asia Minor had no such reservations about his assumption of divinity: the 174 altars and 107 statue bases found among them are frequently to him as Zeus or even as other gods. The largest temple in the Empire, the huge one at Cyzicus, was dedicated to Hadrian assimilated to Zeus-Jupiter.

Perhaps the delirious acclamations of the Greeks, the promises of immortality of Eleusis, the sense and the reality of Olympian power which he wielded had all worked on Hadrian's innate megalomania and turned his head. How deeply and in what form Hadrian believed himself possessed of divinity we cannot tell. Certainly in the divisions of Antinoopolis he automatically associated his own name five times with that and the titles of Zeus and solemnly called himself (as his subjects did) 'saviour of the world'.[16] The name of *Aelia*

Capitolina which he was shortly to bestow on Jerusalem also betrays complete identification between Hadrian and the title of Jupiter, the western equivalent of Zeus. On the official coins he is also sometimes shown with an aureole. Perhaps at this time Hadrian genuinely felt, viewing the universal peace and prosperity all around him and brought by him, that divine providence actually had chosen to work through him for human good.

But, as so often with him, the private and the public selves, the impulsive and the calculated actions, were joined in this assumption of divinity. Hadrian sensed that the Greeks, with their tendencies to anthropomorphism, needed more than a gargantuan temple and an inanimate chryselephantine statue to bind them together and generate feelings of brotherhood – they needed an exceptional being and he alone was that being. By assuming divine status he could kindle in his subjects an enthusiastic awareness of religious community, of common devotion to this god manifest among them: something deeper, more emotionally stirring, more spiritually cohesive than ever the cold cult of Venus and Rome could be. The exhilarated response he elicited shows how shrewdly he knew his subjects. Moreover, Zeus of the Greeks was the equivalent of Jupiter of the Romans and the special protector of the Emperor himself. Subtly, then, the worship of Hadrian-Zeus was also of Jupiter and of the Roman Emperor and thus a new and supreme unity in this trinity of divinities brought the whole Empire, east and west, together at its religious apex.

From 128, it has been said, Hadrian 'belonged wholly to the east', putting all his creative energies into the revival and expansion of Hellenism.[17] There was now a gap growing between the Emperor's personality, actions and preoccupations in the east and his more conformist and limited concerns in the west, a divorce between him and Roman society which had always been latent, would become manifest in the matters of Antinous and Commodus and would later turn to bitter hostility.

Antinous must have been bemused suddenly to find himself the favourite of Zeus and the parallel with Ganymede – which must have been on malicious tongues – was uncomfortable. But a precedent had been established. If Hadrian, with the willing compliance of the Greeks, had been able to elevate himself to divinity as a symbol of unity, so surely, in similar propitious circumstances and with similar support, could he elevate someone else.

In March 129, having devoutly attended the Lesser Mysteries of Eleusis, Hadrian and his suite set sail for Asia Minor.

This was the third of his four visits to the most prosperous, populated and culturally thriving part of the Greek world, indeed of the whole Empire. Grateful for all that he had done, thrilled by his attentive presence, excited by the schemes of panhellenic unity and enthusiastic at his divine pretensions, the cities of Asia Minor responded to the Emperor, his companions and his ideas with a delirious fervour which was to reach its climax of exultation on his fourth visit, shortly after the death and apotheosis of Antinous. Everywhere, in inscriptions, dedications, statues, temples and festivals he was proclaimed Zeus *Olympios* and often assimilated to the other major gods of Olympus into the bargain. Ninety-one altars to him as a god have so far been found in Asia Minor, at least seventy-six cities there celebrated his personal cult and twenty-five of them took his name. Everywhere coins were issued in his and sometimes in Sabina's honour. The presence of this supreme and generous god made everyone more aware of their common blood and heritage. This feeling was expressed on the enthusiastic coins of Pannonia and Bithynia and on the rapturous inscriptions of Magnesia immediately after his arrival.

They travelled in Asia Minor, quickly as always and with the minimum of burden to the locals, for three months. After starting yet more works in Ephesos, they visited other major cities in Ionia. Miletus, which received huge baths and a palaestra, thanked Hadrian as *Olympios*.[18] At Tralles, the Emperor donated 60,000 *modii* of wheat from Egypt to the city. Laodiceia started minting coins in the names of both Hadrian and Sabina. They then moved southwards to the coast of Anatolia. At Patara Sabina was honoured as Hera and Hadrian as Zeus and at Phaselis, exemplifying the unifying impact of this *Olympios*, all the surrounding cities sent statues of him to his temple there.

They then turned on an excursion northwards up into the mountain areas of Phrygia, reaching almost the centre of the peninsula at Synnada. Perhaps Hadrian wanted to hunt: and it is possible that the famous boar hunt with Antinous, commemorated on the tondo, took place in this region. He also took care to visit the tomb of Aicibiades at Melissa where he set up a statue and an annual sacrifice in honour of the fascinating, flawed son of Athens and one of the most famous *eromenoi* of all time.

Returning to the coast in the mounting summer heat the party took ship and sailed to Cilicia and and to the group of cities at the juncture between the loyal Hellenic world of Asia Minor and the more racially and culturally mixed one of the Levant. Here they received a rapturous welcome. Tarsos added Adriana to its name, provided a splendid festival and seems to have taken very special note of Antinous. At Aigeae and Mopsuestia it was Sabina who caught the local imagination, and on the coins of the latter she was transformed into the goddess Artemis. The whole tour must have been deeply gratifying to Hadrian. His policies were evidently working, not only materially but in men's spirits. He had encountered not problems but fulfilment everywhere.

With the arrival of the entourage at Antioch in June 129, which city was to be their base for nearly a year, the atmosphere of the voyage evidently began to turn a little sour. In Syria, Arabia, Palestine and the other eastern regions of the empire now to be visited, the reception was also to be warm. But Hadrian grew to realise that these polyglot regions seething with eastern and fanatical cults like Judaism, Christianity and the worship of Baal, could never be assimilated comfortably, like Asia Minor, into his scheme of a unified Hellenic culture. His coldness to the eastern gods, whose exclusive and separatist claims over their adherents threatened his cherished unity, was to harden into opposition and sometimes to flare into destructive anger.

The visit to the Near East started with an ambiguous portent.[19] Twenty miles south of Antioch rose the bald Mount Casius, 5,300 feet sheer from sea-level. At its peak was a shrine to Zeus. Hadrian, anxious to visit this as well as romantically to see the dawn, made the difficult ascent, perhaps with Antinous and his male retainers, at night. But suddenly a storm arose and in the ceremony of sacrifice at the summit a burst of lightning killed both the sacrificial animal and the acolyte. The gruesome incident was officially publicised as the miraculous recognition by Zeus of his earthly representative. But to some, and perhaps to Hadrian himself, it may have been more perplexing: another omen of death and disaster? Certainly thereafter, perhaps because of exhaustion, recurring symptoms of his former illness or a paranoiac sense of the futility of his mission in hostile parts of this region, Hadrian's perturbation about death seems to have crept back into his mind and, at times, his actions became inordinately suspicious, savage or undiplomatic, betraying otherwise inexplicable lapses in his normal judgement and temperament.

Though he lavished splendid benefactions on Antioch and attended the festival of the nymphs amid the refreshing springs and shady groves of Daphne, the irreverence, febrile gaiety and perhaps malicious gossip of the city irritated him. Like Alexandria and unlike his beloved Athens, there was a turbulent ferment of cultures and an undercurrent hostile to Rome here which was dangerous to his policies.[20] He is said to have grown really to hate the people there and decided to downgrade the city from its pre-eminent metropolitan status. In this connection, it is notable that in the series of coins he later issued to commemorate his visits to the provinces, Syria is significantly left out as though he wanted to erase the memory of his recent stay there.[21] Antioch responded likewise and did nothing to promote the cult of Antinous.

Nevertheless the city with its rebuilt palaces was a pleasant and convenient base for the expeditions which were his main purpose in coming. Sometime in the late summer of 129 he set out north-eastwards for Cappadocia and Armenia and the frontier with Parthia. After reviewing the legions at Melitene, he reached Samosata where, with a great display of pomp and pageantry, he entertained and overawed the client kings and princes of the border lands in a fabulous durbar. Osroes, the Parthian Emperor, did not attend, but Hadrian, as a token to seal the peace which had been established six years before, restored to him his daughter captured by Trajan. Thus in a carefully orchestrated demonstration of military power, riches and diplomacy, Hadrian ensured that peace on the eastern frontier would be maintained.

But while exhibiting such poise and tact, he was busily punishing provincial officials and governors for maladministration and corruption with a brutal severity which struck contemporaries as suspicious or bizarre, as if he deliberately wished to make examples of them by trumping up charges.[22] Something strange seems to have been happening to Hadrian's personality: a brittleness of temperament, a tendency to violent extremes, spasms of withering pessimism seemed to grip him suddenly, transforming the usually rational and benign Emperor into someone altogether less predictable and benevolent.

The winter of 129–30 was spent partly at Antioch and perhaps also south at Gerasa where the inabitants erected a great triumphal arch to him. Better, Hadrian may have felt, to sample the genuine devotion of a minor town than the blistering indifference of the metropolis of Syria. Late in 129 or in the spring of 130, Hadrian, always restless, eager for new experiences and anxious to strengthen fragile bonds with Rome, decided to visit the most easterly and one of the most recently acquired provinces of the Empire, the lucrative land of Arabia. In a brisk journey across the romantic caravan routes of the desert, accompanied probably only by the men in his suite, he arrived at the great trading emporium between the orient and the west, Palmyra. There he was ecstatically greeted as 'Hadrian, the god', 'Lord of the world' and sumptuously entertained by local notabilities in a specially erected camp of tents outside the town.[23] The exotic welcomes continued at Damascus and the remote desert outpost of Petra which added his name to its own to honour him. He must have turned back westwards, crossing the Jordan, well pleased with the sense of a province secure for Rome and loyal to himself.

Already in November and December of 129 officials in Egypt had been forewarned that the Emperor was intending to visit that land and had been making urgent preparations. It may have been on the trip southwards in the summer of 130 or earlier that he made his fateful visit or visits to Jerusalem.

Earlier in his reign Hadrian had shown no particular enmity towards the Jews. However, he cannot have forgotten that it was their coordinated, far-flung and ferocious revolts in 116–17, accompanied by appalling atrocities against the Greeks, which had sabotaged Trajan's Parthian campaign and presented himself with his first grave imperial problems. Of all the alien elements in the Greek east, the Jews were the most recalcitrant, self-consciously, arrogantly refusing any assimilation into Hellenic culture. In Hadrian's eyes they were inveterate oriental barbarians whose fanatical religious and racial separatism posed a perpetual threat to the unity and peace of the empire. Nevertheless, as he travelled down through Judea in 130 he seems to have got on well enough with individuals. We hear him bantering, with typical sarcasm, at the presumption of a centenarian peasant still, hopefully, planting a fig tree. (When, four years later, that same peasant presented Hadrian with a basket of figs from that same tree, the Emperor filled the basket with gold pieces.)[24] We meet him earnestly discussing with a Rabbi the creation of the world and – it is significant of his preoccupations to note – the resurrection of the dead. His actions with regard to the Jewish people as a whole that summer are therefore all the more extraordinary: they can only be explained by the changes within himself.

The chronology of events is confused,[25] but three things certainly happened in 130–31. First, Hadrian banned circumcision, a ritual act practised immemorially by Arabs and Egyptians as well as Jews. The Egyptians were later given some exemptions but not the Jews who were incensed at this sudden and crude violation of their religion and way of life. It seems as though, in a sudden revulsion of horror against such a practice, symbolic of what he conceived as the primitive barbarism of the east, he issued his comprehensive interdict. In earlier, more lucid and tactful days, it is doubtful if he would have done anything so insensitive, so uncompromising, so casually and dangerously provocative.

Next, inspecting the city of Jerusalem still devastated after the catastrophic wars of Titus but still holy to the Jews, he decided to refound it as a Roman colony with a specially imported Greek population. The age-old capital of Jewish religion and culture was to be eliminated and in its place a proud new metropolis created as a bastion of Greco-Roman civilisation dominating and gradually converting this hostile land for Hellenism. Again the sweeping radicalism of the plan – extinguishing thousands of years of history – betrays an astounding insensitivity to the consequences for one usually so attuned to the subtlest nuances of tradition, diplomacy and prudence. The very name of the city reveals Hadrian's ugly megalomania, his divine arrogance of this moment: *Aelia Capitolina*. Here the family name of Hadrian was linked to the Roman title of Jupiter-Zeus. The city of almighty Jehovah was to become that of the still more powerful god, Hadrian.

The third act can only have been taken by one so careless of the feelings of his subjects or so hostile to their faith as to have been almost demented. At this point the dating becomes even more ambiguous. There are grounds for believing that it took place not now in 130 but perhaps a year later on Hadrian's return northwards, his judgement and temper still further eroded by his grief for Antinous, his passion for Greek civilisation, summed up in the now divine ephebe, correspondingly all the more intolerantly fervent.[26] Hadrian, now or then, decided that the sacred Temple of the Jews, their holy of holies, should become the site for a temple to Jupiter-Zeus. It is difficult to see in this deliberate profanation the Hadrian who had, for example, so tolerantly responded to the Christians in Athens and so patiently negotiated with the barbarian Osroes. Perhaps implacable Judaism had become to him such an obsessive symbol of the barbarian threat to his policies that it had to be eradicated altogether and be supplanted by the religion of Greco-Roman unity personified in the trinity of himself, Zeus and Jupiter.

Thus the visit to the east, always somewhat uneasy and fraught, ended with the coarsely insensitive and fatally short-sighted concoction of a disaster in which the sweet civilising mission of Hellenism would have to be imposed only by devastation and hideous bloodshed. For the time being, however, the Jews did not choose to respond overtly to this provocation, biding their time.

Probably proud of his constructions and seemingly oblivious of the consequences, Hadrian now made his way south in the heat of July to the mysterious land of Egypt, the only crucial province of his Empire he had not so far visited.

Perhaps the ladies travelled across to Alexandria by boat. The men, however, despite the gruelling heat, seem to have travelled on horseback down the ancient military road from Gaza, the one used in the distant past by the great conquering or avenging Pharaohs of Egypt: Sethos I, Thutmosis III and Rameses II. No doubt when pausing at the wells or the palm groves or on the banks of Lake Serbonis, which bordered the road, before crossing the final inhospitable tract of waterless desert, Antinous and Hadrian pondered on what awaited them in the strange land where such kings had also been gods.

At Pelusium at the marshy eastern tip of the Delta, Hadrian, before embarking on the imperial barge by canal for Alexandria, stopped to sacrifice and rebuild the ruined tomb of Pompey the Great who had been betrayed and slaughtered there. 'Strange lack of tomb', he mused, 'for someone over-whelmed with shrines everywhere else.'[27]

Thus on the theme of death and immortality, which had pervaded this whole journey, the visit to Egypt also began.

'CLOUDS HIDING THE SUN'

EGYPT, AUGUST–OCTOBER 130

Alexandria, its broad avenues and colour-washed palaces set between a lake and the sea and fanned by cool breezes from the north, must have been refreshing to the travel-worn imperial party when it arrived early in the August of 130.[1] Perhaps Hadrian, like earlier important visitors, was welcomed on disembarking at the quayside of the royal harbour by priestesses gathered in the shade of an enormous awning slung from the pediment of the temple of Isis (fig. 31).[2] Perhaps too, as the coins depicting the toga-clad Emperor in a chariot-and-four greeted by the city seem to suggest, he made a formal entry into this, the second largest and the richest of all the cities of his Empire. Immediately after, we know for sure, Hadrian and Sabina were caught up in a busy whirl of ceremonies. The response of the people, who had never seen him before, was typically ebullient. The personification of Alexandria is shown on the coins presenting him with ears of corn, even bestowing an affectionate kiss. On such an ostensibly cordial note began the visit to Egypt.

In this land Hadrian had no need to borrow regality or divinity: he was, of right, both Pharaoh and god. Since its conquest by Augustus in 31 BC, Egypt had been carefully kept outside the ordinary provincial organisation of the Empire. The abundant crops produced by the miraculous floodwater and silt of the Nile made this country the granary of hungry Rome: he who held it controlled the destinies of the Empire. To save it from ever falling into hostile hands, Augustus had wisely reserved Egypt as a personal possession of the Emperor, who ruled as a direct successor of the Pharaohs, and had excluded everyone of senatorial rank from even visiting it without his special permission. Its administration was entrusted to a viceroy or Prefect of merely equestrian rank. He controlled a tightly-centralised bureaucracy, mainly of Greeks, and two Roman legions to keep the turbulent population in order. Ever since Alexander's conquest of 332–331 BC, and especially since Ptolemy I had seized it on his death, the country had been settled thickly by Greeks and infused with Hellenistic culture. Now, not only in the three Hellenistic colonies of Alexandria, Naucratis and Ptolemaïs, but in all the other cities, it was a Greek-speaking elite, graduating from the ephebate and the gymnasium, which held all the local offices. Other races were excluded from power. And the Egyptian peasantry were kept by taxes and requisitions at perpetual breaking-point, always tilling the rich soil without profit, their abundant produce going to feed greedy Rome, or those other famished cities like Athens, Tralles or Ephesos to which Hadrian airily and generously consigned donations of corn from the sweating fellahin of the valley of the Nile.

Greek was the language of government and educated men. The Museion of Alexandria, with its great library, was the foremost university of the world. The Ptolemies had promoted a syncretic god, Serapis, whose cult had long ago spread to Rome and elsewhere. Other major deities, Isis and Osiris, were also worshipped abroad, identified with Demeter and Dionysos of the Greeks.

In Egypt itself, however, the much older gods, Ra, Horus, Harachte, Set, Thoth and countless others still held sway where, it was reputed, religion and civilisation itself had been born. The huge temples along the Nile still throbbed with life: resounding with the chants of priests, the clang of gongs, the cries of sacrificial animals. 'They are religious to excess', exclaimed Herodotus nearly six hundred years before, '– beyond any other nation in the world.'[3] They still were. Priests, magicians and astrologers continued to perform their immemorial rites. Gods of all kinds and of all animal shapes proliferated: the beneficial Nile itself was a deity. Ancient beliefs, super-stitions, and primitive lores controlled the minds and actions of men perpetually confronted with the inexplicable miracle of life, in the shape of the mysterious river and its thin green fertile plain, winding through the arid desert and stony hills of death. Religion excited a fervour, elsewhere generally reserved for politics, the circus or rhetoric. Riots between the patrons of hostile and jealous cults were common. Even neighbouring towns devoted to rival gods could erupt into pitched battles so frenzied and bloody that they incited a hysterical mass cannibalism.

Little wonder then that Egypt was to leave a profound impression on Hadrian's religious susceptibilities and imagination – almost as great as that of Greece itself. This was his first visit and he had long wished to make it. He came partly to recuperate from that serious illness which may never have quite left him or threatened to recur:[4] the climate and the magic powers of the priests were well known in effecting cures or in averting attacks. He came, as usual, to inspect, restore and reform a province so vital to his Empire, so prone to tension and unrest. He came evidently also to strengthen in this land the claims of Hellenism: and indeed the gods of Greece were now to flourish on its coins as never before, though, in return, the gods of the Nile, Serapis, Isis and Osiris, were to seduce his loyalty. He was intrigued to explore those ancient beliefs, sciences and occult arts which had from long ago drawn Greek scholars and philosophers to this cradle of religion, knowledge and calculation. And, like any vulgar tourist of his generation and of countless since, he came to gaze in awe at the strange, vast and daunting monuments of a civilisation far more ancient than his own, only dimly comprehended and yet, in his day, tenuously surviving.

The effusive kiss of welcome from Alexandria soon savoured of a sting. Because of its endemic turbulence, the largest and most prosperous Greek city in the world had been deprived of its self-government by Augustus, although the Romans fostered local autonomy everywhere else. The numerous Greeks, rich from the trade in corn and with India, bitterly resented this humiliating lack of a civic independence possessed by every other polis in the Greek world and turned their enmity against the authorities of Rome. They used their endless dissensions with the Jews and Egyptians in their midst as a means of attacking the Emperor. Already at the start of his reign, Hadrian had reprimanded the Alexandrians for singing vicious songs and spreading offensive rumours against himself.

Now in 130 his genuine efforts to conciliate the city provoked a similar response because he proffered everything except the autonomy they craved. He embellished the city with temples. He went to the glass and alabaster sarcophagus where lay the mummy of its founder, Alexander the Great, and paid his profound respects to this other propagator of Greek culture and this earlier god acclaimed by Zeus as his son. He began to promote the Alexandrian god Serapis as another of the great centripetal divinities of the Empire, forming a trinity with Zeus and Jupiter.

But that insensitive assertiveness and tactlessness which had sometimes marred his actions in the Levant now reappeared here. In the Serapeum of Alexandria, Hadrian immediately established a chapel to himself as god. He lavished benefactions on the Museion, but promptly appointed to lucrative sinecures there absentee cronies of his own, sophists like Polemo of Smyrna and Dionysos of Miletus, and the poet Mesomedes of Crete, alien appointments which did not endear him to the jealous locals. He spent hours propounding difficult questions to the learned professors, only to affront them by contemptuously providing all the answers himself.

The Alexandrians responded to this mixture of benevolence and ego-centricity in their usual way: public honours, statues and flattery in front of the Emperor's face, scathing ridicule and ribald satire behind (but not too far behind) his back. The jibes were not only directed at his divine and intellectual pretensions but at his sexual proclivities. Hadrian soon became aware of these slanders and, smarting at the Alexandrians' ingratitude, declared them 'most seditious, most deceitful and most given to injury'.[5] Some of this malicious gossip concerned his relationship with Antinous who evidently created an impression in the city. It may also have dwelt luridly on that other male beauty, Lucius Ceionius Commodus, if he had indeed arrived to join the imperial party now.

117

Hurt and resentful, Hadrian and his immediate circle may in late August have removed themselves from the intense and captious city along the canal to the elegant and relaxed pleasure resort of Canopus with its villas, its vine-threaded arches of wicker straddling the water to shade its revellers, and its splendid Serapeum (fig. 32). It was delicious Canopus and not mocking Alexandria which Hadrian was to commemorate so fondly and so magnificently back at the villa at Tibur. Though he was to return to the city for several months early in 131, he evidently felt little relish for the place. Like Antioch, it had resisted, indeed reviled, his blandishments and remained obstinately, perhaps dangerously, outside his scheme of a unified classical culture. As long as Hadrian and his heirs sat on the throne, the city would have to remain deprived of its Council.

Already as August wore on, and the folk of the Delta anxiously peered at the muddy waters and took their measures to ascertain if the Nile's flood was promising or ominous, Hadrian, always restless, must have been longing to get away. Alexandrian scorn had rapidly cut this Pharaoh-Zeus down to puny human size. The time had come for Hadrian publicly to reassert his divine stature and heroic mission.

For a long time the whole land of Libya, to the west of Alexandria, had been ravaged by a lion so ferocious that it had made many places uninhabitable. The beast was enormous, more than two metres long, and of that breed, distinguished by a powerful head, short mane and a tawny-black colour, which Oppian called the kings of all king lions.[6] Here then was a challenge, urgently practical and richly symbolic, which Hadrian could not resist. Taking only his faithful band of hardened companions, he set out from sophisticated Alexandria with relief for the purifying rigours of the Libyan desert, probably in the first days of September.[7]

In the party was Antinous. But this Antinous of 130 was probably of a significantly different appearance from the lad (as shown on the tondo in Rome) who had hunted the wild boar with Hadrian in the highlands of Asia Minor a year before. If the figure appearing at the right hand of Hadrian on the other tondo which commemorates this famous lion hunt *is* Antinous, and we and others have argued earlier that it must be, the elegant youth of the previous year had by now matured into a sturdy and tough young man (fig. 14). This is what we might expect from the prominent role he was to be assigned in this, the most dangerous chase of all.

Antinous must now have been between eighteen and twenty years of age. The onset of bodily hair after puberty, so much deplored in antiquity as the ruin of adolescent beauty ('clouds hiding the sun'),[8] seems to have occurred later in those days than in our own.[9] Now, however, on this sculpture depicting Antinous in September 130, there are signs of down on his cheeks and of sideboards creeping down his face, both indicating a beard perhaps

118

being deliberately cultivated in imitation of Hadrian's own. Above all, the former luxuriant curls have been shorn off in favour of a shorter, more military, hair-style:[10] such a cropping was undertaken at a ceremony deliberately and symbolically marking the advent of manhood.

It would be untrue to say that Antinous was no longer beautiful. He was no longer the smooth ephebe but a hairy, lean and virile young adult. The arrival in Egypt had perhaps coincided with this ultimate (and ceremonial) transformation of his appearance which in itself must have posed anxious problems for his future role and status with regard to his imperial lover. Perhaps Hadrian did not much like the inexorable change wrought by time and happily so long delayed, since it was to be an earlier image of Antinous which he preferred to disseminate later in stone and bronze, after the lad's death. For the time being, however, the living Antinous' evident maturity assured him pride of place in the perilous and manly exploit ahead.

Where they finally caught up with the Marousian lion we do not know. Perhaps they had used footmen to flush out the beast at night with the glare of flaming torches and the din of clanging shields. Perhaps they stumbled upon it by accident in some lair in a palm grove or amid scrub bush. In any case when, in the end, we find them confronting the lion from their specially trained horses, it is from a frontal position, the most dangerous one of all, employed only by the most courageous or the most foolhardy of hunters. For what followed we have the evidence of fragments from the exaggerated and somewhat turgid epic of Pancrates, the poet later commissioned by Hadrian (who doubtless supplied some obviously authentic details) to celebrate the event.[11]

We meet with them after a fierce chase in which Antinous' steed proved, says the hyperbolic Pancrates, swifter even than the famous one of King Adrastus.[12] Hadrian had himself shown later on a medallion also galloping in hot pursuit of the fleeing lion (fig. 41a). Trapped, or perhaps just defiant, the lion suddenly stopped, turned and faced its pursuers, who sharply reined in their horses and prepared, perhaps alone, being way ahead of their companions, for it to spring. '. . . Antinous', continues Pancrates, 'sat in wait for the man-slaying lion, holding in his left hand the bridle-rein, and in his right a spear tipped with adamant. Hadrian was the first to hurl his brass-fitted spear; he wounded the beast but did not kill it, for he intended to miss the mark, wishing to test to the full the sureness of aim of the beautiful Antinous, the son of the Argus-slayer' (Hermes). Thus even in the height of danger Hadrian could coolly, almost callously, try out his younger companion's nerve and skill. But Antinous had no time to aim. 'Stricken,' goes on Pancrates, warming to his theme, 'the beast was yet more aroused and in its wrath tore up the rough ground with its paws and the dust arising dimmed the light of the sun; raging . . . it rushed upon them both, its tail scourging its haunches and flanks . . .' Eyes flashing, foaming at the mouth, gnashing its teeth, hair bristling, the lion

119

'came against the glorious god [Hadrian] and Antinous like Typhoeus of old against Zeus the killer of giants . . .'

At this crucial instant the papyrus (used as a bottle stopper) disintegrates into fragments. We can, however, tell that it was Antinous who bore the brunt of the charge, that Hadrian had to intervene to save him and to give the beast the *coup de grâce* 'with his own hand'.[13] A splendid medallion was later issued to record this very moment (fig. 41b). Below, the lion crouches ready to spring; above, the intrepid Hadrian, his horse rearing up, is poised, spear ready for the final lethal thrust downwards.

By that stroke, Hadrian not only saved his beloved's life, something which must have overwhelmed Antinous with gratitude, but also rid the people of Libya of a lurking menace. Hadrian had always tried to follow his admired Herakles: now he had in fact emulated his hero's conquest of the Nemean lion. His hunts had always been partly designed to stress his affinity with the gods and his civilising mission against encroaching barbarism. Now the new god Hadrian had in fact restored untroubled peace to a land threatened with arbitrary savagery. Zeus incarnate, the god of gods, had triumphed over the king of kings of the animal world.

Full of this manifold symbolism of his achievement, Hadrian swiftly publicised it throughout the world. Official historians solemnly recorded the incident. Pancrates elaborated it into a Homeric epic. Three bronze medallions illustrated and proclaimed 'the courage of the Emperor' (fig. 41).[14] On the appropriate tondo of the Arch of Constantine (fig. 13), one strikingly different in composition from all the rest, Hadrian and Antinous proudly stand in conquest on the mane of the recumbent beast while the Emperor eloquently dilates to his companions on the significance of the event. But by the time that Hadrian, on the next relief, dedicates the spoil in the temple of Herakles, Antinous is no longer shown:[15] just as Hadrian had saved him from dire peril, so by now, perhaps, Antinous had reciprocated at the cost of his own life. The popular memorial of his part in the hunt was to be a wreath of rose-coloured lotuses, the colour of the lion's blood, called the *Antinoeios*.[16]

The lion hunt marked in several senses the climax and the turning point in the relationship between Hadrian and Antinous. It knit them together more closely in a bond of mutual obligation sealed by shared peril and the lion's blood. At the same time it demonstrated the passing of the adolescent beauty which had held Hadrian in thrall. Antinous was outgrowing the established role of *eromenos*. Publicly he was now portrayed as the intimate and equal comrade of the Emperor, yet he knew himself to be ever more his dependent, lacking all autonomy. The texture of their relationship was shifting subtly but quickly to an unpredictable new pattern. For Hadrian too the incident signified a symbolic climax in his reign and the actual peak of his physical prowess: never again would his civilising mission, his heroic mettle, be so succinctly and convincingly exhibited to the world. At this moment he truly seemed possessed of divine mastery and immunity from danger and decline. But how long would that moment last?

The party which assembled at the end of September or the beginning of October to be carried in a flotilla of imperial barges on the cruise up the Nile was much larger than the more intimate group which had toured the Near East.

Hadrian himself was surrounded by officials, the Prefect, army and naval commanders, the head (epistrategos) of each of the three divisions of the country and others. Round him also gathered a literary and scholarly band. The epistrategos of the Thebaid, Gallus Marianus, wrote Homeric epigrams more fluent than those of Balbilla herself. Perhaps the ubiquitous Polemo was present and certainly a poet called Arius from the Museion. Whether the Caesernii and Pedanius Fuscus were still in the party is not known: probably they were.

It has sometimes been claimed that another person, whose company may not have been wholly congenial to Antinous, joined the cruise at this point: Lucius Ceionius Commodus, the good-looking, pleasure-loving aristocrat then aged 29, who was soon to be praetor as the specially recommended candidate of the Emperor and was later to emerge as 'the western favourite' (fig. 36).[17] The evidence for his presence is indirect and flimsy,[18] but there are no insuperable objections to his being there, for impending official and paternal obligations back in Rome patently meant nothing to this exuberant young man avid for enjoyment.[19] His antics must have kept the worried Emperor amused. But if Commodus was there and was eagerly gossiped about by the malevolent Alexandrians as another beloved of Hadrian, then the presence of such a potential rival must have been ominous, even threatening, to Antinous. Perhaps the star of Commodus, whose lineage and rank made him capable of the imperial succession, was sensed to be in the ascendant; that of the socially inferior and ageing 'eastern favourite' flickering towards its decline.

Unlike Hadrian's thoughtful efforts on his previous journeys to spare the locals the burden of his maintenance, here in Egypt it was taken for granted that the enlarged entourage would be fed by the population. Local unpaid functionaries (liturgists) were held responsible for requisitioning provisions from the peasantry and storing them at various collection points. Already, back in November 129, when Hadrian was in the Levant, anxious officials in Thebes had been laying in barley in anticipation of a visit, and yet more supplies were hastily ordered in September and October 130 when the tour to the Upper Nile was confirmed.[20] In two villages on the Middle Nile, near Oxyrhynchus, the local scribe tells us[21] what was already being stored there as early as December 129 in preparation (rather, in apprehension) of the hungry imperial horde: 200 artabae of barley; 3,000 bundles of hay (for pack animals); 372 sucking pigs; 55 artabae of dates; 200 Egyptian sheep; 3 metretae of oil; 7

baskets of chaff; 3 of unripe olives; indecipherable numbers of full-grown pigs; and large quantities of other foodstuffs. We know from a slightly later list of requisitions some of the other things which were compulsorily gathered for the cooks and provisioners of such official visitors:[22] bread, veal and pork; wine, oil and vinegar; geese, other fowl, game and fish; smoked meats and cheeses; vegetables; olives and lentils; wood, lamps and torches; replacement pack animals and their fodder. With whatever relish Hadrian and his party may have looked forward to their trip, it may be doubted if the anxious liturgists and the toiling peasantry of the Nile valley, already over-burdened with taxes and obligations to the brink of breakdown, much welcomed the advent of the Pharaoh-god and his ravenous court among them.

The visitors themselves and especially Hadrian may not have been very happy from the start. The much anticipated voyage up the Nile began and ended in gloom and was punctuated by disaster.

In Egypt there was an old belief that for the Pharaoh to sail on the Nile in full flood was impious and invited retribution. Did Hadrian, who followed in the footsteps of Alexander the Great, know what befell that monarch when he defied this prohibition?

> When the king was sailing down the river, Hector, a son of Parmenion, in the fine flower of his youth and one of Alexander's greatest favourites, desiring to overtake him, embarked upon a small craft, which was overloaded . . . [and] sank. Hector struggled for a long time with the river, and although his drenched clothing and sandals . . . interfered with his swimming, made his way half-dead to the bank; but he was exhausted and struggling to breathe . . . he died. The king was filled with great grief for the loss of his friend, and when his body was recovered, buried it in a magnificent funeral.[23]

Though Hadrian prudently sought to avoid retribution by sailing only when the flood was receding he was to fare no more happily; nor was that later successor of his in the purple, the Emperor Septimius Severus, when he too ventured upon the treacherous waters.[24]

The problem which turned Hadrian's voyage miserable from the beginning was that in the autumn of 130 there was not much of a flood of the Nile to sail on. Already the inundation of the autumn of 129 had fallen far short of the fourteen to sixteen cubits which produced a good crop of grain and scarcity had been the result. The usual festive Nile coins had not been produced. Now, a year later, when the flood waters had reached their height in the September of 130 they were once more seriously deficient. Again in despondency no Nile coins were issued.[25] The imperial visitors should have sailed past plains covered with water, the towns standing on their hillocks like the islands of the Aegean, but this autumn there was more land visible than water.

Everywhere there was anxiety and foreboding. The local people whose livelihood was a second time in jeopardy had only prayers to the gods to rely on.

'Demetrios and Eirene', runs one letter from this time, 'to their dearest Syros, very many greetings. We know that you are distressed at the deficiency of water. This has happened not only to us but to many and we know that nothing has occurred through any fault of yours . . . we hope with god's help the fields will be sown . . .'[26] Two inadequate floods were grim enough, but if there were to be a third in the autumn of 131 then stark famine would grip Egypt and ignite hunger riots if not more problems in Rome and all the cities dependent on that country's corn.

To the ordinary people of Egypt the Pharaoh embodied the fertility of the earth and had powers over the rising of the Nile. 'If thou sayest to the waters', it was said to Rameses ii, for example,[27] ' "Come upon the mountains", the flood comes forth quickly after thy word.' But the word of the Pharaoh Hadrian effected nothing. In past crises the populace had turned on the Prefect in anger. Now, however, in 130, the Pharaoh himself was among them in the valley. The people held him responsible for the river's failure and their desperate plight. Some malediction rested on him, it was thought, and obstructed his powers for good.

The trip on the Nile, now prematurely and rapidly oozing back from the plain to its winter bed, was thus fraught with anxiety, a sense of impending tragedy for Egypt and of dangerous repercussions in other cities of the Empire. Hadrian, who had so easily played the role of the divine benefactor, the 'saviour' and 'redeemer' everywhere else on his tour, found himself practically impotent on a vital matter in which, ironically, his subjects believed him possessed of supernatural authority. The rains which had auspiciously ended the drought and designated his special favour with the gods when he landed in Carthage three years before, ominously failed to greet him now. Every sullen, accusing peasant face, every groaning *saqqia*, every glimpse of the receding waters, must have shrivelled Hadrian's divine pretensions and made him humiliatingly aware of his own weak mortality.

No doubt the learned Balbilla, the scholars of the Museion, the temple priests and magicians whom Hadrian busily consulted, recollected how the distant past had coped with such a disaster. In remote prehistoric times, the Pharaoh himself had been sacrificed to induce the waters to rise, though later a human or animal sacrifice had been made in substitution. An oracle, so tradition went, had instructed the Pharaoh Aegyptus to sacrifice his daughter to stop famine and bring fertility. Having done so, the Pharaoh hurled himself into the river, doubly to appease the giver of plenty. There was another tradition of a gaily dressed young virgin being thrown to the river as its bride to secure a plentiful inundation. In Alexandria as late as 410 AD people still talked about the times when boys of pure parents were also offered to the Nile in sacrifice by its priests on the occasion of the great popular celebration of its flood, the Neilaia, on 22 October.[28] Indeed the idea of the sacrifice of a boy to placate the angry river was to persist down to modern times. Perhaps Antinous heard and brooded on such tales as the Emperor and his advisors discussed desperate expedients to avoid impending calamity.

The party passed through the marshy Delta where the blue lotus flowers poked up out of the water and where they must have been surrounded by inquisitive folk on little papyrus skiffs (fig. 32). The cruise proper started at its southernmost tip, the city of Heliopolis, below which the river ran through a valley only five to twelve miles wide between desert and mountains. It was probably early in October and Hadrian's intention was to proceed leisurely upstream at least as far as the ancient capital of Thebes and perhaps beyond the Philae and the first cataract where the mysterious river, whose source and miraculous flood were still not understood, entered the country. Herodotus tells us that in his day the 552 miles from Heliopolis to Thebes could, given the northerly breezes, be covered in nine days.[29] Hadrian took much longer, perhaps a month to six weeks, before he stepped ashore at the Valley of the Kings on 18 November.[30] On the way there, besides undertaking official commitments, he stopped to visit some of the great monuments of this vulnerable land: their scale, their antiquity, their complacent permanence deeply impressed him and his intimates. Moreover, these great decaying religious edifices were then not, as now, mere barren archaeological sites, but replete with life: served by priests, thronged with worshippers, the air vibrant with the sound of prayer, the incantation of ritual. Soon Hadrian and probably Antinous, standing in the dark, echoing sanctuaries, were gripped by the thrill of these ancient rites and grew anxious to explore the secrets of a religion and spiritual wisdom which had existed before Greece even had gods.

Always intrigued by the occult, and ever keen to venture to the verge of spiritual experience, Hadrian seems to have opened himself, almost credulously, to the priesthood of Egypt, on whom he bestowed privileges. On this trip, with its disturbing contrasts of success and failure, mastery and impotence, he seems to have been peculiarly vulnerable, tense, easily irritated, and arrogant one moment and humbly despondent the next, and not, we may suspect, the easiest of companions for his entourage, Antinous included, to bear.[31] He sought solace in the priests and their expertise in magic, astrology and predictions.

Sacerdotal magic in Egypt was a benevolent skill practised only by the purest of priests. They claimed, through incantation and other rites, to fight evil spirits attacking men by invoking the aid and even the presence of the dead or of divinities. Hadrian, starting his tour at the hill town of Heliopolis, famous in the past for its sciences (which even Plato had come to learn) but now deserted except for its priests learned in magic and astrology, voluntarily underwent a similar experience. There a priest called Pancrates, not the Alexandrian poet of the same name, initiated the Emperor into this divine magic. It was very different from the elevated sublimities of Eleusis. In the dark, cavernous temple of the sun, clouded with incense, Pancrates so convincingly demon-strated his powers of summoning spirits, striking down with illness (in two hours) and even with death (in seven hours) and of descending upon the Emperor in dreams 'that he proved the complete truth of his magic'.[32] Hadrian, probably made all the more receptive by fasting, was deeply impressed, 'admired the prophet and ordered that he be given a double remuneration'. Without doubt, the even more impressionable, wide-eyed Antinous was with him.

Thereafter, the Emperor, always anxious to know what lay ahead, consulted oracles about the future in a land where 'more use was made of omens and prognostications than in any other nation'.[33] So avidly did he learn astrology from the priests of Egypt that he could later dispense with official astrologers and accurately, it was said, cast his own horoscope, even foretelling the very hour of his death.[34]

Death and immortality: those two themes which had woven themselves into the journey since Eleusis raised themselves even more insistently in this valley of the Nile. Where the fertile plain of life ended, the land of death in the shape of the desert and the barren cliffs began. The huge monuments of the past claimed an imperishable eternity. The bound mummies in their painted staring coffins tenuously sustained the immortal souls of the departed.

According to legend, Osiris' death had occurred in the very month of October. His dismembered body had been scattered in the river by his enemies but he had returned, whole and triumphant over death, the bringer of fertility to the land and hope of immortality to its inhabitants. 'Life springs up to us from his destruction,' joyfully ran the Book of the Dead, 'the soul liveth again.'[35]

The holy Nile had long conferred sanctity and immortality not just on Osiris but on all those mortals it took to itself by drowning. Only the priests of the Nile could even touch the corpses of those so sanctified by drowning and they were buried at public expense. Men, women and even children, however humble, who had drowned were venerated in shrines and temples erected especially for them along its shores. Petesi and Paher, two brothers who had drowned in Roman times, one a mere scribe, had an elaborate temple built exclusively to themselves at Dendur. Sometimes the drowned were honoured as gods or identified with them, at others, as with the hundred or so buried at Thebes in Ptolemaic times, they were venerated as martyrs or saints, powerful intercessors with the greater gods. This tradition continued down to the days of Hadrian and Antinous: we know of at least nine people so deified in the imperial period. Indeed immortality conferred by drowning had by then in popular superstition reached ludicrous extremes: drowning in milk or oil conferred some form of immortality and even insects thus killed acquired divine properties. 'If you wish that the gods should come to you,' ran the folklore, 'take a scarab and "deify it" in the milk of a black cow . . .'[36]

Perhaps Antinous, pondering such stories and watching the swirling muddy current from the deck of the gilded imperial barge, contemplated the Nile, which had brought his master such despair, with renewed interest and even dawning hope.

From Heliopolis the flotilla made its way up the current. Normally the houses and temples would have been decorated cheerfully with garlands in tribute to the good flood, but perhaps this year such flowers were not to be seen. Most likely, Hadrian paused at Babylon on the right bank to inspect the Legion xxii Deiotariana which had long been stationed in Egypt. Most of the soldiers now cheering their Emperor were soon to be killed when the legion was wiped out in the Jewish war which his recent policy was to provoke. From the terrace of the fortress there the visitors gazed over to the pyramids at Gizeh which later they are bound to have explored. At Memphis, from which there are indications of a visit, Hadrian must have gone to the sanctuary of the sacred Apis bull, the discovery of which in 122 had caused such trouble in Egypt and himself a precipitate journey. The Serapeum there, with its rows of enigmatic sphinxes half-buried in the sand, must have impressed these visitors as it had done Strabo a hundred and fifty years before. We know that Hadrian paused in the fertile and Greek-populated area of the Fayoum where he granted a privilege to a sanctuary after another visit and consultation with its priests. There the world-famous Labyrinth no doubt intrigued and amazed the whole party. At Arsinoë, another town with many Greek citizens, the Emperor may have inspected the sacred crocodile and seen it fed with cake soaked in honey and wine, while a few miles upstream at Herakleopolis he would have seen, with bewilderment at the contrariness of these Egyptians, the deadly enemy of the crocodile, the ichneumon, venerated instead. The boats glided further south, reaching the midway point between Heliopolis and Thebes around the third week of October.

The imperial party stopped at Hermopolis Magna, the chief shrine of Thoth, the god of philosophy, science, letters and the arts whose equivalent in the Hellenic world was Hermes. His temple had long been a centre for Greek tourists. In addition, Thoth was the god of magic and astrology and there is evidence that Hadrian spent some time in the city deep in discussion with the priests, imbibing more of their occult skills and listening to their advice. Perhaps in the course of their visit he and Antinous saw the tomb of that well-known priest Petosiris, who centuries before had attained immortality and whose aid was still invoked in prayers and inscriptions by devout Greeks. Perhaps also Antinous heard about that fifteen-year-old girl, Isidora, who, only a year or so before, had been drowned in the Nile nearby. But because eternal life was the gift of the river to those who died in it, Isidora had become the centre of a local cult, assimilated to Isis in the Egyptian style or to one of the nymphs of the waters in the Greek one.[37]

Probably while they lingered at Hermopolis the festival of the Nile was celebrated on 22 October and with it the anniversary of the death of Osiris two days later.[38] Usually it was a joyous occasion, welcoming, as the waters declined, the renewal of fertility through the inundation. On land there were solemn ceremonies and uninhibited revelry, and on the river boats, small and large, sparkling with lamps at night, sent sounds of merriment, music and gratitude over the waters to echo away in the mountains across the plains. No such echoes can have been heard in the October of 130. After two years in which the river had refused its blessings, the celebration can hardly have been very cheerful. The hills heard only the wailing and incantations of prayer, summoning Osiris to return again from death, bringing the life-giving flood and fertility to save doomed mankind in the succeeding year.

A little way downstream and opposite Hermopolis, on the right bank of the river where it turned north-eastwards and the currents were stronger, lay an unprepossessing little settlement of mud huts called Hir-wer (fig. 33). Close to the river and its fringe of palms, rose the only notable building in the place, a temple of Rameses ii, modest in scale with typical sloping pylons at its entrance, a halled courtyard with stumpy papiriform columns and a sanctuary beyond (fig. 34). Here, besides Thoth, other gods of old Egypt were honoured: Ra, Hathor and Harachte among them.

But the credulous local folk seemed to have held such an affection for another god, Bes, that they 'exceptionally frequently' incorporated his name with their own, as in 'Besamon',[39] and thereby misled later historians into thinking that the place itself was called 'Besa'.[40] Now Bes was a god particularly adept at warding off danger, the god to whom the poor fellahin frequently turned for protection. By a strange coincidence, this god's name, and therefore his unlikely place on the Nile, connected with Hadrian and his beloved Athens. For it was in a deme called 'Besa' that Hadrian had been enrolled when made a citizen of Athens twenty years before. This district had been specially incorporated into the new phyle of 'Hadrian' created in 124–5 in the Emperor's honour in Athens.

Bes – the god who guarded against danger; and Besa – the deme of Hadrian who already knew and perhaps had just again been warned by the priests of Hermopolis that he was threatened with danger. What possible link could there be between them?[41]

The link – if any – was in the mind of Antinous. For it was near this obscure place, amid the swirling waters of the Nile in the last week of October 130 that Antinous met his death.

DEATH IN THE NILE
OCTOBER 130

'He fell into the Nile.'

Such is Hadrian's own written account of the death of Antinous – at least as it has come down to us in the abbreviation of Dio Cassius' history.[1] Even if the Emperor's original words, in a letter or his autobiography, were more profuse, they evidently satisfied no one at the time and the telegrammatic brevity of what we now read has satisfied no one since. Hadrian's laconic and vague words merely describe, they do not explain. *How*, we immediately ask, did Antinous fall? And *why* – by accident or design? Hadrian's phrase is almost dismissively abrupt; as though he was testily repudiating other explanations being proffered by contemporary gossip without giving anything away himself. From this, the suspicion has always lingered that Hadrian knew more than he was prepared to tell. Perhaps, however, he knew less than posterity is inclined to assume. His few words may reflect nothing more than his own scanty information. Antinous' last moments may have been as much a mystery to him as they remain to us.

The official report being so unrevealing, unofficial ones started at once and have never stopped. Imagination, often lurid and sinister, has taken over where sparse facts leave off, and we have a whole range of explanations of an event depicted as gruesome, sublime or pitifully trivial. Antinous is variously shown floating with a dagger in his back; recumbent with mumbling priests and slavering Hadrian eagerly plucking the entrails from his slit-open body; expiring in agony on the surgeon's table after the removal of his testicles; sinking with heroic resolution and angelic passivity into the murky waters or just slipping helplessly in the mud.

The absence of conclusive proof does not, however, give licence for all or any of these invented deaths. We know enough about the characters of Hadrian and Antinous and the state of their relationship, have enough contemporary clues as to what may have happened, and such abundant evidence as to the consequences, that we can considerably narrow down the range of explanations and, if without reaching final certitude, can at least assess the balance of probabilities, the complex forces which drove or tempted Antinous to his end.

Some things are reasonably certain.

The date of his death has to be calculated from that given for the foundation of Antinoopolis. The *Chronicon Paschale* gives us 30 October as the day of foundation and the year 122 which is obviously a mistake – Hadrian was only in Egypt in 130–31. Though the day and month tally perfectly with the imperial entourage's itinerary, the error in the year has inevitably raised doubts as to their validity also. But such doubts have lately been removed by fresh papyrological evidence, confirming an apotheosis in late October or early November.[2] If Hadrian then formally declared the city founded on 30 October it is reasonable to assume that Antinous died some days beforehand. Weber has proposed 22 October, the day of the Nile festival, with the body remaining in the water three days and nights before its recovery – like that of Osiris. Bonneau suggests 28 October. We can only be sure that it was in the last week or so of that month. Significantly this period coincides with the festival of the Nile and the related commemoration of the death of Osiris (celebrated by the Greeks on 24 October)[3] helps to account for Antinous' actions.

The death was by drowning. This fact needs emphasis as some other rival explanations, ignoring or disparaging Hadrian's words, have Antinous die by other means. Hadrian's own explicit phrase is supported by the vaguer one of the *Historia Augusta* ('he lost his Antinous while sailing along the Nile');[4] by the combination of the name of the drowned god Osiris with that of Antinous in the phyles of his new city and on the obelisk; by water races in his memory on the Nile; by a prose passage, emanating from Hadrian's circle immediately after the death, which compares Antinous with the beautiful youths Narcissus and Hylas, both of whom died in water;[5] and by the naming of the rosy lotus wreath, an attribute of the drowned, as *Antinoeios*; all this apart from Hadrian's own subsequent veneration for the Nile in Egypt, on the obelisk and at Tivoli. This evidence helps to exclude some of the more macabre and bloody deaths on land.

Two such deaths can be eliminated at once.

One is that Antinous was the victim of a court conspiracy, perhaps fomented by Sabina. There is no whisper of such a plot in the ancient sources, always avid for scandal, and no likelihood of it. Antinous may have been prominent, but he was powerless, and his performance of his role and his character threatened no one. With Sabina, as we have seen, his relations seem to have been cordial rather than hostile. The fragmentary sculpture in Rome which shows Antinous' head with the large clenched fist of a colossus resting on it is hardly, as has been suggested, a dramatic depiction of the lethal dagger striking him down. And Marconi's conception of a death 'carried by an unknown hand' is pure unfounded imagination. There is no case for a murder of this kind.[6]

The other is that Antinous died while undergoing voluntary castration with the connivance of Hadrian in a desperate effort to preserve his fading youthful beauty.[7] There can be little doubt that Antinous and Hadrian were perturbed at the favourite's arrival at hirsute manhood and that these reactions did play some part in what finally occurred. It is likely, too, that if Antinous had died under such an operation Hadrian would have hushed the matter up. But Antinous was already between eighteen and twenty and such surgery would have been useless at that age. In any case Hadrian, as we know, had repeated Domitian's ban on castration and extended it to circumcision. Would he have allowed what he regarded as a barbaric abomination to be perpetrated on his beloved – and in the middle of a crowded cruise up the Nile? This grisly fate at least we can be sure Antinous was spared.

Though there are numerous visual memorials to Antinous in sculptures, coins and gems, and references to him in inscriptions, coin legends, and the Christian and pagan authors, very few of them explicitly mention the manner of his death. There is indeed a strange, at first an inexplicable, silence on the matter. Out of about thirty ancient writers dealing with Antinous only three overtly seek to provide any explanation of his end. What they say therefore demands close attention.

The earliest is Dio Cassius who was born only about thirty-five years after the death of Antinous and wrote his history eighty years after that event. His account (as transmitted by the epitome) represents a very early viewpoint.

> Antinous died either by falling into the Nile, as Hadrian writes, or, as the truth is, by being offered in sacrifice. For Hadrian . . . was always very curious and employed divinations and incantations of all kinds. Accordingly, he honoured Antinous either because of his love for him or because the youth had voluntarily undertaken to die for him (it being necessary that a life should be surrendered freely for the accomplishment of the ends Hadrian had in view) by building a city on the spot where he had suffered this fate . . .[8]

Dio categorically sweeps aside Hadrian's account and offers us 'the truth' instead. Antinous was offered as a sacrifice and the word Dio uses (*hierourgetheis*) is that often used for the victim of a ritual sacrifice to ascertain omens by the inspection of entrails. This sacrifice was in connection with Hadrian's magical or religious inquiries, but Antinous' immolation may have been voluntary. The death was on land – where the city was to rise.

All this seems inconsistent with the death by drowning. Dio, however, never explicitly says the sacrifice was of the bloody ritual kind. And if he used the word *hierourgetheis* loosely or figuratively (likewise the site of the event), then his account is not inconsistent with a death in the river. However, the mention of a sacrifice (even by drowning) expands and radically alters the neutral sense of Hadrian's remark. Seventeenth-century and later historians took his words literally, hence the bloody hands fumbling amid the entrails, 'the sacrifice of barbaric curiosity', and Hadrian's guilt for 'a crime the most horrible of which an Emperor was capable'.[9] We shall consider the likelihood of such a ritual sacrifice later.

Our second witness is that of the *Historia Augusta* which, though composed in about 395 AD, derives its material on Hadrian from sources written at about the same time as Dio's original work, again only three generations after the event. It runs:

> He lost his Antinous while sailing along the Nile and wept for him like a woman. Concerning this (*de quo*), there are various reports: some assert that he sacrificed himself for Hadrian, others what both his beauty and Hadrian's excessive sensuality make obvious . . .[10]

This seems to support a death by drowning in the river, at first sight by accident ('he lost'). But when considering alternative explanations for the death (or Hadrian's excessive grief), this writer again introduces a voluntary sacrifice. This, however, is only one explanation for the death: the other seems to hint darkly at suicide.[11]

The third source is Sextus Aurelius Victor, writing at about the same time as the compiler of the *Historia* but using sources we do not know. He is more detailed. Writing of the dedication of the city and statues to Antinous, which some saw as the result of Hadrian's passion, he continues:

> Others see his motives as pious and religious: for when Hadrian was desiring to prolong his life by any means, the magicians proposed that someone should die voluntarily on his behalf; everyone refused, Antinous alone offered himself: from that all the homage rendered to his memory.[12]

Again the voluntary sacrifice theory is given only as an alternative explanation for Hadrian's extraordinary response to Antinous' death. Now, however, it is expressly suggested by magicians as a vicarious offering designed to prolong Hadrian's own obscurely threatened life and rendered all the more heroic by everybody else's refusal to volunteer for it. The manner of death is not specified. Not surprisingly, this passage has once more been interpreted as suggesting the ritual slaughter for *extispicium* – the inspection of entrails.

Our three accounts have enough in common to suggest that they are garbled versions of one earlier source. There are, however, significant variations. There is a hint of drowning by accident in the quoted words of Hadrian and in the opening of the *Historia*. Dio, however, is definite that it was an offering of sacrifice. He and the other two all propose that it might have been a *voluntary* sacrifice as one means of explaining Hadrian's extraordinary response (the other explanation being his equally extraordinary passion). Two of them link the sacrifice with magicians' advice and Hadrian's religious dabblings. One suggests a cause: to prolong Hadrian's life, somehow endangered. Finally, in the uncertain construction of another, there is a hint of suicide provoked by the unbalanced and overpowering relationship of Hadrian to Antinous.

Each of these propositions deserves testing in the light of what we know of the two protagonists, the circumstances of 130 and other evidence.

How easy it was for even the strongest young swimmer to die in the treacherous currents of the Nile has been illustrated in the account of the death of Hector, the young favourite of Alexander the Great. The Nile incessantly claimed such victims. For example, over two thousand years later in 1837, another beautiful Greek lad, Jannis, the page of the intrepid voyager, Prince Pückler-Muskau, stumbled from his boat, fell in the river and immediately disappeared beneath the strongly flowing water, never to be found again by distraught searchers. Only the Arab boatman was pleased. The Nile had received its offering, he commented, echoing the immemorial Egyptian tradition, and the rest of the journey would now be happy.[13]

Hadrian's brief phrase has been said to suggest just such a fate for Antinous. The currents on the bend of the river near Hir-wer were indeed dangerous. Antinous was a lively youth, prone (as we remember from his hunts) to take risks. Weber has even set the scene:[14] the joyous, intoxicating festival of the Nile, Antinous skimming on the river in one of those flimsy papyrus pleasure boats seen on the Palestrina mosaic (and suggested in a phrase of Epiphanios),[15] the boat capsizing in the turbulent waters, the youth being swept away and dragged down. It may have all happened out of sight and earshot of others: hence the mystery surrounding his end and Hadrian's terse and ambiguous phrase. We can indeed be fairly sure that there were few, if any, witnesses to the demise of Antinous, however it occurred.

What mars this accident theory is the lack of any evidence for it at all. Hadrian's phrase, though it is consistent with an accidental fall, could equally apply to an intended one, as can the vague words of the *Historia*. If it was no more than an accident, why should not Hadrian say so openly: at least there would be no need to cover up this mode of death, unlike some of the others which reflect adversely on the Emperor. From the very first, contemporaries suggested that he was holding things back and insisted on the sacrificial explanation, though this might be only to account for his disproportionate response to the death. At least the sacrificial theory has some evidence to support it, though whether that is convincing remains to be seen. It is certainly very difficult to understand the genuine popularity and extent of the posthumous veneration of Antinous if the death which produced it was the result of no more than a slip in the mud or the overturning of a boat.

Weber's beguiling incidentals vanish upon examination. The Nile festival of that year 130 was, as we have seen, anything but joyful. Papyrus skiffs were used on the placid Delta, not on the swift upper river. Epiphanios' 'pleasure boat' refers only to the conventional barque used for the cult or shrine of the god Osiris-Antinous. Other historians have objected that the broad-chested Antinous was probably a good swimmer and was unlikely to have been unguarded: though neither of these grounds precludes an accident.

In the end there is less evidence for or against the accidental explanation than for any other. Certainly there are other interpretations which better fit the known facts, other implications and psychological probabilities. Nevertheless such inexplicable accidents – perhaps isolated and mysterious – do occur and the suggestion cannot be wholly argued away. Behind the more probable deaths postulated for Antinous – more grandiose or profound – this simple one lurks always as an ineradicable possibility.

Dio uses the word *hierourgetheis* which technically means that Antinous was used as a sacrificial victim whose entrails would be searched and interpreted by magicians and priests for omens concerning the Emperor's future. As this explanation has been seized upon by those anxious to depict a gory end and Hadrian's innate cruelty and black superstition, we must consider it as seriously as the others.

Indeed some background evidence lends credibility to this suggestion. The searching of entrails of animals and birds to ascertain omens and auguries was a common practice in Rome. Various Emperors, perturbed about their futures, went further and are said to have slaughtered human beings, especially handsome or noble youths, for this very purpose: Elagabalus (218–22), Didius Julianus (emperor of 193 AD) and Maxentius (306–12) among them.[16] Justin Martyr and Tatian both reprove such practices in the time of Hadrian and Apollonius of Tyana in that of Domitian.[17] Nor can we doubt that Hadrian had grave anxieties in this autumn of 130: he had certainly been listening with avidity and susceptibility to the priests and magicians along the Nile. He was certainly preoccupied with astrology and portents. His character in the last year had undergone some deterioration: he had shown himself capable of astonishing savagery to individuals in the Levant and brutal and reckless insensitivity to a whole people in Judea. Soon his policy towards the Jews would be even more ruthless in its cost of life, and later, when back in Rome, he would cruelly compel former colleagues to 'voluntary' deaths and be accused of indulging in a blood-bath in which numerous Senators, his brother-in-law, his great-nephew and even his wife were swept away. Even his closest friendships were prone to change suddenly into bitter and vicious hatreds.

Admitting much of this, however, it is still not possible to accept that Hadrian allowed Antinous to be used, even with the youth's voluntary consent, as the passive victim of *extispicium*. Such an act is completely inconsistent with their relationship. Maybe that relationship was now altering but there is no evidence that it had soured to the point of hatred, or one where Hadrian's fear for his own life superseded his love for Antinous. Had he not, only a few weeks previously, saved the young man's life? Would he now throw it away at the behest of the magicians? Could the whole apotheosis and the cult around it be solely guilty remorse? Occasionally savage and arbitrary he may well have become, but he was no monster. In his reign the prohibition of human sacrifice, enacted under Tiberius, was more rigorously enforced and bloody cults like that of Mithras were deliberately suppressed. Finally, we know that Antinous died by drowning and, though one antiquarian claims that the lad was bundled up and hurled into the river at the behest of the magicians for the purposes of prediction,[18] this too is a fantasy like the rest, incompatible with the whole quality of Hadrian's character, his relationship with Antinous and his subsequent actions.

The mention of the word *hierourgetheis* by Dio is therefore either a deliberate falsehood, a slander against Hadrian by an historian who did not favour him, or, and this is far more likely, an imprecise and figurative image, a term for an offering or sacrifice of another and much less ghastly kind.

The ancient historians seem to be unanimously suggesting voluntary sacrifice as the cause of death. The idea was enthusiastically taken up by the Victorian apologists for Antinous, such as Rydberg, Symonds and Dietrichson, who seized on its obvious analogies with the sacrifice of Jesus to provide their hero with the halo of near Christian sanctity: as Christ died to save mankind, so Antinous expired for at least the Roman Empire.

The belief that the deliberate, voluntary death of one person could save or restore the life of another, or remove lethal dangers, had firm roots in the mind and practice of antiquity. It grew from a belief in the regenerative power of love, freely given. In the Greek world it was known as anti-psyche (soul for soul) and is celebrated by Euripides in the story of Alcestis sacrificing her life to recover that of Admetus. In the Roman period it developed from an inspiring myth into a practice. In the army such a sacrifice to snatch victory out of defeat, like that of Decius Mus, was honoured as *devotio* (close to the word *devotum* used by the *Historia* of Antinous) and was exempt from the usual taboos and penalties associated with suicide. The general making the *devotio* could also conveniently send a legionary to his death as his substitute. Horace tells us of voluntary sacrifice as if it were an accepted fact in his day.[19] When Augustus and Caligula were ill, people willingly pledged their lives for their recovery and even died in combat in the arena to do so. An inscription on the Capitoline tells of a young wife who believed that her premature death would add the years she had thereby lost to those of her still-living husband. That earlier Prefect of Egypt, Balbillus, had recommended Nero in 64 AD, when the Emperor's life was threatened by a comet, to take the lives of certain noble youths in order to save his own – though whether they died voluntarily is far from certain. (Perhaps his granddaughter, Balbilla, very conscious of her famous ancestor on this tour of 130,[20] reminded the worried Hadrian of this precedent.) Shortly after Hadrian's reign the sophist, Aristeides, boasted that he had been cured from mortal sickness by the deliberate suicide for him of his nurse Philumene and her brother Hermeas.[21] Hadrian and Antinous must also have heard many times the story of Christ's vicarious sacrifice for mankind, sometimes specified as 'the sacrifice of the Son for the Father'.[22] In Egypt too a somewhat similar practice had a venerable history in a voluntary and joyful sacrifice by drowning in the Nile, offered annually in October, like that of Osiris, to ensure abundance and life to the people of the valley. In Roman eyes, for any such sacrifice to be effective it had to be voluntary, preferably deriving from love.

What danger or dangers can have been pointed out by the magicians and priests in October 130 as urgently menacing Hadrian and needing such a sacrifice of a life for their removal?

Some historians have suggested vague political dangers: that Hadrian was grossly neglecting his Empire for the sake of Antinous, which was patently untrue; or that there was seething unrest in Egypt for which there is no evidence, though the situation there must have been tense and disturbing. Others have descried the first rumblings of revolt in Judea which were to erupt into the bloodiest and longest war of the reign, the outbreak of which Hadrian, remembering the fierce strife of 116–17 and the holocaust in the time of Titus, must have dreaded even if he had provoked the trouble in the first place. There is no record, however, that the Jews were stirring at this time. They waited until Hadrian was safely back in Greece in 132 before rising against Rome.

Still others have proposed a deadly comet or a menacing astral conjunction. Hadrian believed in the powers of heavenly bodies over human destiny and could easily have felt doomed by them. But again there is no evidence of a comet at this time or of any such adverse pattern among the stars.

We do, however, have evidence about two possible dangers.

Sextus Aurelius Victor tells us that Hadrian was anxious 'to prolong his life'. The implication is that he was either ill or felt endangered by the prospect of a mortal illness. We know from coins that he had been ill until at least after August 128[23] and Epiphanios explictly connects his visit to Egypt with recuperation from illness. He had been preoccupied by death and survival in the tour of the east and, in the temple of Heliopolis, had rewarded the prophet Pancrates for demonstrating his powers over illness and death. The spasmodic deterioration of his judgement and temper may well have been linked to some recurrence of the earlier malady: one ancient historian tells us that the sickness which was eventually to kill him in 138 had its origins long before, possibly in that of 127–8.[24] Another, Dio Cassius, also confirms that Hadrian suffered from haemorrhages even before the onset of his final illness in 136.[25] Perhaps, affected by the Nile valley's humidity and burdened by the cares of Egypt, the Emperor had another sudden and serious attack. If so, there is no mention of it this time on the coins, though it might partly account for his tarrying in Egypt until well into 131. Much more likely, some worrying symptoms of the long-latent illness may have appeared again, boding evil. Perhaps the magicians saw in these symptoms, and he saw in himself, signs of irreversible physical decline. Hence the suggestion of prolonging his existence by adding to it the vicarious life of a young, healthy and willing human sacrifice. Sextus Aurelius Victor may well have got the subsequent story right. After all, Hadrian had recently saved Antinous from a nasty end. Perhaps, the young man generously and impulsively thought, it was his destiny in turn to save the ailing Emperor. Love and willingness – he was the only candidate who had them both.

The other danger scarcely needs repetition. The Nile flood for two years had been deficient: a third would bring famine to Egypt, trouble in Rome, riots in Hadrian's most cherished cities in Greece. The river's failure made the Emperor-Pharaoh's own failure of divine powers humiliatingly manifest to all. It was as though the godhead in him was moribund or already dead. That Hadrian and Antinous were acutely aware of the need to propitiate the god of the Nile to prevent an impending disaster, the inscription on the obelisk makes perfectly clear.[26] The long and active tradition of sacrificing a young person, distinguished by birth or beauty, to the Nile around 22 October was well known. It may be that by suggesting the revival of this rite the magicians hoped to remove a serious threat to the Emperor and Empire and to replenish his obviously languishing efficiency and power as a god.

What evidence is there to support and to oppose the claims of the ancient historians that the death was such a sacrifice of substitution?

The epitaph on the obelisk hints at something relevant. On the face devoted to Thoth (the deity of Hermopolis) we are told that Antinouss 'received the command of the gods at the time of his leaving life'.[27] Erman, the learned translator, informs us cautiously that, as the Egyptian gods never interfered with the natural demise of a man, this unusual divine intrusion indicates special circumstances surrounding Antinous' death.[28] Earlier translations of these difficult hieroglyphs, however, stress Antinous' deliberate and joyous acceptance of this command, which suggests more convincingly a voluntary sacrificial end.[29] The text also refers constantly to his outstanding moral worth and the love, honour and praise he has aroused in people, all of which suits some noble or exceptional deed. The Nile is also depicted as 'loving' Hadrian and behaving gratefully to him as if for some gift.[30] Even so, there is still nothing straightforward and explicit about the end of Antinous.

Elsewhere on the obelisk Antinous, now deified, is described acting as a god of healing. And this Asclepeian and therapeutic role of his is confirmed by the critical Origen in his account of the cult as it was practised in Antinoopolis about 240 AD.[31] Such evidence certainly lends credence to the idea that the young man was thought to have died voluntarily for the health of Hadrian and, as a god, also acted for the health of humanity in general. The Masson and Fauvel gems and others like them seem to show Antinous contemplating death for a sick-looking Hadrian in the company of the snake of Asclepeios and the goddess of health, Hygeia, herself. But as such gems have disappeared, and their authenticity was in question anyway, they enhance rather than clarify the mystery.

Of the four other writings about Antinous which date from the days shortly after his death, two (the Pancrates poem and the Curium hymn) understandably say nothing about the matter, but the other two can be construed as referring to it.

Arrian, in that interpolation into his Black Sea narrative which does seem to refer to the affair, declares that Achilles died 'in the flower of his youth' and was notable for the 'force and constancy of his love' such that 'he would even die for his friends'. Have we here then, at long last, a definite mention of the voluntary sacrifice for Hadrian? The words used by Arrian for 'his friends' are *paidika*, which would be better translated as 'his young boy-friends' or 'favourites'. This is hardly an apt description of the 54-year-old Emperor of Rome. Perhaps Arrian was using his Greek very freely and some scholars have interpreted (even translated) the passage as talking of Antinous' death for 'his beloved', i.e. Hadrian.[32] But in view of the ambiguity, Arrian's contribution must be inconclusive.

The prose passage deriving from court circles soon after the death and comparing the flower of Antinous, the rosy lotus, with those of the other drowned youths, Narcissus and Hylas, offers its mite of evidence. The flowers of the other youths are wan and death-like in colour, we are told, but that of Antinous is joyful and positive: because he embraced his end willingly.

The numerous coins of Antinous say nothing explicit about his end. On those of Tion he is shown sitting on an altar (a pose from which that on the Masson gem is adapted) and this could certainly be an allusion to his sacrifice. Unoccupied altars appear elsewhere. Oxen occur more often, as on the coins of Smyrna (fig. 48d) and Bithynion, and these sacrificial beasts could again be symbols of Antinous' death. Dietrichson even interprets the hoopoe bird on some coins as symbolic of the devotion of the young to the beloved old. However, all these interpretations could be countered by others equally plausible and we cannot safely invoke the coins by themselves as proving anything.

And so with the 115 or so surviving sculptures of Antinous. Whatever indeed we may be able to *infer* from them, they never openly illustrate the nature of his death. One work, the Ildefonso group in Madrid, was long taken to be conclusive proof of the sacrifice since it ostensibly showed Antinous symbolically preparing to devote his life for an extraordinary youthful Hadrian standing at his side. Much purple prose was expended on its significance. Now, however, we know that a head of Antinous from another source has been grafted on to a quite independent work, Hellenistic or a pastiche, which may originally have shown another pair of lovers, Orestes and Pylades or Castor and Pollux. It has nothing whatever to do with the death of Antinous.[33]

Only one scrap of epigraphic material provides its, typically ambivalent, contribution. An inscription tells us that in the city divisions or phratries of Naples there was one bearing the joint names of Antinous and Eunostos. Now Eunostos, a mythical figure from Boeotia, is said 'in the bloom of his youth free-willingly to have gone to his death' and to have been heroised and honoured with a shrine as a consequence.[34] Is the strange linking of this obscure hero with Antinous because of the latter's similar end? We cannot be sure, for another tradition asserts that Eunostos died unexpectedly and involuntarily as the victim of an assassination plot.[35] Their connection may rather be their shared powers over the fertility of the soil. Thus another fragment of evidence is rendered doubtful if not discredited.

Such then are the only explicit references to a sacrificial death which have come down to us. Their amazing paucity and almost perverse obliqueness at once arouse suspicions. Surely, if Antinous had indeed generously offered his life for that of the Emperor, the literature and artefacts which poured out soon afterwards would have published his noble deed to all the world? Does not the dearth of direct references to the sacrifice cast serious doubts on its reality and suggest that the tales of the ancient historians are mere fabrications or versions of the popular belief that necromancers were responsible for the premature deaths of the young?

To these grave objections we must return when we have considered the other weightier evidence which can be *inferred* from the artefacts and the cult in favour of the sacrificial explanation.

In the light of this proposition, the dating and placing of Antinous' death no longer seem so fortuitous. 22 October or thereabouts, the time of the Nile festival and the commemoration of the death of Osiris, was the traditional period for sacrifices in the river. What more appropriate time for Antinous to offer himself? And what of that other apparent coincidence between the place on the Nile where Bes, the god of protection, was worshipped and Besa, the district which linked Hadrian so intimately to his beloved Athens, to past happiness and fulfilment? Athens summed up the true vitality of Hadrian. The homonymous names and their interlocking associations may have come together in the mind of Antinous. What more propitious spot than this for Antinous to invoke by his sacrifice a divine protection for the continuing life and beneficent activity of the now endangered Emperor?

It is, however, chiefly from subsequent events that historians, ancient and modern, argue most strongly in support of the sacrifice. So colossal was the scale of Hadrian's response to the death – the apotheosis, the cult, the sculptures and coins – that, it is claimed, it cannot all have been the reaction of love alone to a merely accidental loss, but was a demonstration of overwhelming gratitude for the deliberate sacrifice of the beloved for his lover. Such an argument is cogent but not altogether convincing. Hadrian's megalomania, his egocentricity and romanticism, his love of grand theatrical gestures did not need such a motive of gratitude for their exercise. In his unbalancing grief, why should he not, as Alexander had done for Hephaestion, commemorate in as colossal and permanent a manner as possible his great love for Antinous? He had recently promoted his own divinity for a mixture of personal, political and cultural ends. Why not divinise his beloved for the same purpose too? Given the complicated motives which went into their inception and Hadrian's overweening arrogance at this time, the apotheosis and cult do not, by themselves, prove a sacrifice by Antinous to be their cause. Certainly, as far as we know, Hadrian, out of selfishness or shrewdness, never deigned publicly to express his gratitude to his beloved in plain, unequivocal terms.

It is the nature of and response to the cult which provide the strongest evidence for Antinous' offering. After death, Antinous was identified as a god most often with Osiris, Dionysos and Hermes.[36] These three gods had in common powers over the world of the dead. Hermes was the general guide of souls who had restored Persephone herself to the light. Osiris and Dionysos (Zagreus) with whom Antinous was most commonly associated had both suffered, died and been resurrected and both had voluntarily undergone the rigours of the underworld to rescue their kin from death. The parallel with Antinous' own voluntary sacrifice and descent to death to save Hadrian and with his subsequent resurrection is obvious and must have been intended in the persistent assimilation of him to these chthonic deities. It is notable in this respect that Christ, the supreme exemplar of vicarious sacrifice, was himself frequently depicted in his earliest images also as Osiris, Dionysos and Hermes. We know that some sober pagans like Celsus seriously compared Antinous to Christ, possibly because of the analogy between their alleged sacrifices and resurrections.[37] Certainly too the Christian Fathers singled out the cult of Antinous for particular attack, presumably because it in some way competed with their own, though there is only one, very obscure, hint of any sacrifice by Antinous in their invective.[38] In various cult centres mysteries of Antinous were celebrated, akin to those of Eleusis, Dionysos and Osiris. Such mysteries at this time definitely imply a passion or sacrifice on the part of the cult god in which the initiates participated.

The cult of Antinous would not have spread so far and lasted so long if it had not been rooted in some belief about Antinous himself. That he had triumphed over death by himself becoming immortal and a god was self-evident. Was it for this alone that he was worshipped? Or did his legend invest him with the power of bringing others back from death like Hermes, Osiris and Dionysos, because people believed he had in some way saved Hadrian from extinction too? Certainly Hadrian in his epitaph on the obelisk invests Antinous with similar powers to pass back and forth for eternity through the gates of the underworld. Was the warmth of the response to him kindled by his reputation for self-sacrifice, his suffering for the sake of others? The standard image in sculpture created with the Emperor's approval for Antinous' votaries and temples seems to show him contemplating just such a final and difficult act of devotion.

Much then in the cult of Antinous and its duration, if not in its initial creation, remains inexplicable but for the presumption of a death voluntarily offered for the benefit of another or others. This powerful testimony of actual practice and belief, starting immediately after the death, endorses the claims made by historians some generations later and buttresses the frail and wavering statements we have found in the literature and artefacts of the time.

There remains the fundamental objection to the sacrificial theory mentioned earlier. If Antinous had devoted himself to death for Hadrian, why did not the latter say so, indeed trumpet to the world such a sublime abnegation? Surely such publicity would have made the apotheosis all the more welcome among his credulous subjects, all the more explicable to his philosophic critics? Does the absence of explicit accounts from the period when the cult was established, 130–38, mean that there was no such sacrifice and that it was a later invention of historians who could not otherwise explain the scale and intensity of Hadrian's response?

An answer to these objections lies in the nature of this particular sacrificial death and of Hadrian himself. If Antinous had died to save the Emperor from the onset of a lethal sickness or from the consequences of famine in Egypt, or both dangers together, would Hadrian have wished the news of such threats to be broadcast around his Empire? Would someone so independent and proud, recently proclaimed as almighty and bountiful Zeus incarnate, have wished to confess in public and for perpetuity his own impotence in the face of impending illness or death? Would the self-contained autocrat, Hadrian as Emperor, have wished his subjects to know that the future of his reign and the stability of the Empire itself had thus depended on the whim of a mere youth? Would Hadrian, who boasted his independence of astrologers, have desired the world to hear that his fate had been dictated by the gibberings of Egyptian magicians?

However much the sacrifice glorified Antinous, it belittled Hadrian. It exposed his physical vulnerability, the bankruptcy of his divine pretensions, his practical impotence in the face of disaster and his gullible and pathetic dependence. Hadrian thus had every political and personal motive to hush up what actually happened and its causes. The powerful pain of his loss, the self-reproach with which he blamed himself for it, may also have reinforced this political reticence.

Hence the limited and oblique presentation of the sacrifice in the literature which emanated from his court and the symbolical and generalised sacrifice enshrined in the cult. Hence too the brevity of Hadrian's own explanation. It was only after his removal from the scene (and after the artefacts had all been created) that the historians could, with singular unanimity, put forward what had actually occurred.

To sum up.[39] Though we have no convincing proof, there exist more evidence and more compelling arguments in favour of Antinous' voluntary sacrifice than for his death by accident and none at all for his ritual immolation. However, such a sacrifice, by itself, still does not entirely fit everything we know about Hadrian, Antinous and their situation at this moment. There must have been other ingredients in the motives of Antinous as he waded or plunged into the waters.

For a healthy and active young man, scarcely out of his teens, to die for another is credible if this death is heroic, in combat perhaps or in response to challenge, or if it is in company or in public. For such a person in the prime of his life to sneak away alone and to suffocate himself miserably in water, as may well have happened with Antinous, demands a dimension of fixed determination which goes beyond the scope of mere altruism. In dying for Hadrian in such a wretched fashion, Antinous must also have been dying for himself. There were forces which pushed as well as those which pulled him into the river. The sacrifice for the Emperor must have contained elements of genuine suicide, of escape from intolerable pressures to prospective salvation.

Antinous' days as the imperial favourite were numbered if not already over. The inevitable advance of age and changes in his appearance, which Hadrian seemed to have disliked, precluded his continuance as the *eromenos*. Already Hadrian, with an eye to the succession since his illness, seems to have been nurturing a more mature favourite in the person of Commodus, with whose position and social assets a grown-up Antinous could never compete. Commodus might just have been on this cruise: an ominous irritant. In any case Antinous must have felt more than ever insecure and anxious about his own future. Hadrian himself may have been more exacting, difficult and captious on this trip than before and his arbitrariness may have become an ever more threatening cloud as Antinous' own past clear role faded. Perhaps the over-intellectual, jealous and bickering company also grated on the young man's taut nerves. However, it is unlikely that he was filled with disgust at his shameful role or by Hadrian's sexual demands or even at the prospect of becoming a permanent homosexual as some have tried to contend.[40]

The questions posed about Hadrian's future and its dangers raised insistently those of his own. If Hadrian were, as the magicians predicted, to die or to be overwhelmed by disasters, would not that be the end of Antinous too? If the Emperor survived, was there much of a future for Antinous to look forward to anyway? In the oppressive valley with its aura of destiny, its crushingly permanent monuments of stone, in the atmosphere of imminent catastrophe generated by Hadrian's predicament, what value had Antinous' minute spark of life?

He may have seized on the mention of a sacrifice as the means to grasp again, and this time for ever, the waning devotion of his lover, to repay the debt incurred in front of the Libyan lion and, for the first and final time in his life, to achieve something of supreme significance, demanding ultimate courage, independently of Hadrian, on his own. Such a sacrifice also offered a glorious resolution to the squalid and insoluble problem of his own future. Better, he may have thought, to be a dead and hallowed martyr than a living and forgotten has-been.

But would he even *be* dead? Positive as well as negative forces drew Antinous into the Nile. Had he not the resplendent assurance of his initiation at Eleusis that he would triumph over death and find not gloomy Hades but the flower-spangled fields of Elysium? That the confidence of Eleusis imbued his final moments we can be sure, just as its nomenclature and symbols were to invest the city and the images by which he was to be remembered. But more – had not Osiris, the commemoration of whose death fell at this very moment, died in such a manner, only to be reborn and to bring fertility and life to all the earth? Did not tradition promise that if Antinous shared in his suffering and sacrifice he would share also in his triumphant resurrection? The tales and images of Osiris must have echoed in his mind, filled his vision and steadied his nerves as he approached his end. And the Nile itself? He must have heard of the sanctity and divinity which the god of the river bestowed on those he took to himself. If a scribe like Petesi or a girl like Isidora could attain veneration and immortality by a merely accidental death, what more grand destiny might he attain by a deliberate act of sacrifice to the Nile and for the Emperor of Rome? Such may have been Antinous' ultimate thoughts.

If they were, he was to be amply rewarded. Antinous became a god. Hadrian was granted a lease of life so long and so cruelly tenacious that – in the end – he was to beg for death.[41] And in the following season of 131, the Nile god repaid the offering by, to quote the Emperor's own words,[42] rising 'almost higher than any time before, flooding all over the country, causing the production of abundant and beautiful crops . . .'

Though this explanation of a sacrificial death most comfortably fits the facts, the mood and traditions of the time and place, subsequent events and the psychological probabilities, Antinous' death must always remain a mystery, and the faint possibility that it was an accident after all can never be completely obliterated. It must have been as much a mystery at the time. It is likely that no one, including Hadrian himself, fully saw and knew all that transpired in the final moments. Perhaps Antinous, along with Hadrian and others, heard the advice and admonitions of the magicians in the temple and brooded on their implications. Then the young man disappeared. Later his body was found in the river near the township where Bes was worshipped. The Emperor, his jabbering courtiers and bemused posterity were left to deduce what had happened.

LIFE ETERNAL
130–31

Hadrian was shattered. His grief has echoed down the ages. 'He wept like a woman', sneered the *Historia Augusta*, stressing by the comparison not the Emperor's effeminacy but his indecorously public, unrestrained reaction.[1] 'He grieved vehemently', noted a startled St Jerome another two centuries later.[2]

In fact there was nothing unusual in such extravagant demonstrations of mourning by parents or admirers of prematurely dead boys in Rome, as the touching consolations of Statius to the distraught lovers Melior and Flavius Ursus show. The aged Herodes Atticus in a public paroxysm of despair at the loss of his *eromenos*, Polydeukes, commissioned games, inscriptions and sculptures on a lavish scale and then died, inconsolable, shortly afterwards.[3] But these were private citizens and personal affairs.

What alarmed contemporaries and has shocked posterity was the inability of the Emperor of Rome to keep private his grief for a purely personal bereavement. After all, Antinous had been of no public standing or consequence. But now Hadrian sought to involve all mankind and future generations in his own intimate loss as though it were of cosmic and perpetual significance. It is the scale, the elaboration and the staggering presumption of his response which has baffled history.

Flamboyantly histrionic and calculatingly political as were elements in his reaction, there can be no doubt of the genuineness of Hadrian's distress. He had lost the deepest, purest love of his life, and one, unlike his other affections, unsoiled by the manipulations of power. To this overwhelming sense of emotional ruin was added remorse: if the boy had died by sacrifice, by suicide, even by a mere accident, was not Hadrian still responsible? The trivial cumulative incidents which had led to the disaster must have endlessly preyed on his mind, eroding his own confidence in living. Thereafter, as if to efface these painful memories of his great love in its incipient decline or tortured human vicissitudes, he tried to perpetuate it as an ideal, surrounding himself to the end of his days with comforting memorials of his beloved, depicted as devoted, heroic, sublime, unflawed by the ugly problems which the passing of time and the twists of human nature had undoubtedly brought into his relationship with Antinous and into the fateful incident on the Nile.

But the underlying agony told. Hadrian was never to be the same again. The deterioration which had been occasionally detectable before the loss of Antinous now received a precipitating jolt, and for the remaining eight years of his life, Hadrian was gripped by increasing spasms of arbitrariness, savagery, desolate withdrawal and ultimately bleak despair. At first his impulse also to die was revealed only to his close acquaintance, but, with time, his contempt for life became obvious to all. He did not bother to conceal his physical decline. In an unprecedented gesture, the Emperor issued coins and perhaps even sculptures of himself, not as the fastidiously groomed and self-possessed *imperator* of earlier days, but with the dishevelled hair, shaven lips and chin of a grief-stricken mourner: and these coins, dating from years after the death of Antinous, show how long the public expression of his suffering persisted.[4] Another official work, the head now in the Chania Museum on Crete (fig. 35), which may have been sculpted within a twelvemonth of his loss, shows a face, below uncharacteristically tousled hair, distracted, careworn, despondent and suddenly aged.[5] By the time he returned to Rome, in 134, and the moment had come to issue another series of imperial busts, the artists who had produced the serene and majestic one of the *Pater Patriae* only six years before must have been dismayed at the features they now had to reproduce in marble: sunken, haggard, morose, listless and prematurely old: the signs, as Wegner suggests, not of the gradual decay of age, but of a sudden, devastating personal catastrophe.[6]

Whatever the strain, Hadrian did not break. His nature was too complex and supple for that. There were always in him – down to his final moments – qualities which enabled him to see coolly and even to use shrewdly the turbid currents which engulfed other parts of himself. Now, on the banks of the Nile in October 130, amid the tears, the lamentations and torn hair, he unhesitatingly took a series of remarkable decisions.

The first concerns the remains of Antinous. That the corpse was recovered seems certain. The normal Greco-Roman funeral practice would have been for a pyre to be built on the banks of the river, for the body to be placed on a bier and, amid the aroma of incense and myrrh, for it to be ceremonially burnt. The bones would be gathered into a sumptuous casket and taken to Rome for interment. It could therefore be surmised that Antinous' remains were likewise cremated, but for a phrase on the obelisk and items in his cult which strongly suggest something else.

In Egypt, the dead youth was immediately identified with Osiris, venerated as 'Osiris-Antinous the Holy'. Hadrian's epitaph on the obelisk describes him wholly as an Egyptian god, 'Osiris-Antinous the Just', interceding with the other, older, gods of Egypt and honoured in the same ways as them.[7] It tells us specifically that his body was accorded 'all the customs of the ritual of Osiris together with all his secret rites'. Herodotus earlier explained that for anyone drowned in the Nile, foreigner or native,

> . . . there is the strongest obligation . . . to have the body embalmed in the most elaborate manner and buried in a consecrated burial-place, so no one is allowed to touch it except the priests of the Nile – not even relatives and friends. The priests alone prepare it for burial with their own hands and place it in the tomb, as if it were more sacred than the body of a man.[8]

For anyone in Egypt who wished, with Osiris, to attain immortality, it was imperative that the natural body first be preserved from decay and only afterwards, by the ceremonies of opening the eyes and jaws, and by purifications and offerings, could the spirit be released into eternal life. Osiris himself was mummified and went to the grave on a boat-shaped bier and was sustained by the prayers and offerings of food and drink of countless generations of pilgrims at his shrine at Abydos.

This is probably how Antinous' body was treated too. It was, after all, the Egyptians who spontaneously and immediately consecrated him. And there is reason to believe[9] that the Emperor in the first days after the death gladly and gratefully welcomed this prior divinisation by Egypt and only later realised the scope for its extension into the Hellenic world. Accepting this automatic assimilation of his beloved to the great Osiris, Hadrian may well have permitted his beautiful body to be subject to those 'customs' and 'secret rites' mentioned explicitly in his own epitaph, repulsive as they must have seemed. Full mummification entailed the evisceration of the entrails and organs, the removal of the brain by an iron hook inserted through the nostrils, the soaking in natron for seventy days, the binding with bandages steeped in unguents, the enclosure in a splendid coffin, whilst the preserved organs were stored in Canopic jars. The whole process took three to four months and helps to explain a fact which has long perplexed historians – why Hadrian lingered so long in Egypt, apparently aimlessly, until at least well into the spring of 131.

At a splendid ceremony amid the palm groves, perhaps in the old temple of Rameses II, and arranged to coincide with the games of Antinous held on the site of his city-to-be in about March 131, the final ceremony of opening the eyes and jaws and of purification may have been performed in the presence of the Emperor, and the first offerings of meat, bread and drink offered to the new god, the first of half a million such offerings to come. Then, on a boat-shaped bier, the incorruptible, stuffed, swathed and blackened remains of the incomparably handsome ephebe were trundled away for burial. 'Thy body is of gold,' ran the hymn chanted to Osiris, 'thy head is of azure and emerald light encircleth thee . . .'[10]

Contemplating this final, narrowing moment, the Emperor, having had long months to brood on his loss and to devise a new ecumenical cult for Antinous, may have interposed. *He* had claims over Antinous, who may have died for him, stronger than those of the Egyptians. Having delivered over the body to the priests of the Nile for the violations necessary for spiritual perpetuation, was he to abandon it for ever to Egyptian soil? This may have been an ultimate separation which Hadrian found impossible to accept. The ceremonial boat on which the gilded coffin of Antinous lay may have been replaced, in the middle of 131, by a real one on which he was transported, over the seas, to his final resting place.

Before that, in the days following the death, Hadrian had taken two other decisions: to declare Antinous a god and to found a city on the spot in commemoration of him. Both of them may have been impulsive and certainly the implications of both were to be elaborated only over a longer period of time. The city was declared founded on 30 October 130 but was probably inaugurated only four years later when it was still not finished building or fully populated. The apotheosis was promulgated, perhaps by proclamation, throughout Egypt as the obelisk suggests at about the same time – late October or November 130 – but its full ramifications were worked out by Hadrian and his advisors only in the following winter or spring, and were actually implemented in Egypt and elsewhere over the next four or five years.

The deification of Antinous has scandalised Christian posterity from the days of the early Fathers to our own. Raising a mere boy, and one of dubious morals at that, to godhead was seized upon as exemplifying the profane bankruptcy of paganism, especially as the only cause was the Emperor's 'caprice', the 'moral enormity' of his sexual infatuation.[11] Pagan contemporaries seem not to have been outraged so much by the apotheosis as bewildered by its official origins and by the scale, extent and enthusiasm of the cult which followed it and which exceeded that for most divinised Emperors themselves.

In Greek mythology the raising of humans, like Herakles, to divine or semi-divine status as 'heroes' had not been uncommon, and in actual history a favourite like Hephaestion could be made a hero by Alexander and even a wife like Arsinoë could be made a deity by Ptolemy II Philadelphos. Other popular figures, like the thaumaturge Apollonius of Tyana, attained a standing akin to modern canonisation. Nevertheless it has been doubted if the total number of such consecrations in antiquity in any way outnumbered the plethora of sainthoods subsequently bestowed in the Christian epoch. But by imperial Roman times, partly under the influence of Christianity itself, the idea of immortality as the due of any deserving soul had been gaining ground and, particularly for innocent children and the prematurely dead, the certainty of such eternal life, or heroisation, had long been the consolation of grieving parents. Even the rational Cicero, consumed with sorrow at the death of his daughter Tullia and unable to face the prospect of her total extinction, proposed to erect a shrine to her in the belief that she had gained immortality.[12] In the same way, the father of the drowned Isidora of Hermopolis ceased lamenting and built a shrine to his beloved, who, he was convinced, had now become a nymph. Herodes Atticus, always imitating Hadrian, proclaimed his much mourned Polydeukes also to be a 'hero'.[13]

The linked belief that such heroes became stars as symbols of their immortality had never died since the days when Castor and Pollux and Perseus had reached such heavenly permanence. Another Hellenistic queen, Berenice, had been so immortalised amid the stars. The comet which appeared at the death of Julius Caesar was believed to be his soul arriving among the gods. In later days this destiny was less socially exclusive: a twenty-year-old youth from Amorgos, even a child of eight from Miletus, found their scintillating eternal abode in the skies too. It was therefore not too difficult for contemporaries to accept the elevation of Antinous, whether or not his death had been heroic, to the immortals or among the stars.

But public and formal divinisation accompanied by a cult was, in Roman times, quite another matter, far more exclusive, reserved strictly for the Emperor and his immediate family, and conferred by an official edict of the Senate. It was in this august company that Antinous reached Olympus: the last non-imperial mortal to be so grandiosely deified. Hadrian probably issued an edict of deification in Egypt and later sent letters announcing it to the Greek cities. He carefully avoided consulting the Senate in Rome, just as he had ignored that body in his own recent assumption of divinity in the east. He knew how not to offend western susceptibilities. For Antinous the full-scale apparatus of a cult was to be brought into being with temples and priests, images and altars, oracles and mysteries, games and a carefully developed myth. His was the only non-imperial head ever to appear on the coinage.

Why then did Hadrian exalt his beloved to a god? Was it no more than 'an extravagant imperial caprice', 'a folly', 'a whim', as some modern writers have dismissed it?[14] Did Hadrian even seriously believe that Antinous had attained immortality and divinity? Or was the whole apotheosis 'a sham', 'a sort of make-believe', an 'imposture'?[15]

As always with Hadrian we meet his idiosyncratic mix of overt showmanship and deep sincerity, of megalomania and intimacy, of public policy and personal passion. Whatever he decided, Egyptian tradition would have consecrated the drowned lad in any case. This the Emperor may have known before the death and must have been told by the priests of the Nile immediately after. Antinous therefore had gained a form of immortality in Egypt without Hadrian's intervention.

His distraught imagination and shrewd mind turned this modest local sanctification into a spectacular apotheosis of world-wide dimensions. There had always been in him that impulse to express on the grandest scale some of his most private feelings and now, in raising Antinous to a full god in Egypt and Greece, he was demonstrating to the world and perpetuating for all time what – in the exaggerated perspective of his grief – he probably considered an example of superhuman love, dedication and sorrow, on a par with that of Achilles for Patroclus or Alexander for Hephaestion. He had genuinely believed in his own role as Zeus on earth and in Egypt was called 'the glorious god'.[16] Why should he not promote to a similar status the cherished being who had died for him and was already acclaimed as a martyr of the Nile?

Such may have been Hadrian's personal motives. But, as he gradually began to recover his balance, political aims began to interweave with them. The Egyptians were already consecrating Antinous after a fashion. By promoting him officially to a full divinity and developing his cult all over the country was not Hadrian thereby tying the loyalties of these fractious folk closer to himself and to the Empire?

In the autumn and winter of 130–31, as he pondered on the apotheosis and received effusive condolences from his Greek subjects, he began to see in the shining new star of Antinous a bigger and more lustrous destiny. The Hellenic world had undergone a stupendous physical and spiritual revival and was agog with a heady sentiment of unity and confidence. Hadrian's own divinity had been a symbol and an active force in creating this renaissance and togetherness of Hellas. But Hadrian was an ageing Latin, Greek only by devotion. Antinous was a true son of Hellas, embodying the old classical ideal of the divinely beautiful ephebe, who had been seen all over the Greek world, and who had now, by self-immolation, attained immortality. His amazing resurrection from the Nile seemed like a prodigy come miraculously to endow the similar renaissance of Hellas with a divine consecration. Here then, heaven-sent, was a true Greek hero for the new 'age of gold'.

The Greeks had been longing for a symbol, linked to their great common history, round whom they could rally. Antinous was from Bithynion, a colony of Mantineia, a city in that Arcadia from which the earliest Greeks and the first Greek gods such as Hermes are said to have derived. Elaborating the Arcadian origins of this new divinity, identifying him with the earliest of the gods, creating Mantineia as the centre of his cult, Hadrian promoted his consecration in the Greek world as just such a historical symbol of panhellenic unity.

Hadrian had always tried to revive loyalties to the ancient divinities of Olympus. A fresh and youthful recruit to them, whose cult contained discreet and acceptable elements of the new and competing faiths from the east, could only rejuvenate the aged pantheon and kindle the ardour of its devotees.

The apotheosis as a whole in Egypt and in Greece satisfied not only Hadrian's emotional obligations and psychological extravagances, but fitted adroitly his long-term political, cultural and religious programme. The force which started as a spontaneous outburst of passionate gratitude was soon transmitting its energies into grand imperial strategy.

Does this personal and political use of the apotheosis and the later artistic construction of a myth support the view that Hadrian was really only acting out a make-believe, that, inside himself, he knew it was all a sham? Just as there are grounds for accepting that for a time he genuinely believed in his own divine status, so there is no reason to doubt his real faith in that of Antinous. If Hadrian was accused of composing the oracles for Antinous' shrines,[17] does this necessarily prove conscious fraud? There is every likelihood that he felt in some kind of mystic contact with his beloved beyond the grave. If, in the epitaph, he could recount that Antinous appeared after death in dreams to prescribe cures for the sick, why could he not likewise appear to Hadrian to dictate oracles for his petitioners? The Villa Adriana was filled with images of Antinous as a god, sometimes intruded into spaces which Hadrian obviously used privately. Could he have borne the hypocrisy of such endless confront-ations with his great love if the latter's divine trappings had been bogus? It is true that he eagerly accepted and over-generously rewarded any contributions to the myth of his Antinous, however feeble or fictitious. But this proves more the credulity of his faith, his gullible craving for consolation, than any complicity in deceit.

As the years wore on and general disillusion soured the Emperor's hopes and undermined his old confidence in the Eleusinian promises of eternity, he grew sceptical of his own survival after death. But perhaps even then warm memories and mystical assurance made him cling to that of the beloved. Certainly in the years after the death in the Nile, Hadrian seems to have been more convinced than any other man on earth of the divine destiny of his Antinous.

Hadrian also decided to build a spectacular memorial to his beloved adjacent to the spot where he had died: a magnificent new city, to bear his name, to display his countless images, for ever: a truly living memorial.

We can imagine the Emperor striding around the plain where mud-brick Hir-wer stood and with his retinue of architects and engineers sketching out the basic plan and disposition of the principal buildings of the city. The present settlement was to be razed to the ground except for the venerable temple of Rameses ii. The new one was to be grand in its scale, sumptuous in its style and full of images of Antinous so that no one could ever doubt in whose honour it was erected. The plan, district names, constitution and privileges of the city were to evolve more concretely in his mind as the months passed. But perhaps now, in issuing the founding edict on 30 October, he had already decided to hold memorial games in honour of Antinous in the true Greek funerary tradition, in the spring of 131. Certainly an announcement of such games must have gone out in the autumn of 130.[18] It did not matter that the city was still only a dream, that the participants would have to lodge in squalid Hir-wer or over the river at Hermopolis, that there was no stadium: there was the water of the Nile itself for rowing races and the plain for field events.

In creating this new city, Hadrian again did more than react grandiosely to a death. Behind the ostensible object of honouring Antinous, there lurked, as with the apotheosis, shrewd political purposes. Egypt was divided dangerously between the native and the Greek inhabitants. In its three administrative divisions were two Greek cities in the Delta (Alexandria and Naucratis) and one in Upper Egypt (Ptolemaïs), but in the central district, the Heptanomia, where Antinous had died, there was no official Greek centre for the Hellenes scattered in various towns to look to. Antinoopolis would become this much needed bastion of Greek organisation and culture of the Middle Nile, strengthening those forces of Hellenism which Hadrian had spent his life promoting. However, Hadrian, impressed with some of the virtues of Egyptian civilisation also, refused to exclude all local influences from his creation. The ancient architectural style would sometimes be used, even in the temple of the new god. The old cult of Bes and the temple of Rameses would not be eliminated. Above all, the Greek settlers would be allowed to marry Egyptian natives – an innovation unprecedented in the other racially divided Hellenistic settlements. By such means Hadrian hoped to woo the locals into the orbit of Greece, recognising the strengths of this ancient civilisation and people, fusing them harmoniously within the primacy of Hellas and under the aegis of the new god of both nations, Osiris-Antinous.

Once again an apparent arbitrary gesture of overwhelming personal grief turned out to be a clever application of Hadrian's main imperial policies. Antinous the god would serve his maker more powerfully than ever the youth had served his lover.

Hadrian stayed at Hermopolis until he could do no more and, always mindful of his official obligations, decided to resume his journey up the Nile at least as far as Thebes where extensive preparations had been made for him.

It could well have been at this time, while scanning the velvet black heavens and enormous stars of those latitudes, that he descried a star hitherto unknown to him. He consulted the astronomers and mythologers in his suite or from Hermopolis who assured him that this star, between the Eagle and the Zodiac in the Milky Way, was indeed a new one and must therefore be, according to ancient belief about heroes, the soul of Antinous blazing with eternal light. Hadrian exultantly accepted this explanation. And indeed the new star must have seemed to him and to many others the one visible, objective proof of the apotheosis, even if the carping, iconoclastic Alexandrians were to cackle that it was a fiction. The star of Antinous became a widely accepted article of his faith all over the east – it appears on the coins of Tarsos in the south-east corner of Asia Minor, on those of Bithynion and of Amisos up on the Black Sea, and of Nikopolis far to the west on the Greek mainland (figs 48a, 47b, d). It remains notably absent from those of Alexandria. It twinkles, still bearing his name and undimmed by modern scepticism, in the night sky to this day.

Hadrian and his courtiers, wary and perplexed at his vulnerability of mood, now made their way once again up the Nile, arriving at Thebes, city and burial place of ancient kings, on 18 November.

Apart from his official activities there, Hadrian was anxious to visit the colossi of Memnon, two seated statues, fifteen metres high, on the fringe of the desert, guarding the valley of the tombs. They were in fact of the Pharaoh Amenophis III but had become confused with the Ethiopian hero of the Trojan war, another Greco-Egyptian amalgamation which Hadrian encouraged. At dawn, as the sun's rays warmed its broken stones, one statue emitted a strange sound, 'like the twang of a broken harp string'.[19] To hear Memnon 'sing' had become a religious-touristic experience for visiting Greeks and Romans, 108 of whom left their names or impressions carved on the colossus. For Memnon to remain silent was a bad omen.

On 19 November Hadrian duly appeared at dawn and the colossus insolently and ominously made no sound. On the 20th it emitted one cry when Sabina and Balbilla arrived early and two more when Hadrian came an hour later. Next day, democratically, it sang for the entranced Balbilla alone. The whole sequence was recorded by her in archaistic epigrams carved on the god's left foot or ankle, the one concerning her private visit displaying the largest lettering of all. Apart from exhibiting Balbilla's own vanity and erudition, and her flattery of 'the amiable beauty'[20] of her mistress, the poems disclose, between the lines, the mood of Hadrian. He was conspicuously irritable, quick to take offence, vulnerable to adverse portents, anxious to be seen to be in favour with the gods, striking fear by his imperious demeanour. He was clearly still in turmoil after his loss.[21]

From Thebes, and no doubt a visit to the Valley of the Kings, the party may have gone upstream as far as Edfu and beyond even to Philae. From there, preoccupied with the honouring of the drowned, the Emperor may have ordered the rebuilding of the temple to the two drowned brothers Petesi and Paher, long ago sanctified, at Dendur in Nubia, a temple which ironically was later to be drowned itself.[22] On the other hand, papyrological evidence suggests that the Emperor turned northwards after Thebes, reaching the town of Oxyrhynchus on 29–30 November and entering Tebtynis on 1 December 130. He then may have spent some time in the Fayoum, visiting Arsinoë, and from there have made his way back to Alexandria by the end of the year.

In Alexandria the trail peters out, though a visit across to the Greek city of Cyrene in Libya is not to be entirely ruled out. When exactly he left Egypt is also a mystery. He was certainly gone by August 131, most probably during or after March of that year. What he was doing for three or four months has sometimes puzzled historians.

★   ★   ★

Hadrian was not wasting time. While waiting for the body of Antinous to emerge from the process of mummification and for the funeral games to be prepared, the Emperor, aided by the scholars, poets and mythologers of the Museion, was systematically working out and propagating the cult of the new god.

About this time he began to disseminate the deification and cult of Antinous in the Greek lands.[23] It is unlikely that he did anything so crude as to issue orders or edicts: they were not necessary. He probably sent letters, like the one referred to in a document from Athens, telling about the new hero and requesting divine honours, and, later, religious ceremonies and cult statues for him. Though a few Greeks may have been offended by the idea, most official bodies responded warmly, even more so when, from the summer of 131, Hadrian travelled among them actively promoting the cult by his example and donations.

At this stage Hadrian clearly presented Antinous, the boy whose Bithynian roots went back to Arcadia, as chiefly identified with the god Hermes, who was reputed to have been born in Kyllene in Arcadia. The city of Mantineia was probably now told it was to become the mainland centre of the new god. The deme names which Hadrian was devising for that district of Antinoopolis called 'Osiris-Antinous' demonstrate the links now being forged or fabricated between Antinous and the earliest Greeks: they were 'Bithynia', 'Kleitor', 'Parhasos' (the latter two mythical brothers of the founder of Mantineia and themselves founders of cities in Arcadia) and 'Hermes', one of the original gods of Arcadia and therefore of all Hellas. No doubt the learned mythologers helped Hadrian work out these abstruse and meaningful connections. Hermes also had his cult centre in Egypt (as Thoth) in the city from which Antinous went to his doom. Though the Greeks were to accept this identification of Antinous with Hermes, most, as we shall see, preferred to see in him the alternative also offered by Hadrian in the shape of Osiris-Dionysos, and it was in this latter form that his veneration spread most popularly, willingly supported by the Emperor.[24]

In Egypt some form of proclamation had already been issued: as the obelisk puts it, 'he, the king, has for all men founded a doctrine in the temple'. The Egyptians scarcely needed such official bidding to raise Antinous to full divinity. 'Temples are built to him and he is as a god honoured by the priests and prophets of Upper and Lower Egypt so many as they are . . .'[25] Temples, altars, priesthoods, oracles, inscriptions, games and statues were soon being set up for Antinous throughout the land. Apart from the cult centre of Antinoopolis, with its temple 'of good white stone', surrounded by sphinxes, statues and columns in a mixture of the Greek and Egyptian styles,[26] evidence of his cult has come to us from Hermopolis itself, from Alexandria, Oxyrhynchus, Tebytnis, Lykopolis and Luxor. Perhaps now in Alexandria, where a temple and priesthood had been established, may have begun the production of the first sculpted images of Antinous. The colossal head in sandstone from the Nile (now in Dresden (fig. 57)) may well date from this time and shows Antinous transformed by geometrical simplifications into the remote and inscrutable grandeur of an ancient Egyptian divinity. Other statues of him in the hieratic manner may also have been started. It is even claimed that his standard image as a Greek deity, exemplified in the fine head as Apollo (now in Berlin) was made in Egypt at this time, though this is improbable (fig. 25).[27] It is unlikely, however, that Hadrian waited until he reached Athens in the autumn of 131 before commissioning some Egyptian and *ad hoc* classical images of his beloved. The issue of coins had to wait until 134.

Round the story of the youth a myth began to be woven in which many writers had a hand. Antinous already had a star. Others discerned him on the moon as well, and the belief spread to Smyrna, Ancyra, Nikopolis and Hadrianotherai.[28] Some earlier heroes who had died sacrificially had had symbolic red flowers named after them: Adonis and Ajax among them. Now the resourceful local poet Pancrates pointed out to Hadrian a rosy lotus which usually grew in the swamps in the summer and declared, with a tenuous poetical fancy which Hadrian was gullible enough to applaud as 'original', that the flower had sprung from the swamp of blood which had gushed forth from the Libyan lion in the desert when it was slain.[29] He proposed to call the flower after Antinous, an ingenious idea which deftly knit together Hadrian's heroics on the lion hunt and Antinous' in the Nile. The rosy lotus, a bloom symbolising immortality and the mystic marriage of Isis and Osiris, thus became the flower of Antinous, shown on some of his coins, paintings and sculptures. The wreath of his flower, a symbol of the drowned, and called the *Antinoeios*, was awarded at his games.

Pancrates was duly commissioned by Hadrian to write a Homeric epic on the subject of the lion hunt and the flower. Athenaeus, who wrote down the story in 192 AD, called it 'not inelegant', faint praise in which he has been followed by some modern critics who regard its surviving hyperboles, preciosities and conventions as stale, static and turgid, though some others find in it, surprisingly, force and imagination.[30] Hadrian professed to do so too, and rewarded Pancrates with a life fellowship at the Museion.

Other writers rushed in to celebrate Antinous. Numenios of Herakleia, a rhetor, composed a consolation which was probably declaimed to the mourning Emperor. Mesomedes, a freedman from Crete and a friend of Hadrian, well known for his odes set to the lyre, composed a special hymn of praise to Antinous. This may well have been performed at the inaugural games of Antinous in 131 (for such literary encomia became part of his festivals), and reflections of it found their way into the citharodic hymn sung on Cyprus somewhat later. Hadrian, like the later Emperor Caracalla, was deeply impressed by Mesomedes' art and assigned him an exceptionally handsome pension at the Museion as well. This was too much for his frugal imperial successor Antoninus Pius, who reduced the pension with the unaesthetic comment 'that there was nothing meaner, nor more unfeeling than the man who nibbled away at the revenues of the state without giving any service in return.'[31] Caracalla made posthumous amends by erecting a cenotaph to the poet.

Meantime, too, Hadrian must have been gradually devising that list of ten phyles and fifty demes in which Antinoopolis was later to be subdivided on the pattern of the Athens of Cleisthenes.[32] The names of the ten phyles were of those dear or important to Hadrian who had attained some form of divinity: Athena; his imperial predecessors, Augustus, Nerva and Trajan; Matidia and Sabina; himself and his family (Aelius); his recently dead and probably consecrated sister, Paulina; and Osiris-Antinous alongside them. Into the deme-names were blended all the themes which most mattered to him: allusions to Athens and its history; to the policies of peace and security of his predecessors and mentors; to the great gods of Egypt; to the Zeus with whom he was identified and to other unifying deities of Greece; and, above all, to the goddesses, fruitfulness and experience of redeeming Eleusis. It was in this mental matrix of the Emperor that the divinity of Antinous had its roots.

So extravagant had been Hadrian's response to Antinous' death that the Alexandrians began to make invidious comparisons with the meagre honours he had bestowed on Paulina, no more than some form of local consecration in association with Isis and a set of funeral games. Hadrian must have been aching to leave a place on which he had conferred so much and from which he had received so little.

By late February or early March, the remains of Antinous must have been ready and, it is fair to conjecture (there is no proof), the Emperor probably travelled back to Antinoopolis to attend the ceremony in which the coffin-case in the shape of Osiris, standing on its clumsy wedge feet, was purified and given the offerings by which the spirit within could be released to eternal life. The first annual games were celebrated at the same time and the Emperor probably presided as agonothete.

Then, after returning downstream, in the late spring of 131, Hadrian finally set sail from Alexandria in the galley shown on coins, heading first to Syria and Judea and thence back to the consolations of Hellas. His mind and his imagination were full of his mission for Antinous and for the unification of all the Greeks.

THE SECRET OF THE TOMB

What happened to the mortal remains of Antinous? This simple question immediately involves us in one of the most fascinating of his many mysteries.

The obvious place for them to have been deposited was Antinoopolis itself and for nearly two thousand years this was presumed. Strangely enough, however, there is little evidence of a tomb of his there. The obelisk, though it describes the temple and the cult in the city never mentions a grave in Egypt. Clement of Alexandria does refer to 'a tomb of the boy beloved' but seems to separate it from his city.[1] The only literary evidence comes from the highly unreliable Epiphanios, writing about 370 AD, who tells us that Antinous, lying on a pleasure boat, was buried by Hadrian in his city.[2] From this, some have argued that the actual sarcophagus was in the shape of a boat. It is, however, much more likely that Epiphanios is confusedly referring to the processional boat of Osiris on which the coffin was borne to the grave or, more likely still, to that in which the image or oracle of Osiris-Antinous was carried in procession by his priests.

No archaeological confirmation of such a tomb has been unearthed. In 1798, Jomard, the French surveyor, found the low ruins of a massive building thirty-four metres square, surrounded by an arcade, with doors at the angles, and which terminated the northern main street of Antinoopolis, and suggested tentatively that this might have been the tomb. But by the time that the next archaeologist, the fanciful Gayet, started his capricious excavations a hundred years later all traces of these ruins had disappeared. Dietrichson confused these remains with those of the newly found temple of Rameses II near the Nile which he thought was the site of the burial (fig. 34). Gayet, who falsely claimed to have discovered the temple himself, also unhesitatingly declared it to have been used as Antinous' funerary chapel if not his actual tomb – though, characteristically, he produced no evidence.[3] Later scholars have easily dismissed his theories.[4] Nevertheless, some shrine containing relics if not the body of Antinous must have existed in Antinoopolis, as is suggested by the miracles he is said to have wrought there and by the half a million jars containing the offerings of pilgrims which Gayet claimed to have discovered filling a whole valley nearby.[5]

However, if, as the obelisk indicates, the funerary rites followed ancient pharaonic practice, Antinous would not have been interred in the city at all. As a god, his sumptuous coffin would have been buried in a vault cut deep into the rock of the mountains, perhaps, according to the precedent of Osiris, even on the west bank of the river. Similar vaults with shafts fifteen metres deep were found by Gayet himself in the mountains near the city. They led him to speculate that Antinous was buried

> . . . in some lost corner of the mountains; and that his body, embalmed with care, could one day be rendered back to us. What a revelation for the scholarly world would be this reappearance of a face so familiar! What a surprise, if it was found little to resemble the type consecrated by Greek statuary, and gave the denial to the artist who bequeathed us the image of the beautiful ephebe of effeminate traits and with a brow crowned with vine leaves![6]

This picture of the swathed body of the young god lying in its staring coffin, inviolate in its dark airless vault and still awaiting discovery, has haunted modern historians and novelists.

Such alluring fantasies and the traditional assumptions about the burial were challenged in 1896 when Erman produced the first thorough translation of the difficult hieroglyphs of the obelisk standing on the Pincio in Rome. On the fourth side, the German scholar deciphered the words: 'Antinous, who is here, and who rests in this place which is in the border-fields of the lady of . . . Rome'.[7] This passage then turned by deliberate geographical contrast to describe the cult of the god 'in the holy places of Egypt'. Now the phrase 'who is here' is a standard euphemism for 'deceased', and 'who rests in this place' is one for 'is buried' or 'entombed'. The precise translation about 'the lady of . . . Rome' eluded Erman and it seemed that here the hieroglyphs contained a clumsy circumlocution for a specific Latin or Greek term.

Up to this revelation, it had always been assumed that the obelisk had stood near the tomb in Antinoopolis and had been transported to Rome by an Egyptophile Emperor, such as Septimius Severus. Some historians now hastened to explain that the newly translated phrase did not contradict that view. After all, 'the border-fields of . . . Rome', they contended, was but a metaphor for the frontiers of the Empire of which Egypt was one and therefore perfectly consistent with the obelisk's alleged origins in Antinoopolis. However, virtually all the modern Egyptologists who have studied the text are firm in asserting that 'border-fields' denotes a delimited country domain, and that 'Rome' is the specific city, not to be construed as the general 'Empire'. Moreover, both the language and the style of script on the obelisk are too unconventional, faulty and peculiar to have been composed authentically in Egypt itself: they are the work of scholars and craftsmen in Rome simulating Egyptian phraseology and graphology. Admitting these Italian origins of the obelisk, some writers still maintain that it must have been part only of a cenotaph, an empty tomb serving as a memorial in Rome. The real grave was in Antinoopolis.[8] However, the words 'who rests in this place' are explicit and cannot be so easily argued away. The obelisk seems to be telling us clearly that Antinous is definitely buried where it was erected originally, on the outskirts of Rome.

Did Hadrian, then, send the body back to Rome? Given the way in which in his last years he obsessively surrounded himself with portraits of Antinous, it is quite credible that in his shattered grief of 130–31, he could not bear to be parted finally from all that was mortal of his beloved. Perhaps after his visit to the opened tourist-ridden tombs in the Valley of the Kings he doubted the security even of a secret mountain vault in Egypt for the precious remains. It is, however, difficult to reconcile this transfer with Egyptian funerary beliefs, Antinous' posthumous rites and veneration as Osiris in Egypt and the pilgrimages and offerings to him in his city there. It is just possible that Hadrian brought to Rome only the Canopic jars containing the heart and other organs of the youth, leaving the body in its distant mountain tomb.[9] Or did he leave some such relics for the Egyptians, keeping the embalmed corpse for himself? The claim of the obelisk to guard the body seems more cogent and authentic than Epiphanios' confused and belated testimony about a boat and a tomb in Antinoopolis.

If it could be shown exactly where the obelisk stood in antiquity the issue might be resolved: indeed the remains of Antinous might even yet be found.

Its history was first properly traced by the German topographer Hülsen in 1896.[10] The Popes had been given it by the Barberini princes in 1770, in the courtyard of whose palazzo it had lain in pieces since having been acquired from the vineyard of the Saccocci family in 1633. This was just outside the walls, in the south-eastern corner of Rome. There the brothers Saccocci proudly claimed to have re-erected the obelisk in 1570 to perpetuate the memory of 'this circus of the sun' on the ruined walls of which their commemorative tablet was placed. Various earlier maps, drawings and topographical accounts record the fallen and broken obelisk in that area, again in connection with the ruins of a circus, the earliest being that of Antonio di San Gallo in 1525 who saw it in 'a naval circus'. As no archaeological proof of the existence of such a circus existed before 1922, Hülsen naturally concentrated on the relation of the fallen obelisk to the nearby road, the Via Labicana, not far from the Porta Maggiore. As burials were banned within the sacred precinct of Rome (the *pomerium*), tombs were normally placed alongside such suburban highways. Here, then, concluded Hülsen, south of the Via Labicana, was the original site of the obelisk and of a grand mortuary edifice to Antinous, with perhaps a tomb-chamber below in the tufa of the hill. Indeed in 1917, after a sumptuously decorated basilica fourteen metres underground had been discovered nearby, beneath the Rome–Naples railway, he suggested that its desecrated and empty chambers might be the long lost sepulchre of Antinous.[11] It is, however, now accepted that this building is of the first century. In view of the absence of any other trace of a monument to Antinous in this area, other sites, even more implausible (including Hadrian's mausoleum and the Temple of Roma) have been proposed. Nevertheless there remain some archaeologists who are satisfied that the monument to Antinous, containing the obelisk and perhaps his actual body, was constructed on the south side of the Via Labicana.[12]

Such a proposition may appeal to archaeologists, but it can scarcely satisfy those who seriously consider Hadrian's relationship to Antinous. The Osiris-Antinous god of Egypt, the Dionysos-Hermes deity of Greece, the focus of a cult over half the Empire, the greatest love of the Emperor's life – lying alongside the suburban clutter and plebeian memorials of one of Rome's less well-known highways? Is this compatible with Hadrian's sense of scale, self-respect and taste, his megalomaniac devotion to his divinised beloved? The answer is no, for we can be sure that he would want those hallowed remains – if indeed they were in Italy – to be as near him as possible, honoured in a splendour commensurate with the divine dignity which Antinous had attained in death and placed in an ambience redolent of the happiness they had enjoyed together in life.

We must return to the enigma of the obelisk for more convincing solutions.

In recent years it has been indubitably shown that a circus did exist in antiquity south of the Via Labicana, probably built in about 200–220 AD by the Emperor Elagabalus or a predecessor.[13] It is now clear that the Renaissance writers and cartographers and the brothers Saccocci were right in their statements that the obelisk in their day lay within the walls of this circus and had indeed, in Roman times, stood on its central spina, the traditional place for displaying plundered obelisks since the age of Augustus, where it still remained in pieces in 1570. The hypothesis of its decorating a tomb *outside* the circus and between it and the Via Labicana, always unsupported by archaeological and documentary evidence and psychologically unconvincing, can therefore be abandoned. Like the other obelisks decorating circuses, this one had been brought from another original site. And where was that?

Very recently a minute study of the crucial phrase on the obelisk from actual photographs of the inscription has rendered more precise Erman's original translation from a defective text. The words 'border-fields' turn out to be (as was originally proposed by Müller in 1898) 'country estate', and the vague circumlocution rendered as 'our lady of . . . Rome', is a faulty reading of the title of the Emperor: *imperator*. As reconstructed, the whole phrase now runs: 'O, Antinous! this deceased one, who rests in this tomb in the country estate of the Emperor of Rome'.[14]

This indication that the obelisk and the tomb of Antinous were located in the Villa Adriana at Tibur is neither novel nor surprising. Here, if anywhere, was possible that combination of public splendour and private significance, of official tribute and intimate association, which Hadrian would have chosen for the loved-one become god.

Over the centuries, considerable quantities of Egyptian sculpture and mosaics have been excavated and dispersed from the villa. Some are genuine ancient sculptures of Osiris and Isis and other gods, while many others are Hadrianic creations in the older idiom. At least eight Egyptian-style sculptures of Antinous himself, rendered chiefly as a pharaoh-god, wearing the calantica and uraeus, have come from the villa, two as colossal Telamones supporting the lintel over an entrance. Whether some of these Egyptianising works formed a coherent ensemble cannot now be known: it is tempting to think that they did. Even Canopic jars were discovered long ago.[15] Their precise finding-place and contents, if any, are not recorded; but could they have possibly once held the precious organs of the beloved?

If some or all of these dispersed fragments had once been part of a funeral monument at the villa, that would have been most likely to have been located in that area known as the Canopus (fig. 37). It consisted of a long canal (120 by 19 metres) with a curved loggia at one end and, at the other, a temple made up of an exedra and an amazing scalloped semi-dome, enlivened with baroque effects of lighting and ingenious use of water. Though the dating of this construction is puzzling and controversial, it must logically have been finished and decorated after Hadrian's visit to Egypt.[16] It clearly symbolises the Nile with Alexandria or Canopus represented at its mouth. Huge figures of the Nile and Tiber, and a great fountain in the shape of a crocodile, have recently been found in the canal. The extraordinary semi-domed structure at the end is usually called the Serapeum, but no statue of Serapis has ever been found there or anywhere else in the villa.[17] It has more recently been suggested that the whole area was Hadrian's posthumous monument to Osiris-Antinous and the Nile and that within the semi-dome, at the far end of the dark grotto-like tunnel, theatrically lit by concealed apertures, stood a colossus not of Serapis but of Osiris-Antinous himself.[18]

Excavations began here in 1952. They unearthed, apparently violently flung into the canal, a group of sculptures from a position on its side which, if the canal were symbolic of the Middle and Lower Nile, would roughly have corresponded with the position of Antinoopolis on its east bank. There stood two colossal Sileni bearing baskets of fruit and four caryatids, Roman copies of those on the south side of the Erechtheion on the Acropolis of Athens (fig. 38).[19] Carefully spaced, they all seemed to have borne a stone canopy as entrance to some monumental composition which extended back from the canal into an area which has not yet been excavated.

Now here, it has been claimed, could well have been the original home of the obelisk and the site of Antinous' tomb.[20] As these figures seem to have been vigorously hurled into the canal not long after its creation, it has been suggested that the tomb of Antinous was deliberately destroyed by Hadrian's successor Antoninus Pius as part of his efforts to stamp out pederasty. This is hardly credible.[21] More likely, the tomb was destroyed and the obelisk removed by Elagabalus to decorate the spina of his private circus in the new palace at Rome.

But what have these Sileni and caryatids to do in this Egyptian and Nilotic setting? What connection can they have with Antinous? Both Sileni and these Greek maidens had long been used to bear canopies over graves: their combined presence thus strongly indicates a sepulchre. Moreover, Silenus was the tutor of Dionysos whose form Antinous most frequently took in Greece, and similar Sileni are found on the Dionysian screen of Athens where Antinous is also said to appear and on coins which are specifically devoted to him. Silenus in Egypt was also approximated to Bes, and this immediately establishes another connection with the place on the Nile where Antinous died. The caryatids reinforce this because, representing Athens, they symbolise not only the happiness of Hadrian and Antinous there but the link of Athens to the death in the Nile, in the homonymous names Besa and Bes. In addition these formidable maidens were in mythology the daughters of King Erechtheios, one of whom, Chthonia, sacrificed her life to deliver her father from a peril predicted by an oracle – a clear parallel with the end of Antinous.

These fragments, then, though they prove nothing, are by no means meaningless or alien as possible elements of a vast funeral monument in a mixed Greco-Egyptian style (like the temple in Antinoopolis) dedicated to Osiris-Dionysos-Antinous, the sacrificial god. An excavation of the whole site has been urged and this – if it found the destroyed tomb – could at long last provide a final answer to the entire puzzling problem. Who knows what the earth of Tivoli may yet have to tell us of Hadrian and Antinous?

Until further secrets – if any – are revealed, it is wise to be cautious in conclusion. It is possible that Antinous was mummified and not cremated. It is unlikely that he was interred inside Antinoopolis. His body may well still rest, encased in the gilded form of Osiris, in some undiscovered mountain vault or long ago have been torn to pieces by the axes and prying fingers of tomb-robbers. In this case, the edifice near Rome was either an empty cenotaph or guarded some easily transportable relics only. There is, however, a greater probability that the obelisk marks, as it says, a definite tomb; and Antinous' last resting place can most credibly be postulated in the lavish, eclectic grandeur of Hadrian's villa.

The strange twists of this story engender a tantalising suspicion that others are yet to be encountered . . .

XIII

THE BITTER END
OF HADRIAN, 131–8

It was back to the sympathetic lands of Greece that Hadrian now hastened. The tragic role he was publicly playing, accompanied by inner feelings of guilt and also of relief at the transmutation of a decaying affair into a sublime devotion, inspired in him a final burst of creative activity before the clouds of war, deranging sickness and bloody dissension gathered to cloud the sunset of his reign. He would now do what even Pericles and Alexander had failed to accomplish: realise the ancient ideal of panhellenic unity of which his new god Antinous would for ever be a symbol.

The precise route of Hadrian's last peregrination in peacetime is lost to us. We do not even know if Sabina was still with him. He seems to have landed in Syria in the spring of 131 and may fleetingly have visited Judea. It may indeed have been now rather than in the previous year, acting under the strain of Antinous' death which had recharged the fervour of his philhellenism, that he took the fateful decision to build the temple of Jupiter on the site of that of the barbaric Jehovah. From that alien and now seething country, he made his way rapidly up to the more congenial provinces of Asia Minor. Possibly he visited some cities in southern Anatolia before pushing north-eastwards along the frontier lands of Cappadocia.

This was his fourth visit to Asia Minor. But none of the fervour and enthusiasm with which he had been greeted in the years before had yet abated. Indeed, the prosperous cities, perhaps well aware of the great climax to which this tour was a prologue, ecstatically showered on the Olympian deity among them yet more dedications, altars, statues, temples and fulsome titles. His presence and propaganda, reconciling old inter-city differences, stirred again proud and exultant sentiments of being Greek. And the beautiful youth, himself from the region, now resurrected as the hero-god Antinous, whose cult the Emperor everywhere promoted, seemed a miraculous embodiment of this transcendent spirit of renewal, this resurgent sense of an ancestry, history and culture common to all the Hellenes. Out of gratitude to Hadrian, and out of buoyant self-consciousness, they readily accepted the new god as their own.

161

After visiting the frontier garrisons, Hadrian reached one of the easternmost outposts of Greek civilisation, Trapezus on the Black Sea, below the brooding Caucasus. The populace, which in the distant times of the ancient hero Xenophon had been grudging towards Greek religion, was now swept up in the universal enthusiasm for its latest incarnation. Spontaneously, they commissioned a sculpture of the Emperor placed on a commanding site and pointing out to sea. No doubt financed by him, they began to erect a handsome temple dedicated to Hermes, almost certainly to Antinous as Hermes,[1] and adorned it with more statues. Hadrian must have left well pleased at these monuments to civilised ardour arising on the very borders of oriental barbarism.

Some years later, however, he heard from his friend Arrian that the locals' aspirations to classical culture had outrun their primitive skills. The statues both of Hadrian and of Hermes (Antinous) were such vile travesties that Arrian begged the Emperor to send out replacements worthy of their subjects and their respective sites. Even at its remotest extremity Hellenic civilisation was not to be tainted by the barbarism it confronted.

Travelling eastwards along the Euxine coast via Amisos, Hadrian most probably stopped at the town of Bithynion.[2] This was his first return to the birthplace of Antinous since their meeting. It is easy to imagine the extravagant reaction of the publicly grieving, somewhat posturing lover to this hallowed spot. No doubt the excited inhabitants, proudly erecting statues to 'the new god Antinous'[3] and to the Olympian Emperor, already knew that their town was to become one of the chief centres of the new cult. While in their midst, Hadrian and his experts probably elaborated on the rites to be instituted and sketched out plans for an ambitious sanctuary for himself and his beloved with a monumental gateway and an octostyle temple to be erected in crisp red limestone.

Perhaps promising to return to consecrate the finished shrine in a few years' time, the Emperor made his way in the autumn sunshine over land and sea to his beloved Athens.

The third winter spent in Athens brought to a climax Hadrian's whole policy for Greece and launched the cult of Antinous in the motherland.

He arrived in September–October of 131, in time to participate once more in the revitalising mysteries of Eleusis, and sought thereafter to use the magnetic force of those immemorial rites to enhance the cohesiveness of his panhellenic structures and the spiritual authenticity and community of his new cult.

After so many centuries of vain aspiration, the vast gleaming temple of Olympian Zeus at long last stood complete: a towering witness to the revival of the fortunes and resources of Greece (fig. 22). In a final spectacular ceremony, attended by representatives of the entire Greek world, the great edifice was solemnly consecrated. Snubbing the local sophist, Herodes Atticus, Hadrian chose his old companion, Polemo from Smyrna, to pronounce the oration. He 'delivered a long and wondrous discourse from the base of the temple', which, with typical modesty, he 'declared was not without divine impulse'.[4]

The human crowd in the sanctuary must have jostled against the one of stone. For already, stirred by the passage of the living *Olympios* among them, the cities of Greece had seized upon this holy place as the centre of their common aspirations and identity. As tokens of this, they had begun to deluge the precinct with statues. Beneath the gargantuan Corinthian columns stood bronze images personifying the ancient Greek colonies and all the way round the half-mile perimeter wall were ranged countless marble images of Hadrian. Four large statues of him – two in the Egyptian style and stone and perhaps from Greek cities there – stood near the entrance. Athens, not to be outdone, had erected a colossus of the Emperor near his altar behind the temple. The whole Greek world was coming together in religious harmony and exultation around its ancient supreme god and his modern representative.

In this euphoric atmosphere, Hadrian decided to go further and to realise the aims of Isocrates and Pericles which Plutarch had recently propagated – to bring each of the scattered city-states of Greece within a political and cultural union based on Athens. Already in 125 he had contemplated such a confederation by using one of the old existing leagues. Now, in 131–2, he launched something totally new: the Panhellenion.

Though it kept close religious ties with the Olympeion, the new organisation was provided with a substantial sanctuary of its own immediately adjacent, where perhaps the centripetal cult of Hadrian could decently be given more prominence. It consisted of an elected President and a Council of delegates from each genuinely Greek city or colony. An annual celebration and a more important four-yearly festival were started, called the Panhellenia. From the beginning, Greek communities all over the world vied with each other to join. It seems, however, that Alexandria and Antioch, whose allegiance to Hadrian's cultural mission had always been suspect, stood apart.[5] Elsewhere, the leading magistrates of the member cities eagerly competed for the honour of being elected to the Council or the Presidency. The primacy of Athens was recognised, and all the cities contributed regular donations to the shrine of Demeter at Eleusis which Hadrian thereby made the central mystic cult of all Hellas.

Of course the Panhellenion did not amount to self-government for the Greeks. No Roman Emperor, however philhellene, could contemplate that, and the Greeks themselves, flourishing so markedly under the imperial aegis, no longer demanded it. The Union remained loyal and subordinate to the Emperor and through him to the whole polity of Rome. Much of its time was spent on trivia: checking credentials, organising festivals, superintending the sanctuaries. But Hadrian and his two successors regarded it very highly and it did possess significant religious, cultural and even political functions.[6] It fostered Greek self-consciousness, promoted the ancient gods, diminished the immemorial feuding between the cities and adjudicated between them, represented the whole Greek world in its embassies to Rome, advised the Emperor and recruited able men to the imperial administration and the Senate.

Honoured and active, it continued to flourish as long as traditional city-life itself, until the troubled times of the late third century.[7] It was one of the steps by which the centre of the Empire moved from the increasingly moribund and endangered Rome to the vital and enduring east. The Panhellenion really only got going after the election of 134 and the completion of its sanctuary in 137, too late for the doomed and preoccupied Hadrian to fashion it. Nevertheless the ebullient Greeks in gratitude jubilantly added another to his many titles: that of *Panhellenios*. It had taken an Emperor of Rome to realise, in however limited a form, the ancient Greek dream of unity at the very end of the pagan epoch, before the rise of another more potent form of unity in the shape of the Christian Empire of Byzantium.

While bringing the peoples of Hellas together Hadrian did the same for their gods. He decided to erect an imposing temple to all the gods of Greece, thereby stressing their common links and origins and the power and centrality of Zeus. We do not know if Antinous qualified for a niche within the enormous building, larger than the Parthenon itself. On its walls the Emperor, imitating Augustus again, proudly had inscribed his innumerable benefactions to all the cities of Greece and even to the barbarian nations.

After yet more munificent gifts to Athens, the visit came to an end in the spring of 132 with Hadrian, clad in Greek costume, presiding 'brilliantly' (as Dio admits) in the ancient theatre below the Acropolis at the great festival of Dionysos.[8] Boasting thirteen statues of Hadrian, the theatre had been rearranged to provide a new imperial box and seats newly inscribed for the priests of Demeter and Eleusis, of Hadrian, of the Olympeion and of Antinous. It was a microcosm of the spiritual world Hadrian had created around himself. Nearby, a large altar was to rise bearing reliefs of the Athenian and Eleusinian deities, of Antinous and Dionysos as a memorial of this final ceremony of Hadrian's life in his cherished city.

Meanwhile the citizens had complimented the Emperor by adding the deme of Antinous to the phyle bearing Hadrian's name. Now, in the Stoa Basileios in the heart of the city, they erected yet another statue of Hadrian significantly next to that of Zeus the Bountiful. It belongs to a series of at least seventeen such statues in armour issued about this time, the decoration of which eloquently sums up Hadrian's imperial policy.[9] On the Emperor's cuirass, flanked by attributes and Victories, appears the ancient image of Athena (the Palladion) standing upon the recumbent wolf of Rome suckling Romulus and Remus. Nowhere is more succinctly proclaimed Hadrian's belief that the material power of Rome existed to sustain the superior civilisation of Greece. Among other details recalling Hadrian's attributes, the sculptors introduced a notable variant on the head of the Medusa which had traditionally adorned the uniform's fringe of lappets. Instead of the feminine profile seen on the similar statue at Olympia or that of an Alexander-like Hermes shown on the one at Corinth,[10] here in Athens, above the necklace of snakes, appear the unmistakable features of Antinous (fig. 40). In profile and hair-style with a fillet, it is almost identical with the idealised statue of him as an ephebe later to be raised at Olympia (fig. 26).[11] By such subtle means and in the midst of their bustling city, the Athenians paid their special tribute to the realisation of a noble ideal and to the passing of a great love.

All the time Hadrian had busily been promoting the cause of his new panhellenic deity. If the Emperor had been in South Anatolia in 131, his own impact may account for the major cult of Antinous which soon developed at Tarsos.[12] Perhaps in the temple established there was one of the oracles with which the Greeks said Hadrian occupied himself. At Trapezus, he no doubt founded the temple and priesthood of his beloved as Hermes. In Bithynion he had done the same, but adding the regular celebration of mysteries and of commemorative games.

Once back on the mainland of Greece, Hadrian carefully planted the new cult in each of the venerable sanctuaries of Hellas. In Athens, for the 16–18-year-old ephebes in their gymnasium, he established an annual festival, the *Antinoeia*, held each October. At Eleusis, also exclusively for the ephebes, a similar annual festival was set up, so that for at least a century and a half afterwards, Antinous was the only individual to be honoured each year in the city-state by two such separate celebrations, reflecting his own interests in life.[13] An ephebe was allowed to be president (agonothete) of the games and priest of Antinous: another notable glorification of youth. In the city, Hadrian encouraged the Dionysian artists (artists, poets and musicians connected with the theatre), who had formed a mystic synod after their initiation at Eleusis, to set up their own cult of Antinous-Dionysos, with a priest, doubtless a chapel and sacred image, and a seat in the theatre reserved for the 'priest of Antinous Choreios' (fig. 39).[14] On the great altar or memorial near the theatre, it is claimed, a stocky Antinous is possibly portrayed being presented by Demeter and Persephone to the enthroned Dionysos.[15] The erection of a statue of the youth as Dionysos Zagreus in the outer sanctuary of Eleusis itself and his regular ephebic festival imply the starting of a cult to him there, linked in some way to that of Demeter.

At this time too Hadrian must have approved a basic model of the new god for the Greek sculptors to reproduce and distribute to cities far and wide. At Delphi, the council seems to have commissioned one of the earliest life-size sculptures of Antinous and perhaps erected a small temple for his cult. At the ancient panhellenic sanctuary of Olympia another statue, very similar to that of Delphi, was either ordered locally or presented by the Emperor, while a recumbent figure of Antinous as the river god Alpheios was sculpted there for the festival games at which the new god was commemorated in 133.[16]

There can be little doubt that Hadrian himself travelled down to the Peloponnese and visited again the walled city of Mantineia. Here, to crown his earlier benefactions, the Emperor founded a temple and priesthood to Antinous who became 'the local god'.[17] Annual mysteries and initiations were to be celebrated and, every four years, major games, perhaps given in the specially enlarged stadium outside the walls. A chapel devoted to Antinous, adorned with his sculptures, fine stones and paintings to him as Dionysos, all of which impressed the critical Pausanias, was begun in the gymnasium.[18] At nearby Argos, other games were established. On the journey, Hadrian probably paused at Corinth where another temple, priesthood and sacred images of the beloved as Hermes and Dionysos were soon to appear.

By the time Hadrian left Athens in the spring of 132 on a high tide of political, religious and cultural exaltation, the cult of Antinous had been judiciously planted in fertile soil from which, nurtured in such a sympathetic climate, it would rapidly grow and spread of its own accord.

Where exactly Hadrian was between the spring of 132 and that of 136 we cannot tell. We only know that he was at Rome, writing a letter, on 5 May 134. Some historians have him touring the eastern Mediterranean yet again, then going on to the Jewish war and finally settling in Rome in 134, but others send him there in 132 and despatch him to Palestine from mid-134 to late 135 or early the following year. The latter chronology is marginally the more plausible. In Rome, Hadrian completed his great legal codification and his equally monumental and more enduring mausoleum on the banks of the Tiber, another structure in which can be seen his debt to Augustus, his megalomania and his histrionic posturings with death.

From such activities he was called away to the war in Judea. After Hadrian's provocations, the Jews, surreptitiously gathering weapons, had lain low until the Emperor was safely away and then, in 132, rose furiously in open revolt supported by agitations in Jewish communities elsewhere. Led by Simon Bar-Kochba and fanatical priests, they seized Jerusalem which they held for three years and fought a savage guerrilla war, avoiding set battles. Nonplussed by these tactics, the Roman legions suffered heavy losses – the XXII Legion Deiotariana was wiped out. Only when Hadrian anxiously brought Julius Severus from Britain to take command did the Romans slowly begin to gain control, but, even so, progress was slow and the slaughter and devastation hideous.

Hadrian, the streak of ruthlessness in his nature coming ever more to the fore as he aged, was determined to settle the Jewish problem once and for all, a problem which had so long threatened material order and classical culture in the east. With the cause of the latest Greek god, Antinous, in his heart, he had even less time for the exclusive and jealous one of the Hebrews. Leaving Rome in the middle of 134 – if we accept one chronology – he probably took part in the siege of Bettir in 135. On the loss of that stronghold, the Jewish cause collapsed. Already over half a million of them had died in the field and a thousand towns and villages had been destroyed. Now Hadrian exacted a terrible revenge on the living; the leaders were cruelly executed, prisoners were sold off cheaply in hordes to miserable slavery, the edicts against circumcision were rigorously enforced. Above all, the Jews were completely excluded from their sacred city of Jerusalem except for one humiliating day in a year. Hadrian vigorously recommenced the building of *Aelia Capitolina*. In the obliteration of the city of Jehovah, some of the holy places of Judaism and of Christianity were deliberately desecrated. Judea, henceforth known as the province of Palaestina, lost its status as the Jewish homeland; it was as if its ancient religion and culture had never existed.

The Jews were never to regain the position they had held in Palestine in 130 until our own times and all hopes of reconciliation between them and the Christians were now terminated. The consequences of Hadrian's precipitate actions in 130–31 have therefore been incalculable for mankind. The whole appalling episode – as was to be seen again soon in Rome itself – seems to have derived from the ageing Emperor's impulsive intolerance of opposition, especially to his obsessive cultural mission. The impact of the death of Antinous and the conviction of the ideals he had come to represent only hardened Hadrian's attitudes. To the Jews he was henceforth 'Hadrian the wicked' and introduced by the imprecation, 'may his bones rot'.[19] Soon the Senators of Rome would be using similar phrases. Even he seems to have been ashamed of the devastation and bloodshed, at least among his own armies.[20]

It was deeply ironic that this destructive war should be the cause of his last foreign journey. He returned to Rome broken in health, morally disillusioned, anxious to retire from the harsh reality of public affairs into the warm glow of private memories.

One of those memories was Antinous. On his way out to the battlefield it is possible (though not proven) that Hadrian stopped off again in Greece.[21] In the autumn of 134, the first great penteteric games of Mantineia in honour of Antinous were celebrated, the thirty or more cities, as if in unison, issued medallions and coins in the new god's honour.[22] The group of consummate medallions issued by cities of the Peloponnese seem to be the work of a court artist and may have been commissioned by local notables expecting a visit from the Emperor. And could Hadrian easily have resisted presiding over the festival commemorating the death of his beloved in the very cult centre which he had designated? Indeed, he may even have gone on by sea to that other centre, Bithynion, to consecrate the now completed temple there.[23] Maybe, too, as part of the orchestrated programme of celebration, the city of Antinous on the Nile was also declared officially inaugurated at this time, but claims that Hadrian himself returned there as well have even less evidence and plausibility to support them.[21]

Back in Rome, which he had never liked and which may never have much liked him, Hadrian spent his time preparing for the succession and publicising his past achievements. Now turned sixty, he had reigned longer than any Emperor since Tiberius – an odious comparison which was rapidly to acquire topicality. Sick in body and tired in mind, he now enjoyed the retrospect of the past rather than any prospect of the future. He lived, even in winter, in the marbled fantasy of the villa at Tibur. He busied himself by turning the Canopus area into a memorial for his beloved whose images as hero or god, commissioned by the Emperor or sent by flattering Greek cities, were to be found everywhere, set sometimes in sacred groves. He ate solemn cult meals beneath the statue of Antinous as Dionysos which he installed in the summer triclinium or participated in his mystic rites below the melon-shaped semi-dome of the Canopus temple. He dictated his memoirs, exculpating himself from the deaths of the four consulars of 118 which suddenly in 137 men had urgent cause to remember, and defended himself against rumours about the death of Antinous.[25] In this connection, he commissioned coins to the god of the Nile and issued an edict flattering that god and remitting taxes in Egypt because of another cyclical failure of the river to rise. Memories of Eleusis made him dabble at introducing the cult of Demeter in some way into Rome itself. And echoes of the great sophists, the schools and the Museia of Hellas, prompted him to found in Rome an Athenaeum for lectures and debates, the first university in the west.

On 21 April of one of the years 136–7, the enormous temple of Venus and Rome was finally consecrated. The official coins had a valedictory air, rehearsing some of the earlier slogans of the reign but now as goals achieved: peace, stability, prosperity and unity all attained. *Tellus stabilita* proclaimed a notable coin bearing an image of Herakles: the whole earth was abundantly fruitful and comfortingly stable, thanks to the efforts of this Emperor so much like Herakles, 'the great adventurer, traveller and friend of men'.[26]

His vicennalia in 137 seems to have passed without much official rejoicing: perhaps because of the tense political situation in Rome. But Hadrian had already designed the supreme and characteristic monument to his achievement. Not for him a vulgar column or a forbidding arch; instead, he issued around 136–7 a series of beautiful medallions which, circulating the world, made everyone aware of the scale and nature of his imperial endeavour. The people of the west often seemed to ignore the meaning of his years of travel. These exquisite medallions conveyed the message subtly to them. By now Hadrian had visited thirty-eight of the forty-four provinces of the Empire. The medallions illustrated his arrivals, his restorations of whole countries, his cherishing of their individuality and his prudent care for their defence. In the series, national ethnic groupings as well as imposed administrative units, rough local auxiliaries as well as crack Roman legions, all were carefully recognised. Italy was ranked as no greater than any other province of the Empire. The entire series articulated Hadrian's view of his Empire as a brotherhood of equal members whose individuality and inherent diversity were to be encouraged as contributing to the vitality of the whole, as a unity sustained by the reciprocal partnership of all rather than by the oppressive dominance of one.[27] It was a generous ideal which Hadrian's incessant labours had brought far to realisation, though it is doubtful if the Senate or his less cosmopolitan successors ever understood or tried to follow it. He probably realised that the fragile balance he had created in the Empire would pass with himself.

Deliberately, too, in Rome he promoted the cult of Antinous. It is sometimes said that Rome was hostile to the new god, but this is to misunderstand its response, different in kind from that of the east. The Emperor himself felt it incumbent to discard his own divinity on Latin soil. Probably there were no official promulgation of that of Antinous either. Inevitably there were no coins for Antinous from cities which did not possess the eastern right of minting. Nor could it be expected that this panhellenic hero, this Greco-Egyptian divinity, would arouse the same ecstatic acclaim in Italy as in the lands of his birth and death. But, as we shall see in Chapter 15, outside official circles a religious cult of Antinous flourished with individuals and groups. Thus in Rome itself, doubtless with the Emperor's blessing, the local branch of the world-wide union of Dionysian artists followed the example of their brethren in Athens by setting up a statue of the beautiful Antinous (as Hermes), appointing a priest to him and arranging the ritual of his long-term worship.[28] Again probably with official blessing, an altar was set up on the Campus Martius with an inscription by the priest of Isis in which Antinous was equated with the great gods of Egypt. A similar cult started at Ostia. Not far from Rome, at Lanuvium, probably in 136, a temple to Antinous was consecrated, perhaps in the presence of the Emperor.[29] The survival from Rome and its immediate environs (but not from the Villa Adriana) of eighteen busts and statues, seven of which are of colossal dimensions, suggests that there were yet other cult centres of which we have no trace.[30] By the death of Hadrian the people of Rome must have been at least as aware of the features and divine status of Antinous as those of Athens. In his very last days, 137–8, Hadrian was constructing a chapel or large altar in the centre of the city, commemorating his hunts as symbolic of his whole imperial mission. Here Antinous appears in human retrospect simply as an intrepid youth. Hadrian was not, as has been claimed, concealing the lad's divinity here to flatter Roman susceptibilities. On the contrary, when compared with the imposing cult statues of the new Dionysos and Hermes to be seen elsewhere in the city these historical reliefs of Antinous, the young man, must have brought home the fact of his apotheosis all the more strikingly.

★   ★   ★

Temporum felicitas, *Roma felix* exulted the coins of these years. But the last months of Hadrian were to be anything but felicitous and were to bring not happiness but stark terror to Rome.

Hadrian had returned in 135–6 exhausted and seriously ill. He was in the grip of a spasmodic, painful and lethal illness: a type of arteriosclerosis with haemorrhaging. Though he was lucid and active at some moments, at others he was prostrated and unbalanced by pain. The strain on his already precarious stability was too much. It can be seen in the sunken, furtively mistrustful, disillusioned portraits of his last phase, and in some of his actions which are otherwise inexplicable.

For all the benefits he had brought to Rome, one was lacking: an heir. Sabina, we recollect, had seen to that. Hadrian had been grooming his only male blood relative, his great-nephew Pedanius Fuscus, for the succession. He was aged twenty-three in 136.[31] Perhaps Hadrian had contemplated some sort of regency of the young man's ninety-year-old grandfather, Servianus, who had belatedly been honoured with a third consulate in 134. No doubt, the Emperor wished to keep the principate within the Ulpian-Aelian dynasty. Fuscus, however, given to 'passion and gladiators' and easily swayed by unscrupulous people, seemed by 136 to Hadrian's jaundiced mind unsuitable as a successor, and he had always harboured a grudge against jealous old Servianus.[32]

In December 136 Hadrian announced his adoption as heir of the 35-year-old aristocrat from Etruria, Lucius Ceionius Commodus, who now took the title of Lucius Aelius Caesar. The news was greeted 'by the opposition of everybody'.[33] Hadrian had to distribute 300–400 million sesterces to placate the troops and the populace. However, those who knew the Emperor's personal preferences could scarcely have been surprised. Ever since the death of Antinous, Commodus had been in the ascendant. He had became praetor as the Emperor's own candidate and Consul later in 136. In the year before, his elder daughter had been betrothed at Hadrian's insistence to the precocious fifteen-year-old darling of intellectual society, a distant in-law of Hadrian, Marcus Annius Verus, known to history as Marcus Aurelius. This deliberate linking of the old senatorial family of Commodus with the powerful provincial clan of the Annii created a formidable alliance and power-base for the new Aelius Caesar in the Senate.

Nevertheless, everyone was shocked. Commodus' breeding was impeccable but his unsuitability for the job rivalled even that of the superseded Fuscus. He was already afflicted by some serious malady. Well educated, elegantly dressed and affable, he dabbled in poetry and was an avid conversationalist.[34] His main interests seem to have been sex and eating. It was he who spurned his wife's reproaches at his numerous infidelities with the memorable phrase: 'to be a wife is a duty not a pleasure'. His chief claim to fame had been the invention of a cunningly-blended meat pie to which Hadrian was very partial. He had a taste for luxury and sensuality: his bed was stuffed with rose petals and his coverlet was of lilies and he smothered his body with the rarest perfumes of Persia. He decked his pages with wings and expected them to perform his errands as quickly as the winds after which each was named. No doubt these foibles were harmless enough in imperial Rome but they scarcely constituted qualifications for the exacting role of *Princeps* as indefatigably and austerely performed by Hadrian. Commodus, it has been well said, was Hadrian's 'last great insult to Rome'.[35]

What everyone agreed was that Commodus did possess ' a regal beauty' (fig. 36).[36] It was very different from the rounded, sinuous, oriental kind of Antinous. Commodus had clear, aristocratic features, sharply delineated: an arched nose, full lips, straight eyebrows and widely spaced eyes and cheekbones. His hair was rich and wavy and a thick curly beard covered his cheeks and was allowed to dangle in a luxuriant mass below the jaw. He marked the advent of a new ideal of masculine beauty in Rome, derived not from Greece but from the conquered Germanic races of the north.

Some historians assert that Hadrian deviously and wickedly promoted this mortally sick man in the anticipation that he would die soon after succeeding, leaving the throne for Marcus.[37] It has even been suggested that he sent Aelius off to chilly and damp Pannonia as Governor to hasten his end. But Hadrian had not thought that Aelius' illness would prove fatal: in the event the end was sudden and unexpected. Hadrian's grief then was genuine. Nor when Aelius was Caesar was Hadrian already planning beyond him to Marcus. Aelius had a young son of his own, another Lucius, whom Hadrian was fondly rearing in his own household: the throne would descend naturally to him.

More plausibly, it is argued that Hadrian sought by the adoption to conciliate a powerful group in the Senate connected to Aelius.[38] But it is not clear why he should have needed to do this in 136 and still less if any such powerful group actually existed or operated as such. Indeed this controversial selection may have alienated more than it conciliated: it certainly prompted appalling dissension at the heart of government. And if Hadrian *was* trying to recruit senatorial allies by a politically advantageous adoption, why choose someone who was obviously inadequate and widely opposed?

What was also obvious was that between Commodus and Hadrian there existed some very intimate relationship. The young man had only to ask for something – even by letter – for the Emperor immediately to grant it. So close were they that men whispered of some secret bond or pledge between them. Evidently Hadrian had found in this beautiful, lively and amusing young man something like the *rapport* he had enjoyed with Antinous.

Evidently here we encounter another of those cases where Hadrian's private inclinations spilled over into his political actions. Though there may well have been devious political motives for his choice, it can only be satisfactorily explained by a personal preference, an emotional bond so overriding that it swept away all the inadequacies and dangers embodied in Commodus. Such a deep, heedless and unconcealed bond could, under the circumstances, have only two alternative origins. Commodus must have been either Hadrian's son or his beloved.

Carcopino has brilliantly and ingeniously proposed that the young man was Hadrian's bastard. Relying heavily on the letter to Servianus and elaborate interpretations of a few words in the *Historia Augusta*, he proposes an adulterous liaison between the just-married Hadrian and a society lady called Plautia in about 100 AD. Most scholars consider the letter to Servianus a fake and there can be little doubt that Carcopino's interpretations strain the other more authoritative texts. Moreover, when so many contemporaries (at least Plautia's three husbands) must have been in the know about the Emperor's alleged illegitimate son, it is amazing that no hint of such a juicy scandal ever reached the alert ears of the ancient writers. The only concrete evidence in support of the theory is Hadrian's loyalty towards the little son of Commodus, later to become the Emperor Lucius Verus, for whom, on the premature death of his father, he tried to reserve the principate by secondary adoption, a strategic marriage alliance and depiction as the chosen successor on the last great monument of the reign, the dynastic frieze at Ephesos.[39] Such obvious affection, however, given Hadrian's usual strong loyalty to the dear departed and his obsessive desire to perpetuate their memory, does not necessarily entail any kinship on his part. 'Let the Empire retain something of Commodus', explained the fond and grieving old man.[40]

We are left with the hypothesis that Commodus was, or had been, Hadrian's beloved. If Hadrian could elevate another *eromenos*, a mere provincial nonentity into a god, surely it is credible that he, in his illness and ultimate solitude, could raise the only other person he seems to have created an intimate relationship with, and who was into the bargain of consular rank and politically well-connected, into his heir? That Commodus was Hadrian's beloved suits all that we have discussed about the Emperor's sexual preferences. It is powerfully supported by the precedent of Antinous. It explains the universal opposition to Commodus' adoption and the favours he had received before. It is also explictly mentioned as the only cause in the *Historia Augusta* which three times says that the only reason for the adoption was Commodus' physical beauty and Hadrian's sexual attraction to it.[41] What exactly the ageing, grief-stricken Emperor found in this young man, besides his good looks, vitality, literary cultivation and exotic tastes, it is difficult for us to surmise. No doubt his wit and good humour cheered the disconsolate mourner of Antinous; because, however much in these suffering and lonely last years Hadrian was drawn to Commodus, this new experience never obliterated the memory of and yearning for the perhaps more fulfilling love of the past.[42]

In the end all the turmoil went for nothing. Aelius was only Caesar for a year.

33 The Nile near where Antinous died

34 The temple of Rameses II

35 Hadrian, shattered and grieving after the death of his beloved, *c.* 131-2

36 The 'western favourite', Lucius Ceionius Commodus as a young man

37 The Canopus canal at the Villa Adriana, looking towards the temple

38 The Caryatids and Sileni on its west bank: was or is Antinous buried behind them?

39 The chair of the priest of Antinous in the
theatre of Dionysos, Athens

40 The cuirassed torso of Hadrian from the Agora,
Athens: Athena stands above Romulus and Remus,
profile of Antinous on the lappet

41 Hadrian (a) pursues (b) confronts the lion of Libya, bronze medallions (not actual size)

42 'Antinous the god', a final pagan challenge to Christianity? Contorniate of *c.* 384

43 The infamous ephebe-god of Antinoopolis reconciled with Christianity? (Stele from Antinoopolis)

44 (a) Entrance gate of Antinoopolis as seen by Jomard in 1798–1800

44 (b) The entrance to the theatre

45 (a) 'A perpetual peristyle', the ruins of Antinoopolis, looking east from the river, as seen by Jomard

45 (b) All that was left of the main street in 1913

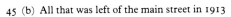

46 Medallions and coins of Antinous:
from Arcadia (a) (b) (c) (*above*); from Chalcedon (d) (*right*); from
Alexandria (e) (f) (*below*) (not actual size)

47 Medallions and coins of Antinous:
from Bithynion (a) (b) (c) (d) (*above*); from Tion (e) (*below left*); from Corinth (f) (*below right*)
(not actual size)

48 Medallions and coins of Antinous: from Tarsos (a) (b) (*above*); from Smyrna (c) (d) (*below*); from Adramyttion (e) (*bottom left*); from Stratoniceia (f) (*bottom right*) (not actual size)

49 Early bust from Patras by a Greek artist

50 Early bust from Patras by a Roman artist

51 Portrait or caricature? The bust now at Kansas City

52 A fifth-century BC inspiration: the Apollo of the Tiber, Roman copy

53 Statue of Antinous now in the Bank of Italy, Rome

54 Another fifth-century BC inspiration: the Doryphorus of Polycleitos

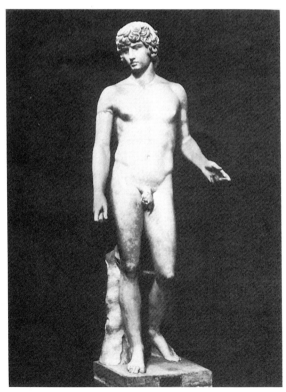

55 Statue of Antinous, 'the Farnese'

57 Head of Antinous as Egyptian god from Dresden

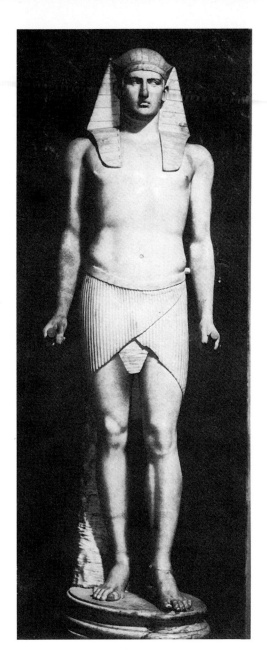

56 Antinous as an Egyptian god

58 The serene and compassionate god-man;
refined and smooth workmanship from Rome:
detail of the Sala Rotonda Dionysos

59 The innocent and divine adolescent: crisp and
lively workmanship from Greece: detail of the
Delphi statue

60 Antinous the god: the colossal statue of Antinous-Dionysos in the Sala Rotonda of the Vatican, 'the Braschi'

In the offices of Consul (for the second time) and Governor of Pannonia he acquitted himself with average success. His illness recurred. 'We have leaned against a tottering wall', complained the Emperor, himself weakening visibly and now even contemplating the young man's demotion.[43] In the end he was spared such a calamity. After taking an overdose of medicine to strengthen himself for the speech of thanks on his adoption that he was to deliver to the Emperor and Senate, Aelius Caesar died on the night before 1 January 138. His ashes were the first to be placed in the new mausoleum. For Hadrian, already disillusioned and despondent, this was a final blow. He was deeply affected, but went through the rituals of grief and commemoration as if he were mourning Antinous yet again.[44]

The adoption of Commodus had precipitated a crisis in the imperial family and in governing circles. We have no knowledge of the manoeuvres for the succession after the Emperor's return from the east, but he had evidently encouraged several hopefuls besides his relatives. The advent of Aelius Caesar dashed such expectations and his demise raised them all again. At some point, in 137 or possibly early in 138,[45] the passed-over Pedanius Fuscus, spurred on by omens, prophecies and unwise counsel, seemed to be hatching a plot to secure the throne. Hadrian, now mentally overwrought, responding violently to the slightest implied threat, peremptorily had his only male relative and former heir-presumptive executed. Everyone whose imperial pretensions he had encouraged now became a menace to his paranoiac, some say deranged, mind. On very flimsy pretexts he demanded the suicide of his innocent ninety-year-old brother-in-law Servianus. In complying, the old man pronounced a curse on Hadrian: 'may he long for death but be unable to die'.[46] At about this juncture, probably in 137, Sabina died.[47] It is generally assumed that she had bitterly opposed Commodus' adoption. Her aptly-timed death was her final disservice to her husband, for though it is highly unlikely that Hadrian chose to dispose of her after enduring thirty-seven years of unhappy wedlock, it created the impression that she too had been forced to suicide or, worse still, had been secretly poisoned by him. Hadrian granted the defunct Empress the minimal honours of divinisation and burial in the Mausoleum that a cold etiquette demanded.

Anyone left close to Hadrian or who had ever been led to aspire to the succession now felt in danger. Hadrian, seeing only enemies in former friends and suffering hideously after a near-fatal haemorrhage, lashed out with incoherent threats and wild penalties. To terrified Rome it seemed that the last days of those reputed blood-stained monsters Tiberius and Domitian were about to be re-enacted. Men remembered with dread the killings for which Hadrian had been held responsible in 118. There seems little doubt that he turned viciously against his former literary cronies, Favorinus, Heliodorus and Valerius Eudaemon. He persecuted his eminent old ally Turbo and leading

Senators such as Ummidius Quadratus and Terentius Gentianus, and may have exiled Titianus.[48] It was claimed that he had driven others who had once served him, like Polemaeanus and Marcellus, to suicide too. Senators vanished secretly from Rome in droves; executed, it was rumoured, at Hadrian's command.[49] A reign of terror seemed suddenly to have extinguished the 'times of felicity'.

Hadrian was not always so demented. On 25 February 138, gathering the quaking rump of the Senate around his bedside, he announced fresh arrangements for the succession. He was to adopt the respected Senator later known as Antoninus Pius, who at fifty-two, he said, was neither 'young enough to be reckless' (like Fuscus) 'nor old enough to be neglectful' (like Servianus).[50] Antoninus was indeed temperate, simple, conservative, able in administration and insular in his attachment to Latin traditions: much that Hadrian was not. He was also without surviving sons and Hadrian evidently hoped that this successor only a few years his junior would be a stop-gap holder of the status quo. The real heir to the Empire was to come from the two secondary adoptions which – in an extraordinary act – Hadrian now insisted that Antoninus make in his turn: of Aelius' seven-year-old son Lucius, who was now in token of his pre-eminence betrothed to Antoninus' own daughter, and of the seventeen-year-old Marcus. The arrangement of two such junior heirs was fraught with prospective contention, but perhaps Hadrian included Marcus in the settlement to satisfy the clan of the Annii.

Though this arrangement, born surprisingly in the turbid circumstances of early 138, smoothly settled the succession of the Empire for two generations, and has been hailed as Hadrian's final masterstroke, it did not exactly turn out as he had planned. Antoninus Pius proved no short-term stop-gap: he was to reign longer than Hadrian himself, for twenty-three serene but undynamic years in which the Empire was soundly administered but left to stagnate, its inherent problems becoming more acute. Lucius, whom Hadrian had probably wished to succeed, and who would have proved an even more unsuitable ruler than his father, was deftly demoted as heir by Antoninus soon after Hadrian was dead in favour of Marcus who thus became his son-in-law and official heir as Caesar. In some respects the earnest, dutiful Marcus was better fitted to rule the Museion than the slowly crumbling Empire he inherited. However, on his accession, and out of deference to Hadrian, he did associate Lucius as his junior partner in the *imperium* and even called his own disastrous son after Commodus.

Hadrian no longer cared. He handed over affairs of state to Antoninus and retired to the villa. His illness was now complicated by dropsy and his agonies were hideous. It seemed as though the sacrifice of the beloved Antinous to prolong his life had been cruelly twisted into the curse of Servianus for him never to be able to die. *Patientia*, the coins soothingly urged. But Hadrian had lost the will to endure. Now he longed for death and it would not come. Unable to bear his torments he tried to kill himself but the dagger was snatched from him. Antoninus, either in attendence or in correspondence, would not, out of humanity or political prudence, allow the Emperor to die unnaturally. Hadrian persuaded his strong and faithful huntsman, Mastor, to stab him through a circle carefully painted over his heart; but in the event the servant recoiled in horror. Hadrian demanded poison but the doctor took it himself rather than administer it. In his ravings Hadrian threatened with death those who thwarted him, complaining bitterly that he had power to kill everyone but himself. Antoninus discreetly countermanded his orders.

Finally, seeking relief from the summer's heat, he somehow travelled down to the resort of Baiae on the gulf of Naples. There, watching the glittering sea and being watched by the ever-attentive Antoninus, he waited for death. It still refused to come. Loudly cursing, not for the first time, the uselessness of doctors, he deliberately flouted their prescribed regimen, gorging and quaffing the wrong things in order to force death upon himself. Thus, perverse and arrogant to the last, he met his end on 10 July 138. He was sixty-two and a half and had reigned just under twenty-one years.

In the few moments of lucidity of his final months he had composed a last poem. Gone now was the pretension to Olympian divinity, even the mystic Eleusinian assurance of immortality. A lifetime's restless searching in the sanctuaries of all the world for convincing proof of the after-life ended in a cool, mocking scepticism. Never lacking in courage, Hadrian went to the grave doubtful if his soul, though destined for official divinisation, would rise to perpetual light like that of Antinous. His verses, with their allusions to the archaic poet Ennius, their delicate melody of plaintive diminutives, their subtle ambiguity of mood and of sincerity, sum up the always elusive spirit of the man. They can scarcely be rendered into English.

> *Animula vagula, blandula,*
> *hospes comesque corporis,*
> *quae nunc abibis in loca*
> *pallidula, rigida, nudula,*
> *nec, ut soles, dabis iocos.* *

On any reckoning Hadrian was one of the greatest rulers Rome had ever known. It is therefore a supreme irony that he died 'hated by all'.[51] So convinced was the Senate of the fact of the recent slaughter for which this monster had been responsible that it refused him divine honours and prepared to damn his memory, rescind his acts and deface his monuments as if he had been another Caligula or Nero. Antoninus, cremating the body in the grounds of Cicero's villa at Puteoli, was forced to inter the ashes there, though later they

* 'Little spirit, gentle and wandering, companion and guest of the body, in what place will you now abide, pale, stark and bare, unable as you used, to play?'

were to be transferred to the Mausoleum. Gradually, however, it transpired that the Senate and public opinion were mistaken. Most of the alleged victims of Hadrian's bloodlust, who had suddenly or sinisterly vanished, now reappeared in Rome, alive and well. Many had sneaked away into hiding of their own accord, fearing the danger of proscription; others had been smuggled to safety by Antoninus. The so-called reign of terror had therefore been a mental condition rather than an actual holocaust. Reluctantly, the Senate was at last forced by Antoninus to grant the usual divine honours to one who for ten years had been a god to half of his more grateful and perceptive subjects. Even after death Hadrian, like Antinous, belonged more unstintingly to Greece than to Rome.

XIV

THE NEW GOD

The young Bithynian had now been elevated to Olympus. In such superhuman and famous company this obscure *parvenu*, it might be expected, would immediately shrivel into insignificance and indistinctness. What then was to be Antinous' standing, nature and role among the more celebrated gods? And by the humans down below was Antinous to be accepted as a genuine immortal or as no more than a flimsy and ephemeral fantasy of the imperial imagination? Could such an upstart deity hope to survive the lifetime of his fabricator, Hadrian the Emperor?

Though Antinous had been made a god largely, but not entirely, at Hadrian's behest, he was never to be the same as the ordinary imperial *divi*. True, he was sometimes closely linked with the imperial cult: his statues occasionally hint at such dependence, his altars sometimes shared the official sanctuaries, his temples might rise in the same street as Hadrian's and his profile appear on coins where the Emperor's should have been. But from the outset Antinous displayed a personality, nature and activity as a god far removed from the cold, impassive and formal divinity assumed by the consecrated imperial family. The difference is summed up in a phrase of the time. Men soon began to act upon 'a belief in Antinous' and even to compare it with a 'faith in Jesus'.[1] No one ever developed 'a belief in' the divine Sabina, for example, or even in her august and reluctantly divinised spouse. Always dependent upon his imperial lover in life, Antinous leapt to a vigorous autonomy after death.

One factor in Antinous' impact as a god on the people of the second century and beyond is obvious. He had been a man like them and was never to forfeit in his divinity his human form and personality. Even in the most Olympian and remote depictions of him as a god his distinctive physical features and powerful enigmatic personality are never lost. Here was no fanciful personification of an abstraction, no variable embodiment of a creature of myth, as with the other gods. In Antinous the ancient classical idea of the divine immanent in man received a final and spectacular affirmation. The very idiosyncrasies of his mortal body, the inscrutable mystery of his human character, never to be obliterated by his new divinity, invited other mortals to identify all the more readily with him. He was a man-god. And he thereby offered all other men the hope of a similar immortality.

Antinous' godhead took four forms, each theoretically distinct, but in the practice of his times and of his devotees not much separated.

He was, first, the divine ephebe. Ancient Greece had seen in the beauty of innocent youth a spiritual element, blooming, fading and always mysteriously renewed and therefore deserving of veneration. In sculpture, poetry and literature this divine adolescent (often shown as Dionysos) had long been celebrated. Now in Antinous it achieved a last consummation. More than half of the existing sculptures show him without the emblems of godhead.[2] And even when he is shown with them, as in the statues of Delphi and of the Bank of Italy, he is still the naked resplendent ephebe, replete with the divine spirit, to whom the trappings of deity, such as laurel wreath or thyrsus, are almost superfluous and interchangeable. Pausanias and Dio tell us that his statues were both of this human-divine as well as of a more specifically godly character.[3] Hence he was called by five communities on his coins simply 'Antinous' or nothing at all: his divinity (and he was worshipped as a full god in these places) needed no further appellation.[4] Some scholars have anxiously tried to extract identifications with other gods from the meagre details on such images, but this is not necessary. His divinity was self-evident to his contemporaries in his form as a beautiful ephebe. Over and over again his beauty was extolled by them as a prime ingredient in his divine make-up.[5] Even the Christian opposition generally conceded that he possessed this significant quality, though, like Clement of Alexandria, they refused 'to worship' his beauty as did the pagans because it was blighted by his impure morals.[6]

When Antinous' immortal status *was* defined, it was most often as that of a 'hero'. Twenty-two of thirty cities called him that on their coins. One of the thirty-eight extant busts of him is overtly dedicated 'to the hero Antinous', implying (as do the many coins on which the busts are shown) that most of the others show him also in this heroic guise. Even the temple erected by Hadrian and Aelius Caesar to him at Socanica in 137 was dedicated to him as a hero. A 'hero' was a human being who through virtue had attained immortality, like Achilles and Herakles. To ancient writers like Hesiod or to later purists like Plutarch, 'heroes' had not the status of full divinities though they could mature to it.[7]

However, in the days of Antinous no necessary inferiority of status was implied in being a hero. Herakles, for example, was both hero and god. So was Antinous. At Bithynion he was dubbed a 'hero' on some coins and a full 'god' on others and also on the inscriptions beneath his statues in the town. At

Tarsos he is called 'hero' on one side of the coins and the 'new Apollo' or the 'new Iacchos' on the other. At Tion and elsewhere he is described as a 'hero' on the obverse and identified with Dionysos or other major divinities on the reverse. The frequency of his designation as a hero does not therefore suggest a reluctance to grant his full divinity so much as a desire to retain certain attributes of heroes dear to his followers: for these human-immortals approximated to the canonised mortals, the saints, of later Christianity. Having been mortal they remained closely concerned with those they left on earth. Heroes could readily be summoned by sacrifice and supplication to bring succour and protection to the living, to utter oracles and work miracles and to intercede with the supreme divinities of Olympus. A hero was more immediately approachable than these distant gods, more likely to respond positively and actively to his votaries' prayers. It was a role which was particularly to suit the hopes and claims that people attached to Antinous.

Nevertheless he was frequently regarded as a true god, most often assimilated to one of the greater gods of paganism. On 53 of the 115 sculptures of him he displays the attributes of such gods, and 20 of the cities issuing coins associated him with them. To the Dionysiac artists of Rome he was 'the new god Hermes', to other devotees there and in Ostia he 'sat with the gods of Egypt'.[8] At Adramyttion he was 'Iacchos-Antinous', in Antinoopolis 'Osiris-Antinous'.[9] Many of the associations on the coins are loose and express no more than a desire to commemorate local deities alongside this new one. But with certain gods there is a widespread and deliberate identification: Antinous' divine nature evidently shared certain important features of theirs. In such assimilations Antinous may be subordinate to the main god, but, throughout, he retains his own identity, possessing a godly character more sharply delineated than the gods of variable myth to whom he was so linked.

He was, however, also a 'pure' god, a full divinity entirely in his own right. As such he appears on the coins of Bithynion, Nikopolis and Ancyra, on inscriptions from Mantineia, Bithynion, Alexandria, Leptis Magna, Antinoopolis and Lanuvium, twice on the obelisk, in the words of Pausanias and in the accounts of the Christian Fathers. In this form, which theoretically was of a higher status than the others, Antinous kept his same godly personality. Obviously he did not rank on a par with the twelve original gods of Olympus or the ancient deities of Egypt. Indeed, he is shown on the obelisk as a junior god, interceding with the greater divinities of the Nile. Nevertheless, contrary to what has sometimes been asserted, he did possess a dimension as an independent and full divinity in the pagan pantheon.

Antinous' godhead thus assumed four layers which adhered harmoniously together or separated in people's minds according to their culture, location, rank or needs. This diversity of status, always compatible with a unity of nature, helped to confer on him a real vitality and popularity. Among the aristocracy of Italy, for example, his grand godly character was in vogue; in

Greece his ephebic or heroic role was popular with all groups. In Egypt, alongside the pure or assimilated god of the official cult, he was invested by the common people with yet another form: the daemonic. In Plutarch's philosophic hierarchy 'daemons' are closer to full gods than 'heroes' and it is in this sense that Antinous was termed a 'daemon' by Celsus.[10] To ordinary folk, especially on the Nile, daemons were often the spirits of prematurely dead youngsters which remained on earth, housed in temples, and were very active: inspiring prophetic dreams, working miracles, healing and mediating between mortals and more aloof gods. Usually they were benevolent and protective to their votaries, but they could be avenging, afflicting transgressors or enemies of their cult with dire pains and penalties. In the hands of necromancers they could become agents for evil. It is easy to see how the benevolent 'daemon' of Antinous in the popular pagan mind was later to be twisted into the foul fiend or 'demon' of Christian denigration.

Sometimes historians have contended that Antinous' godly nature was so various and fragmented as to lack all unity.[11] On the contrary, if we bring together those identifications on coins and sculptures which are certain and relate them to inscriptions and other evidence from his cult, a rich but distinct and coherent nature emerges which remains consistent from Luxor in south Egypt to Aquileia on the north Adriatic, from Tarsos and Amisos in the east to Caesarea in Mauretania and Lyons in Gaul in the west.

Of the 53 sculptures which show him with divine attributes, about 41 are of him as Dionysos-Osiris, 4 others as divinities of fertility linked with the Dionysos myth,[12] 3 as Hermes, 2 as Apollo and 3 as other deities. We know from coins and inscriptions that there were relatively more sculptures of him as Hermes in antiquity. Of the thirty cities which issued his coins, nine linked him firmly with Dionysos, six with Hermes, five with Apollo and eight with miscellaneous symbols or gods of fertility such as Pan. Of the 143 series of coins actually issued, 58 identify him as Hermes (but 49 of these issues come from only three places, Alexandria, Mantineia and Bithynion), 21 as Dionysos, 5 as Apollo, 2 as Iacchos, 2 as Pan and 6 with miscellaneous deities. Overwhelmingly, then, Antinous was conceived as Dionysos, to a lesser extent as Hermes. Only rarely was he identified with other gods of which the fertility group and Apollo alone have numerical significance. This conclusion is supported by other evidence from which we know that Antinous was worshipped as both Dionysos-Osiris and also Hermes at, for instance, Antinoopolis, Alexandria, Mantineia, Corinth, Bithynion and Rome. Though Hadrian and his mythologers may have preferred the association with the Arcadian Hermes (as the heavy bias of the coins of Alexandria, Mantineia and Bithynion suggests), it was with Dionysos that Antinous was to be linked throughout the Empire.[13]

These identifications were not haphazard. They simply equate the central features of his story and growing myth – his own triumph over death and his sacrificial rescue of Hadrian from death – with similar features in the myths of the two greater chthonic deities. In one myth of Dionysos, locating his origins in Asia Minor, he was a god of fertility, of the cycle of the seasons and also 'lord of souls' in the lower world. In the potent and widespread Orphic myth, he was the 'divine child', Dionysos Zagreus, offspring of Zeus and Demeter (or Persephone), torn to pieces by the Titans and reconceived through Semele. Later the grown-up Dionysos ventured down to Hades to bring his mother Semele back to Olympus. The links between this legend and that of Osiris, including the latter's journey to the underworld to rescue his brothers, need no further elaboration. Even Apollo was linked to the fate of Dionysos Zagreus.[14]

Hermes too was a god of fecundity and procreation: as Hermes Nomios he was protector of crops and flocks and father of that other Arcadian god of rural fertility, Pan (fig. 47 b, d). As herald of the gods, he too was an intercessor. He was closely linked with Dionysos whom he had twice rescued from perils as a lad before handing him over to the care of Demeter. Above all, Hermes had powers of passing back and forth through Hades as the conductor of souls. It was he who had led Persephone up from its gloom to the embrace of her overjoyed mother. Through this connection of Dionysos and Hermes with Eleusis and its seminal myth of suffering, renunciation, death and resurrection, and of the whole cycle of earthly fertility, the godhead of Antinous received fundamental nourishment.[15]

That Antinous was regarded principally as a conqueror of death is made abundantly clear by the obelisk: 'the guardians of the gate of the kingdom of the underworld say "Praise to you!", to him. They loosen their bolts and open their gates before him, many years long, daily, as his duration of life is the sun, never in eternity elapsing.' It announces his 'salvation', his being 'raised again to life'.[16] On the coins he is shown as the chthonic riding-god Hermes with a caduceus, or symbolised by a funerary horse (fig. 46 b, f). The Curium hymn also refers to his underworld presence. Perhaps because he was famed for saving Hadrian from death and because of his own attainment of immortality, Antinous became in the popular mind a god who assured the souls of his devotees a similar 'rejuvenation' (to quote the obelisk again), 'salvation' as his adherents at Lanuvium put it.[17] Little wonder then that his name or image was nailed in hope to the coffins of the dead, that symbols of resurrection decorated his shrines at Tibur, that his medallions were worn on the body as a protection against the vicissitudes of fate. Thus, too, a mourning father in Mantineia could commend the soul of his dead young son to the immortalising care of 'the god Antinous'.[18] Whether as god, hero or daemon, Antinous offered to other mortals, as he had been, the prospect of life eternal.

This faith in his resurrective powers was matched by one in his general benevolence. He possessed *kalokagathia* in the ancient sense of beauty of body and soul, as his Dionysian worshippers in Rome recognised. To the folk of

Curium in Cyprus, he was 'blessed', to the artists of Rome 'holy', to the people of Hadrianotherai and Juliopolis 'good'.[19] When he was depicted as a daemon in sculpture and cameos it was as *agathos*, benevolent. Some ingredient in his story, no doubt his voluntary sacrifice, justified this stress on his moral virtue which led to comparisons with that other god of vicarious sacrifice, Christ. As such he was an active worker for good when invoked, healing the sick in dreams, working miracles, counselling through oracles – as the obelisk proclaims and Origen confirms. 'He grants the requests of those who call upon him.'[20] Ordinary people wore this good god's likeness as a talisman against evil or called upon him in their most trivial need. For example, an obsessive and desperate lover called Serapamon from Antinoopolis invoked this benevolent daemon and other chthonic gods to secure an indifferent woman's affection for himself.[21]

To this role was added that of a god of nature. His beauty as the divine ephebe was symbolic of the eternal pattern of waxing and waning of the earth. As a god, his powers of renewal and protection extended, like those of Dionysos and Hermes, to crops and animals. It is Antinous' powers of rejuvenation, deriving from his chthonic character, and not his alleged pastoral origins, which explain his appearance in statues as Sylvanus harvesting the vine and as Aristaios the sturdy peasant, on coins as Hermes Nomios or Pan tending flocks, and on an inscription (from Leptis Magna) as 'Antinous the god of fruitfulness'.[22] His association with rivers not only hints at the manner of his death but at the restorative power of water.

Far then from being vague and disintegrated, Antinous' godly nature was clear and cohesive: through sacrificial goodness he had conquered death and now he offered similar salvation, protection and good works to all men and fertility to their crops and animals. At least 117 of the 143 issues of coins proclaim this coherent nature.[23] He was not just the pale reflection of greater deities. His own legend, elaborated in poems, hymns and prose, and in the repeated encomia of his festivals, symbolised in flower, moon and star, embodied in his unique beauty and in the intense mystery of his personality, gave this chthonic god an unmistakable identity of his own.[24]

Above all, he was an *active* immortal, compassionately 'carrying out his work among the living', as the obelisk says. Like Dionysos and Demeter in particular, he appeared as a dynamic god of change who underwent suffering, abnegation and triumph. In this way Antinous differed from some of the fading, static, self-concerned gods of the old hierarchy, 'that ancient aristocratic senate in the heavens',[25] and approximated to the now ever-more-popular mystery-gods of ancient times or the newer, increasingly compelling, deities of ecstasy and revelation from the orient. Of course his cult did not, like the new faiths, offer omniscient explanations of the universe, claim exclusive and monotheistic powers over its adherents, impose creeds, pietistic practices and moral codes or segregate its priests and its brethren from the profane herd. But his cult did, like theirs, offer salvation in the life to come, instil revelation and bliss through mysteries and initiations in the present, provide a moral exemplar to follow, support believers with supernatural aid and punish transgressors with divine retribution. In Antinous the old and the new forces of religious experience briefly met. It was this infusion of warm oriental energy, mysticism and transcendence into a cult which vividly re-embodied the most ancient and profound myths of Greco-Egyptian religion and remained comfortably accommodated within the chilly classical pantheon, that gave the 'belief in Antinous', 'the worship of Antinous', a real vitality, a deep and wide appeal to people of all ranks and sensibilities in the second century and later.

XV

'A BELIEF IN ANTINOUS'
THE CULT

The cult of Antinous never became one of the greatest of its time. It in no way
rivalled the elaborate cosmopolitan cults of Zeus or Dionysos, Demeter or
Asclepeios, for example, or those of the now fashionable Isis and Serapis. It
was much less extensive than the official imperial cult for Hadrian himself,
though it probably proved more lively and durable than that. Minor in stature
and limited in scale by such comparisons, it was nevertheless in its own right
more widespread in scope, richer in manifestations, more varied in its hold
over men's minds and spirits and more tenacious in duration than has
previously been supposed. Antinous' face, if not his faith, became one of the
most widely known in late antiquity. It reached the extremities of the Greco-
Roman world, from the east in the shape of the statue at Trapezus to the west in
the guise of the Arcadian coin found in the mud of Godmanchester in Britain;
from the northern frontier lands, where bronze vessels and coins of Antinous
have been discovered at the mouth of the Rhine and right across central Europe
to the mouth of the Danube, to the southern perimeter of civilisation, the
North African coast, where depictions of him have been found from modern
Algeria to Alexandria and even, it is claimed, in oases deep in the Sahara.[1]

Traces of some definite public cult or veneration come from some seventy
cities.

In Egypt his chief cult centre was, of course, the extraordinary city of
Antinoopolis where he had two temples, but we know of substantial cults with
temples and priesthoods to him at Hermopolis, Oxyrhynchus, Tebtynis and
Alexandria and some form of veneration in at least two other places. On the
Greek mainland we know that at least thirteen cities honoured him. Chief
among them was the mother city of Mantineia with its two temples and
numerous images and coins of its 'local god'. But the activity in Athens should
not be overlooked – it boasted two cults, priesthoods and chapels to him, and
annual games, and at least four sculpted images of him have been found there.
A cluster of cult places were in the Peloponnese, like Corinth or Argos, and
others were in famous sanctuaries, like Delphi, Olympia, Eleusis and

Epidauros. Yet more were scattered northwards, such as Nikopolis on the west coast, the spa and hunting resort of Aidepsos on the tip of Euboea or Hadrianopolis up in Thrace. Asia Minor, his homeland, was enthusiastic for the new god. Many of its booming cities have not been excavated enough to yield much evidence. Nevertheless, we know of twenty-seven of them where he was honoured.[2] In the north, his proud birthplace, Bithynion, had the most vigorous cult, but it was rivalled by the official capital of the province, Nikomedia.[3] On the west coast, Smyrna, grateful to Hadrian and the home of his friend Polemo, acted as a major centre for the dissemination of the cult. On the south, Tarsos had at least one temple and two styles of worship, and rapidly developed a creative ardour for the new god. We learn of the cults in the twenty-seven cities mainly from the coins and the sculptures which they commissioned of Antinous and can be sure of only seven temples among them, but there must have been many more.[4] In Italy, apart from that city-in-miniature the Villa Adriana, there were ten other places from which his cult is attested, boasting among them at least seven temples and attendant priest-hoods. Clearly, then, as Hadrian had intended, the god Antinous helped knit the Greco-Egyptian-Roman Empire together.

Elsewhere, the traces of his cult are more isolated, though the important discoveries recently of a temple at Socanica in Dalmatia and a festival at Curium in southern Cyprus prove that it existed in areas where its penetration had not previously been suspected. There is evidence of some form of honouring at Caesarea, Carthage, Leptis Magna and Cyrene along the coast of North Africa and from Malta in the Mediterranean. Only one sculpture has been found in the Levant, in the Lebanon, and the great metropolis of Antioch seems to have ignored him, perhaps out of its spite for Hadrian. The small bronze from Lyons (Lugdunum) in Gaul comes from a private rather than a civic cult there.[5] The fourteen or more small bronze jars, used for incense or for anointing-oil, which show his type if not his actual portrait in a debased form, come from North Portugal, Holland, the Rhineland, central Germany, the Danube and the Black Sea and seem to have been propagated from Alexandria and Asia Minor where his cult was strongest.[6] Thus they are not evidence of specific veneration of him in the places where they have been found, but, in view of their religious and agonistic uses, do testify to the widespread, if imprecise, dissemination of his image and story and recognition of his supernatural powers.[7]

What, then, did the worship of Antinous consist of?

Of the twenty-eight or more temples for which there is evidence not one survives in any form.[8] Those in which Hadrian had a direct involvement, at Antinoopolis, Mantineia and Bithynion, must have been fairly grand – that in the home town stood on a high podium and boasted a portico of eight tall Corinthian columns.[9] If the statue from which the colossal Mondragone head comes stood in a temple at Frascati, that too must have been on an impressive scale. But generally Antinous' buildings were more modest: four columns sufficed for the porticoes at Tarsos, Philadelphia and Lanuvium, for instance. Probably he also had other, simpler chapels like the one in the gymnasium at Mantineia or in the sanctuary at Delphi. Sometimes his chapels, altars and statues would be erected in or near the temple for the imperial cult or those for Dionysos and Hermes. We know the names of some of the priests who served him: Hostilius Marcellus at Corinth, for example, or Isidoros Didymos at Alexandria. The priest of his Dionysiac cult in Athens was important enough to have a central chair in the front row of the theatre there, and that of the similar group in Rome, Nikias, acted as their representative to the imperial court. In Athens and Eleusis different ephebes could act as his priest annually. Though many of the local cults were financed civically or by sponsors, Antinous seems to have had a special appeal to specific groups who enjoyed celebrating festive, mystic or artistic rites: like the Dionysiac artists, the college of Lanuvium, the miners of Socanica, the cultores at Curium and the bands of pilgrims to Antinoopolis with their wild orgies.

His worship was often assiduous, varied and even spectacular. At Oxyrhynchus the days of both his consecration and birth were solemnly kept by special horse-rites. At Delphi his statue was ritually polished with subtle oils for so many generations that even now it possesses the lustre of alabaster. According to his obelisk and archaeological discoveries in Egypt, he was the subject of daily offerings of food and drink there and, no doubt, in the Greco-Roman cities, of libation and sacrifice.

But this god and his worshippers were active beyond such sedate norms. Both the *Historia Augusta* and the obelisk speak of his oracles being pronounced in temples and in dreams as if they were a fairly widespread phenomenon. Origen discusses those given in Antinoopolis and it has recently been proposed that a priest delivered his oracles there from the hollow rear of a huge cult statue of him.[10] There is evidence of oracles at Tarsos and perhaps in Rome itself.[11] No doubt it was through these pronouncements and visitations that he wrought miracles and healing for which he evidently became famous in the east. Perhaps too his powers were exercised, like those of Demeter and Dionysos, through those initiations and mysteries which were basic to his faith. Again they seem to have been fairly widespread, though we only have definite evidence of them from Mantineia where they were annual, from Bithynion where they were supervised by a person of consular rank, at Rome and Athens where the mystic synods celebrated them, and at Eleusis and Stratoniceia. His initiates re-enacted with drama and music his passion, descent to the lower world and resurrection, obtaining thereby an inner assurance of a similar immortality. But those at Antinoopolis, his 'sacred nights' as they were called, became downright notorious.[12] Celsus, the Platonist, declared that few devotees of a daemon 'go astray in evil ways and wander around in greater darkness, more iniquitous and impure than that of the revellers of Antinous in Egypt'.[13] The Christian, Clement of Alexandria, called these celebrations 'really shameful' and implies that they were marked by 'fornication' and flagrant and uninhibited homosexual orgies.[14] Juvenal describes a similar festival in the Nile valley:

> . . . these revellers, slurred of speech and lurching from booze, as they danced
> To some blackamoor's piping, all greasy with rank pomade and
> Sporting garlands galore, wreaths all askew over their heads . . .[15]

One of the strengths of the 'belief in Antinous' was its appeal to the most sensitive and inward of mystical natures as well as to the exuberant, joyous and ecstatic sides of human experience.

His official festivals and games possessed an unusual artistic element. At the theatre in Curion the festival was begun under the open sky by the citharode-priest, clad in gold and purple and plucking his gilded and ivory-inlaid lyre. His song alternated with that of a choir which he had specially trained in hymns to Antinous composed on the model of Mesomedes, whose encomium on the new god must have enjoyed a wide reputation. Poetry and music played a prominent opening part in the games of Athens, Eleusis, Antinoopolis and elsewhere.

The four-yearly games at Mantineia and the annual ones at Antinoopolis became some of the most famous in the Greek world, attracting competitors, athletic, poetical and musical, from all over the east and offering substantial prizes: not just the wreaths of Antinous and honorary citizenships, but money and even free maintenance for life. We find a twice-successful boxer selling his prize of civic sustenance at Antinoopolis for one thousand drachmas cash in the year 212.[16] The games there were the most important in Egypt and included rowing-races in honour of the death in the Nile and horse and chariot races in the hippodrome, and these horse events may have been a feature elsewhere. The games at Athens and Eleusis, besides also being annual, were reserved only for ephebes and, though long celebrated and recorded, were not of international standing. In all, there is evidence of games to Antinous in nine cities, including Bithynion.[17] All of these were in the Greek east.

This brings us to the problem of the cult in the Latin west, in Italy in particular. Because there were no such games, no coins and no *senatus consultum* for the deified Antinous there, some historians have concluded that his cult was disapproved of in conservative official circles and was negligible in extent. Even those who recognise the profusion of sculpted images of Antinous in Italy often maintain that he was admired aesthetically, not religiously: though such a modern distinction may not have applied to philhellenes at that time. On the contrary, what evidence we have shows that the cult was by no means insignificant when compared with that from the mainland of Greece, for example. If there was 'a powerful opposition' among conservatives to Hellenism and to the veneration of a humbly-born Greek youth in Rome, then it signally failed to deter Hadrian and other devotees of Antinous.

Of the seventy sculptures of Antinous, the finding places of which are fairly well attested, forty-four were found in Italy (half from the Villa Adriana), twelve in Greece and Asia Minor and six in Egypt.[18] If we compare the sculptures which seem to have been made in Italy with those from Greece, proportionately more show Antinous with divine attributes: as though for the Latins his overtly godly nature was more stressed or required.[19] If we look at statues of Antinous, which are colossal and which must often therefore have had a public or religious function, ten (or twelve if we include the controversial Vertumni from Ostia) were found on Italian soil, two elsewhere and none at all in Greece. The head of Antinous found at Frascati (the Mondragone) must have come from a statue at least 5–6 metres high, and this enormous godly image must have had a religious significance as did the 3.5 metres high Dionysos from Praeneste and others.[20]

For someone whose divinity is said to have been frowned upon or illegal, Antinous the divine was brazenly prominent. There are no signs that the apotheosis of Antinous was surreptitiously concealed. Putting aside the huge and hothouse cult in the Villa Adriana, we know that Antinous was proclaimed 'the new god Hermes' and 'enthroned with the gods of Egypt' in inscriptions in public places in the heart of Rome, that he possessed two priests there, possibly two chapels or temples and was to be seen in no less than eighteen still extant sculptures, mainly of him as a god. At Lanuvium he was venerated publicly along with Diana as a god of salvation by a club possibly formed in August 132 only twenty months after his death.[21] The town of Lanuvium also had its temple to him and two sculptures have been found in the vicinity. At Ostia, his image in priestly guise was found in a religious precinct and nearby two colossi of him as Vertumnus and a now-lost colossal head as well as an inscription which repeats the Egyptian assimilation of that of Rome. It is reasonably claimed that there must have been a sanctuary to him at Ostia.[22] In Greek-speaking Naples there are indistinct traces of a serious cult – a section of the city was named after him and there is evidence of a temple and at least one statue.[23] At Aquileia, at the head of the Adriatic, where the Caesernii brothers came from, he was venerated popularly: as is shown by terracotta plaques bearing his image (from coins of Bithynion which evidently reached there), by an extant bust and by his identification with Belenus, another fertility god especially worshipped there.[24] In the south, there are indications of his veneration at Pozzuoli and Brindisi.[25] Throughout the peninsula, it is said, his name was commonly given to children.[26]

No doubt all this is puny when compared with the other mighty cults of popular deities at the time. No doubt too in Italy Antinous was venerated more by small religious groups and individual households than by whole confederations, cities or mass congregations as in Greece and Egypt. After all, the Latins had no political or national motives officially or communally to exalt him. But there can also be no doubt that Antinous, as a god of salvation in his own right, or as identified with Dionysos or Hermes, with the gods of Egypt or of fertility, found many devotees at all social levels in Italy and that their loyalty proved some of the most intense and persistent of all.

The coins of Antinous are another witness to the penetration of his cult in the east. Over thirty-one cities issued them, all, except for Alexandria, in Asia Minor or on the Greek mainland, and there were an astonishing 143 different issues, chiefly concentrated in the years 134–5.[27] Eighty-five of these issues came from the major cult centres of Alexandria, Tarsos, Smyrna, Bithynion and Mantineia. But not all the places which honoured Antinous issued coins: there are none from Athens, Eleusis or Aidepsos, for example. Circulating the whole Roman world, the obverses of these coins propagated the titles and the distinctive features of this young hero and god who usurped the place hitherto exclusively and jealously reserved for the imperial family. Antinous' religious impact is illustrated by the way the cities hastened on the reverse sides to depict his cult or godhead and to associate him with their own local gods or heroes. The coins were probably struck to commemorate the first games of Antinous at Mantineia and local festivities elsewhere. As such, many of them were medallions, not regular currency and a few are rare works of art. Some pieces were struck only on one side and left smooth on the other: deliberately made to be worn. Many were pierced by holes and hung from the neck as talismans: Antinous' image offering protection against evil, sickness or death. Some of these might even be souvenirs from pilgrimages or initiations at his shrines. Others were set in frames of wood or glass or impressed into terracotta plaques for votive purposes in the home or the funerary chamber. Some were buried with the dead to invoke the god's aid on the perilous journey into the unknown.

The coins were rivalled in quantity by the sculptures. These, too, ever since an object of aesthetic admiration, were conceived at the time essentially as religious objects. Even the apparent portrait busts were, as the coins of Mantineia and Bithynion prove (figs 46–8), intended to display Antinous as hero or god. It has sometimes been said that we possess more sculptures of Antinous than of any other individual in antiquity.[28] This is not so. True, we have a goodly 115 of Antinous, but over 250 of Hadrian and still more of Augustus. Nevertheless, his image was reproduced in amazing quantities in the few years 130–38. In addition to those still preserved we know of at least another eighty-three which formerly existed.[29] If the Napoleonic surveyor, Jomard, is to be believed, there were at least another 1,344 busts or statues of Antinous in the two main streets of Antinoopolis alone.[30] This gives a total of around 1,550 sculptures of which we have some knowledge, which makes de la Maza's estimate of 2,000 sculptures being produced in these years not as

---

BELOVED AND GOD

incredible as it at first seems. We also know from Pausanias and from coins that numerous paintings existed of the young god – at Mantineia, Bithynion, Chalcedon and Tion, for example. Dietrichson lists also eighty-eight incised gems, many of which derive from the sculptures.[31] Perhaps never in antiquity had so many varied images of one individual been produced in such a short span of time.

The demand on the workshops of Greece, Egypt and Italy for images of Antinous in the years 130–38 must have been enormous. There can have been few sanctuaries to Hellenic or Egyptian gods which did not possess a likeness of this new one, however remote from the original it may have been, like the bust now in Kansas City or the draped priest-Antinous from Cyrene. Sometimes in the eagerness to display an Antinous the authorities had to improvise, as at Leptis Magna where a mask of the youth's face was hastily fitted to an existing statue of Apollo. The large proportion of busts (38 definite and 42 possible of 115 works) indicates that the cult was also widespread in more domestic settings where the god brought more personal protection and inspired more intimate devotion. His face became so popular that it established a fashionable type for a generation or two. Little wonder that the Christian Fathers scattered in Carthage, Alexandria, Rome, Byzantium, Cyprus, Antioch or Bethlehem all knew of Antinous' beauty and could not forget his divinity or his aggravatingly persistent cult. And when the 'belief in Antinous' ultimately perished it was the numerous images which it had produced which were to hand on his memory to posterity.

Who, then, and how sincere were these believers?

Hadrian and his mythologers had promoted the cult and people hastened to respond from a variety of motives. The thirteen men who commissioned the issues of coins on which their names appear represent very much the official response. Aristotimos the priest of Delphi and Polemo of Smyrna acted no doubt more out of loyalty to Hadrian than any sudden faith in Antinous. Others like C. Claudius Julianus of Stratoniceia or Julius Saturninus of Ancyra were probably magistrates anxious to please the Emperor and to enhance their standing and that of their cities. Perhaps the more modest Veturius of Mantineia and the Hostilius Marcellus who announced himself as 'priest of Antinous' on the coins of Corinth display somewhat more conviction in him. Whatever the calculating motives of such sponsors, the diversity and abundance of the coins, the association of local gods and attributes, however humble or incongruous, with Antinous suggest a considerable and genuine enthusiasm for him on the part of the populace. In Egypt the Aurelius Horion who founded games in Oxyrhynchus and the epistrategos of the Thebaid, Julius Fidus Aquila, who erected a colossal bronze staue of 'Antinous *Epiphanios*' at Antinoopolis, may have acted from motives in which piety played little part.

Elsewhere among the upper classes we do get a feeling of more conviction in

190

the new god: from that M. Domitius Euphemus who organised the mysteries at Bithynion or the C. Julius Eurycles who generously dedicated an Ionic portico in Mantineia 'to the local god'.[32] In Italy, the owner of the villa outside Lanuvium who so carefully cherished and repaired the Sylvanus relief must have observed some form of cult for Antinous, as did the L. Funisulanus Vettonianus who kept the colossal Antinous-Dionysos now in the Bank of Italy at his villa at the eighth milestone on the Via Nomentana near Rome.[33] Assiduous private devotion of this kind flourished especially in Italy.

Among the middling ranks there are also signs of a genuine belief in Antinous. The father, Isochrysus, who set up a bronze of his dead son, Dochis, in Mantineia, sincerely believed that the god Antinous would cherish and save the lad's soul. The M. Lukkios Flakkos who unusually dedicated a bust 'to the hero Antinous' also seems to have possessed ardour. Indeed the domestic busts of him must have been the focus of a cult to him in many well-to-do households, just as the exquisite gems provided spiritual support for those too fastidious to hang a vulgar talisman around their necks. Some of these devotees evidently could not bear to be parted from the beneficial and reassuring presence of their Antinous and therefore had small, light-weight travelling busts or bronzes made to accompany them on their journeys.[34] One such bust in alabaster and from Egypt conveniently collapsed into five pieces for its peregrinations.[35] There seems little ground to doubt the faith of the Dionysiac artists in him – of that Nikias, for example, who took on the duties of his priest and curator for life and without any remuneration, or of the citharode of Curium who organised such an elaborate festival and gushed forth such a rhapsodic encomium for 'the blessed Bithynian'.[36]

More humble folk widely separated in different parts of the Empire seemed genuinely touched by Antinous. The small artisans and slaves of Lanuvium may have enjoyed their 'good amphorae of wine' at their six annual feasts more than the solemn funerary business of their club, but that is no reason to doubt their faith that Antinous would help them gain 'salvation' when all earthly festivities were over.[37] Likewise the temple erected in such an unlikely place as Socanica in Dalmatia some years after the death (137) must have been intended to tap a similar devotion to Antinous among the colony of silver miners there, themselves perhaps exiles from his native Bithynia.

The frequent use of his medals as talismans or amulets demonstrates a widespread faith in his powers in Greece, Asia Minor and Egypt. In Alexandria, indeed, after two large emissions of thirty different bronze medallions, a third in cheaper lead had to be made to meet the demand for the image of Antinous as Osiris and the chthonic riding-god Hermes. Even this did not satisfy the demand and an enterprising workshop used a mould to reproduce illicitly yet more crude and cheap medallions of this hero whose images, miracles and protection were obviously sought by countless poor folk of faith or superstition. Far away at the north end of the Adriatic his profile was pressed into leaf-shaped terracotta plaques which either served votive, healing and miraculous purposes or were attached to the coffins of the dead to ensure them safe passage to eternity. Far to the south, on the Nile at Luxor, Antinous' name, written on wooden tablets, was fixed to mummy cases for similar purposes of redemption. All over Upper and Lower Egypt, in Athens, Macedonia and Italy, children were now given his name to protect them in this life or the next.[38] The lovesick man, Serapamon, who lived in Antinoopolis in the third century, and who in a ritual incantation invoked the daemon Antinous to help him capture the body and the love of the woman Ptolemaïs, may have degraded the standing and function of the sublime hero but exemplifies the common faith in his efficacy and in his ready response to mortals in any kind of distress.[39] The fourteen bronze jars found scattered over Europe indicate a popular if vague recognition of his divinity among small folk in unlikely areas. But those other jars, the half a million large (one metre high) amphorae, which Gayet found in 1896 literally paving a whole valley north-east of Antinoopolis, more distinctly show how vast the pilgrimages of believers to his shrine were and how seriously they took the obelisk's injunctions to make pious offerings.[40] Some other words of the obelisk obviously did not exaggerate: 'Love of him is in the hearts of his servants and fear of him commands all people and his praise is with all mankind and they praise him . . .'[41]

It is impossible to quantify all this fragmented evidence. It is, however, clear that at widely different social levels and in widely separated parts of the Empire the cult of Antinous became far more than merely official. This new god satisfied some deep cravings within many people at the end of paganism. From the start, Antinous took fire in their hearts, hopes and convictions, and faith in him as a divinity or daemon flourished of its own accord long after the original promoters of his cult were dead. It has even been contended that confidence in his self-devoted sacrifice, the basis of his worship, actually grew and became more explicit with the generations.[42] Indeed, the popular vigour and genuine conviction of the 'belief in Antinous' were widespread and persistent enough to provoke the scorn of some sophisticated pagans and the anxious and unremitting indignation of most Christian apologists for two and a half centuries to come.

The apotheosis of Antinous was outrageous enough to attract the censure of even some pagan writers. Pausanias (c. 160) seems to be sceptical about it, the Sybilline Oracles (c. 170) attack it as part of their general opposition to Hadrian, and Lucian (c. 180) wittily and obliquely parodies the credentials of the new god.[43] As late as 360 AD, the Emperor Julian, who had tried to restore paganism in the face of the now nearly triumphant Christianity, mocked the whole story: he depicted the long-bearded Hadrian anxiously searching for Antinous on Olympus, only to be rudely and pointedly told by Silenus that the youth had never been admitted there.[44] Much more serious was the argument of Celsus, an advocate of restrained philosophic paganism, who in about 176 published an indictment of Christianity. He criticised the flourishing new cult of Antinous for its dangerous oriental dynamism, flaunted in the shocking debauches of its devotees in Egypt.[45] He also sensed that this cult threatened the settled old hierarchy of gods. Moreover, this new god, argued Celsus, was a powerful daemonic force and instructor, leading people into evil ways, into mystic and turbulent darkness – just like Christ. Indeed Celsus saw little distinction between these two new sects: the honours paid to Jesus, he declared, were 'no different from those paid to Hadrian's boy-favourite'.[46]

Such comparisons stung the already hypersensitive susceptibilities of the Christians to the quick. In the later second century the Church was still a struggling minority and its ultimate ascendance nearly two centuries later could by no means be foreseen. Though the new cult of Antinous was never in numerical scale, spiritual depth or personal impact a major rival to that of Jesus, its buoyancy in various parts of the world aroused jealousy for a long time to come. Moreover, the parallel between the beautiful, self-sacrificed and immortal youth from Bithynia and the immaculate, self-sacrificed and resurrected redeemer of Calvary, though a caricature, was uncomfortable and grating.

Thus almost all of the Christian writers down to the final conquest of their faith (c. 390) never failed to attack Antinous and his cult. Some writers could not leave Antinous alone. Tertullian returns to the attack in four different books, Origen five times in the same work, the serene Jerome in four separate books, Epiphanios in three.

The tone in the first six writers after the death of Hadrian is circumspectly muted.[47] But with the disintegration and collapse of the Antonine dynasty under Commodus, such caution was thrown to the winds, Hadrian was openly named and the charges luridly elaborated. In the polemics of the recent convert, the virulent Tertullian of Carthage (written 197–207), Antinous is compared with public harlots, corrupted Ganymede, and bizarre recipients of ludicrous consecrations, including mountains, granaries and even the sewers.[48] This reaction of indignation mixed with salacious charges continued down to the attacks of Athanasius who wrote in Alexandria in 350 and of Prudentius composing in Rome in 384. Clement of Alexandria, writing in about 190, treated the matter with a pained and sorrowful sensitivity, stressing the sexual and aesthetic violation,[49] while his pupil, Origen, who had had himself castrated in order to demonstrate his own purity and wrote also from Alexandria in 249, argued with vehement theological reasoning.[50] The later authors either repeat the earlier ones or are more factual. Jerome, who wrote about 381, though he does once equate Antinous with a public concubine, is generally more benign.[51]

Four principal charges were developed. The apotheosis and cult, it was alleged from the very first attack by Justin in *c.* 150, had been imposed by fear of the Emperor, supported by bribery and perjury (Tatian) and maintained by tyranny (Epiphanios).[52] Almost all of the Fathers rallied to the second charge: Antinous had been a mere mortal and therefore unqualified to be honoured as a god, and his human sinful origins cast doubt on the supposed supernatural origins of all the other pagan gods. The third indictment concerned Antinous' morals. At first the Fathers were discreet, but with the *Book of Wisdom* (*c.* 180), Tertullian and Clement, the denunciations blared forth. This was the deification not of love, but of lust, of fornication, buggery and pederasty. The theme was rumbustiously taken up later by Athanasius and luridly illustrated by Prudentius. The final charge went deeper. Already Tertullian had called Antinous *infelix*, meaning unblessed.[53] Origen, admitting the extent and vitality of the cult in Egypt and Greece in his day, claimed that these were the products of evil, 'of magic and spells', of sorcerers and cheats. Origen cleverly twisted the popular conception of Antinous as 'blessed', 'holy', 'a benevolent daemon', into one of a restless, arbitrary, deluding and vengeful creature of black necromancy, the wicked demon of later medieval fantasy. Nothing could be further from this damned and earthbound spirit, he declared, than the sublime son of God, Jesus.[54] There can be little doubt that this denigration of Antinous had some impact on his more credulous believers who, like Serapamon the lover, began to see in him a daemon of magic, albeit benevolent, rather than of spiritual power.

The repeated stress on Antinous' beauty as a major element of his cult produced a strange reaction on the part of some Christians. So as to emphasise that they did not worship such evanescent externals, they depicted Jesus as almost physically ugly or commonplace by comparison, contending that his true beauty was spiritual and not visible to those purblind enemies who reviled him.[55]

Of the immediate effect of the Christian offensive, regurgitated in numerous compilations for a thousand years, we have no evidence. No doubt it helped erode the faith of believers in Antinous, especially in the late third century and beyond.

How long, then, did the 'belief in Antinous' last? Is it true that 'Antinous' star quickly lit up and as quickly went pale', that 'his life as a god was almost as short as his life as a man'? These two verdicts sum up the common view that the cult of Antinous was a very transient phenomenon of less than a decade, that 'Hadrian took his beloved into death'.[56]

It is indeed true that the manufacture of his artefacts in large quantities seems to end with the Emperor in 138. Though a couple of cities issued the odd coin of him in the next two reigns, only loyal Bithynion continued to mint them down to the reign of Caracalla (died 217).[57] We have no idea how long the busy Alexandrian counterfeiter continued at work. But by 138 there were clearly enough of his medallions in existence to satisfy demand. The sculptures also seem to stop around that date. There are only six which probably come from the following twenty years,[58] though considerably more which reproduce his type in a religious or mythological context and which may therefore witness to the lingering pervasiveness of his faith. Nevertheless, the sudden and enormous creative upsurge of the 130s was certainly over. But if there are no visible signs of the cult expanding thereafter, there are equally few of it contracting dramatically for many generations, until in fact the whole of Greek and Roman city life and culture were convulsed by the barbarian invasions after 250 AD. Even then a faith in Antinous survived surreptitiously or belligerently for another century and a half, down to the last struggles between the pagans and the Christians.

Everywhere his games continued to thrive, and these, it should be stressed, were not mere gatherings for pleasure but also dutifully perpetuated his memory and myth in their encomia, and were linked to priesthoods and the religious cult. Those at Mantineia, Antinoopolis and Bithynion were still famous in the early third century when we last hear of them. The ephebic games and priesthoods of Athens and Eleusis were in full vigour when records stop in 266–7, and seem to have continued well after that date. Those in Argos may have gone on to just before the reign of Julian in 360, that is about two hundred and twenty years after they started.

When Origen attacked Celsus in 249 the cult in Egypt, with its temples, oracles, miracles and orgies, was obviously flourishing and he mentions the 'belief in Antinous' among the Greeks as though that too was unabated. Athanasius' denunciations of a century later seem to be directed at a cult still very much in practice 'in our own times'.[59] Epiphanios' comments of about 367 confirm this.[60] Some of the sarcophagi and other objects which reveal Antinous as a popular saint also date from the third and fourth centuries.

With the depredations of the barbarians in the late third century, his cult may have withered in Greek and Italian lands if not in Egypt. Everywhere in late antiquity images of Antinous were destroyed or mutilated, by barbarians and Christians alike. The head at Cherchel was deliberately defaced by deep, precise incisions, the statue at Leptis Magna had its nose and genitals ignominiously removed, that at Eleusis was flung and smashed to pieces in the taurobolic ditch by Alaric's men in about 395. At the Villa Adriana, Gavin Hamilton, excavating in 1769, found a huge pit in the Panatello area, formerly a sacred grove, in which at least forty-five sculptures, several of Antinous, had been thrown after prior desecration.

In fact it is the history of some of his sculptures which most vividly illustrates the affection and veneration in which Antinous was held in at least some places until the final convulsions of classical civilisation. The statue at Delphi, lovingly polished for centuries, was, in some barbarian incursion, toppled over, losing both its forearms. Afterwards, however, it was gently raised and re-erected without its arms in another chapel further up the sacred way, where it was found, still standing, its knees and ankles now broken under the weight of the earth on top of it, in 1893 (figs 1–2). The colossal statue at Frascati was abandoned to the iconoclasts but only after its godly head had been cut off and buried so reverently that the silver film and palombino marble of its eyeballs were still partially intact when it was dug up fourteen hundred or so years later.[61] Other smaller heads like the Florence bronze were similarly preserved. Busts were sometimes buried for safety in fields or woods, where Lanciani about 1900 discovered one:

> I remember, in the woodland of the Isola Farnese, where a labourer had just struck with his plough the left shoulder of a bust. I helped disengage it from the earth, and shall never forget the sight of that lovely face suddenly appearing amidst such desolate surroundings and looking at us with a melancholy expression, as if we had disturbed the peace of his grave.[62]

Even the Antinous-Dionysos of the Vatican, all 3.5 metres of it, was laid down so carefully near Praeneste that, despite its angular pose and vulnerable extremities, nothing was seriously damaged when it was found in 1795 (fig. 60).[63] Near Lanuvium, the relief of Antinous-Sylvanus was carried out from the villa, laid face downwards on a bed of specially sifted soil in a trench one metre deep, and then covered over.

Perhaps the motives for such acts of preservation were sometimes purely aesthetic or material. But obviously too they were religious, the last acts of loyalty to the old gods by devoted bands of votaries or pious households, mainly in Italy. Antinous seems to have been a special object of such concern: that, it is said, is why relatively more statues of him survive in a fair condition compared with those of some other, greater gods.[64]

His images survived publicly till the very final prohibition of paganism under Theodosius in 391. Not until that time was the colossal bronze of him in Antinoopolis taken down and its base re-used. In Rome, as the fortunes of the beleaguered pagans and the triumphing Christians swayed back and forth in the years 360–91, Antinous seems to have been pushed to the fore as the last symbol of the old classical culture under assault. Hence the particularly vicious outburst of the Christian poet Prudentius against him in his denunciation of the head of the pagan party, Symmachus, in 384. Indeed, at this very time a final set of images of Antinous was boldly and defiantly issued. They are a series of seven contorniates (large medallions with a deep indentation within the rim). They were new creations but evidently derive in part from medals of Mantineia, Bithynion, Smyrna and Cyme of the years 134–6. We do not know where they came from, but they seem to refer to the struggles in Rome in the 370s and 380s between the pagan and the Christian factions over the removal from the Senate House of the Altar of Victory, a focal symbol of the old paganism erected by Augustus himself, the final eviction of which in 384 marked a decisive victory for the Christian party.[65]

In these crude medallions, Antinous, meticulously named, is chiefly recognisable by his hair-style and massive chest. He is shown draped, holding the pedum or the caduceus, once as a tense funerary charioteer, or accompanied by his old emblem, the bull. As if designed flagrantly to affront the Christians, he is deliberately associated with some of the principal pagan immortals in history: Achilles, Hermes and Dionysos. To provoke them more, he is shown with the pedum and unflinchingly identified by name with the notorious god of fertility, Pan – whose libidinous and immoral activities the Christians especially loathed. On one coin (fig. 42) Antinous appears in full military uniform, evidently as a champion, shaking his upraised hand as if in farewell to the classical world and in defiance at the Christian one in which he was an early demon. The legend, as aggressive as his posture, proudly proclaims for the last time: 'The country of Antinous, the god'.

XVI

THE RISE AND FALL
OF ANTINOOPOLIS

One thousand six hundred years after it was built, the city of Antinous on the banks of the Nile still stood intact enough to astound intrepid travellers. 'The moment one enters,' exclaimed the Jesuit missionary Sigard, who was there in 1715, 'it offers to the eyes noble and regal buildings . . . This town was a perpetual peristyle.'[1] At the end of the same century, a member of Napoleon's expedition to Egypt in 1798–1801, the surveyor Jomard, was dazzled: 'masses of ruins, constructions among the palm trees . . . standing out white against the dark groves and the blue skies'.[2] Once in the centre, he could only utter rhetorical questions: 'What are we to make of these magisterial streets, as long as the new city itself, which divide it in two and are, from one end to the other, just immense colonnades?'[3]

But eight decades later the scene had changed and evoked not wonder but despair. For example, when in 1880 Dietrichson sailed by on a cruise without stopping, his response was not disappointment but almost relief. He noted: 'I did not complain too much that I was prevented from wandering among the endless rubbish tips which stretched beyond the splendid palms . . . where at the very most here and there a hardly recognisable stone was to be found.'[4]

At the end, the desolate scene must have been very like that at its birth in October 130 when Hadrian contemplated the spot where Antinous' body had been brought ashore. Here, 360 miles from its mouth, the Nile swung north-west and then north-east in a large bend (fig. 33). From its right bank a sandy plain ran 1.5 kilometres eastwards to the craggy, grey-white escarpment of the desert which rose parallel to the river for some time and then swerved round to meet it at the north-west. On this plain there were traces of an ancient pharaonic settlement of some substance which had degenerated into poverty and virtual extinction in Ptolemaic times. Inscriptions on the papiriform columns of its surviving temple near the river show that it had probably been called 'Hir-wer'. The temple, though very modest by Egyptian standards, was the only building left of note. It bore the cartouches of the great Pharaoh

Rameses ii (1298–1235 BC) who had re-used materials from an earlier temple deliberately destroyed after the death of its heretic founder, the monotheist Pharaoh Akhenaten (1379–1362 BC) (fig. 34). A religious, indeed a mystically heterodox spirit, was always to impregnate this spot.

Perhaps the body of Antinous had been carried past the sloping pylons of the temple to lie in its cool sanctuary before being taken back over the river to Hermopolis. No doubt too Hadrian rested in its halled courtyard on his several visits to discuss the new city which was to rise on the almost deserted plain outside. From gratitude and respect, he left the temple standing, indeed may even have embellished its precincts with statuary and paving.

For though the new foundation was to be ostensibly Greek, Hadrian intended to incorporate some of the strengths of the Egyptian culture he had lately come to admire. The city, as we have seen, was not to be just a personal memorial to his lost love or a cult centre for the risen god but a political bastion of Hellenism in Middle Egypt. 'The new Greeks of Antinous', as the Emperor officially designated those recruited to this impressive new metropolis,[5] were to embody the civic and cultural values of Hellas which he had done so much to revive. At the same time, the ancient culture of the Nile which, after all, had first recognised the divinity of Antinous as Osiris, was to be honoured and indeed, through an approved admixture of native blood in the citizenry, to be fused into that of Greece.

Hadrian officially declared the city founded on 30 October 130, but it was still not completely built or settled at the time of his death eight years later. To demonstrate its pure Greek roots (and his own antiquarianism) he took some of its laws and its archaic municipal calendar from Naucratis in the Delta, the oldest Greek settlement in the land. A core of its citizens were chosen by lot from Ptolemaïs, the Greek city on the Upper Nile which prided itself on its purity of blood. Yet more were recruited from the Greek elite scattered in the towns of the Fayoum. Others were taken, sometimes by compulsion, from Oxyrhynchus and Herakleopolis and other cities of the north. The obelisk declares that veterans of the Roman army and navy, who were at least nominally Greek, were also enrolled as citizens and given land (perhaps elsewhere) upon completion of their service. There is little papyrological evidence of this happening in Hadrian's time but more signs of veterans arriving in the 140s and 150s.[6] Evidently the settlement took time and may have been somewhat reluctant. The earliest surviving records of Greeks enrolling, from Arsinoë in the Fayoum, is from the spring of 133. Some people took the citizenship of the new city but then went back to their old homes. Indeed it has even been argued that the special privileges with which Hadrian endowed the city were proffered, between 132 and 135, only when it had become clear that some special inducements were needed to draw in more settlers.[7] Be that as it may – and the matter is disputed – by the Emperor's death Antinoopolis was thoroughly established and continued to grow, well into the Byzantine era.

Using limestone from quarries to the east and granite from Syene, the physical construction of the city must have been pushed on apace. The first annual games, or *Antinoeia*, were held in the spring of 131, no doubt in primitive camping conditions and amid the mess of builders. But by those of 134 the city had risen far enough to be formally inaugurated: at least such an event can be deduced from the presence in the area in that year of a contingent of high-ranking Roman officials and the dedication about that time of a colossal bronze statue to 'Antinous *Epiphanios*' by the then *epistrategos* of the Thebaid, Julius Fidus Aquila. Even so, the new road with its watering-places and guard-houses, which Hadrian drove across the bandit-infested desert to link with the port of Berenice and the lucrative Indian trade of the Red Sea, was not to be finished until February 137. And the theatre, which no respectable Greek city could be without, was still being constructed a year later.

Antinoopolis was laid out on the gridiron plan typical of Hellenistic cities like Alexandria. One main thoroughfare, 1,308 metres long, ran parallel and fairly close to the Nile, roughly north to south. It was crossed by the second main street, 954 metres long, from the quayside on the west to the eastern perimeter. These divided the city into four main, though unequal, districts (or *grammata*). Within and across them smaller roads ran in parallel grids, forming the blocks (or *plintheia*) by which groups of houses were numbered. The whole city, trapezoid in shape, 1.5 kilometres square and 5 kilometres in circumference, was surrounded on three sides by a huge brick wall, a structure, now so demolished that it appears as a dry moat, which poses unsolved problems of dating, position and function.[8] Beyond the wall, on the uninhabited half of the plain to the north and east, were cemeteries for ordinary citizens of Greek or Egyptian religion. The rich were entombed more exclusively in deep shafts sunk in the mountains nearby.

Hadrian was determined that no visitor should ever forget this city or the person and love it commemorated. His instinct to symbolise his feelings in constructions of megalomaniac scale and stunning impact found here another expression. The boring layout was to be transformed by the architecture and decoration.

Coming up the steps of the quay, the visitor to Antinoopolis found himself in a vast courtyard.[9] On either side stoa, each of at least forty columns of red granite topped by Corinthian capitals of limestone, extended to the river bank. Facing him, and flanked by similar colonnades, towered the principal gate of the city, 18.75 metres high and 17.37 wide (fig. 44a). With its mixture of Doric and Corinthian orders, of severity and richness, of gabled domestic gate and military triumphal arch, it epitomised the eclectic idiom of this place and Hadrian's usual style of civic porticoes. Before it, on two great plinths, stood colossal statues, possibly of Antinous.

Once he had passed under its three arches and moved up the western arm of the main transverse street to its junction with the main north–south one, the visitor, even sixteen hundred years later, let out a gasp of astonishment. Not only were these two boulevards majestic in their breadth, twenty metres wide (including the walkways), as wide as those of the great Alexandria and more than twice those of Pompeii, but on either side ran covered arcades supported by polished limestone columns of Doric profile with Corinthian capitals.[10] These endless colonnades were only interrupted where the elaborate façades or grand propyleia of impressive buildings intercepted their stately procession. On the north–south street Jomard calculated that there were at least 772 such columns and on the transverse one another 572 and concluded 'that this multitude must have produced an effect as if of magic' (fig. 45a).[11] Given the 80 or more columns at the entrance, another arcade near the theatre and 365 or so columns surrounding the hippodrome, little wonder the city, even in its ruin, was declared 'magnificent . . . a perpetual peristyle'.[12] At the corners of the two main crossings of the north–south street rose four yet more imposing Corinthian pillars, eighteen metres high and bearing colossal statues. Those at the chief crossing may have been of Hadrian. Those at the one further to the north were erected in 232 AD to celebrate the victory of the Emperor Alexander Severus over the Persians.

But it was not these imperial images which were the most striking. Over each column on the north–south street, and probably over those in the transverse street as well, stood sculptures of Antinous, his name inscribed on the entablatures below. The tragically mutilated fragments of these statues or busts, of a standard form, strewed the main street from top to bottom in Jomard's day and Sigard had earlier been able to read the inscriptions. Thus in the two principal streets alone there were probably repeated 1,344 images of the beloved and god: 'a prodigious number', exclaimed Jomard.[13] In addition, there were in public places free-standing sculptures of Antinous, with higher artistic pretensions, of which we have traces of three.[14] No stranger would ever have had a moment's doubt whose city this was.

The vistas along the 'immense colonnades'[15] terminated in spectacular buildings, climaxes of stone. The main transverse street ended at the east in a massive propyleion which straddled its width and of which Jomard saw enormous Corinthian shafts still standing. This may have been a later rebuilding of the Hadrianic original for another celebration in 282 AD. At the southern end of the main street rose a still finer and richer Corinthian gateway, twenty metres high, which led into the spacious courtyard of the theatre (fig. 44b). The proscenium of this was seventy-four metres wide and from the hemisphere of marble seats beyond, the spectators had a splendid view over the whole city to the north, to the arid mountains on the east and to the lush Nile valley on the west. More than three-quarters of a mile away, at the northern end of the same street, loomed a massive quadratic building, thirty-four metres square and surrounded by an arcade, of which only the foundations remained for Jomard to inspect. He conjectured that it might well have been the mausoleum of Antinous. Given that there must have been some shrine or cenotaph, if not an actual tomb, of his in the city, this monumental construction, placed at the end of a vista of nearly a thousand of his images and on the same side of the town as the field of offerings found by Gayet, might well have been it. Only excavation could clarify the matter and this, as for so much else of importance in the city, has never been attempted.

The sumptuous remains of many other columniated buildings, basilicas or courtyards met Jomard's eyes. The materials were everywhere lavish – not just polished limestone and red granite but porphyry and the pure or veined marbles of Italy and Greece. The baths of the south side of the east street were certainly among the most magnificent edifices in the city: 78.5 metres wide and 68 deep, sheathed with marbles and segregated for men and women strictly according to Hadrian's prudish precepts. We know that the city possessed a gymnasium for its educational needs, an agora for its social and political life, a market for its economy and a praetorium and a Caesareum for administration. Gayet discovered near the eastern gate two magnificent temples of Isis and Serapis with columns eleven metres high and gilded capitals.

As was usually the case with such cities, the domestic dwellings were more humble, honeycombed together, three storeys high, of brick, with internal courtyards and decorated with mosaics, like the one recently uncovered of Diana the huntress.[16] On the plain, beyond the eastern wall, stood the hippodrome, 307 metres long and 77 wide, with a race track wide enough for six chariots abreast. In 1714, Lucas counted eight tiers of seats still remaining and in 1829 Prokesch saw the rump of a colossal sphinx still decorating its spina. It was enclosed in a palisade of at least 365 columns of red granite.

The whereabouts of the centre of Antinous' cult has, until recently, been a mystery. The obelisk talks of a temple to him in the city built in a mixture of classical Greek and archaic Egyptian architecture and surrounded by statues and sphinxes. A papyrus mentions an *Antinoeion*, which implies a temple to him exclusively as an Hellenic god. Perhaps there were two temples, just as there were to be two basic kinds of sculptural image: one to him in a mixed style as Osiris-Antinous and served by Egyptian priests who were not citizens, and another in the classical idiom to him as the divine ephebe or Dionysos of Greece and administered by the civic hierarchy. We know that his cult was endowed with lucrative estates – 'the holy ground of Osirisantinous'.[17]

The site of the Greek temple of Antinous has recently been established. Italian excavators in 1965–8 discovered a fragment of sculpture in Parian marble, part of the naked right shoulder (0.93 metres long and 0.43 high) of a huge statue which bears indications of having been the chief image of the Greek cult of Antinous in the city.[18] If it is, it represents the largest sculpture of him so far known and must have been broken up on its original site. Now this, in turn, corresponds exactly with a remarkably elaborate temple which Jomard explored and sketched. It lay at the very hub of the city, at the south-east corner of the main crossing, and consisted of a noble Ionic propylaion, 11 metres deep, fronting a splendid façade 25 metres wide, all resting on a substantial podium. Its marble columns of the Ionic order and 8.5 metres high were of exceptional workmanship. Not far away, Jomard himself found a marble life-size torso, 'pure and youthful', which seemed to show Antinous in the nebris of Dionysos like that from Aidepsos. Here, no doubt, in the heart of the city, was the centre of the Greek cult of Antinous, though whether his notorious mysteries were enacted there or his oracles intoned from within the hollowed back of the great cult image must remain more doubtful. The home of the healing and miracle-working 'daemon', praised by the obelisk and denounced by Origen, may rather have been in the other, more fantastic Greco-Egyptian temple, and this is not likely to have been the somewhat poky and peripheral chapel of Rameses ii down by the river. Its location, like so much else of interest at Antinoopolis, waits to be discovered.

Hadrian endowed the city with a Greek constitution and administration equipped with Roman municipal powers and privileges. Presided over by a Senate and possessing the usual array of civic magistrates and functionaries, the city was autonomous in its self-government, independent of the district administration and responsible directly to the governor (*epistrategos*) of the whole Heptanomia. Every citizen had to be enrolled in one of the ten phyles and fifty or more demes, the names of which had been drawn from the personal experience and public aspirations of the Emperor. They did not correspond to the geographical divisions of the city but grouped the citizens for civic functions and obligations.

What made the city exceptional among those in Egypt and Greece and more Roman in its character were the extraordinary privileges which Hadrian bestowed on it, partly out of generosity of sentiment, partly as a shrewd means to swell its population. Most unusual was the right conceded to both Greek men and women[19] to marry Egyptians and have their children qualify for the citizenship. Such a policy realistically recognised the existence of mixed marriages in areas like the Fayoum from which the city hoped to attract colonists. But, deriving from Hadrian's sympathy for provincial cultures and new-found respect for that of Egypt, it optimistically hoped to infuse native strengths into the Hellenic polity. Some of the more purist Greek councillors may soon have found it degrading but as the centuries wore on, the self-conscious Greek elite which they represented disappeared eventually in the racial and cultural amalgam and under financial pressures.

Chief among the other privileges was the exemption of Antinoites from civic obligations (liturgies) outside the city in other districts where they possessed property. Over the years they vigorously fought to preserve this right against jealous local officials; with decreasing success in the third century. Another lucrative privilege was the right of citizens who had their children registered within thirty days of birth to have them maintained out of funds specially set aside by Hadrian for the purpose on the model of the Italian *alimenta* system. There were also desirable exemptions from poll-taxes, from property-transfer and import dues, and from expensive guardianships; and, among other privileges, special powers were given to Antinoites over their creditors. No wonder the rolls of the citizens soon inflated with cunning opportunists who took the citizenship for its privileges but continued to live elsewhere.

Much of the bustling life of Antinoopolis over the centuries has been preserved for us in the abundant writings of its citizens, but that life was not remarkably different from other Greco-Egyptian communities at the time. It is not clear that the city ever became a major commercial centre, though it did possess private banks. The new road never succeeded in diverting much trade from the Red Sea and there was little fertile land in the vicinity. Its undoubted prosperity and expansion may have come more from its role as a religious centre and as an ever-more-important seat of government. Certainly the grand and expensive buildings erected in the mid- and late third century, when Greek cities everywhere were being reduced to ruin, testify to its economic buoyancy. The cemeteries which have been so extensively excavated have lain bare the corpses of its embalmed middle and ruling classes equipped with all the paraphernalia requisite for eternity. There were hosts of trade guilds and craftshops – gold-beaters, weavers, leather workers, seamstresses – to equip them in this life and to rig them out for the next. Indeed, as the centuries of Rome became those of Byzantium, the stuffs which the citizens wore for the grave became ever more majestic in design, though the pottery they took with them ever more crude.

Hadrian, however, would have had little to complain of in the devotion of the 'New Greeks' to their Hellenic heritage. From extensive but fragmentary finds of papyri from various centuries we hear of schools teaching Greek grammar and official shorthand and find the citizens reading, among other things, the philosophy of Plato and Xenophon, the history of Thucydides, the speeches of Demosthenes, Homer's *Iliad* and *Odyssey*, poems by Pindar and Callimachus, dramas by Euripides, comedies by Aristophanes and Menander, as well as scientific works by Hippocrates and Galen. The most important find has been of a sixth-century codex containing sixteen idylls by Theocritus, coming from a Byzantine library in the town, the earliest surviving manuscript of the work.

The visual arts flourished, too. The complete destruction of the statuary does not enable us to know if there were local workshops in the classical style, though there were plenty of vigorous if crude carvers of images at work in the Coptic period.[20] Splendid line drawings of charioteers and botanical specimens appear in the papyri. Portrait painting, if only for mummy effigies, started immediately after the foundation – over forty-two such portraits have been recovered by an estimated fourteen different artists.[21] Wall-painting also developed richly as the fine and well-preserved frescoes found in the tomb of the sixth-century woman Theodosia in 1937–8 bear witness.

Much of the prosperity and the singular prestige of Antinoopolis came from its religious character as 'a holy city'.[22] It was never to lose its reputation as a centre of wild, profound or useful religious experience – of miracles, of the occult and, more sinisterly, of magic. Even deep in the Middle Ages the Arabs still muttered that it was 'a place of sorcerers' – the very words used of it by Origen a thousand years before.[23]

'The most great god Osirisantinous', as he was called,[24] was the chief god of the city on whose name (and that of the Emperor) solemn oaths and legal documents were sworn. The frequency of his name attests his popularity. The obelisk's panegyrics and Origen's denunciations all powerfully suggest a highly charged atmosphere, mystic, excitedly awaiting on supernatural manifestations, breaking out at special festivities into unbridled ecstasies. The cult of Eleusis was not only commemorated in the phyles and demes but seems to have had its fervent devotees in the city and may have been linked to that of Antinous.[25] However strict his worship according to Greek and Egyptian rites may have been, many more practitioners of magic and necromancy must have swarmed to the city eager to provide credulous believers, like the love-sick Serapamon, with incantations, spells and charms and avid to prey on the countless pious pilgrims who flocked there with their offering jars and hopeful prayers.

In addition to the pilgrims, ambitious competitors and spectators came from all over the Greek world for the great games or *Antinoeia*, the most important in Egypt, and notable for being held every year. They were unusual, too, in their scope, comprising artistic and musical festivals, athletic events, and chariot and equestrian competitions. Rowing races were held on the Nile in honour of the new Osiris, or, it has been proposed, inside the specially and ingeniously flooded hippodrome itself.[26] The prizes – citizenship, money, tokens and free maintenance for life – attracted competitors of international standing.

It is not surprising, therefore, that devotion among the citizens to Antinous persisted at least until the official imposition of Christianity in about 392. It was about that time that the colossal bronze erected by Julius Fidus Aquila was wrenched from its red granite base, which was frugally turned round, re-inscribed and used for a marble figure less offensive to Christian suscepti-bilities. The Greeks, unlike the local Egyptians, clung to their pagan gods, Bes, Isis, Serapis, Hermes and Aphrodite among them, until well into the Christian era. There may have been violent friction, even outraged destruction of monuments or even of quarters in the notorious pagan city when Christianity finally became the official religion. As perhaps a token of reconciliation, the local sculptors produced, in the fourth century grave steles depicting a naked ephebe, with a form and a hair-style resembling those of Antinous, holding aloft in one hand a cross and in the other the grapes of Dionysos.

Orthodox Christianity indeed took long to establish its hold over the city. There was a bishop there in the second century and rival ones in the next. But the Christian minority were so heterodox that the Emperor Valens (364–78) could comfortably banish his theological enemies there to simmer impotently among the eccentrics. In Byzantine times the strange religious fervour of the place continued. We hear of a dozen convents, and Gayet dug up the mummies of colourful anchorites and dramatically converted courtesans. Christian churches replaced the temples: Sigard saw their marbled ruins and recent excavations have uncovered a fifth-century one on the site of the old temple of Isis.[27] The district produced a rich crop of canonisations, even other miraculous recoveries from the Nile. Colluthus, a doctor from the area who was martyred in the persecutions of the governor Arrianus, became a prominent local saint. The tradition persisted into the Moslem era: the very name of the squalid village presently on the site, Sheik Abadeh, 'the pious Sheik', is said to come from an Arab chieftain martyred there upon his conversion to Christ. Sacrifice, devotion and consecration haunted the place to the end.

Antinoopolis grew steadily bigger and more important as the Empire of Rome crumbled and turned into that of Byzantium. The city expanded southwards of the wall. In later centuries it became the seat of a *Dux* who combined military and civil power. After 535 it was still the seat of the *Dux et Augustalis* but capital only of the Lower Thebaid. The Coptic and Egyptian culture had now obliterated the last vestiges of Hellenism and the city was no longer particularly distinct in its privileges and organisation from others in the province. The proud title of 'Antinoite' ceased to be used in the fifth century.

At first, the Arab invasions of 639–42 had little impact on its status. Over a century afterwards we find it still a flourishing centre of Moslem administration. It then disappears into the obscurity of the Middle Ages in Egypt. Saladin (1137–93) emerges in the chronicles to order the great doors of the theatre arch to a gate in Cairo where they were still to be seen in the eighteenth century. More ominously, he is said to have ordered the city's demolition, though other Arab writers speak contradictorily of its extensive remains.[28]

The final destruction is charged indubitably to modern man.

When Sigard toured the city in 1715 it was already in ruins. For centuries the locals had used it as a quarry for their homes, mosques and cemeteries. The north and east gates were piles of stones, the colonnades mainly fallen, but the western and southern gates stood substantially intact, architectural features were everywhere visible and even the minor streets could be discerned.

Jomard came in 1798–1801 on five visits, armed with 'a good metric chain' and a blunderbuss.[29] Despite the wavering and soon catastrophic military situation of the French, marauding Bedouin and mishaps like getting lost in gloomy catacombs, he produced a lucid account of the city, full of accurate measurements and data, with illustrations, sections and plans which put even the most recent archaeological reports to shame.[30] Much had gone since Sigard's day: the ruins of the north and east gates, for example, the traces of the minor streets, the seats of the hippodrome. But the standing ruins were still very moving: the cluster at the theatre gate formed 'a very beautiful ensemble', the west gate and its surroundings and the Alexander Severus quadrivium were impressive. Everywhere the fallen or broken monuments begged for reconstruction or excavation which Jomard had not the time to make. Already, however, the forces of rapid destruction were at work. In the theatre the chalk oven 'of the barbarians' was already burning the limestone (of which the city was chiefly built) and marble to powder. Outside on the plain handsome crops of sugar cane infiltrated the very city limits.[31]

It was this sudden and short-lived prosperity which swept the splendid remains of Antinoopolis off the face of the earth. Under the independent dynasty of Mehemet Ali, after the 1820s, intensive agricultural production was encouraged. The columns, panels and architectural blocks of the city were smashed up and carted away to build a sugar factory opposite at El Rodah, highways, and later a dam at Assiut. The rest was consigned to the ovens for chalk and lime. When Mariette, the great French Egyptologist, arrived on a visit to the already despoiled area in 1863–4, he came across the red granite base of that statue of Antinous erected by Julius Fidus Aquila in 134, standing outside a factory. He was told that it had recently been purloined in the search for building materials:

'And the statue?' asked Mariette.
'But it was there too.'
'What's become of it then?'
'Oh, it was in marble and has been turned into good lime.'[32]

Even the nitrous soil, rich with papyri, was carted off in loads to supply a gunpowder establishment or nibbled away by the ever-active nitre-gatherers of the valley, the *sebbakhin*. By the 1880s Dr Freund, reporting back to Dietrichson, wailed: 'the Egyptians seek the last stone, the last piece of burnt brick'. He encountered great piles of recently smashed up stones and shafts. Nevertheless there were a few stumps of columns still obstinately standing and 'everywhere fragments of lovely marbles, remains of panels from houses and splendid remains of columns'.[33] When in 1913 Johnson took the first photographs, Antinoopolis had vanished along with the meretricious local prosperity which had consumed it. His prints reveal a ravaged landscape of rubbish and shard tips and of trenches, like a torn battlefield of the coming

World War, across which some paving from the great thoroughfare, now shrunken to a ghostly path, arbitrarily and sadly makes its way (fig. 45h)

By the irony of time, the scene which meets modern eyes at that bend of the Nile – with its desolate plain, fringe of palms, miserable village and archaic temple – has reverted back two millennia to that which Antinous may well have glimpsed in his expiring struggles before his head sank finally beneath the waters.

'THE CROWN AND GLORY OF SCULPTURE'

Antinous inspired the final great creation of classical art. Fired by the religious and political ecstasy ignited by his death and symbolic resurrection, excited by countless enthusiastic commissions and working hectically in the short span of only eight years, the sculptors of the imperial world, themselves mainly Greek, fashioned the last in that long and consummate series of sculptural types of human and divine beauty which had first taken shape seven hundred years before in the workshops of Argos and Attica. Yet, though nourished by classical art, the sculptures of Antinous embody aims and techniques fresh enough to make them something powerfully original, unforgettably distinct and of their own time.

The originality of the achievement is partly explained by the unprecedented circumstances these artists faced. The older gods of Olympus had, after all, never existed as living human beings and had long ago been reduced to iconographic types. The Hellenistic ruler-gods, such as Alexander the Great, had had their human features transformed into energetically heroised idealisations. The traits of the Roman imperial *divi*, consecrated after death, were known only too precisely from their numerous realistic portraits from life. The divine images of them therefore tended to be but these portrait likenesses, scarcely idealised, blown up into colossal proportions perhaps, adorned with godly trappings and sometimes incongruously grafted onto gracious bodies copied meticulously from famous types of the divinities of mythology.

Antinous presented a different problem. Here was a youth, recently a living being, whose very individual physiognomy and style of beauty had been widely seen, admired and noted all over the Greek world and which Hadrian wished to be perpetuated. But here too was a new god whose following and faith attracted a fervour which eclipsed the tepid formalities of the imperial cult and rivalled those of the more vital gods of sacrifice and salvation from antiquity and the orient. Moreover, here also was a story, a myth in the making, fresh in the minds of contemporaries, which combined the two most potent mysteries –

love and death – as well as more humdrum elements of character, adventure and relationships.

How could all this be summed up in works of marble or bronze without incongruity, prolixity or incoherence? How convincingly to suggest both the transient physical form of the actual youth and also the ageless immortality he had now attained? How to keep his humanity while expressing the transcendence of his new divine status? How to isolate the crucial mysteries of his myth from the trivialities of his story and reputation? The creation of the image of Antinous was thus a formidable challenge. Fortunately, the antitheses it posed – of realism and idealism, humanity and the divine, carnality and spirituality, history and myth – were just such as the minds and creative energies of the time loved to grapple with. And in responding to the challenge the sculptors of the last days of Hadrian at their best devised the last masterpieces of classical art.

Where and how did the present images of Antinous originate? Though some may be variants of *ad vivum* portraits now lost and others worked up from the memories of artists who saw him in life and tried to piece together his characteristics after death, it is clear that a substantial core, indeed a majority, are closely related to each other. This similarity, almost identity, can be seen most closely in a group of busts of Antinous. For other works the affinity can be traced not so much in the facial expression and bodily posture, which differ subtly or widely, but most consistently in the hair-style. It is extremely unlikely that an artist will invent a hair-style and disposition of individual locks for a portrait identical with another of the same subject without first having seen that work or a model from which it derives. The detailed study of the hair has thus become a recognised method of establishing affinities and common derivations between groups of sculptures of the same subject, even enabling sequences in time or in style to be established which can be traced back to one prototype.

On the basis of a study of this kind published in 1966, Clairmont has concluded that forty-seven of the sixty-one sculpted heads of Antinous which he discusses derive from one and only one such prototype.[1] But long before his detailed analysis confirmed the theory, art-historians had been convinced that most or all of the sculptures of Antinous had been based on one such model or *Urbild*.[2] The problem was, which one, and where and how was it created?

Though Hadrian may have commissioned sporadic sculptures of Antinous during his last months in Egypt in 130–31, it is more probable that he waited until his return to his beloved Greece in 131–2 before approving a definitive image in the classical style which would serve as the authorised model for the cult he was so busy founding. The visual sources of that fundamental work we cannot guess, except that Hadrian must have scrutinised and agreed every detail. We know from coins that such an image was in existence before mid-133, when Hadrian still may not have returned to Italy. That this seminal work was made not in Italy but in Greece is rendered likely by Hadrian's presence there after the apotheosis, by the rapid spread of the cult in the east in 131–3, creating obvious demands for an authentic image of the new god, and Antinous' own special appeal to Greek cultural and national susceptibilities. It has nothing to do with an alleged repudiation of Antinous by Italian artists on moral and religious grounds: on the contrary, once a model was available they avidly copied and elaborated it.[3]

Clairmont has argued from the hair-style that a group of four Greek works – the Delphi statue, the two Patras busts (figs 2, 49–50) and a head in Athens – are the closest surviving replicas of a model, now lost.[4] They relate closely to the fine medallions depicting busts of Antinous produced in the Peloponnese in 133–4. These medallions are said to be the work of an artist from the group from Aphrodisias in Caria now settled in Rome, patronised by the Emperor for coins and sculpture and now commissioned to come to Greece to cut the dies.[5] What could be more natural than to assume that this virtuosic artist who so cleverly depicted busts on his coins was none other than the man who also carved the original sculpture on which those busts were based? But attempts to identify this man by relating the relief of Antoninianus of Aphrodisias, and the sardonyx with the tantalising signature 'Ant[o]', to the busts shown on the coins have failed on the grounds of basic differences of hair-style among all three productions, which are unlikely to have occurred if they all had the same author.[6]

It is generally agreed that the prototype was a full-size statue of Antinous, possibly in bronze. Clairmont thinks that this was created in the Peloponnese in 131–2. But though the busts shown on the medallions may well have been early versions of this statue, this is not reason enough to believe that the statue itself was erected there, still less that it was made there.[7] It is more likely that it was fashioned under the Emperor's careful eyes in Athens in 131–2 by an outstanding master, perhaps indeed by an artist of the Aphrodisian school specially brought over from Rome for the job.[8] This artist or his colleagues may well have gone on later to work on the medallions and replicas of the Peloponnese.

Even the four so-called replicas of this original are so dissimilar that it is difficult to reconstruct it precisely from them. Probably it was a statue of Antinous naked as the divine ephebe, without specific godly attributes. Its head was lowered and turned to the left above its powerful chest and slender thighs. Whether its left shoulder was raised or its arm rested on a plinth is not clear.

From this model, using wax, plaster or terracotta casting or the pointing process, copies were made for distribution all over the Empire, to clients or workshops. At the latter, yet further copies would be carved. Such replicas might be fairly exact or widely divergent from the original. Some of the series of closely related busts of Antinous, hollowed out for easy transport, and truncated copies of the original statue or an early version of it, may have been distributed from Greece as models for further copies. The unusual form of these busts, displaying the lowered head to the left, wide shoulders, stumps of arms (the left often raised), broad chest carved down to beneath the nipples, gave distant sculptors enough information about the scale, nature and posture of Antinous' body for them to work up full-size statues of him if so desired. There can be no doubt that some of these busts which found their way to Italy provided sources for Italian-made statues and reliefs.

Clairmont's list of works with hair-styles derived from the original model falls into three different series, the last of which, following the example of the Naples Farnese statue where the head turns to the right (fig. 55), is mainly confined to works of Italian manufacture. Though without doubt the prototype was widely influential, too much can be made of its impact, which subsided like the ripples on a lake. Of the forty-seven works given as dependent on it by Clairmont, fifteen have hair-styles differing so widely from the presumed archetype that some (e.g. the Berlin head) can be considered as independent or only vaguely related to it.[9] Another fourteen are admitted to be altogether independent and these include some of the most notable works of Antinous – the Sala Rotonda bust, the Museo delle Terme head, the Mondragone head and the Lansdowne Dionysos among them. If we take into account factors other than hair-style – facial features, expression, posture, and the group of works in the Egyptian style – then over 50 of the 115 works listed in Appendix 1 differ markedly from the standard model with the downcast head, sombre expression and raised left arm seen in abbreviation in the busts or in full elaboration in the Vatican Dionysos.

The variety within the type, even within those which follow the model, and putting aside the Egyptianising works, has not been stressed enough hitherto. Sometimes the posture is varied: the introspective bowed head gives way to a challenging stare or to an upward gaze; the arms stretch up or out; the body twists or is frontal, in repose or movement. The hair varies from the thick, standard curls of the model to the crinkly woolly cap of the Kansas City bust, the corkscrew ringlets of the Sala Rotonda bust, the decoratively woven festoons of the Cherchel and Mondragone heads. The age alters from the little boy of the heads of London and Ostia, the sylph-like adolescent of the Conservatori Museum, to the virile man of Copenhagen (no. 685). The expression ranges between extremes: sometimes diffident and insecure (the Delphi and Eleusis statues), frequently brooding and withdrawn (the busts, the Vatican Dionysos), occasionally disdainful and aloof (the Albani relief, the Mondragone head), sometimes with a tinge of sensuality (the Sala Rotonda bust, the Copenhagen head no. 686), at others fierce, alert, even aggressive (the Museo delle Terme head, the Bank of Italy statue). The body changes from the drooping languor of the Sylvanus relief to the gladiatorial athleticism of the Berlin statuette.

Why so many variations? Some occur because the works are genuinely independent creations derived from imagination or sources other than the standard model. Others stem from the functions or symbolism of the particular sculpture or the attributes of the hero or deity with whom he was being associated. Many are just the arbitrary decision of the sculptor or are consequences of his skill or lack of it. Some characteristics are regional: the virile ruler-heads seem a product of Asia Minor. Roman workshops preferred a high finish and an introspective mood. Some works (e.g. the Knole and Mondragone heads) may be replicas of bronze originals, hence their bland and inexpressive smoothness.[10]

Only one work of Antinous is signed, the relief by Antoninianus, though a heterogeneous variety of other works have been ascribed to him. No doubt he and other artists from the school of Aphrodisias in Rome played a major part in producing images of Antinous, but, apart from technical facility, their individual styles are too diverse to form a distinctive and recognisable Aphrodisian version of him.[11]

One other factor accounts for the forms and the variety in the images of Antinous: the artists' debts to the past.

The Romans had long surrounded themselves with copies of famous Greek sculptures of the past. Now in the reign of Hadrian there was a renewed interest in the art of the fifth century BC in particular: the age of classicism and of Athens. Partly this was a reaction in taste against Flavian realism and towards idealism, partly it arose from the enthusiasm of the Emperor to unify the Greco-Roman world by evoking the style and the elevated spirit of its fresh and matchless prime.

Once a sculptor commissioned to produce a work of Antinous had ascertained from copies the facts of his subject's physiognomy and from the client the symbolism or godhead required, he had to choose a posture or corporeal expression for such facts and ideas. It happened that Antinous' broad and somewhat stocky figure matched the physique preferred in much of the art of the years c. 460–440 BC, the late archaic and early classical periods of ancient Greece which had now come back into Roman fashion. Consciously or not, the Hadrianic sculptors turned to types from that period on which to base their images of Antinous.

Much ingenious scholarship has been expended in tracing these sources, two of which seem fairly prevalent. One group of Antinous sculptures looks back – via copies – to a work of the earliest classical period (c. 480–460 BC), an Apollo, best known now in copies at Cherchel and Rome. From this elegant young Apollo of the Tiber (fig. 52), it has been claimed, derive some of the major statues of Antinous as Dionysos or Apollo: those of Delphi, the Bank of Italy, the Vatican, Copenhagen (the Casali) and Berlin among them.[12]

A second group derive from a later work of around 440 BC by Polycleitos, his

Doryphoros (fig. 54). This classical portrayal of a square-built and vigorously muscular athlete is more dynamic and complex than the earlier Apollo. From this model derive another series of major works of Antinous: the Naples Farnese statue, the Sylvanus relief, the Aidepsos and Naples Dionysoi among them.[13]

Other sources have been proposed for other works. The Mondragone head, it is said, derives from a Roman copy of the Athena Lemnia of Phidias and, more probably, from Apollonian and Dionysian heads of his period.[14] The general scheme of the Sylvanus relief is drawn from the funerary steles of the fifth and fourth centuries BC down even to the sniffing dog. In addition, some historians rightly detect in the works of Antinous influences of later artists of the fourth century BC, Praxiteles, Lysippos and Scopas, especially in the supple treatment of the flesh, the pathos and expressiveness of the heads and eyes.[15] Some of the proud heads of Antinous reflect the imperious or passionate, open-mouthed and wild-haired images of Hellenistic ruler-gods.

From all this one might dismiss the sculptures of Antinous as no more than eclectic pastiches of borrowed forms and expressions, fabricated in copies of copies. Such a conclusion would be emphatically wrong. For the artists of Antinous were not content slavishly to copy or indiscriminately to borrow, but tried to interpret their subject not only in the light of the whole gamut of past traditions but also in terms of their own sensibilities, needs and techniques.

Thus on a closer examination the two basic statue prototypes provided only general starting points. The Bank of Italy Antinous, which is supposed to be closely based on the Apollo of the Tiber, follows its general posture but is fundamentally different in its bold athleticism, tense musculature, swelling chest, strong abrupt neck and outward-looking, extrovert head capped with richly textured locks not found in the classical work (figs 52–3). The Delphi statue is even more distant from this model. That other precedent, the Doryphoros of Polycleitos, seems to be even more removed from the works supposed to be based on it – except in general posture. In the Naples Farnese statue or the Sylvanus relief, for example (figs 5, 55), the hefty, muscular young adult of Polycleitos is replaced by a distinctly younger, more slender youth of gracious gestures, coiling posture, languorous mood, smooth and voluptuous flesh and fused lines of energy. Perhaps the Albani relief does exude an air of deliberate classicistic imitation, but even this is belied by its gross realism and smooth handling.[16] The imperious heads, too, tend to differ in the richness of their modelling, their portrait realism, from some of their Hellenistic models. In the Mondragone head the thick nose, the powerful curving lips, the audacious declivities below the nose and at the chin are completely original and crucial features.[17]

The variations tell us that the artists of Antinous did not copy. According to taste and need, they absorbed into their own idiom and fused into the distinct form of Antinous the influences of ancient art: the structural geometry of the archaic masters, the serene and dynamic equilibrium of the classical ones, the surface subtleties, sentimental or vehement expressiveness of the Hellenistic sculptors. To this they added a Roman concern for character and the portrait, for realism of physique and detail and a specifically Hadrianic love of rich effects. Inevitably, the results differ in their emphasis and success of realisation. At their best, however, the sculptures of Antinous are a convincing and original synthesis, unmistakably of their own time and of one distinct personality but organically imbued with the stylistic resources and iconography of an immemorial Greek tradition.

In one group, however, the synthesis notably fails: the ten sculptures (five statues and five heads or busts) in the 'Egyptian' style. Only two of these seem to come from Egypt itself, the rest being carved in Italy, mainly for the Villa Adriana. They have always been thought to be exceptional in the *oeuvre* and indeed have been dismissed by one scholar too sweepingly as later fakes.[18] They all depict Antinous wearing the calantica head-dress of a Pharaoh-deity and in the statues he wears a pleated loin-cloth. The posture and profile are borrowed from the archaic Egyptian style of rigid frontality, one foot placed flat before the other, arms held stiffly to the sides, face erect and staring into infinity, hair hidden under the severe shapes of the head-dress. Instead of treating the body with the abstraction and flat planes demanded by this hieratic model and suggested by the clothing, the Hadrianic artists could not forego their beloved naturalism. In the Vatican statue, for example (fig. 56), the muscles and details of the body (such as the knees) are knowingly carved within a stance which renders them paralysed. Antinous is given a somewhat corpulent stomach and his broad shoulders are thrown so far back to fit the rigid scheme that the carefully carved nipples almost disappear under the armpits. The attempt to render his expression as impassive severity results in only a frozen scowl. In these works the taste for naturalism, for archaic models and the need to divinise all fail to cohere.

Two of the fragments are more successful. In the Louvre bust some robustly carved locks of hair (based on the Greek model) protrude from under the head-dress and the modelling is so bold, the planes so simplified, the features so crisp that – despite the hybrid style – that Antinous attains an intense majesty. This is even more the case with the Dresden head (fig. 57), which seems to come from Egypt and may well have crowned an enormous colossus of the new god. Here naturalism is abandoned, detail minimised, modelling simplified, symmetry imposed. Only the eyebrows, the broad nose, the strong and disdainful mouth derive distantly from the living Antinous. This work, along with the Mondragone head in the classical idiom, reaches the highest degree of abstraction and idealisation in the whole *oeuvre* of Antinous. Here indeed he becomes an inscrutable and remote god of the Nile, 'Osiris-Antinous the just', the judge of souls.

Before we can define the elements which unite the other sculptures into a unique type expressive of a man-god and his destiny, we must first introduce them in their variety of form, content and quality.

The core of the busts, which form so large a proportion of the works of Antinous (thirty-eight), are those without attributes. They constitute a virtually new art-form.[19] Seldom before in naked busts had so much of the chest and arms been shown and with such deliberate effect. Also the bowing and turning of the head in three-quarter profile, the raising of the left arm and lowering of the right introduce new movement into the genre. The monumentality of scale suggested by the massive shoulders, swelling chest and thick arms is offset by the intricate and lively detail of the hair as though the head was coyly lowered just to show it off.

By no means all are aesthetically successful or even faithful portraits. That now in Kansas City, for example, is so stylised in its cap of knobbly curls, so bold in its simplified planes and so truculent in its stare that it seems almost an aggressive and misinformed caricature (fig. 51). At the other extreme is the equally idiosyncratic Sala Rotonda bust in which high finish, colossal scale, minute detail and unfamiliar features combine into a work of arresting and disturbing power.

The heads (forty-three), whether broken or sculpted for insertion, are too diverse to classify. They vary from the primitive yet lively young heads of Ostia and London to the elaborately wrought and serene Dionysian heads of the British and the Fitzwilliam Museums. Some stress the voluptuous beauty of Antinous and are in a corresponding florid style, others emphasise his intelligence and energy and are more incisive and dynamic in treatment. Indeed the Copenhagen head has been proposed as a forerunner in technique and sensibility to the 'David' of Michelangelo (fig. 24).[20] Some artists attempted a haunting intimacy of mood as expressed in the soft forms of the Berlin head or the more acute poignancy of form and feeling in the Dionysos of Leningrad. The Mondragone itself, once lauded by Winckelmann as 'one of the finest things in the world' (fig. 8),[21] tends in its immaculate yet cold handling, its academic dependence and remoteness of feeling, to produce not unbridled rapture but reactions of unease, dissociation and repulsion mingled with admiration among more modern critics.[22]

The same response occurs in front of that other work, the Albani relief which Winckelmann included in 'the glory and crown of sculpture in this age as well as in all others' (fig. 9).[23] Its smooth, precise finish, its large and somewhat empty planes, its remorseless realism and the withdrawn and supercilious expression of its fleshy Vertumnus are not so much to modern taste as are the softer forms, nervous technique, rhythmic vitality, deft expression of textures, volumes and space, the mood at once languorous yet electric of the Sylvanus relief by Antoninianus (fig. 5). This is universally regarded as a masterpiece of the *oeuvre*, of Hadrianic, indeed of Greek art.

So great has been the demand since the Renaissance for images of Antinous that some earlier works have been mistakenly dubbed with his name (e.g. the Capitoline 'Antinous') and many others have been deliberately faked or ingeniously converted.[24] Scholars still argue over the identification and authenticity of several works. Is the dull statue of Antinous as Vertumnus in the Lateran old, modern or a drastic restoration? Is the damaged running Hermes from Mantineia really of him? Though there are similar doubts about two late works, the vigorous Androcles-Antinous of Ephesos and the pensive ephebe of Olympia (fig. 26), it cannot be denied that they are very close approximations to his portrait and have a strong claim to be included in the canon.[25]

Not all the statues accepted as Antinous are great works of art. The Dionysos-Antinous of Copenhagen (the Casali), a version of the Apollo of the Tiber, is flaccid and coarse, though it has been further spoilt by restoration. The Antinous clad as Aristaios in the Louvre lacks vitality and feeling and fails to solve the problem posed by its flat hat. Even the Eleusis statue is mediocre in workmanship and details but is redeemed by its potent expressiveness.

We are left with a group of statues which by any yardstick are outstanding. The Delphi Apollo-ephebe, for all its ungainly contrast between broad chest and slender thighs, has a crispness of realisation, a softness of modelling, a relaxed dynamism of posture all fused into a glowing tenderness of mood (figs 1–2, 59). That Italian-made work, the Bank of Italy statue, whether finished or not, refreshingly reinvigorates its prototype with its athletic stance and musculature, its alert and textured head (fig. 53). The Naples Farnese statue has long been recognised as another of the outstanding and perhaps the most seminal images of Antinous produced in Italy (fig. 55). The balanced rhythms of its Polycleitan posture are softened and sensualised by the elegant curve and swing of the hips and legs, by the supple musculature and smooth polished skin, and are relieved by the rich, stylised cascade of hair which frames a face and profile carved with perfect lucidity into an expression of resignation tinged with bitterness. In the huge, half-draped Dionysos of the Vatican a similar cool virtuosic technique transforms the diffident Attic model into a monument of Olympian repose and detachment (figs 58, 60). Here the features of Antinous – broad shoulders and face, severe profile and forceful lips – create one of the most virile of Dionysoi. Between the contrasted masses of undulating flesh, of textured drapery and hair, between the rhythmic sweep of the cloak and the poised stance of the body, between each clear element of the face, a complete and secure equilibrium is established which issues in a mood of sublime and ineffable harmony.

What qualities, then, have these works in common which make them into the last of the great and unmistakable types of classical art, that of the man-god Antinous?

The physical features of Antinous stamp the type throughout and created a new style of masculine beauty. The high, domed head covered with luxuriant curls which spill down the neck and cluster low over the brow, the broad, squarish face, the imperceptibly curved but prominent eyebrows, deep, widely spaced eyes, thick nose close to the arched and protuberant lips, reappear throughout his works however varied by individual artists. They comprised a new kind of handsomeness readily applied to other subjects: so that we cannot be absolutely sure that the statues of Ephesos or of Olympia, for example, are really of Antinous himself or represent others in his style.

With the distinctive head went an equally unique body. The bodies of ancient Greek gods had been pure invention. Those of the Roman *divi* had been copies of these ancient types to which portrait heads were added, however grotesquely. In the case of Antinous, however, the body itself was as much a portrait as the head, and some or all of its salient features were usually expressed: the broad shoulders and swelling chest, the prominent breasts and nipples, the short thick neck, the long thighs. It has been possible to recognise even headless busts and statues as those of Antinous from such constantly preserved features.

However much they were to be idealised or divinised, the face, the individual physical presence, the peculiar beauty of Antinous was never lost. For the first time since the fourth century BC a new type of beauty was created in art, based on an actual person and not on a copy book.

These physical properties are all the more pronounced in the works because they so perfectly suited the aesthetic taste and sculptural techniques of the day. To Hadrianic artists, seeking effects of contrast between broad scale and arresting details, smooth surfaces and rich textures, refractory polish and inviting shadow, the form of Antinous offered a splendid opportunity for their realisation. The new techniques of deep-drilling the hair, plastically indicating the eyebrows, giving the eyes vitality and expression by incising the irises and pupils and even flashes of light, boring out the nostrils, sharply outlining the edges of the lips, polishing the surfaces to a porcelain lustre were all eagerly lavished on the type of Antinous. The hair of Antinous emerges as perhaps the most abundant and luxuriant in the art of antiquity, the eyebrows among the most subtle and incisive, the lips the most generous, controlled and enigmatic. The enthusiastic combination of new techniques with the physical facts of the subject enabled the artists to invest the face with layers of shadows, veiling the brow and then the eyes, deepening the lips, powerfully charging the mystery of the expression. The contrast between the decoratively textural, richly detailed and yet enticingly ambiguous head and the smooth, clear yet subtle body is another essential ingredient in the type of Antinous.

Within this style, however, there are significant differences which make for the vitality of the whole *oeuvre*. These variations are sometimes explained in national terms, 'Greek' and 'Italian'.[26] But such simplistic categories will not do. Among the works indubitably produced in Greece there is a wide divergence in style: compare the Delphi and Eleusis statues, for example, or the two busts from Patras, one of which is so 'Italian' in style that it has been ascribed to a Latin sculptor working in Greece (figs 49, 50). Likewise among the works found in Italy, many must have been made by Greek artists resident there or have been imported from Greece. Can the Sylvanus relief, for instance, probably made in Italy by a Greek and combining 'Greek' sensibility with 'Italian' detail, be classified as exclusively one or the other? The question is almost irrelevant, anyway, as so much of the inspiration and influence affecting imperial sculpture came from Greece in the first place. Even the vivid realism so beloved by the Romans originated in Hellenistic portraiture.[27] It is more illuminating to think of a general imperial style profoundly shaped by Greece which varied according to the highly sophisticated, even mannered tastes of the court and the more direct and less fastidiously stylised ones of the provinces.[28]

If we compare, for example, the Sylvanus and Albani reliefs, the Delphi and Naples Farnese statues, the two Patras busts, the Aidepsos Dionysos and its replica in Naples, it is clear that two different idioms went into the making of the Antinous type. Associated especially with the court in Rome went a taste for high finish, meticulous refinement, polished surfaces, poised equilibrium and detachment of mood (figs 55, 58). It seems part of the preference there for colossal and divinised images of Antinous. Outside imperial circles, both in Italy and in Greece, the approach was less consciously artificial: the chisel strokes on the Sylvanus relief are short and nervous, the surface of the second Patras bust breathes with unpolished nuances, the body of the Aidepsos Dionysos is summary and immediate and even the by-no-means-underfinished Delphi statue mixes incisiveness of outline with softness of modelling (figs 49, 28, 59). But both idioms have their merits and their own contribution to the art of Antinous.

What also distinguishes this art from much of the rest of its times is its deliberate effort to rise above all-prevalent realism to idealism. Partly it was a response to the aspirations of Hadrian and to the ancient prototypes being followed, but mainly it was an attempt to convey the spirituality which set the divinised Antinous apart from other mortals. It is one of the unique achievements of his type that, though we are always aware of his unmistakable portrait, it is so generalised that we are seldom diverted away by petty details of human character and physiognomy from the prevailing mood of elevated and enigmatic resolution, the detachment of his spirit from the very carnality so sensuously displayed in his naked body.[29] Of course not all works achieve such a successful fusion of the portrait and the ideal. The heroic scale and hair-style of the Sala Rotonda bust do not redeem the face from the suspicious petulance of a spoilt adolescent. The pitiless realism of the gross breasts and nipples of the Albani relief counteract any glimmer of spirituality in the face which is said to display 'a grimace of satiety'. Too often the effort to idealise, to avoid the explicit or the detailed, result in hermetic or gloomy withdrawal as in some busts, or in vacancy as in the Cyrene statue, or in woodenness as in the Louvre Aristaios. In the Mondragone head idealisation reaches such an extreme that, at first glance, it is difficult to recognise the usual features and nature of the human Antinous. In many works, however, a unique blend is accomplished between dynamic or contemplative spirituality and a very earthy presence, as in the Copenhagen and Berlin heads.

This, then, was the delicate and difficult solution applied to the problem of representing a well-known human being who had now become a hero and god: not to evade Antinous' mortality but to distil the human elements to their spiritual essence. It is another of the achievements of the Antinous type that this divine essence is communicated not so much by imposed trappings or iconographical allusions as by extracting inherent qualities and inner express-iveness. Very few works of Antinous are not to some degree removed from common mortality: though that degree varies. The Delphi statue suggests its divinity in its innocent radiant nudity. Some of the busts are elevated by heroic scale and lofty self-absorption. Some of the heads exude a superhuman energy and disdain, others a mystic spirituality, or a rapt meditation. In these works the frailties and the vicissitudes of the human Antinous have dropped away. But it is evident that the artists, like the people who shared in the cult, did not want to envisage Antinous as some remote and abstract deity, awe-inspiring, indifferent and unapproachable – a conception realised only in the exceptional Mondragone head or the Dresden Osiris.[30] After all, it was through Antinous' very humanity that they could connect beneficially with this new curing, intercessory and redeeming divinity who, as the obelisk stressed, 'carried out his work among the living', who 'granted the requests of those who called upon him' and who was 'loved' by them in return.

The simple man-god of Greek antiquity was thus revived in a very particular form and to satisfy very contemporary needs. The achievement is most fully seen in the Vatican Dionysos where the distinctive figure of Antinous has attained an Olympian grandeur and a sublime serenity without losing, in his divine reverie, remembrance of the mortal he had once been or compassion for the plight of those other mortals he has left behind him (fig. 58).

And it is thus, and finally, that the art of Antinous celebrates his story and his myth. The astonishing quality is its deliberate reticence. In an age in which works of painstaking realism and of contrived allegory proliferated, here was one ripe subject which the artists refused to illustrate literally or to elaborate fancifully. We are shown no tragedies of sacrifice, no dramas of devotion, no miracles of consecration. By refusing to be explicit, by knowing exactly where to stop, the artists charged their works with a potency and a magnetism which endure. The sculptures are content to do no more than hint variously at sorrowful devotion, serene resignation, ineluctable fate, heroic action or triumphant resolution. They exhibit the most superficial attractions but suggest the most profound experiences. They are impregnated with a beauty at once voluptuously carnal and yet austerely spiritual. Their attributes connect with fundamental themes of love and death, redemption and immortality. These lucid yet baffling works invite our questions but refuse all answers. Their tantalising enigma may therefore conceal everything or nothing, plenitude or vacuity, the cosmic or the trivial. We can never know. Antinous remains in them, as he remains at the end of our researches and as he may always have been in life to the fascinated Hadrian, an ever-perplexing but ever-inviting mystery.

CONCLUSION

The story of Antinous is more than a mystery of love and death through time by the megalomaniac grief of Hadrian. Antinous' own enigmatic personality, the unexplained death, Hadrian's obsessive passion would always have made the tale unusual. What raises it to significance are the forces which shaped it and the repercussions it generated.

Antinous the god was not just the creation of imperial fantasy, fashionably re-enacting the pederastic heroics and superhuman myth-making of epic days. He was a symbol of the whole triumphant, if somewhat faded, efflorescence of Greek civilisation in his time and of the harmony which it had temporarily established with the power of Rome. But for the Hellenic revival, promoted from Rome itself, his divinity would have had no meaning, durability or artistic progeny, would scarcely have taken root and would have withered rapidly wherever it did.

But Antinous was also the creation of the religious yearnings and compromises of the time: of those sensibilities dissatisfied with the old pantheon but not yet prepared to dispense with it, drawn to the newer creeds offering salvation, participation and bliss but reluctant to surrender to them.

The protégé of the Emperor who brought Rome to its zenith of peace, stability and prosperity, Antinous, both as a human being and as a god, represented a moment of balance between the forces of old and new, past and future, between Roman organisation and Greek culture, classical religion and eastern faiths, traditional society and provincial blood. But it was with the Greek world from which he sprang, and some of the ideals of which he personified, that the future lay. It was the newer beliefs, partly exemplified in his divinity, which were to capture the spirits of men. And it was the provincial, even barbaric blood which flowed in his veins and formed his singular style of beauty, which was to transform and to disintegrate the body-politic of Rome.

Designed to reinvigorate classical paganism, the apotheosis of Antinous, by its apparent preposterousness, its uncomfortable parallels with the story of

Christ, aroused the indignation of the early Fathers and provided damaging ammunition and a focused target for the attacks of Christianity. Ironically, therefore, it aided the ultimate triumph of the type of faith it was set up to oppose.

Contributing in life to the serenest and most tolerant moments of the Emperor, in death Antinous helped to precipitate the ruthlessness and intolerance which led Hadrian brutally to extinguish the Jewish presence in Palestine, with consequences which remain to this day.

The story of Hadrian and Antinous is therefore something more than a bizarre and intense drama of homosexual love which left behind a juicy scandal and the last great works of classical art. The tragedy on the Nile, so long ago, so seemingly personal and insignificant, contributed unexpected energy to the forces which were to bring the dominance of Rome and the world of paganism to an end and, thereby, in its small and distant way, helped fashion our own.

THE SCULPTURES OF ANTINOUS

Below are listed those sculptures which can, on scholarly grounds, be accepted as images of Antinous of the Hadrianic period. There are plenty of other works of the Roman epoch which borrow his features or type and still more which are indubitably of him but are modern, Renaissance in date or later: neither of these latter categories is included. This list derives from the fundamental one of Marconi (1923) as modified by H. Weber (1956) and Clairmont (1966). Though I have included all the additions the latter two scholars have made to the canon, I have not accepted their excisions of certain works which other authorities believe to be of Antinous. Such controversial works are clearly indicated, with their chief academic supporters. I also add a supplementary list of some major works long thought to be of Antinous and, indeed, still displayed in museums and books as being of him, but which are now generally doubted. Some of the works listed as seen by Marconi are not discussed by the later writers and I have let them stand, though they have probably disappeared.

In her review of Clairmont's books, Helga von Heintze (1971) sweepingly dismisses all ten Egyptianising works of Antinous and excludes another twenty from his catalogue as unauthentic or not of Antinous. Her views, for example, on the Egyptianising works or on the Antinous-Mondragone head have been challenged (see Chapter 17, p. 216, note 22) and are not yet supported by detailed evidence. I have therefore not followed her excisions but noted her objections to the individual pieces.

This compilation is not a fully argued catalogue but a checklist for the convenience of the general reader. In each case reference is given to the discussions in the catalogues of Marconi (= M), Clairmont (= Cl) and de la Maza (= Maza) and, where necessary, to other scholars and to the text of this book. To aid the reader I have starred those works which seem to me of exceptional artistic or historic interest, adding brief notes of explanation.

ALGERIA

CHERCHEL: MUSEUM
  1 *Head from a statue of Antinous–Dionysos*

Cl – 42. From Caesarea. Deliberately mutilated work identified by the hair- style.

AUSTRIA

VIENNA: KUNSTHISTORISCHES MUSEUM

2 *Bust of Antinous*

M – 127; Cl – 50; Maza – 25, page 245. Maza, understandably, doubts the identification of a work so unlike its subject whatever vestiges of similarity in the hair-style.

DENMARK

COPENHAGEN: NY CARLSBERG GLYPTOTHEK

3 *Statue of Antinous as Dionysos (the Casali) 548*

M – 92; Cl – 26; Maza – 47, page 371. Found in Rome, formerly in Villa Casali. Colossal statue of a somewhat adipose Antinous, marred by heavy restoration and overworking.

4 *Head of Antinous 685* (fig. 24)*

Cl – 6; Maza – 17, page 227. Acquired in Rome but of Greek workmanship. Vital work showing Antinous as a virile, energetic and intelligent hero, loosely based on Hellenistic prototypes from Asia Minor.

5 *Head of Antinous 686*

Cl – 8bis. From Tivoli near Rome. Upper head severed. Somewhat florid style and sensual depiction of the subject.

COPENHAGEN: NATIONAL MUSEUM

6 *Head of Antinous on a modern base 1024*

Cl – 21; authenticity doubted by von Heintze, 1971, page 397.

Though the hair-style relates to the basic model, the facial features are scarcely recognisable as those of Antinous.

EGYPT

CAIRO: COLLECTION DROVETTI

7 *Bust of Antinous*

M – 124; Dietrichson – 133. (Now lost?) From Lycopolis in Egypt.

FRANCE

PARIS: LOUVRE

8 *Head of Antinous as Dionysos (or Apollo) 1205* (fig. 8)*

M – 61; Cl – 58; Maza – 45, page 357. Authenticity doubted (with no evidence) by J. Chartonneaux, *Sculpture Grecque et Romaine . . . du Louvre*, Paris, 1963, page

165 and von Heintze, 1971, page 397 but reaffirmed by Kraus (in H. von Heintze, *Römische Porträts*, Darmstadt, 1974, page 424). Found near the Villa Mondra gone, Frascati, between 1712 and 1728 and from a colossal statue. One of the most idealised and god-like of Antinous' images, much praised by Winckelmann. Looks back to Phidias and other prototypes of the fifth century BC.

9 *Statue of Antinous as Aristaios or Sylvanus Ma 528*
M – 62; Cl – 23; Maza – 37, page 314. Artistically undistinguished but interesting as showing Antinous with an ephebic hat (*petasos*) and boots and as a divinity of the fields.

10 *Head (and statue?) of Antinous*
M – 63; excluded by H. Weber and Clairmont, accepted, after examination, by Maza, – 28b, page 268. Authenticity doubted by von Heintze, 1971, page 397. From the Villa Adriana. The head is accepted by Marconi and Maza who also thinks the body (nominally of Herakles) could be his.

11 *Statue of Antinous as a Priest 1781*
M – 65; Cl – 55; Maza page 381. From Cyrene. Colossal and fully draped with mantle over head. Only a vague likeness.

12 *Bust of Antinous as Osiris**
M – 66; Cl – 6, page 16; Maza – 41, page 432. Authenticity doubted by von Heintze, 1971, page 397. From the Villa Adriana. Wearing the calantica in the Egyptian style but fully modelled and majestic. Rather hard restorations.

13 *Head of Antinous as Dionysos Ma 238*
M – 68; Cl – 70; Maza – 469, page 366. Authenticity doubted by von Heintze, 1971, page 397.

14 *Bust of Antinous*
M – 69; Dietrichson 93.

15 *Bust of Antinous*
M – 70.

16 *Relief with figure of Antinous*
Identified by Clairmont, page 57. Antinous with Mondragone-style hair, in the company of other Egyptian gods. Doubted by von Heintze, 1971, page 394.

PARIS: COLLECTION DU CLERCQ
17 *Bust of Antinous*
M – 129; Cl – 9. The bust (but not the dedication on the plinth) is not considered authentic by von Heintze, 1971, page 397. From the Lebanon. The only inscribed bust; 'Dedicated by M. Lukkios Flakkos to the hero Antinous'.

GERMANY

BERLIN: STAATLICHE MUSEEN R 59
18 *Statue of Antinous Agathodaimon*
M – 93; Cl – 19; Maza – 38, page 319.
From Rome and colossal. Only the head of this composite work is definitely of Antinous, though Maza thinks the body is from another sculpture of him.

19 *Statuette of Antinous R 56 (fig. 27)*
M – 94; Cl – 41; Maza – 14, page 216. Formerly in the Grimani collection, Venice.

An even more muscular version of 59 and deriving from the same classical prototype.

20 *Head of Antinous (as Apollo?) R 57* (fig. 25)*

M – 55; Cl – 16; Maza – 12, page 204. Acquired in Cairo, possibly from a statue of Antinous as Apollo. Sometimes, wrongly, considered one of the earliest works of Antinous, but undoubtedly, in its subtle simplifications and haunting poignancy, one of the most poetic.

21 *Bust of Antinous R 10*

M – 96; Cl – 10; Maza – 28c, page 270. Authenticity doubted by von Heintze, 1971, page 392.

22 *Head of Antinous (Dionysos–Hermes) R 58*

M – 98; Cl – 59; Maza – page 361. Authenticity doubted by von Heintze, 1971, page 392.

BERLIN: COLLECTION VON STRAUSS

23 *Head of Antinous*

M – 97; Cl – 60. Authenticity doubted by von Heintze, 1971, page 397. Dull version of the Louvre Mondragone head.

DRESDEN: ALBERTINUM

24 *Head of Antinous or Osiris* (fig. 57)*

M – 106; Cl – 5, page 16; Maza – 42, page 332. Authenticity doubted by von Heintze, 1971, page 394. From Egypt and a colossal statue. The most effective of the Egyptianising works of Antinous in its bold abstractions of form, abbreviations of detail and godlike remoteness and majesty of feeling.

25 *Head of Antinous*

M – 104; Dietrichson – 114.

MUNICH: GLYPTOTHEK

26 *Bust of Antinous 400*

M – 101; Cl – 12; Maza – 23, page 241. From Verona.

27 *Statue of Antinous as Osiris*

M – 103; Cl – 52; Maza – 44a, page 340. Authenticity doubted by von Heintze, 1971, page 394. From the Villa Adriana. Noted in the seventeenth century. In red marble.

28 *Head of Antinous 286* (fig. 16)

M – 102; Cl – 52. Authenticity doubted by von Heintze, 1971, page 397. A young-looking head; the attribution to Antinous is dubious.

MAINZ: MUSEUM

29 *Bronze head of Antinous*

M – 107. This is one of the bronze incense jars discussed in Chapter 15, p. 185 and note, showing heads close to Antinous. In view of their cult uses they may have been meant to be likenesses of him but could also have been mere approximations to his type.

DARMSTADT: FORMERLY COLLECTION BARON HEYL

30 *Head of Antinous*

Cl – 22bis, page 60. Authenticity doubted by von Heintze, 1971, page 398.

FULDAI SCHLOSS FASANERIE

31 *Head of Antinous*
   H. von Heintze, *Antike Porträts in Schloss Fasanerie*, Mainz, 1967, no. 33, plate 57.
   The cranium is partly severed but the work is recognisable and of good quality.

GREAT BRITAIN

LONDON: BRITISH MUSEUM
32 *Head of Antinous as Dionysos 1899*
   M – 75; Cl – 37; Maza – 46c, pages 368–9. Found near the Villa Pamphili, in Rome
   and from a colossal statue.
33 *Head of Antinous 1900**
   M – 76; Cl – 22; Maza – 1, page 153. Crude work depicting Antinous as a boy.
34 *Statue of Antinous as Osiris*
   M – 82; Cl – 4, page 16. Authenticity doubted by von Heintze, 1971, page 394.
   From Egypt and formerly at Osborne House. Work in the Egyptian idiom.

BOWOOD, WILTSHIRE: LANSDOWNE COLLECTION
35 *Head of Antinous as Osiris*
   M – 81; Cl – 16, page 8. Authenticity doubted by von Heintze, 1971, page 394.
   From the Villa Adriana.

CAMBRIDGE: FITZWILLIAM MUSEUM
36 *Head of Antinous as Dionysos (known as the Lansdowne Antinous)*
   M – 80; Cl – 55; Maza – page 366. Von Heintze thinks (1971, page 397) that it is 'a
   modern contamination of the Antinous–Mondragone and the Antinous Braschi'.

CHATSWORTH HOUSE, DERBYSHIRE
37 *Bust of Antinous as Dionysos*
   Cl – 30; Vermeule, 1955, page 139, accepts and von Heintze, 1971, page 397,
   doubts.

DEEPDENE, SURREY: FORMER HOPE COLLECTION
38 *Bust of Antinous as Osiris*
   M – 79; Cl – 7, page 16. Authenticity doubted by von Heintze, 1971, page 394.
   From the Villa Adriana.

HEVER CASTLE, KENT
39 *Bust of Antinous*
   Cl – page 58. Rejected as unauthentic by von Heintze, 1971, page 398.

KNOLE HOUSE, KENT
40 *Head of Antinous*
   M – 87; Cl – 35. Vermeule, 1956, page 331, accepts and von Heintze, 1971, page
   397, rejects its authenticity. From the Villa Adriana.

PETWORTH, SUSSEX
41 *Bust of Antinous*
   M – 90.

PORT SUNLIGHT, LADY LEVER ART GALLERY
42 *Statue of Antinous (as Ganymede?)*★
M – 78; Cl – 39. From the Villa Adriana. Formerly at Deepdene. The assimilation to Ganymede is doubtful as the arms are restored and the attributes they bear are therefore of questionable authenticity. Typical work in the fluent, slightly chilly style of artists associated with the imperial court. Von Heintze thinks the whole is a fake – 1971, page 397.

GREECE

ATHENS: NATIONAL MUSEUM
43 *Bust of Antinous 417* (fig. 49)★
M – 112; Cl – 3; Maza – 20, page 234. Found at Patras. Considered one of the earliest works of Antinous and in an accomplished, smooth style which implies a sculptor from imperial circles.
44 *Bust of Antinous 418* (fig. 50)★
M – 113; Cl – 2; Maza – 20, page 234. Found at Patras. Also considered an early version but fresher, more spontaneous and more organic in style than 43. Despite its mutilations it remains an outstanding work by a Greek master.
45 *Head of Antinous 518*
Cl – 4. Another early version of original model.
46 *Statue of Antinous as running Hermes 698*★
Cl – 64 excludes this work but it is accepted by Lippold, 1923, pages 183, 192; Holm, page 13; West, page 35; H. Weber, pages 135–136; Vermeule, 1966, pages 488–489, and von Heintze, 1971, page 398. From Mantineia. Sadly fragmentary but important as the only surviving work from the Greek cult-centre and linking via coin images with the other centre of Bithynion in Asia Minor. (A related head, A 1273, is also accepted by von Heintze.)

ATHENS: HADRIAN'S LIBRARY
47 *Statuette of Antinous 495*
Cl – 56. Found in 1960 in a cistern in Hermes Street.

ATHENS: THEATRE OF DIONYSOS (ACROPOLIS)
48 *Dionysiac frieze: Antinous being presented by the goddesses of Eleusis to Dionysos*
Graindor, 1934, pages 277–9; Geagan, page 148. Headless work which Graindor ingeniously argues is Antinous and not, as sometimes thought (e.g. Cook, 1914, page 710, and Kraus, *Römische Weltreich*, plate 213), Theseus. The torso makes the identification possible, the legs much less so.

ATHENS: AGORA: STATUE OF HADRIAN
49 *Relief of Antinous on the cuirass* (fig. 40)
There is a remarkable similarity between this profile on the lappet and the Olympia head of Antinous (55). Could it be a subtle Athenian compliment to the Emperor? (See Chapter 13.)

CHALKIS: MUSEUM
50 *Statue of Antinous as Dionysos 32* (fig. 28)★

M = 111; Cl 36; Mana page 369 Found at Aidepsos, north Euboea, in 1907. Despite its damaged state, it reveals the succinctness and crisp vitality of a Greek master-sculptor.

DELPHI: MUSEUM

51 *Statue of Antinous (as Apollo?) 1718* (figs 1, 2, 59)*

M – 109; Cl – 1; Maza – 52, page 385. Found on the site in 1893. One of the earliest works of Antinous, depicting him as the divine ephebe. Though carefully finished, the subtlety of modelling and nuance is entirely Greek.

ELEUSIS: MUSEUM

52 *Statue of Antinous as Dionysos Zagreus* (fig. 30)*

M – 108; Cl – 14; Maza – 8, page 174. Artistically inferior but compelling in its evocation of Antinous the adolescent about to confront the supreme mysteries of death and resurrection.

KIFISSIA (ATHENS): PRIVATE COLLECTION

53 *Bust of Antinous (as Osiris?)*

Cl – 15. Von Heintze, 1971, page 397, denies its authenticity. From Egypt and in alabaster. Small and collapsible into five pieces for travelling. Suggests the domestication and popularity of the cult of Antinous.

OLYMPIA: MUSEUM

54 *Torso said to be of Antinous*

M – 110. Both H. Weber (pages 138–140) and Clairmont (page 58) reserve judgement on the identification until the head is found. Found at Olympia, 1878. This headless, fragmentary work is much debated. Some scholars identify it as Antinous from the chest alone and claim that it is identical with the Delphi statue or is from the same workshop.

55 *Statue of an ephebe (Antinous?)* (fig. 26)

Cl – page 14, note 1 and H. Weber *passim* do not think it is Antinous. Vermeule, 1966, pages 488–9, accepts it as 'a very ideal' Antinous. Maza – 7, page 167, also accepts. See Chapter 17, p. 217, note 25. Found in 1939 at Olympia and a late work (140 AD). The profile, facial features and expression are very close to 20, though the hair-style, neck and overall height are unusual. Despite its date, it seems to merit inclusion in the canon at least as much as the accepted but even more idiosyncratic 2 and 28. A borderline case between an idealised version of Antinous and an ephebe portrait strongly influenced by his type.

HOLLAND

THE HAGUE: ALLARD PIERSON MUSEUM

56 *Head of Antinous 192*

M – 91; Cl – 32. Either from Hermopolis (modern Ashmunen) or Antinoopolis and in alabaster. Sadly mutilated and insignificant in scale and workmanship. Its interest lies in its being possibly the only sculpture left of the huge number which adorned the city of Antinous.

ITALY

ROME: ARCH OF CONSTANTINE

57 *Boar Hunt Tondo* (figure in middle looking left) (fig. 12)*
M – 29; Cl – 57; Maza – 29. The only work where, it is generally agreed, Antinous is shown as a human being, albeit retrospectively and on the basis of the posthumous standard and idealised image.

58 *Lion Hunt Tondo* (figure on viewer's left holding horse) (fig. 13)*
M – 30; Kähler, 1950, page 154 and note 151; Maull, 1955, *passim*. Considered by some but not all scholars to be a depiction of Antinous as he was shortly before death with cropped locks and hirsute and far from the posthumous ideal. Chin damaged in last hundred years.

ROME: BANK OF ITALY

59 *Statue of Antinous as Dionysos* (fig. 53)*
M – 28; Cl – 28, Maza – 49. Made in Italy and found in Rome in 1886; derived from the prototype of the Apollo of the Tiber. Fine realisation of Antinous as the vigorous hero-god.

ROME: BANCA ROMANA

60 *Relief of Antinous as Sylvanus* (fig. 5)*
M – 23; Cl – 5; Maza – 9. Found in 1907 at Torre del Padiglione and formerly in the Istituto dei Fondi Rustici. The only signed work of Antinous, by Antoninianus of Aphrodisias. Major work of refined sensibility and consummate technique based on classical grave steles. Antinous as the languorous ephebe-god.

ROME: CASA DI VICOLI DEL DIVINO AMORE

61 *Head of Antinous*
M – 42. (Now lost?)

ROME: COLLECTION TORLONIA

62 *Bust of Antinous as Dionysos*
M – 26; Maza – 46, page 365.

63 *Bust of Antinous as Dionysos–Osiris*
M – 27.

64 *Bust of Antinous*
M – 25; Maza – 27b, page 257.

ROME: ENGELSBERG

65 *Head of Antinous 130*
Cl – 46. Authenticity doubted by von Heintze, 1971, page 397. From a herm.

ROME: MUSEO BRACCIO NUOVO

66 *Head of Antinous as Osiris*
Maza – 43, page 326. Egyptianising work, first identified by Maza in 1966, doubted by von Heintze, 1971, page 394, accepted by Roullet – 103, page 87.

ROME: MUSEO CAPITOLINO

67 *Head of Antinous (as Apollo or Dionysos) 43*
M – 14; Cl – 17; Maza – page 365.

ROME: MUSEO NAZIONALE DELLE TERME

68 *Bust of Antinous*
M – 17; Maza – 27, page 257. Excluded by Clairmont, page 58, as practically modern. In fact, the chest (described by Maza as 'magnificent') and the cranium are ancient and the identification is certain from these two.

69 *Head of Antinous 200* (fig. 23)*
M – 18; Cl – 49; Maza – 4, page 161. From the Villa Adriana. Powerful conception of an alert, incisive Antinous based on Hellenistic ruler images and relating to a coin of Adramyttion in Asia Minor.

70 *Head of Antinous wearing diadem 341**
M – 19; Cl – 45; Maza – 3, page 158. From Ostia. Vigorous work of a very child-like Antinous wearing a priestly diadem bearing obscure images.

71 *Head of Antinous 128576*
Cl – 54. Von Heintze doubts the identification, 1971, page 398. From Tivoli.

ROME: MUSEO NUOVO

72 *Head and statue fragment of Antinous**
Cl – 29; Maza – 16, page 224. Subtle but mutilated work which relates to the harder 59.

ROME: PALAZZO DEI CONSERVATORI 65

73 *Head of Antinous as Dionysos*
M – 15; Cl – 43; Maza – 2, page 153. Boyish head with Eleusinian wheat ears mounted on a torso which is not that of Antinous.

ROME: VATICAN MUSEUM

74 *Unfinished relief with head of Antinous in profile*
Identified by Clairmont, page 20, note 4.

ROME: VATICAN: MUSEO CHIARAMONTI

75 *Head of Antinous (as Attis or Ganymede) 625*
M – 6; Cl – 24; Maza – 33a, page 304.

ROME: VATICAN: MUSEO GREGORIANA – EGIZIO

76 *Statue of Antinous as Osiris 99* (fig. 56)*
M – 10; Cl – 3, page 16; Maza – 44, page 340. Authenticity doubted by von Heintze, 1971, page 394. From the Villa Adriana. Colossal work of Italian manufacture in the archaic Egyptian style.

ROME: VATICAN: SALA A CROCE GRECA

77, 78 *Two Telamones of Antinous*
M – 11 & 12; Cl – 1a & 1b, page 16; Maza – 40, page 329 (disputing the identification). Von Heintze disputes identification too, 1971, page 394. Accepted by Roullet, 101–2, page 87.

ROME: VATICAN: SALA ROTONDA

80 *Bust of Antinous 540* (fig. 6)*
M – 2; Cl – 47, page 248. Found in the Villa Adriana, 1790. Italian work of Antinous as a somewhat overweight and sullen adolescent with corkscrew ringlets. Much debated as to its being *ad vivum* or posthumous, realistic or idealising, early

or late in manufacture and innocent or depraved in sentiment.

81 *Statue of Antinous as Dionysos (known as the Braschi) 545* (figs 58, 60)★
M – 1; Cl – 27; Maza – 54, page 398. Found in 1795 in the imperial villa at Praeneste. Outstanding work of the smooth and refined imperial court style depicting Antinous on a colossal scale as a deity of Olympian serenity.

ROME: VIGNA CASALI
82 *Herm of Antinous*
M – 40; Dietrichson – 33. (Now lost?)

ROME: VIALE DELL'OBELISCO, PINCIO HILL
83–85 *Obelisk of Antinous: Three reliefs, Antinous as a Pharaoh-god*
M – 32–34.

ROME: VILLA ALBANI
86 *Relief of Antinous as Vertumnus* (fig. 9)★
M – 20; Cl – 25; Maza – 10 page 193. Found in the Villa Adriana. Cool and sophisticated Italian court work of trenchant realism much admired in Winckelmann era, less so nowadays.

NAPLES: NATIONAL MUSEUM
87 *Statue of Antinous (known as the Farnese) 6030* (fig. 55)★
M – 43; Cl – 33; Maza – 13, page 193. Formerly in the Domus Flavia (Vermeule, 1960, page 4) and in the Farnese Collection in Rome. Seminal work for the Italian-made sculptures of Antinous in the highly finished court style. Based on the Doryphoros of Polycleitos. Arms restored and possibly not in original posture.
88 *Statue of Antinous as Dionysos*
M – 44; excluded by H. Weber and Clairmont, accepted by Maza – 48, pages 373–4 and by Holm, pages 28 & 36. Formerly in the Farnese Collection. Though heavily restored (see Maza's examination), this is basically authentic and a colossal Roman version of the statue from Aidepsos, 50.

FLORENCE: PALAZZO PITTI
89 *Head of Antinous*
M – 48: Dietrichson – 70. (Now lost?)
90 *Bust of Antinous*
M – 49; Dietrichson – 69. (Now lost?)

FLORENCE: UFFIZI
91 *Bust of Antinous 327*
M –45; Cl – 11; Maza – 22, page 239. Found in Rome in 1671.
92 *Head of Antinous from a statue as Triptolemos 364.*
M – 46; Cl – 18.

TURIN: MUSEO CIVICO
93 *Head of Antinous 128*
M – 51; Cl – 31.
94 *Head of Antinous*
M – 52; Dietrichson – 73.
95 *Statuette of Antinous as Dionysos*
M – 53; Dietrichson – 76.

VENICE: ACCADEMIA
96 *Bust of Antinous*
    M – 56; Dietrichson – 77.

PARMA: MUSEO
97 *Bust of Antinous*
    M – 57; Dietrichson – 80.

CATANIA: COLLECTION BISCARI
98 *Bust of Antinous*
    M – 59; Dietrichson – 137. (Now lost?)

LA VALLETTA (MALTA): COLLECTION BARBARO
99 *Bust of Antinous*
    M – 60. (Now lost?)

POZZUOLI: ANTIQUARIUM
100 *Head of Antinous*
    Cl – 44. Von Heintze is doubtful of the identification, 1971, page 398. From near Naples.

TARANTO: MUSEO CIVICO
101 *Head of Antinous*
    Cl – 53, von Heintze doubts the identification, 1971, page 398. From Brindisi, via Casimiro.

LIBYA

TRIPOLI MUSEUM
102 *Head of Antinous added to a statue of Apollo Lykeios**
    Cl – 38; Maza – 53, page 397. From the baths of Leptis Magna. An idealised mask of Antinous applied to an existing statue of Apollo. Late work.

SOVIET UNION

LENINGRAD: HERMITAGE
103 *Head of Antinous*
    M – 119; Cl – 39; Maza – 466, page 366. From near the Villa Adriana. Poignant work.
104 *Bust of Antinous (as Hermes?)*
    M – 120; Dietrichson – 126. From the Villa Adriana.
105 *Bust of Antinous (as Dionysos)*
    M – 121; Dietrichson – 127. From the Villa Adriana.
106 *Statuette of Antinous as Dionysos*
    M – 123.

SPAIN

MADRID: THE PRADO
107 *Head of Antinous (the Ildefonso group)*★
M – 114; Cl – 40; Maza – 28, page 267. Head of Antinous inserted on a Hellenistic or pastiche group of Orestes and Pylades. Formerly thought to be Hadrian and Antinous and contemporary evidence of the latter's devoted sacrifice for his lover, a theory unconvincingly revived recently (see Iwas, *passim*).

108 *Bust of Antinous 235*★
M – 115; Cl – 13; Maza 24, page 243. From Rome. One of the most majestic of the series of busts, despite incongruous facial restorations.

MADRID: ACCADEMIA ARTISTICA
109 *Bust of Antinous*
M – 116; Dietrichson – 83. From Rome.

SEVILLE: COLLECTION MEDINA CELI
110 *Head of Antinous*
M – 117; Dietrichson – 84.

PALMA: MUSEO
111 *Bust of Antinous*
M – 118. From near Rome (Aricia).

SWITZERLAND

BASEL: SALEROOM (1967)
112 *Head of Antinous as Dionysos*
Vermeule, 1966, pages 488–9. (Now lost?)

TUNISIA

TUNIS: BARDO MUSEUM
113 *Head of Antinous*
Cl – 7; Maza – page 381. From the Odeion in Carthage. Another sensual, boy-like image.

TURKEY

IZMIR: MUSEUM
114 *Statue of Antinous as Androcles hunting*
Rejected by Clairmont – 66 and Maza – 35, pages 308–9 but accepted by Hahland *passim* and Inan and Rosenbaum, 1966 – 37, pages 73–4 and by von Heintze, 1971, page 398. From the Gymnasium at Ephesos. There is a strong facial resemblance to Antinous, an iconographical link through the coins of Ephesos (Holm, page 18)

and Antinous' own reputation as a hunter: all grounds for believing that this work of the 150s AD is meant to show Antinous as Androcles and is not just a borrowed type. (See Chapter 17, p. 217, note 25.)

UNITED STATES OF AMERICA

KANSAS CITY, MISSOURI: NELSON GALLERY AND ATKINS MUSEUM (fig. 51)
115 *Bust of Antinous**
Cl – 48; Vermeule, 1960, *passim*. Identification rejected by von Heintze, 1971, page 397. Scarcely recognisable as Antinous in either the hair-style or expression but undeniably vigorous Greek work. Probably late.

Some works thought to be of Antinous but now generally not accepted

FRANCE

PARIS: LOUVRE
a *Bust of Antinous*
M – 67; Maza – 21, page 237, who thinks it is a perfect and authentic work. Generally considered to be a fine work of the sixteenth century.

PARIS: BIBLIOTHÈQUE NATIONALE
b *Statuette of Antinous as Hermes*
M – 73; Maza – 29, page 322. Both the attribution to Antinous and its Roman dating are doubtful.

GERMANY

DRESDEN: ALBERTINUM
c *Statue of Antinous as Dionysos*
M – 105; Maza – 50, page 379. A headless colossus to which a modern head of Antinous has been added, though there are no grounds for believing the trunk to be his.

GREAT BRITAIN

MARBURY HALL
d *Statue of Antinous as Vertumnus*
M – 86; Maza – 36b, pages 310–312. Accepted by Calza – 121, page 82. Found at Ostia in 1775. More recognisably Antinous than the other Ostia work (f, below) though heavily restored also.

ITALY

ROME: MUSEO CAPITOLINO
  e *Statue of an ephebe or Hermes*
    M – 13; Maza – 15, pages 221–3. Found at the Villa Adriana, 1738, and long believed to be Antinous and much copied as such. Now generally held to be a Hermes of the Flavian period. Maza thinks the body is Antinous'.

ROME: MUSEO LATERANO
  f *Statue of Antinous as Vertumnus*
    M – 16. Dismissed by Clairmont as modern (page 13, note 2 and page 58) but accepted by Calza – 130, page 81; Maza – 36a, pages 310–312 and von Heintze, 1971, page 398. Found at Ostia in 1798. Heavy restorations make the work almost modern and very wooden. It may, however, be of Antinous and derive from the cult to him in Ostia.

FLORENCE: ARCHAEOLOGICAL MUSEUM
  g *Bronze Head of Antinous*
    M – 47 is doubtful but the work is accepted as authentic by Holm, page 36 and West, page 138 and Maza – 5, page 164. A bronze replica of the Naples Farnese head (87) which may be Roman or of Renaissance date.

THE COINS AND GEMS

Some thirty-one cities or confederations struck coins to Antinous of which at least 143 different issues are known. Apart from Alexandria in Egypt which alone minted over 32 issues and six cities or confederations on the mainland of Greece which together produced another 30 issues, the remaining twenty-four minting cities were all in Asia Minor and account for the other 80 issues.

Antinous' coins date from well after his death. The heads or busts of him which decorate their obverse sides usually derive from images of him which already existed in sculpture, as do some of the more fanciful works depicted on their reverses. They are therefore relative late-comers in his cult and must have been prompted by some special event or events rather than a sudden, spontaneous and random desire tardily to honour him. A couple of coins, from Olympia (Elis) and Alexandria, may doubtfully be assigned to the year 133. But the first definitely dated coins are those of Amisos of 133–4 and Alexandria of 134–5, though, owing to the different modes of calculating the calendar in these two cities, both issues could well come from September or October 134. We know that Alexandria emitted at least another large issue in 136–7, and Olympia possibly one in mid- or late 135. The only event in the autumn of 134 which could have prompted the first great issues was the inauguration of the major four-yearly games commemorating Antinous' death and held in Mantineia, the chief cult centre on the mainland. Perhaps other cities all over the Greek world held local festivals and struck coins to coincide with, or to follow, that principal one.

Certainly the limited number of issues produced by most cities indicates one specific and transient occasion as their cause: twenty-one cities made three issues or less. The coins themselves, in bronze, are also eloquent of their festive and cult origins. The majority are sizeable medallions, 30–40 mm in diameter, and designed for commemorative purposes. The largest and the best among them are rare and superbly worked pieces for presentation to favoured individuals in the games, the cult or the city. One third of the cities issued medallion types alone, more than a third produced such medallions along with smaller pieces of mundane currency, and only half a dozen or so confined themselves to this Antinous small-change. The exceptional quality of the designs also makes many of these coins out of the ordinary.

As do their origins. For though many were produced by cities in the normal eastern way, others are in the names of whole confederations (Achaia, Arcadia, Bithynia), and in thirteen centres civic worthies dedicated the coins to their compatriots, paying for the engraving and even perhaps the whole production.

Five cities between them emitted more coins than all the rest put together. Alexandria produced over thirty-two issues, ranging from fine bronze medallions, through cruder copies of them, still coarser ones in lead, to small coins for circulation. On the Greek mainland, Arcadia (Mantineia) accounted for twelve, the cities of Argos and Corinth (Achaia) for another six of the thirty issues from the mother country. Again these Peloponnesian coins were of distinctive design and superlative quality and had a far-flung influence. In the north of Asia Minor, Bithynion produced thirteen issues, less unique in design and technique than those of its Arcadian mother, but more varied and livelier in content. The other cities of Bithynia put out eight issues in honour of a favourite son. In the south of Asia Minor, Tarsos took the lead by making thirteen issues, again of a distinctive style and content, while on the west coast Smyrna accounted for fifteen issues of a narrow and comparatively dull range of designs. Among the cities making a moderate number of issues, Delphi (with six) produced an elegant design of its own, Tion in Pontus on the Black Sea (with five) favoured a rich if derivative set of motifs, while Nikopolis confined itself to half a dozen mediocre but varied and enthusiastic pieces of ready currency.

Not every city had its own die-cutters and mint. It is said that between five and seven such workshops sufficed for the whole of Asia Minor. Some designers evidently travelled from place to place and used existing coins or uniface specimens from other cities to copy from. There are, therefore, often unexpected similarities of design from places far apart. The many obverse sides of the coins with heads or busts of Antinous are in fact often local copies or elaborations of about five basic images produced by a few great centres, whereas the reverses are equally often designs special to each city.

Some scholars see Alexandria as the starting point for the design of the whole coinage as it had been back in 130–31 for the cult. But though its coins were widely copied, the images of Antinous they purveyed suggest the same sources as those of the medallions of the Peloponnese: similar models in sculpture must have been available in both places by 133–4. It is therefore dangerous to assign any priority in design. Occasionally some such priorities can be ascertained: obviously the head of Antinous with the uraeus from Tarsos followed the similar one of Alexandria, the busts on the medals of the Peloponnese and Chalcedon precede the crude imitations on those of Cyme, Hadrianotherai and Nikopolis. No doubt some of the biggest issuing centres like Arcadia and Alexandria and to a lesser extent Tarsos had a powerful impact, but others like Smyrna and Bithynion had relatively little. The web of interacting influences is difficult to disentangle.

Most of the images of Antinous on the obverse of his coins are based on his early sculptures, as the hair-style proves. But though the coin types which result are limited in number, there is the widest disparity in interpreting the original sculptural models. On those from Arcadia we encounter typical busts of the young ephebe depicted with an astonishingly accomplished realism, rendered in a crisp, deep and delicate relief (figs 46a, c). Moreover, the bust is shown virtuosically in the different medals from different angles including an artistically daring and original view from behind and above Antinous' left shoulder.

At the other extreme from this Roman portrait realism rendered with Greek fluency and subtlety are coins like the one from Adramyttion which hark back to an older

Hellenistic tradition (fig. 48e). Here we confront a proud, vigorous, indeed imperious hero or god, condensed into an erect head, with a sharp profile and wide eyes and poised on a long neck. The rendering is in flat planes and linear. This Adramyttion image might seem a pure creation of the engraver's imagination and technique. But not so. In fact, as Holm long ago showed, this particular obverse is clearly related to a sculpture: the head of Antinous now in the Museo delle Terme once in the Villa Adriana (fig. 23).

The types of Antinous' head found on the obverses fall into five groups each possessing common characteristics which derive from one designer, one workshop or, in the later groupings, extensive copying from certain coins of other cities.

The first and most famous group is that from Arcadia and Achaia which stylistically relate to some very distinctive coins of Hadrian produced in Rome and Olympia, including one of Antinous as the Elean river-god Alpheios. Though there are some differences on the busts shown on the medals of Arcadia and Achaia, they are probably by the same hand which cut the outstanding Olympian and Roman series of dies (figs 46a, c). It is suggested that this consummate artist, himself a Hellene, was brought over from Rome to prepare the Greek coins for the great festival at Mantineia in 134 and may have tarried there as late as 135, as a later series from Olympia indicates. This artist, it has been proposed, was none other than the one who signed the remarkable intaglio sardonyx of Antinous with the letters 'Ant[o] . . ! (fig. 7). And he in turn was none other than that Antoninianus of Aphrodisias who sculpted and also signed the celebrated relief of Antinous as Sylvanus (fig. 5). In fact, however, both the disposition of the hair and the strong, incisive style of the sardonyx differ notably from that of the relief and of the coins and it is unlikely that the same Antoninianus created them both or all. Moreover, the relief with its schematic, dull hair is less like the Peloponnese coins and the busts they portray than are some other sculptures and, again, Antoninianus may not be their creator. However, it remains possible that an artist from the Aphrodisian school in Rome did cut the dies for all these coins and that he or another fellow artist may even have created, earlier, the basic model from which most of the sculptures and the coins derive.

The second group derives from Alexandria: strongly modelled heads on draped shoulders (fig. 46e). These are close in mood and posture to those on the Peloponnese busts but are richer in style and are most likely based on similar sculptures available in Egypt. They produced offspring in the coins of Tion (fig. 47e) and Bithynion (fig. 47a-d) and, from a cruder Alexandrian variant, also at Tarsos.[1]

Much more extensive is the third group. This comprises thirteen profile heads of Antinous on a prominent neck without shoulders or drapes and designed in the erect, alert, staring-ahead manner of older ruler images. They range from a cluster in a style of pronounced modelling and soft outlines[2] to those of a flat, sharp, graphic character (fig. 48a, e, f).[3]

The fourth and fifth groups merge. The first shows Antinous' head on draped shoulders and strongly in relief. A small coin from Alexandria may be the source from which similar coins of Mantineia, Tmolos and Ancyra are based, though the latter is in a very refined and attenuated manner.[4] The fifth group shows the same draped shoulders but with the erect, ruler-hero head and varying in the flatness and linearity of the design (fig. 47c).[5]

Indeed the styles of these obverses vary more than the images they portray. Those from the Peloponnese and Chalcedon aim at a gracious and generous realism, a high relief, a delicacy of detail and nuance of planes which blends the best of Roman and Greek medallic art into a truly imperial Hadrianic style. Those from Alexandria are plastically richer and more robust in manner, more exaggerated in the outlines, the play of light and shade, and in the rhythms. In this style they were followed, somewhat more coarsely, by the series from Tion. Bithynion produced a strong relief style too, striking in effect and sure in composition but less delicate in the modelling and details than some others. By contrast, Tarsos' coins display a more graphic style of smooth contours, without drama of light and shade, relying on subtlety of line and the sensitive juxtaposition of flat planes (fig. 48a, b). This idiom reaches its extreme in the barely modelled head of Stratoniceia, sharp in outlines on its elongated neck (fig. 48f).

These Antinous emissions helped to push the recently developed art of the medallion towards its classical zenith. The harmonious Peloponnese obverses and reverses have long been admired as masterpieces of this art form. But so, in their very different way, are the reverses of Alexandria, Bithynion, Tion and Tarsos, in which varied, often complicated and dynamic subjects are integrated with detail and lettering into a satisfying wholeness of composition entirely appropriate to the scale and shape of the medallion and its immediate comprehension.

The reverses are far more varied, presenting each city's own response to the Antinous ephebe-hero-god so uniformly depicted on the obverse sides. As such there is much less borrowing of other cities' images. Though some of the reverses must have derived also from existing sculptures, reliefs and paintings, many must have come solely from the imagination of the engravers. As a whole, they constitute a rich, delightful and idosyncratic tribute of the localities to the new hero-god.

Many of course directly illustrate his cult. Some of these present only symbols of his cult, divine nature or apotheosis: for example, the star and crescent moon of Nikopolis, the chthonic caduceus of Alexandria, the oracular dove, laurel and tripod of Delphi and Tarsos, the bull marked on the flank with a crescent moon (fig. 48d) issued by several cities and representing fertility or sacrifice rather than the Egyptian Apis as is sometimes proposed. Others illustrate some aspect of his cult: for example, an armed combatant and a rudder signifying the games at Argos and Corinth, the temples of Bithynia, Tarsos and Philadelphia, the altar at Nikopolis. Some ten actually show the local cult statues of Antinous. At Corinth one exquisite medallion shows a statue of Antinous as Hermes (fig. 47f) and another of him as Dionysos, though the latter is more likely to be an invention of the engraver.

More inventive are those reverses which attempt to explain Antinous' active godly nature. They may be borrowed from reliefs or paintings but are often the pure conceptions of the designers. On the series from Alexandria, Antinous is shown as Hermes-Thoth, bearing his caduceus as the chthonic god. In the series from Bithynion, deriving possibly from reliefs, he is Hermes-Nomios, the protector of beasts and crops, with winged feet, clutching a pedum, leading an ox while his star gleams in the heavens above. At Tion and Tarsos he is shown as Dionysos riding in languorous dignity on a magnificent panther.

Less often the reverse images do not illustrate the cult but bear witness to the desire to associate existing local symbols and gods with this new hero. Thus the Corinth artist took a revered local image of Poseidon (with whom Antinous had nothing icono-graphically to do) and incongruously gave it Antinous' head on his coin in tribute. In some cases only local civic symbols are shown: the bear of Hadrianotherai, the prow of Smyrna, the city gate of Nikopolis, for instance. Locally venerated gods are also paraded: obscure civic deities from Philadelphia or Nikopolis, local heroes from Cyzicus and Ephesos, the river gods of Tarsos and Amisos (though these may allude to Antinous' death). A whole range of Olympian deities whom Hadrian sought to promote in these regions are introduced. With some of these Antinous was clearly linked, though in these cases such a connection was implied rather than illustrated. Demeter, Dionysos, Silenus, Pan and Apollo appear several times in their own right without his features. Other locally worshipped gods with whom he had less to do also make their appearance: Herakles, Tyche and Asclepeios among them.

A brief review such as this can scarcely do justice to the variety and inventiveness of these reverses. They communicate much of the enthusiasm and local patriotism with which these diverse communities embraced this new Greek hero-god, symbol of their own political and cultural renaissance. His particular religious role as a benevolent god of fertility, nature and death overwhelmingly pervades the series, however unrelated may be some of the deities with whom he is occasionally associated. On the obverse side of his coins his portrait as beautiful ephebe or commanding hero is only rarely – at Alexandria and Tarsos – dignified with the attributes of deity, and in the legends he is most often described as 'hero'. It is left to the images on the reverse vividly to announce, to explain and to illustrate his divine status and its active nature.

Our notice of the gems of Antinous must be only a short footnote. These valuable works of art, scattered over many private and public collections, have never been studied as a whole except by the indefatigable Dietrichson who compiled a list from earlier catalogues and literary authorities. Of the 134 given, he accepts only 88 as probably authentically antique, but, since half a dozen of these show the Capitoline statue which is no longer thought to be of Antinous, and a similar number seem to be repetitions of the genuine Marlborough sardonyx, doubt must persist even about his alleged genuine works. Indeed, perhaps in no area of ancient art is it more difficult to distinguish authentic classical works from later imitations or inventions, especially the excellent ones of the late eighteenth and early nineteenth centuries. Many copyists proudly added their names to their works, but others did not. The numerous copies from the Renaissance onwards, along with those of the coins and sculptures, bear witness to the early impact of Antinous' kind of beauty, and of the compelling, revived classical style in which it was originally expressed, on sensibilities newly awakened to the charms of antiquity.

The gems also confirm the potency of his image in his own times. Most of them (sixty-nine) are of him, as on the coins, without attributes as an ephebe or hero. Only a few provide divine attributes and these of little meaning. Most are engraved on semi-precious stones: carnelian, agate, sardonyx, amethyst; others are cameos. A few signatures are listed by Dietrichson: of Teucros and the well-known Gnaios, both engravers, and of Hellen, probably an owner. There is no reason to doubt that the best artists were employed in this area of tribute to him as in that of coins, or that they frequently took as models the busts or sculptures.

Fortunately, the most notable of the gems is not in dispute, though damage to it poses tantalising problems. This is the famous black sard, once in Venice, then in the Marlborough collection and now in that of Giorgio Sangiorgi back in Rome (fig. 7).

Small in size, 5.2 × 5.7 cm, of the intaglio technique, mounted as a gold ring, it presents with consummate skill and accuracy one of the freshest and most convincing portraits of Antinous. He is shown wearing a chlamys and with a staff borne on his left shoulder. The neck is thick and powerful, the head only slightly inclined. The vigorous swirling patterns of the luxuriant hair, the deep-set eyes, the full, firm mouth and emphatic line of chin and jaw all make this one of the most alert, energetic and forceful of Antinouses.

To the left, broken by damage, is the beginning of an inscription with the letters 'ANT' followed by a vertical stroke with an oblique shaft which could be the start of the Greek *omega*. Some have reconstructed this as 'Antinous' or less plausibly as 'Anteros', a gem-cutter of the Hadrianic period. More excitingly it has been suggested that it is none other than the signature of Antoninianus, the sculptor of the Sylvanus relief. But close comparison between the relief and the sardonyx dispels such an identity of authorship. Perhaps it is the work of another artist of the school of Aphrodisias with the same name or bears a later signature of attribution. Whoever was its creator, it is a masterpiece. More perhaps than colossal or elaborate works of Antinous, this miniature one brings us closest to the singular looks, the powerful and enigmatic character of the young man whom Hadrian loved and mourned.

NOTES AND REFERENCES

Modern works are indicated by the author's name. The full title, place and date of publication are given in the bibliography. Different works by the same author are given by year. Items from Clairmont's catalogue are cited as 'Cl. no.' and from Marconi's as 'M. no.' Ancient texts are given with the author's name and the title abbreviated according to academic practice. Translations or special editions are noted when used.

CHAPTER ONE

 1 Stocklein, quoting Sigard, 1716, 59.
 2 Coins: Hadrianotherai, Juliopolis as *agathos*. *IG*, XIV, 978a as *kalos* in the sense of beautiful and good. Statue as Agathodaimon in Berlin.
 3 Maza, 114.
 4 Clem. Alex., *Adhort. Gks.*, IV.
 5 By Dietrichson, 98.
 6 Jerome, *Comm. In Ies.*, 2; *Interpr. Chron. Eus.*, 130–1, ann. 13.
 7 Tertullian, *Apol.*, 13, 1, f; *De Corona Milit.*, 13; *Ad Nat.*, II, 10, i, f.
 8 Prudentius, *Contra Symm*, I, 273–7.
 9 *Op. cit.*
10 By S. Parker, 258–9, of Athanasius, *Contra Gentes*, 9.
11 Suidas, ed. Berhardy, 1853, under *paidika*.
12 Tournemine, 42; I. Weber, 21; Stocklein, quoting Sigard, 59.
13 *Decline and Fall*, 1771 edit., vol. 1, 92.
14 Levezow, 16; Bayle, 242.
15 1898 edit., 307, 349.
16 Riencourt, 2–3, 31; Tristan, 549; Millin, 155; Bayle, 243.
17 By Dubois, edit., Sextus Aurelius Victor (SAV), *De Caesaribus*, 461.
18 Dietrichson, 213; Maza, 239.
19 Laban, 6–10.
20 *Anmerkungen*, 1767, 2, 123; *Hist. Anc. Art*, trans. Lodge, 2, 335.
21 Grosskürth, 187–8.
22 Reinach, 1885, 359.
23 pp. 65–6.
24 pp. 42, 48.

25 *Ibid*, 55.
26 Rydberg, 194.
27 Symonds, 1879, 49.
28 Stahr, 386–7.
29 p. 168.
30 Kishor, 280. Her account is based on Lanciani's.
31 1909, 186.
32 C. Tennyson, *Alfred Tennyson*, London, 1949, 395.
33 Marconi, 244; E. Clark, 137.
34 Vermeule, 1969, 488; Toynbee, 1934, XXVI.
35 Taylor (Hausrath), 5.
36 Marconi, 298.
37 E. Clark, 166.
38 Vermeule, 1960, 2.
39 E. Clark, 165; Rydberg, 188.
40 Marconi, 244.
41 *Ibid*, 299.
42 Weber, 1937, 148, 225.
43 *HA.Had.*, XXV, 7.

CHAPTER TWO

Principal sources: for Bithynia: Strabo; Pliny's *Letters*; Frank; Magie; Bosch; Dörner, 1949, 1952; Millar; Vidman; Polverini. For the Greek world: Suetonius; Pausanias; Aristeides; Philostratus' *Apollonius* and *Sophists*; Syme, 1958, 1957–60, 1965; Jones, 1974 and *Greek City*; Toynbee, 1934; Millar; Bengtson; Bowersock; Benjamin and Raubitschek; Oliver, 1953 and 1968.

1 Strabo, XII, 4, 7.
2 Calculated from the coin issues in Bosch, 96–7.
3 Smallwood, 1966, no. 163; Mommsen, *De Coll.*, 114; Symonds, 1879, 71; Gregorovius, 311.
4 *Pap. Oxyrhyn.* XXXI, no. 2553. The date of Antinous' birthday is here mistakenly given as 30 November.
5 E.g. Magie, 1190–1; Pausanias, ed. Levi, VIII, 9, 7 note 71.
6 Weber, 1907, 186–8; Holm, 5, 13.
7 K. Clark, 44; Salmon, 306; Laban, 46.
8 E. Clark, 165; West, 129, 141.
9 Symonds, 1879, 48–52; Stahr, 387; Dawes, 233.
10 Erman, 1917, 16, IIId; 43, IIId.
11 E.g. Malaise, 422–3. Beaujeu e.g. 242, 245, 246 etc. Dietrichson, 36. *Contra*: Maza, 22; Kishor, 287.
12 Beaujeu, 245. According to Momus in Lucian's *Convention of the Gods*, 232, Zamolxis, a slave of Pythagoras, had become a Thracian god. Herodotus, IV, 94, 95, describes the barbarous sacrifices of this god. Apuleius, *Apologia*, 290. Zamolxis later seems to have been freed and rich.
13 Eusebius, *Eccl. Hist.*, IV, 8, 2. The passage was later quoted by Jerome, *De Vir.*

III, *22*, 'servus Hadriani Caesaris' and repeated by Nicephoros Kallistos in c. 1400, *Eccl. Hist.*, III, 26. Henderson, 130, note 1.

14 *Ibid.*

15 Jerome, *Comm. Ies.*, 2; *Interpr. Chron. Eus.*, 130–1, ann. 13; *Adv. Iov.*, 2, 7.

16 Frank, 691–2, 839; Vidman, 83.

17 Alexander, 158; Henderson, 209; Salmon, 306, note 2; von Premerstein, *Hermes*, LVII, 1922, 271, col. III, lines 24–31.

18 Maza, 29. Dietrichson, 137, thought that the fact that the Lanuvium burial club had Antinous as a patron god implied that he had been a slave. There is no evidence that the members of this club, however poor, were mainly slaves or that Antinous' status in life affected their choice. They chose him as the newest god of salvation.

19 Weber, 1907, 186–7; Holm, 22; Robert, 1943, 184, note 9.

20 Justin, *1st Apol.*, XXIX, the sneer 'who he was and whence he came' could be directed against his Greek origins. Kishor, 288; Levezow, 8.

21 *Convention of the Gods*, 2, 88. It is disputed if this really does refer to Antinous. Arrian, *Black Sea*, 34, refers to the 'noble birth'.

22 Written, it is thought, about 350 AD by the 'pseudo-Lucian'. Text: Lucian, ed. M. D. Macleod, VIII, *Affairs of the Heart*, para. 45. I have slightly amended the translation given on p. 219.

23 Dietrichson, 35; Maza, 153.

24 Suetonius, *Claudius*, XXV, XLII.

25 Pausanias, VII,17,1.

26 Hammond, 1957, 77, 79; Grenoble in *Aufstieg*, 367; Syme, 1958, *passim*.

27 Horace, *Epodes*, II, 1, 156. Marrou, 357–66.

28 Juvenal, *Satires*, VII, 114; III, VI, both *passim*. Pliny, *Nat. Hist.*, XV, 5, 19; Tacitus, *Annals* (Penguin edit.), 323; Syme, 1958, 512, 517; 1965, 247.

29 Flacelière, 1971, from *Pyth. Orac.*, 408b–c; Syme, 1958, 504; 1957–60, 573–5.

30 Oliver, 1953, Aristeides, *Rom. Or.*, 28, 36, 60, 69, 71, 94 etc.

31 Oliver, 1968, Aristeides, *Panath. Or.*, 38 and *passim*. Even Plutarch refers to 'the Romans' as if they were different and somewhat inferior (e.g. *Erotikos, passim*); Jones, 1974, 102.

32 Philostratus, *Sophists*, 531–5.

33 *Rom. Or.* 100.

34 Frank, 442–52; Weber, 1907, 195–6; 217–18, 219; Henderson, 111; Oliver, 1970, 94.

35 Oliver, 1951(b), 348.

CHAPTER THREE

Principal sources: *HA*; Dio; SAV; *Epitome*; Fronto; Pausanias. Weber, 1907, 1937; Henderson; Orgeval; Kähler, 1950; Beaujeu; Syme, 1958, 1964, 1965, 1971, 1972–4; Carandini; Temporini; Thornton; Waters, 1974; Garzetti; Guarducci, 1949, 1965; Strack; Mattingly; Wegner, Aurigemma; Gusman; Graindor, 1934; Oliver, 1965, 1978.

1 Pausanias, 1,5,5.

2 Strack, 93, 124–5.

3 Fronto, Loeb edit., vol. I, 111; vol. 2, 207; M. Aurelius, *Medit.*, XVI; Henderson, 266.

4 *HA.Had.*, XIV, 11; *Epitome*, XIV.

5 Weber, 1937, 125–8, 145, 149–50. Throughout this book I refer to Weber's original essay on Hadrian published in German in 1937, not to the abridgement in the *Cambridge Ancient History*.

6 Syme, 1964, 144; 1965, 246.

7 Weber and others assume that the mention of Rome as his birthplace by the *HA* is an error (e.g. Eutropius, VIII, 6; Weber, 1907, 14; 1937, 125; Henderson, 10), but this is now generally accepted as accurate (e.g. Syme, 1964, 142–4 etc.) However, if we are to accept the sentence of the *HA* including the birth in Rome as accurate, we must equally accept its subsequent phrase that Hadrian 'returned to Italica' (*rediit*) which Syme tries to explain away. The phrase makes it clear that Hadrian was probably in Italica in infancy and before his return there at the age of fifteen.

8 *HA.Had.*, III, 1. This is sometimes construed as if Hadrian spoke Latin with a Greek accent (e.g. Weber, 1937, 129) but the adjective in the *HA* is *agrestius*.

9 Syme, 1958, 39.

10 Pliny, *Letters*, X, 40. Cramer, 163.

11 Fronto, *loc. cit*; *HA.Had.*, XXVI, 3.

12 *HA. Had.*, III, 3; V, 1; VI, 1; IX, 1–2; Dio, 68, 13, 6; 69, 4, 6. Carandini, 26, 67; Fronto, Loeb edit., vol. 2, 207; Mattingly, CXXV.

13 *HA. Had.*, II, 7. Perowne, 1974, 115–18, 120; Maza, 57; Dawes, 232, even suggests 'he gained his preeminent position by the prostitution of his body' to Trajan.

14 Syme, 1971, 126; Temporini, 128–34; *HA. Had.*, II, 7, 10; III, 3, 7, 8, 11; IV, 8.

15 Strack, 40.

16 E. Clark, 167.

17 *HA. Had.*, XX, 9–11.

18 *HA. Had.*, XI, 7; XV, 1–3; XVI, 4; Amm. Marcellinus, XXX, 8, 10; *Epitome*, XIV; Dio, 69, 3, 1–6.

19 Syme, 1958, 245; Strack, 39, 117; Temporini, 161, 173.

20 *HA. Had.*, XIV, 11.

21 Especially, Salzman, *passim*; Dietrichson, 82; Weber, 1907, 174, 269; 1937, 207–10, 222; Kähler, 1950, 157; Taylor (Hausrath), 7; West, 104. Guarducci, 1941, *passim*, and Beaujeu (115, 166, 174, 235–6, 246, 277) take a more balanced view and see Hadrian's religious interests as sincere, even mystic, but as less intense and consistent than the former authors.

22 E.g. Henderson, 112, 238–40 ('religion was not one of Hadrian's hobbies'!); Salmon, 306; den Boer, 123–5, 135; Garzetti, 433, 697; Boissier, 268.

23 Smallwood, 1966, 114. *HA. Had.*, XI, 3–4. Temporini, 169–73; Carandini, 59, 64. Mommsen, 1905, 424.

24 *HA.Had.*, XI, 3–4. Carandini, 64–6, tries to translate the words *morosa et aspera* as 'rebellious and traditional' and casts Sabina as a member of a clique opposing Hadrian's peace policy. There is no evidence for this.

25 Kähler, 1950, 159; MacKendrick, 295.

26 E. Clark, 139.

27 Aristeides, *Rom. Or.*, 82.

28 Alexander, 155.
29 Strack, 61, 62. Historians disagree as to whether Sabina accompanied him on all or part of this journey: there is some slight evidence that she may have been on the western voyage but nothing for the eastern one: Carandini thinks she remained in Rome from 121 to 125, pp. 64–5, 69, 80; *contra*: Temporini, 88, note 389, 116.
30 Sardinia, Corsica, three Alpine provinces and perhaps Cyprus, Strack 144–5; *Epitome* XIV.
31 Quoted in Henderson, 121; Beaujeu, 278; Weber, 1937, 147.
32 I follow chiefly Weber, 1907, though he sometimes tends to confuse visits made in 129 and 131 in Asia Minor and the mainland with those of 123–5.
33 Weber, 1907, 121.
34 *HA. Had.*, XX, 12–13; Kähler, 1950, 151; Gusman, 275.
35 Flacelière, 1971, 177–8; Follet, 1976, 109–10.
36 Alexander, 154; Weber, 1907, 192–6; Benjamin and Raubitschek, 73; Oliver, 1970, 132.
37 Strack, 73, 105–7; Beaujeu, 159–60.

CHAPTER FOUR

Principal sources: Obelisk: Erman, 1896, 1917; Marucchi; Iversen; Derchain; Kähler, 1975 (see chap. 12). Tondi: Bieber, 1911; Hoffa; Bülle; Buschor; Blumel; L'Orange; Kähler, 1950; Aymard; Maull; Condurachi; Bonanno. Sculptures: Clairmont; Marconi; Maza; Lippold, 1923; Kraus, 1959; Vermeule, 1960; West (see chap. 17). Ancient historians: Syme, 1968, 1971 and in *HA Colloq.*, 1976, 306–9; Hammond, in *Aufstieg*; Gaden; Barnes, 1967, 1978; Momigliano; Benario; Millar.

1 Attempts have been made to date the obelisk to 133–4 on the basis of a coin of Hadrian with his foot on a crocodile which is said to be based on a sculpture connected with the obelisk (Levi, 30–8; Clairmont, 19). There is no reason to connect this coin and the obelisk, or to suggest any such dating.
2 Erman, 1917, 14.
3 Dietrichson, 135.
4 This is Aymard's objection, 535. Bonanno denies that it is Aelius Caesar, 102–3, 105–6, but Hannestad, 91, no. 2, accepts it in his catalogue of portraits of Aelius.
5 Carandini, 39.
6 By Maull, 57.
7 On the tondo the lower face is now missing, so comparisons must be made with Reinach, 1910, no. 8. There are close similarities between this and the heads given in Clairmont, nos. 7 (Tunis), 20 (Louvre).
8 E.g. coins of Sardis, Blum, 1914, 51; pl. III,16; of Amorium, *ibid*, 50. The profile of this latter coin is very similar to that of Antinous on the lion hunt tondo (Reinach, 1910, no. 8).
9 He sees, as have other scholars, Antinous as the graceful youth on the left of the departure scene, older as the rider on the far left in the bear hunt, older still in two of the scenes of sacrifice, though not in those of Apollo and Artemis. Maull, 57, sees a clear chronological growth of Antinous throughout. There are indeed correspondences between these heads and other sculptures – compare the profile of Reinach no.

17 with Cl. nos 5 and 23; Reinach no. 26 with the Marlborough sardonyx and with Cl. nos 7, 13, 28; the hair of no. 26 on the tondo is damaged and originally came down over the brow. But the facial features and hair-style on the tondi are not consistent. Maybe the discrepancies are due to the small scale and the participation of two workshops in their carving (H. Weber, 132; Aymard, 529; Bülle, 141; Bieber, 1911, 224). Certainly there is as much diversity among the full-size sculptures accepted as Antinous (e.g. compare Cl. no. 3 with 48, 50 or 54). By 136–8, the features of Antinous had become a fashion and figures *like* him on the relief may not be *of* him. His absence from two of the tondi also argues against Kähler's case that the series specifically commemorates his life.

10 1805 trans. The final word in Greek is *paidika* which implies boy-friends or favourites.

11 Tristan, 542. There are wide variations in the translations and interpretations of this passage in Arrian (*cap.* 33–4). Maza, 19–20, claims that Patroclus is Hadrian, but Yourcenar (Penguin edit., 221–2) presents Achilles as Hadrian and Patroclus as Antinous in a very free version of the text. Homer tells us that Patroclus was older than Achilles, but as he died *before* the younger man he can scarcely be Hadrian. Nor can Hadrian be the younger of the pair, who, Arrian tells us, died in the flower of his youth for his friends. Perhaps Arrian did not intend individual comparisons but only one with the quality of the friendship. Para. 34 in this report is such an extraneous intrusion into the narrative that it must have been intended as a flattering consolation for Hadrian. Most of the characteristics of Achilles suit Antinous (beauty, untimely death) but one seems to suit Hadrian alone (devotion to *paidika*). Again perhaps Arrian left the analogy deliberately vague, applicable to both, implying heroic devotion in both the Emperor and his dead beloved.

12 Gallimard, 1974 edit., 338.

13 Dietrichson, 76–7, 267 no. 10, 268–70 no. 12, 273 nos 34–5; Montfaucon, 1719, Suppl. (II), pl. 27 no. 3. Blum, 1914, 46 and pl. III/6. The gem could have been a pastiche based on these coins.

14 Dio, 69, 3, 2; 4, 2; 7, 4; *HA. Had.*, XIV, 8. *Epitome*, XIV.

15 Vermeule, 1960, 2, suggests that an archetype was made in Athens before 130.

16 *HA. Had.*, XIV, 10.

17 Pausanias, VIII,9,7, admits that 'personally I never saw him [Antinous] in his lifetime' which implies that others did and remembered him as notable. Hahland, 63–5.

18 The group in which he appears boy-like are: the heads from Tunis, Cl. no. 9; Amsterdam, Cl. no. 32; Engelsberg, Rome, Cl. no. 46; Munich, Glyptothek 286, Cl no. 52; Rome, Conservatori Mus. Cl. no. 43; London, British Mus. 1900, Cl. no. 22; Rome, Mus. delle Terme, Cl. no. 45. The Olympia statue (Appendix 1, no. 55) may also show him as a youth as also the more doubtfully attributed bronze from Lyons (now in Paris, Appendix 1, b) – Maza, 320.

19 Burckhardt in Laban, 34; Marconi, no. 2, pp. 255, 281ff; Maza, 250.

20 The ringlets may be those of Apollo (Kraus, 1959, 64) or Osiris (? West, 137; Jücker, 1961, 88, no. 34). There are no further versions, as one might expect if this was an original *ad vivum* work. The style, with its hard metallic rendering of the hair and boring of the eyes etc., puts it in the 130s. Its colossal scale and whole conception derive from the posthumous model of the new hero or god: Clairmont,

35; Maza, 249; Kraus, 1959, 64–5; Jücker, 1961, 89; Lippold, 1923, 193.

21 I. Marriott, *JRS*, LXIX, 1979, 65–77.

22 Syme, 1971, 283.

23 *Ibid*, 34.

24 Syme, 1971, 33. Benario, *passim*.

25 *HA. Bonosus*, VIII; Dietrichson, 46–8.

26 Syme, 1968, 60. Recent authorities who dismiss the letter are Beaujeu, 274, note 1; Schwartz, 1968, 167; Hohl, 42.

CHAPTER FIVE

Principal sources: mainly indicated below. Paedagogium: Jordan; Lanciani, 1897; Lugli, 1929, 1970; Platner; Arias. Africa: Weber, 1907; Henderson; Brusin; Bülle; Chawen.

1 *HA.Had.*, XIV, 5.

2 Dietrichson, 36–7; cf. Reinach, 1885, 360.

3 Rydberg, 191.

4 Yourcenar, Penguin edit., 1978, 127; Gallimard edit., 1974, notes, 335.

5 Carandini, 77.

6 E.g. Graindor, 1934, 14; 59, note 2; 129–32; Guarducci, 1949, 152; Carandini, 35; Beaujeu, 168–9.

7 Perowne, 1960, 100. Carney, 12; Weber, 1907, 85, note 287 dismisses a connection so early. Gascou, *Latomus*, XXXVII, 2, 1978, 436–44 contends that Suetonius' work was published between 123 and 129, which makes allusions to Antinous more possible.

8 Erman, 1917, p. 16; IIId. As Antinous was not 'raised up' or 'taken away' from his birthplace by the gods, it must have been by Hadrian.

9 Weber, 1907, 126, note 438. The most recent discussion of the vexed chronology of Hadrian's journeys is in Garzetti, 387ff. According to this (391) and other authors (e.g. Henderson, 86) it could have been in 124 that Hadrian visited Claudiopolis. Beaujeu, 242, accepts 123.

10 Tertullian, *Apol.* XIII, 9.

11 MacKendrick, 291–2; E. Clark, 165.

12 The deliberate alteration of the 'Latin Library' and erection of a statue of Antinous there after 130 could imply some specific commemoration of his earlier presence in a room which hitherto had been a small summer triclinium: Kähler, 1950, 110, 156.

13 E. Clark, 165.

14 Thus Boucher-Colozier, 76, who also says there was a statue and temple to Antinous there. The discovery of such a head in a place by no means automatically implies a visit to it. However, we can be fairly sure that Hadrian was in Mauretania in 128 (Chawen, 323–4; Brusin, 219ff; Weber, 1907, 203) and possibly at Caesarea with Antinous. The head might therefore be a response, after 130, to his earlier presence as well as to a desire to please the Emperor.

15 Bardon, 437. Syme, 1958, 500. If Syme, 1958, 517–19, can contend that Tacitus is really referring to Hadrian when discussing Nero, the same might plausibly be argued in the case of Juvenal who was early disenchanted with the philhellene

Emperor.

16 Kaibel, 811; *IG*. VII, 1828: 'you, wise Eros, extend to him [Hadrian] the favour of Heavenly Aphrodite'. See Beaujeu's perceptive note 2, p. 163. In the Curium poem Antinous is seen as Eros: Lebek, 130, line 14. Aymard, 526, thinks the poem is a pastiche of pieces from the *Anthology*. There is perhaps a connection with Hadrian's admired Xenophon in his *Banquet*, VIII, 3–15, where he discusses the 'Heavenly Aphrodite' and the grace she bestows in aid of spiritual love, love of friendship and noble conduct – all in the context of pederasty. The dialogue on homo- hetero-sexual love of Plutarch (*Erotikos*) is also set at Thespiae.

17 Yourcenar, Gallimard, 1974 edit., 335.

18 *Bull. Comm.*, 1893, 248ff. and Lanciani, 1897, *loc. cit.* Lugli, 1970, pl. 146–7.

19 Winckelmann, 1767, vol. 2, 236; Riencourt, 21.

20 E. Clark, 169; Vermeule, 1960, 1–2; Marconi, 298.

21 Symonds, 1879, 65; Rydberg, 191; West, 108, 130; Taylor, 8.

22 Erman, 1917, 15; IIa; Kishor, 298.

23 Arrian, *Black Sea*, para. 34.

24 Erman, 1917, 15; IIb; Kishor, 303–4; The festivals established for Antinous had music and poetry competitions (e.g. Graindor, 1934, 101–2).

25 Coins of Hadrianotherai and Juliopolis; statue in Berlin, Marconi no. 93; obelisk, Erman, 1917, IIc.

26 Condurachi, 453ff.; Strack, 92, no. 485a; Aymard, 173; Bieber, 229; Maull, 66; Magnaguti, 83; Gnecchi, nos 95, 96.

27 Hahland, *passim*.

28 Xenophon, *Cyn*. XVII, XXI.

29 *Pap. Oxyrhyn*. VIII, no. 1085, 8–10.

30 Laban, 68 and *passim*.

31 Levezow, 9, 21; E. Clark, 167; Gregorovius, 351; Montfaucon, vol. 2, II, 323, 'this effeminate Antinous'; Symonds, 1879, 48; Gayet, 1897, 17; Stahr, 388; Marconi, 230, 244, 298–300; Poulsen, 1920, 324; Kraus, 1959, 56.

32 Levezow, 9; Kishor, 295.

33 Prudentius, *Contra Symm.*, I, 272ff: 'illum purpureo in gremio spoliatum sorte virili'.

34 Michaelis, quoted in Laban, 43, and H. M. Stanley, *ibid*, 58.

35 The Aidepsos Dionysos (Cl. no. 36) is in the Chalkis Museum. The headless figure on one of the scenes in the frieze in the theatre of Dionysos in Athens has been claimed as Antinous by Graindor, 1934, 171, 277–9, supported by Geagan, 1952, 148. Cook, 710, thinks the figure is Theseus, which Graindor refutes. Pickard-Cambridge, 262, repeats Cook as does Kraus, *Römische Weltreich*, pl. 213. Other athletic statues are: the Roman copy of the Aidepsos statue at Naples, Marconi, no. 44, Maza, 373–4; the Mantineia Hermes Antinous in Athens, Cl. 64 (excluded by him but accepted by Lippold and Vermeule etc, see Appendix One); the Dahlem bronze, Maza, 166 (a very doubtful identification); the Herakles-Antinous of the Louvre, Maza, 268 (another doubtful attribution); and the torso found in Antinoopolis by Jomard, relating to the Aidepsos type, Jomard, 26, pl. 59/4–5; Maza, 90.

36 Marconi, 255, 267, 283 etc; Strong, 1907, 250; Heibig in Laban, 51.

37 Clem. Alex. *Protrepticus*, IV. Also Tatian, *Addr. Gr.*, X, I: 'a beautiful youth';

Jerome, *Interpr. Chron. Eus.*, 130–1, 'an extraordinary boy of exceeding beauty'.
38 Lebek, 130, line 12.
39 p. 150.
40 Symonds, 1879, 49.
41 Marconi, no. 38 at the Palazzo Pacca in Rome.
42 Lebek, 130, line 14.
43 Erman, 1917, 15; IIa.
44 E. Clark, 148; Aurigemma, 177–8; Gusman, 102.
45 Strack, 92–3, 122; Wegner, 60; Weber, 1937, 187; *IGR*. 1, 1049.
46 Epiphanios, *Weights and Measures*, XIV. See also the Syriac version edit. J. E. Dean, 1935, 29–30. *Contra*: Weber, 1907, 205, note 732.
47 *Epitome*, XIV, 9. Kähler, 1950, 158.
48 Henderson, 95.
49 Fifth speech to the cavalry of the 16th Commagenian cohort.
50 Strack, 168; Vogt, 102; Smallwood, 1966, no. 118; Kühn, 126, note 6.
51 Phyle, *Sabinios*; deme, *Harmonieus*.
52 Erman, 1917, 14; 1e and p. 30.

CHAPTER SIX

Principal sources: Philostratus, *Letters*; *Apollonius*; Lucian, *Dial. Gods;* Pseudo-Lucian, *Amoribus*; Plutarch, *Erotikos; Lives*; Greek Anthology; Arrian, *Discourses*; Strabo; Cicero, *Ad. Fam*; *Tusc. Disp.* Tacitus, *Ann. Hist.* Pliny, *Letters; Panegyrics;* Suetonius; Valerius Maximus; Dio; *HA*; Fronto; Martial; Juvenal; Statius; Tibullus; Horace; Catullus.

Symonds, 1908; Kiefer; Meier; Dover; Eglinton; Marrou; Sherwin-Bailey; Flacelière, 1952; Robinson and Fluck; Carney. Commodus: Carcopino, 1949, 1965; Grenade; Hohl; Pflaum; Syme, 1957 (see chap. 13). Trajan: Waters, 1974; Syme, 1958.

1 Dietrichson, 48, 50; Reinach, 1885, 359; Gregorovius, 130–1; Perowne, 1960, 100, 155, 156; Salmon, 306; Taylor, 7, 9; Marconi, 242, 282; Farberg, 52; Moreau, 25.
2 Dietrichson, 48, 52–5; Schiller, 1883, vol. 1 (2), 625; Henderson, 133; Kiefer, 338; Rydberg, 188, 192; Vermeule, 1960, 1; West, 109; Symonds, 1879, 65; Schulz, 74; Stahr, 382.
3 Dietrichson, 38; Dover, 1.
4 Henderson, 23–4.
5 Syme, 1958, 249. He is more open about Trajan, e.g. *ibid*, 41. Beaujeu, 242–3, accepts Hadrian's homosexuality.
6 Dietrichson, 38–56.
7 p. 55.
8 Perowne, 1960, 155–7; 1974, 121.
9 *HA.Ael.*, V, 2.
10 See Carcopino's scanty treatment of the homosexual explanation, 1949, 289–90. In his 1965 article it is not mentioned at all. Grenade dismisses it in a footnote, p. 261. Hohl, 42, raises the issue of a sexual connection but does not pursue it. Pflaum, 1963, 100, finds 'nothing surprising' in the allusions to sex between Hadrian and Commodus, but prefers his own fantastic and melodramatic theories of political and

dynastic intrigue. Champlin, 1976, 89, gives no reason for the 'startling and inexplicable' adoption. Hannestad, 70, thinks that Hadrian was infatuated with Commodus.

11 Hohl, 42.

12 Philostratus, *Letters*, 306.

13 E.g. Xenophon, *Banquet*, 468–71. The same ideas are expressed by the protagonist of pederasty in Plutarch's *Erotikos*, 750, some five hundred years later: 'Love [Eros] is it that attaches himself to a younger talented soul and through friendship brings it to a state of virtue'.

14 Marrou, 70.

15 *Erotikos*, 754.

16 Pliny, *Letters*, X, 40; Marrou, 202–3, notes that the gymnasia lasted longest in Asia Minor, also 349, 365.

17 Strabo, X, 4, 21.

18 Plutarch, *Erotikos*, 750.

19 Cicero, *Tusc. Disp.*, XXXIII, XXXIV.

20 Philostratus, *Love Letters*, no. 64. Eglinton, 358ff., vastly exaggerates the moral decline and increased sensuality of Hellenistic and later Greece.

21 769, 770.

22 The authorship is uncertain, the style is based on Lucian, the title is *De Amoribus*. For dating, see Loeb edit., Lucian's *Works*, VIII, 147.

23 Cicero, *Tusc. Disp.*, XXXIII; Marrou, 365; Meier, 186; Robinson and Fluck, 24–5.

24 Catullus, *Poems*, nos 28 and 10. Catullus was attacking Memmius who had once denounced Caesar for homosexuality but had now joined his party. Even if Catullus' charges are fabrications, they show the uses to which the patronage system could be put.

25 Mommsen, 1899, 703. The law (variously spelled, see Meier, 178) was in existence by 170 BC. It does not seem to have been a general prohibition of homosexual acts so much as a protection against unsolicited assault. The later moral laws of Augustus did not concern homosexual acts. Mommsen, *loc. cit.*; Sherwin-Bailey, 69.

26 Tacitus, *Histories* (Penguin edit.), 165, 212.

27 Dio, 62, 6, 4.

28 67, 11, 4.

29 Symonds, 1908, 294.

30 Statius, *Silvae*, II, i, vi. Martial, VI, 28–29, I, also on Glaucias and Melior.

31 E.g., 88; VI, 52, 68.

32 Marcus Aurelius, *Meditations*, 1, 17; Fronto, 23–9. This *erotikos* is a literary exercise only, but it does indicate how common it was for boys of high rank to have lovers and how pederasty had become a commonplace in Rome; 221, 81, also 31–3.

33 By Suetonius, *On Grammarians*, 467; Eglinton, 283–4; Meier, 187.

34 Kiefer, 282. A comparison between the pederastic and heterosexual epigrams of Martial leads to the conclusion that the former were the more deeply felt and based on genuine emotional experience. Martial, XII, 18, implies that Juvenal was a pederast. The latter's pathological hatred for women, disgust at overt homosexuality and tender references to boys suggest a repressed pederasty: e.g. VI, 35ff.; XI, 147ff.

35 Carney, 7, note 5.
36 *Claudius*, XXXIII.
37 Vespasian, VIII, XIII.
38 Tacitus, *Annals*, 232.
39 Suetonius, *Nero*, XXIX; Dio, 62, 13, 2; 63, 22, 4; Tacitus, *Annals*, 362.
40 *HA. Had.*, II, 7–8; IV, 5–7.
41 Dio, 68, 7, 4; Martial, XII, 15, could be hinting at Trajan's pederasty.
42 Dio, 68, 10, 2; Smallwood, 1966, no. 173; Fronto, Loeb edit., vol. 2, 9, para. 4.
43 *Caesars*, 35, 406–7.
44 *Pap. Oxyrhyn.* III, 1903, 471; Schubart, *Griechische literarische Papyri*, Berlin, 1950, 90–4; Musurillo, 152–6; Syme, 1957 (*Historia*, VI), 480–7; Schwartz, 1952. I accept Schubart's view that the boy was probably the Theon mentioned in his fragment. There is no evidence that Vibius Maximus was being prosecuted for *stuprum cum puero praetextato* as Musurillo, 156, claims, but on other charges including bribing the boy's father.
45 Temporini, 176–7; Pliny, *Panegyric*, 83–4; *Letters*, IX,28, 1.

CHAPTER SEVEN
1 E. Clark, 164.
2 *HA.Had.*, XIV, 5–9, 10–11; *Aelius*, III, 8. SAV, XIV.
3 *HA.Had.*, XI, 7–9.
4 Origen, *Contra Celsum*, III,36.
5 'Ex erotikes philias', Dio, 69, 1, 2; 10, 3.
6 E.g. Carney, 12, talks of his 'vigorous sexual athleticism among Rome's society dames'.
7 Letter of *c.* 121 given in Henderson, 51. Syme is suspicious about the relationship, 1958, 249. Temporini, 19.
8 Fleres, *Atti Acad. Peloritana*, Messina, 1951–64, 48, 199ff. Temporini, 156, 180; Cramer, 170; Pliny, *Panegyric*, 83–4.
9 Perowne, 1974, 120.
10 Henderson quoting Dositheus, 185, letter of 121 AD; *ibid*, 51. Temporini, 164.
11 Smallwood, 1966, 114; Temporini, 169–70; Bardon, 404.
12 Bernand, no. 30, poem by Balbilla on the statue of Memnon.
13 *Epitome*, XIV.
14 Juvenal, VI,596.
15 *Epitome*, XIV.
16 E. Clark, 152; Mattingly, 1936, CC.
17 Aurigemma, 1961, 17; Gusman, 278–9. The figure of twenty-two works so retrieved is my own calculation.
18 Weber, 1907, 85, note 287. Jerome, *Chron.*, 120.
19 II, 7–8. Temporini, 80.
20 IV, 5–7. Benario, 59.
21 XI, 7–9. Maza, 58; Benario, 90.
22 XIV, 9–10. Defence of Apuleius, *Apologia*, 254–5.
23 SAV, XIV, 'iniecisse stupra puberibus'.

24 *Meditations*, Bk. 1, 16, 12–13.
25 Suetonius, *Augustus*, VII.
26 Bülle, 153; Aymard, 533.
27 Graindor, 1922, 180, 220; 1934, 12–17; Alexander, 153, quoting letter of 131–2.
28 There are ten principal pagan sources and nineteen principal Christian ones.
29 Pausanias, VIII,9,7.
30 *Contra Celsum*, III,36; V,63.
31 Lucian, *Dialogue of the Gods*, V. The references to the 'soft Phrygian boy', 'this youth, effeminate, a foreigner, soft and girlish', 'the handsome youth with the flowing locks' are usually taken as referring to Antinous by editors but there seems no reason why they should. That in the *Convention of the Gods*, concerning the origin of upstart deities, seems more pointedly directed at Antinous.
32 69, 11, 3.
33 *HA.Had.*, XIV, 6. Another adjective may well have been lost between *Antinoum* and *suum*.
34 SAV, XIV.
35 *Adhort. Gr.*, IV. Dulière, *passim*.
36 *Loc. cit.*
37 Tertullian, *Apol.* XIII, 12; *Ad Nat.* II, 10.
38 *Contra Celsum*, III,36. He calls Antinous *paidika* twice and *meirakion* (young man) once. The context is clearly the licentiousness of Antinous compared with the purity of Christ, *pace* Perowne, 1960, 155.
39 Athanasius, *Cont. Gen.*, 9; Prudentius, *Cont. Symm.* 1, 267–77.
40 Jerome, *Cont. Jov.*, 11, 7. Usually Jerome refers to Antinous as *in deliciis* (= *paidika*). Once, however, he links his role with that of a public male concubine – *Comm. In Ies.*, 2. *De Vir. Ill.*, 22; *Interpr. Chron. Eus.*, 130–1, ann. 13.

CHAPTER EIGHT
Principal sources: *HA*; Dio; SAV; Pausanias. Personnel: *PIR*; Carandini; Cramer, Bernand; Bülle; Brusin; Champlin. Eleusis: Mylonas; Méautis; Bianchi; Guarducci, 1949; Nilsson; Beaujeu; Kienast; Weber, 1907. Athens: Graindor, 1934; Liegle; Follet, 1968, 1976; Oliver, 1941, 1965, 1970; Beaujeu; Metcalf; Benjamin, 1963; Benjamin and Raubitschek; Travlos. The east: Weber, 1907, 1937; Le Glay; Vermeule, 1968; Strack; Garzetti; Woodward: Mattingly; Stinespring. Jewish policy: Weber, 1907, 1937; Beaujeu; Follet, 1968; Smallwood, 1976; Barnard.

1 *Satire* VI,434ff.
2 Champlin, 84.
3 Henderson, 79. The original inscription (*CIL*.VI(2) 8991) does not specify Hadrian as the Emperor.
4 *De Legibus*, II, 14.
5 E.g. Graindor, 1934, 14; Guarducci, 1949, 152. Supporting a connection of Antinous with Eleusis are: the statue and games of his there; the statue in the Museo Chiaromonti (Cl. no. 43) with a wreath of wheat ears (Maza, 153); the relief in Athens of him being presented by the goddesses of Eleusis to Dionysos (Graindor, 1934, 277–9; Geagan, 148); the heads of Leningrad and Florence with ears of corn

(Cl. nos 18, 34); the coin of Adramyttion where he is identified with Iacchos and Demeter is shown on the reverse (Blum, 1914, 47–8) and those of Tarsos where he is also identified with Iacchos (*ibid*, 52). One of the demes of the phyle of Antinous at Antinoopolis is 'Hermes' with whom Antinous was also identified frequently on his coins. Hermes descended into Hades to conduct Persephone back to Demeter. There was therefore in Hadrian's mind a link between Antinous and Eleusis in the use of this name as there were in the various Eleusinian references in the names of the demes belonging to the tribes of Hadrian, Sabina and Matidia, and Augustus. Cf. Beaujeu, 168–9, 196 note 7, 250; Dietrichson, 161. The assimilation of Antinous to Dionysos also links him with another major associate of the Eleusinian cult: Geagan, 148–51; Graindor, 1934, 131–2, 154, 277–9 and note at rear to p. 168.

6 Quoted in Méautis, 67.

7 Geagan, 148; Bianchi, 8; Graindor, 1934, 262–7; Lenormant, 219; Marconi, no. 108; Maza, 176–8; Clairmont, no. 14, follows Lippold, 192 and Holm, 39, in seeing Antinous as Asclepeios. The Delphic omphalos at his left foot is, however, the tomb of Dionysos Zagreus. In the Orphic myth Zeus and Demeter were the parents of Persephone and she gave birth to Dionysos who was torn to pieces by the Titans and later resurrected, this time as the son of Semele.

8 Clairmont, *loc. cit.* and Marconi think the work is 'elegant'. In fact the hands and feet are crude. It is not a good likeness: the eyes are too prominent, the nose too long, the mouth too full, and the chest too narrow. The statue was discovered in several pieces in 1860. The cranium, nose, parts of the drapery and feet are restored. The statue is remarkably lacking in depth, though very successful in disguising this fact: it evidently stood flat against a wall. See Maza's penetrating interpretation of the work, 176–8. Also West, 109; Guarducci, 1949, 152.

9 Quoted Graindor, 1934, 122; Weber, 1907, 168, 207; Guarducci, 1949, 150–1. We cannot be sure if this refers to his first or second initiation. The reference to his benefactions might make the later date marginally more likely.

10 Kienast, 61–9; Beaujeu, 166–73; Guarducci, 1949, 151–3.

11 The aqueduct was begun in 124–5 or 128–9 though not finished till 140 (Graindor, 1934, 44; Travlos, 253). The library may have been begun in 128–9 and finished in 132 (Graindor, 1934, 54) or only started at the latter date (Travlos, 244).

12 *HA.Had.*, XIII, 6.

13 Metcalf, 62–6; Beaujeu, 178–81, 200–9, 278; Weber, 1907, 212; 1937, 152, 205.

14 *Roman Oration* (Oliver, *Ruling Power*), 31–3, 103.

15 Graindor, 1934, 170; Beaujeu, 201; Benjamin, 1963, 58–9; Raubitschek, 130.

16 The phyle Hadrianios has the demes: Zenios, Olympios, Capitolieus, Sosicosmios and one Mousegetios (Apollo) and the phyle Aelieus has a deme of Zenios (Polieus). Nothing could be further from the truth than Henderson's claim that Hadrian was 'amused' (239) to find himself a god. He both promoted the claim and evidently took it very seriously indeed. Beaujeu, 184.

17 Weber, 1937, 217; Beaujeu, 220.

18 The following itinerary and details are from Weber, 1907, 212–31.

19 Henderson, 127; Weber, 1907, 236. The *HA* dates this incident as in 129 (XIV, 3); Dio at the beginning of the reign (69, 2, 1). Beaujeu, 269–70; Schulz, 77; West says Antinous was with him on the summit, p. 109.

20 *HA.Had.*, XIV, 1. *Contra*: Gaden, 141. Carandini, 84; Plew, 18, note 2;

Henderson, 126; Weber, 1907, 233–4.

21 Mattingly, CLXXII. The Syrian legion alone is commemorated – Strack, 141.

22 *HA.Had.*, XIII, 9–10.

23 Weber, 1907, 237; Starcky, 38–9; Garzetti, 686.

24 *Enc. Judaica*, 7, col. 1055.

25 Follet, 1968, 71–2; Beaujeu, 261. The *HA* (XIV) gives the banning of circumcision as the cause of the later war and places it in the period 129–30. Dio sees the founding of Aelia Capitolina as the cause of the war after the visit to Egypt (69, 12). Epiphanios places the founding of Aelia Capitolina on the 130 journey (*Weights and Measures*, XIV).

26 Dio clearly places the founding of Aelia and the temple of Jupiter there after the visit to Egypt of 130–31 but before the Jewish war broke out in 132. The decision was probably taken then. Some scholars think the temple was founded only after the war was concluded – Follet, 1968, 71–2; Smallwood, 1976, 434–5.

27 Dio, 69, 11, 289; Strabo, XVI, 2, 33; XVII, 1, 21.

CHAPTER NINE

Principal sources: Herodotus; Strabo; Juvenal; *HA*; Athenaeus; Pancrates; Q. C. Rufus; *Pap. Oxyrhyn.*; *Pap. Milano*; *Pap. London*; Plutarch, *Iside*; Weber, 1907, 1911; Vogt; Bonneau, 1964, 1966; Lindsay, 1963, 1965; 1968; Malaise; Milne; Jouguet, 1911; Sijpesteijn; Hoffa; Follet, 1968; Wainwright; Rowe; Morenz; Graindor, 1932; Eitrem; Calderini; Kühn; Roeder.

1 The coins of Alexandria permit an approximate dating. One announces Hadrian's arrival in his fourteenth regnal year in Egypt (i.e. on or before 28 August 130), others in his fifteenth year (i.e. on or after 29 August) – Vogt, 102–3. Using this, some historians place the arrival early in August (Weber, 1907, 247; Beaujeu, 228); Sijpesteijn, 111, at the end of the month. The earlier date seems more consistent with coin-issuing practice and what we know of Hadrian's later programme.

2 I have used details shown on the mosaic of Praeneste (now at Palestrina) throughout this chapter as evidence of the Nile scene at the flood period. I follow Bonneau, 1964, 90–4, in accepting that this mosaic is Roman, though the dating is uncertain (Augustan or Tiberian most probable). The dating of 280 BC in the latest study by Steinmeyer-Schareika, 1978, 54–5, is unacceptable.

3 Herodotus, II, 143.

4 Epiphanios, *Weights and Measures*, XIV, '. . . as a result of the illness which befell him, he went on a journey to the land of Egypt'.

5 *HA.Bonosus*, VIII, 5. The words are from the alleged letter of Hadrian to Servianus. Though the authenticity of this letter is very doubtful, its report of Alexandrian mockery and Hadrian's reaction is probably true and is based on its fourth-century fabricator's reading of earlier sources (*ibid.*, VIII, *passim*). It is confirmed by Dio, 69, 11, 4. Beaujeu, 274, note 1.

6 Athenaeus, *Deipn.*, XV, 677d, e, f. Bülle, 150; Aymard, 395–7.

7 In his article on Hadrian's visit to Egypt, Sijpesteijn, 1969, 115, places the lion hunt in December 130 in the Fayoum. As Antinous is known to have taken part and was dead by 30 October, and as Athenaeus says that the rosy lotus which grew from the

dead lion's blood grew 'in the summer season', such a dating is unacceptable. The early part of September fits Athenaeus' season, Antinous' life and Hadrian's movements far better (Follet, 1968, 67 note 1). Athenaeus also tells us explicitly that the hunt took place 'in the part of Libya near Alexandria' (*loc. cit.*) and not down in the Fayoum.

8 Philostratus, *Letters*, nos 13, 58; Plutarch, *Erotikos*, 770. Much pederastic poetry of early and Roman vintage concerns the ending of a boy's beauty by the onset of facial and bodily hair: e.g. *Pal. Anth.*, XII, nos 4, 12, 25–7; Martial, IV,7, Horace, *Odes*, IV,10. Lucian in his *True History*, 28, says 'never have commerce with a boy of more than eighteen years'.

9 Pausanias, ed. Levi, II, 219 note 74. Martial, IX,76 tells us that Camionius, who was twenty, had shaved but once; Statius, *Silvae*, V,11, says that Vettius Bolonus, who was sixteen and entering the army, still had no sign of down on his cheeks. Eglinton, 244.

10 Above Chap. 4, Kähler, 1950, p. 154 and note 151; Reinach, 1910, no. 8. Blum, 1914, 51; pl. III/16, coin of Sardis; 50, coin of Amorium.

11 *Pap. Oxyrhyn.* VIII, 1085. The details of the different spears sound very authentic, as do the roles of Hadrian and Antinous.

12 Adrastus was saved by his horse Arion in the expedition of the Seven against Thebes.

13 *HA.Had.*, XXVI, 3; Hoffa, 98–9; Aymard, 181.

14 Gnecchi, III nos. 95–6; Strack, 129 and nos 450, 468, 499; Magnaguti, 117–18; Aymard, 152; Condurachi, 455–6.

15 Hoffa, 100. Kähler and Maull claim that Antinous is shown as in Reinach, 1910, no. 13. Above, Chap. 4.

16 Athenaeus, *loc. cit.*

17 Carandini, 39. West, 110; Kübler, 7; Gregorovius, 129; Cramer, 172, 175.

18 The flimsy evidence for his presence is: his appearance on the Masson gem (now disappeared); on the lion hunt tondo (but this may have been because the tondo was created in his Caesarship in 137 and his identity there is disputed by Bonanno, 102–3, though accepted convincingly by Hannestad, 91, no. 12); and the mention in the letter of Hadrian to Servianus (considered mostly as a fake). All of this is very dubious indeed but might just reflect a tradition of his being on the Nile journey.

19 As even Hadrian had been away from Rome for six months in his praetorship (Temporini, 131), it is unlikely that Commodus as praetor would have felt obliged to forego a holiday in the Emperor's company for such official duties; and, as his scornful attitude to his wife indicates, he would hardly have felt it incumbent upon him to tarry round the child-bed (his son was born on 15 December). The Aelius chapter in the *HA*, though highly suspect in its anecdotes (Hohl, 43–8; Syme, 1971, 54–77) does convey a convincing flavour of his character.

20 Viereck, no. 141 (two receipts); Wilcken, 1912, no. 412; Sijpesteijn, 109, 116–17.

21 Van Groningen, 253–6.

22 Wilcken, 1912, no. 415. A visit by the Prefect to Hermopolis between 145 and 147.

23 Q. C. Rufus, IV, VIII, 7–9.

24 In 199–200 there was a bad flood and Severus also encountered plague.

25 Bonneau, 1964, 23, 346, 351; 1966, 379; Lindsay, 1968, 12–14. The evidence for the insufficient flood of these two years comes mainly from the absence of the usual

Nile coins: Vogt, 52–3, 101, 103, 104.

26 Quoted Lindsay, 1968, 12.

27 Wainwright, 72–3, 90–2.

28 Hopfner, 617, quoting Servius of 355–410 AD; Eitrem, 321–2.

29 p. 132; Bonneau, 1966, estimates the journey, Alexandria to Thebes, as 500 km and taking fourteen days.

30 Sijpesteijn, 112, note 23. We know that he was off Hermopolis on 30 October. He therefore took nineteen days to reach Thebes, a journey which normally would have taken four or five. True, he probably delayed at the site of Antinous' death, but the implication of this speed is that the journey before the death was leisurely also: hence my assumed starting date of early October. I do not accept Sijpesteijn's view, 111, note 19a, that Hadrian only visited antiquities on the return journey which seems implausible. Sijpesteijn ignores the strong evidence for visits to Hermopolis and Memphis, to Denderah (cartouches, buildings and sculptures), and the more debatable evidence of an expedition beyond Thebes via Edfu to Philae (Greppo, 221; Weber, 1907, 257–8; 1937, 221; Wegner, 37, 61; Beaujeu, 228). Most important tourists, like Lucius Memmius and Septimius Severus, visited Memphis, the pyramids, the Labyrinth and Thebes. Hadrian must have seen at least these, and not all on the return down the Nile.

31 The Balbilla inscriptions on Memnon indicate his anxiety to demonstrate publicly that the gods still cherished him (Bernand, no. 28), his easy irritability and arrogance (no. 30 and Bernand pp. 20, 27). The Pancrates 'testing to the full' also implies tension and his behaviour at the Museion was arrogant.

32 Preisendanz (1973 edit.), 148–9, lines 2445–6 of this magical papyrus now in Paris.

33 Herodotus, II, 159.

34 *HA.Had.*, XVI, 7. Beaujeu, 238.

35 Budge, 1895, LIV; 1911, 1–17; Rowe, 3; Wainwright, 96.

36 Morenz, 141.

37 Graindor, 1932, 97–100. Eitrem, 314–20.

38 Weber, 1911, 22 and note 13. Bonneau, 1964, 346. Plutarch, *De Iside*, 356c. Graindor, 1934, 153, 159. See below, chap. 10.

39 Calderini, 75, 79, shows the name of 'Bes' being used there in the second century. Kühn, 10. Other examples: Pistorius, nos 140–6. Milne, 46, notes the traces of identification of Antinous with Bes. Lindsay, 1965, 217.

40 Photius, writing around 890 AD, refers to a writer Helladios of about 310 AD as coming from the city of Besantinous. Ever since, historians have assumed that the name Besa was that of the settlement before Antinoopolis was founded. This view is held by Dietrichson, 98–9; Weber, 1911, 20, 21 note 9 and more recently by Graindor, 1934, 14; Beaujeu, 192, 245; and Follet, 1968, 62. However, in 1913, Kühn, 10–20, concluded that Photius had mistaken the personal name 'Helladios son of Besantinous' for the name of the place and therefore no such place-name as Besa previously existed there, though the personal name 'Besantinous' was 'exceptionally frequently' found in Antinoopolis. In this he has been followed by Pistorius (1939), 50, and Calderini (1966), 75, 79. However, the unusual frequency of the name of the god Bes there does imply a flourishing cult of that god there. We know that in Roman times his cult spread widely along the Nile, ousting that of Serapis from primacy at Abydos, establishing itself in the Serapeum of Memphis

too. He had oracles and spoke through dreams and was a widely invoked protector against evil, in amulets, tokens etc.: all identical features of the cult of Antinous which was established at Antinoopolis and which may well have taken over elements from that of Bes already there. Amm. Marcellinus, XIX, 12, 3. Milne, 46. Hastings, VI, 383a, article by Milne.

41 An intriguing question first posed by Graindor, 1934, 14, who was going to answer it (*ibid.*, note 1) but never did; cf. Beaujeu, 245 note 1.

CHAPTER TEN

Principal sources: *HA*; Dio; SAV; *Epitome*; Athenaeus; Arrian; Plutarch, *de Iside*; Epiphanios, *Weights*; *Ancoratus*; Suetonius; Origen; Aristeides; *Pap. Oxyrhyn.*; *Pap. Milano*. Symonds, 1879; Dietrichson; Weber, 1907, 1911; Kishor; Erman, 1896, 1917; Hermann; Blum, 1914; Marconi; Perowne, 1960; Kühn; Dulière; Cumont, 1949; Beaujeu; Bonneau, 1964; Follet, 1968.

1 69, 11, 2.
2 *Pap. Oxyrhyn.*, XXXI, no. 2553, lines 1–3. In this calendar of cult offerings the entry concerning the apotheosis occurs three entries before Antinous' birthday (27 November). This obviously strongly supports the *Chron. Pasc.*'s dating of late October (III Kal. Nov.).
3 Plutarch, *De Iside*, 356c, gives the death of Osiris as occurring on 17th Hathyr (Budge, 1911, 4). Graindor, 1934, 153, 159, points out that the Athenians and the Greeks celebrated this anniversary on 24 October (13 Boedromion).
4 *Had.*, XIV, 6.
5 *Pap. Milano*, 1, 1937, 181, 176.
6 Marconi, 299; Dietrichson, 76.
7 Kishor, 295. She seems to be relying on Prudentius' extremely vague phrase about Antinous losing his manhood.
8 69, II, 2–3.
9 Riencourt, 31, 3. E.g. also Le Menestrier, 129; Millin, 155; Tristan, 541, 549; Dubois, ed. SAV, 461; de Tillemont 246; Bayle, 243, note B.
10 *Had.*, XIV, 6.
11 Kishor, 294. It is not clear if the *de quo* in the text refers to the death of Antinous or to Hadrian's grief. If the former, then the second alternative seems to imply a suicide provoked by Hadrian's excessive lust. If the latter, then the alternative says the excessive grief was the product of homosexual passion and not gratitude for sacrifice. On the contrary, Dio tells us emphatically that the death was a suicide, but says that Hadrian's extravagant reaction was caused either because the sacrifice was voluntary or because of Hadrian's love. See Plew, 19.
12 Section on Hadrian, XIV. Author's translation of this very condensed Latin.
13 Pückler-Muskau, 1, 259–60. E. M. Butler, *Tempestuous Prince*, London, 1929, 115–21. A section is quoted by Clairmont.
14 1911, 21.
15 *Ancoratus*, 106, i, f.
16 *HA. Elagab.*, VIII, 1–2; Dio, 74, 16, 5; Eusebius, *Eccl. Hist.*, VIII,14. For similar offerings to gods: Tertullian, *Apol.*, 9; Lactanctius, *Div. Inst.*, 1, 21.

17 Justin, *Apol.*, 9; Philostratus, *Apollon.*, VIII, 15; Tatian, *Cont. Graec.*, 165.

18 Le Menestrier, 129.

19 *Carmina*, III, 9 *ad Lydiam*. Also Juvenal, XII, 115ff.

20 She mentions 'Balbillus the wise' in her private poem carved on the colossus of Memnon. Bernand, 86ff., no. 29.

21 Aristeides, *Sacred Talks.*, V,24. Dietrichson, 79; Symonds, 1879, 59; Beaujeu, 243.

22 Dulière, 216; Dietrichson, 81–2.

23 Strack, 92–3 and no. 499, coin bearing the legend *Salus* and the emblem of Asclepeios bears also the title *Pater Patriae* and must therefore be *after* August 128.

24 *Epitome*, XIV. Dietrichson was also at Antinoopolis in October (1880) and vouches for the trying climate at that season (p. 76).

25 Dio, 69, 17, 1.

26 Erman, 1917, 1f.

27 *Ibid.*, IIa, p. 15.

28 *Ibid.* Erman is unable to accept the idea of *extispicium* and therefore thinks it means a command of the gods that Antinous be brought to their ranks.

29 Quoted in Dietrichson, 323, 'His heart triumphant, letting fall the arms, he received the commands of the gods as it were his joy'. *Ibid.*, 72, 73; Kishor, 295. Cf. Beaujeu, 244.

30 Erman 1917, 1c, 1f.

31 Origen, *Contra Celsum*, III,36.

32 Maza, 19; Tristan, 542.

33 Dietrichson, 72 and sculpture no. 81. Marconi, 114. The recent attempt by Iwas, 1976, 485–8 to contend that the sculpture is Hadrianic and may therefore refer to the death of Antinous, is unconvincingly based on stylistic analogies alone. Clairmont, no. 40; Maza, 267. Symonds, 1879, 85–8.

34 Schiff in PW, VI, I col. 1136 under 'Eunostidai'.

35 *Ibid.*, under '*Eunostos*', col. 1136. Plutarch, *Greek Questions*, 40; Beaujeu, 256, note 13.

36 Osiris descended for his brothers, Dionysos for Semele, Hermes for Persephone. Dietrichson, 160–1.

37 Origen, *loc. cit.* Dulière, 216.

38 Dulière, 216, notes that Clement of Alexandria talks of the order to mourn Antinous like a son and connects this with the phrase in *Hebrews* that Christ was 'a son sacrificed voluntarily for the father'. Hermann, 163.

39 There are two other minor objections. First, the absence of any mention of the sacrifice in the Christian writings raises doubts. But for them to mention such a thing would at once have created uncomfortable analogies with Christ and have rebounded in Antinous' favour when their aim was denigration. Second, the prohibition of the burial of suicides in the rules of the Lanuvium fraternity seems to invalidate a sacrificial suicide on the part of their patron Antinous. (Column II, v.5, Mommsen, 1848, 100.) But such a sacrifice or *devotio* was not considered an ordinary suicide in Italy at this time; it was in another and religiously permitted category. Bayet, 171, 175; Beaujeu, 244, note 3.

40 Heinse (Laban, 14); Kishor, 291, 294–5, 307 (Hyse); Plew, 19; Marconi, 242, 244, 282–4, 298–300.

41 *HA.Had.*, XXIV, 8ff.

42 *Pap. Oslo*, 1936, no. 70. *Alexander*, 165–6, The phrases on the face concerning Hadrian on the obelisk (Erman, 1917, 1f.) also seem to refer to a good inundation achieved after Antinous' death and perhaps because of it.

CHAPTER ELEVEN

Principal sources: *HA*; Dio; Herodotus; Pancrates; Pausanias; Athenaeus; Suidas; *Pap. Oxyrhyn.*; *Pap. Soc. Ital.*; *Pap. Oslo*; *IGR*; *CIG*; Symonds, 1879; Weber, 1907, 1911; Bracker; Wegner; Erman, 1917; Budge, 1895, 1911; Gayet, 1897; Follet, 1968; Sijpesteijn; Kühn; Jouguet; Cumont, 1949; Beaujeu; Blum, 1913, 1914; Milne; Graindor, 1934; Orgeval; Breccia, 1957; Lindsay, 1965; Hermann; Bernand; Le Glay.

1 *HA.Had.*, XIV, 6. *Muliebriter* was used by Tacitus even of himself when convulsed with uncontrollable emotion. It is not a reference to effeminacy. Plew, 20; Weber, 1907, 244, note 901; 1911, 21; Maza, 17.

2 *Interpr. Chron. Eus.*, 130–1, ch. 13, *vehementer deperiens* (variant, *diligenter sepeliens*).

3 Robert, 1979, 160–5. Polydeukes died in 173–4 when Herodes Atticus was about 73. Vermeule, 1960, 7; H. Weber, 145–6.

4 Bracker, 75–7, 80–2 and *passim*. Bieber, 1970, 95; Hannestad, 95.

5 Wegner, 42–3, 62. Wegner suggests that the head found in 1913 at Dictynnaion in Crete is Athenian work of 131–2. Vermeule, 1968, 391, no. 7, thinks the cuirassed statue to which it was attached (but to which it may not originally have belonged) and which has now been destroyed was later than Hadrian. He thinks even that the head could be of Antoninus Pius, though to the present author the features, especially the nose and lips, are very much Hadrian's. Inan and Rosenbaum, 1966, 69.

6 Wegner, 25, 62, 71.

7 Erman, 1917, IVc, 1a, IIa, IIb, p. 34.

8 II, 90; p. 161 (Penguin edit.).

9 From the exclusively Egyptian cult expounded on the obelisk, and from the Egyptian elements of the cult in the Villa Adriana and in Rome itself.

10 Budge, 1895, 254.

11 Gregorovius, 307.

12 Cicero, *Ad Atticum*, XII,12, 18, 20.

13 Robert, 1979, 160–5. He had done the same for his wife.

14 Maza, 93; Marucchi, 134; Symonds, 1879, 63.

15 Symonds, 64–5.

16 Pancrates' poem: *Pap. Oxyrhyn.*, VIII, 1085, line 25.

17 *HA.Had.*, XIV, 7.

18 *Pap. Soc. Ital.*, III, no. 199. Robert, *REG*, 1952, 192–3; Follet, 1968, 63–4.

19 Pausanias, 1,42,2.

20 Bernand, no. 30. Balbilla's vanity: nos 29 and 31.

21 Bernand, p. 85; pp. 20, 21. Hadrian's mood: nos 28, 30.

22 Blackman, 2, says it was built by Augustus but Rowe, 22, gives Hadrian's dates. It is difficult to see why Augustus who never left Alexandria should have honoured two obscure drowned men in Nubia. Hadrian was closer and clearly had a motive. The

temple was submerged in the creation of the Aswan Dam earlier this century.

23 Oliver, 1941, 77, no. 33; Kähler, 1950, 153.

24 As the Antinous-Dionysos sculptures found in the Villa Adriana indicate. See below chap. 14.

25 Erman, 1917, 1b, IIb; p. 16.

26 *Ibid.*, IVa.

27 Holm, 33–4; Hahland, 62–3; Kraus, 1962, 134–5; Clairmont, 15, 17, 26 and no. 16; Dietrichson, 247, 263, nos 110, 134.

28 Tatian, *Add. Gks.*, X. Blum, 1914, Nikopolis, no. 6; Smyrna, no. 8 etc.; Hadrianotherai, no. 2; Ancyra. Dietrichson, III.

29 Athenaeus, *Deipn.* XV, 677d–f. As the lotus was a water plant and the lion was killed in the desert, one has to assume the poetical licence of a swamp of blood from which it grew (Hoffa, 98).

30 Athenaeus, *loc. cit.* Page, 517; *Pap. Oxyrhyn.*, VIII, 73; Bardon, 430, are very critical. Garzetti, 399; Henderson, 18; Maza, 13, admire the poem.

31 *HA.Antoninus*, VII, 7–8.

32 The names do not appear to have been used in Antinoopolis before 133 – Follet, 1968, 65. Kühn, 128–9. For these see: Weber, 1907, 251–5; Beaujeu, 167–9, 184, 237, 252, 277; Bell, 1940, 140–1; Pistorius, 42–4, 125–6; Calderini, 106–9. Also Guarducci, 1949, 152; Carandini, 36; Graindor, 1934, 6–11, 14.

CHAPTER TWELVE

Principal sources: *HA*; Clem. Alex; Epiphanios, *Ancoratus*; Dietrichson; Erman, 1896, 1917; Hülsen, 1896, 1919; Gayet, 1897; Jomard; Kühn; Calderini; Donadoni, 1938, 1939, 1945; Marucchi; Müller; Malaise; Iversen; Derchain; Kähler, 1975; Follet, 1968; Budge, 1925; Lugli, 1970; Lanciani, 1909; Nash; Colini; Gusman; Aurigemma.

1 Clem. Alex., *Protrepticus.*, IV. He says, translating literally: 'There is a tomb of the *eromenos*. A temple of this Antinous and a city.'

2 *Ancoratus*, 106.

3 Dietrichson, 106, 136, 318, Gayet, 1897, 16–23, 50–4.

4 Kühn, 17; Donadoni, 1939, 666–7; Beaujeu, 255, note 1.

5 1897, 50–1. Erman, 1917, IIb and c; Origen, *Contra Celsum*, III,36. Calderini, 88, says there was a mausoleum of Antinous at Antinoopolis but the tomb was in Rome.

6 1897, 17.

7 1896, 119; 1917, IVa. All references are to this later and somewhat revised translation. Erman could not accept Marucchi's 1898 translation (based on Birch): 'the divine Antinous, buried in this city, in the middle of the fields of the domain of the powerful Lord of Rome' (p. 132ff., cf: Erman, 1917, 11, note 2), though this has proved to be more accurate (Kähler, 1975, 40–1). There seems to be a deliberate geographical contrast being made here between the obelisk and tomb in Rome and the honouring of the god in Egypt. Why should the obelisk so elaborately describe the tomb in Antinoopolis if it stood there? The implication is that the obelisk and this text were always far removed from Egypt.

8 E.g. it seems, Weber, 1911, 21, note 9. Follet, 1968, 59, note 7; Beaujeu, 255.

9 Budge, 1925, 240, 342. The Egyptians would have wanted the organs preserved

near the body. Kübler, 21, suggests that the body rested first at Antinoopolis and then was transferred to Rome.

10 Hülsen, 1896, 123–7; Iversen, 164–6.

11 Hülsen, 1919, 259–64.

12 Nash, 253; Lugli, 1970, 519; Clairmont, 19.

13 Colini, 169–74; Lugli, 1970, 519; Iversen, 162–6; Kähler, 1975, 37–8.

14 Kähler, 1975, 41; Derchain, 811–13.

15 Gusman, 314, 317.

16 Aurigemma, 1961, 25, 127, claims that from the brick stamps the Serapeum and Canopus were completed by 127 (Gusman, 145, says 123–6). But as Kähler, 1950, 28, has pointed out, this dating may be illusory as the bricks may have been stored for years at the bottom of the piles and only used after 128 (p. 28). He thinks the Canopus was chiefly built during the second journey and was still unfinished in 134 (1950), 28ff, 138; 1975, 42 and note 8). As the Canopus area is one of the very few in the villa which clearly refers to a geographical location, the Nile valley, it would indeed be extraordinary if it had been created *before* Hadrian visited that location in 130–1 and not after. The Nilotic sculpture there must surely derive from the visit to Egypt, as did Hadrian's devotion to the Nile thereafter. Kähler, *Encyc. dell'Arte Antica*, 1, 80; Bonneau, 1964, 349–51.

17 Malaise, vol. 2, 102–4.

18 Sweet, 229; Gusman, 147, 153.

19 Aurigemma, 1961, 109. Van Buren, *AJA*, 59, 1955, 215, 216.

20 Kähler, 1975, 42–4; Derchain, 810.

21 Kähler argues (1975, 42–4) that because so little mud or sediment was found between the toppled Sileni and caryatids and the stone bottom of the canal, they must have been thrown in 'fairly soon' after it was constructed. His view of Antoninus Pius as violently anti-Antinous is not convincing. We know, for example, that Antoninus probably finished the relief cycle on which Antinous as well as Aelius Caesar and himself are shown and may have approved the erection of the statue of Androcles-Antinous at Ephesos (Hahland, 76–7). There is no evidence that he took measures to stop the cult or the further issue of sculptures in his reign. The Villa Adriana was left full of sculptures of Antinous undamaged by his act. It is also notable that the Christian critics of the pederastic relationship between Hadrian and Antinous kept very muted in the reigns of Antoninus and Marcus Aurelius, as if they knew they could expect no public sympathy from these Emperors, whatever their private sentiments may have been on the matter. The destruction of the tomb or this part of the Canopus is yet another mystery and seems more consistent with the behaviour of the Emperor Commodus or Elagabalus himself.

CHAPTER THIRTEEN

Principal sources: *HA*; Dio; *SAV*; *Epitome*; Arrian; Philostratus, *Sophists*; Pausanias; Eusebius, *Eccl. Hist.*; *IGR*; *CIG*; *IG*. Eastern journey: Weber, 1907; Le Glay; Magie; Garzetti; Dörner, 1949, 1952; Beaujeu; Benjamin 1963; Robert, 1943, 1952. Panhellenion: Weber, 1907; Graindor, 1934; Tod, 1922; Fraser; Larsen; Follet, 1976; Oliver, 1941, 1951, 1953, 1970, 1978. Cult: Graindor, 1922, 1934; Geagan; Beaujeu; Blum, 1913, 1914; Seltman; Toynbee, 1944; Weber, 1907, 1911; Guarducci, 1949.

Jewish war: Weber, 1907; Henderson; Smallwood, 1976; Follet, 1968; Barnard; Strack. Last days: Toynbee, 1934; Strack; Carcopino, 1949, 1965; Pflaum; Hohl; Syme, 1971, 1979; Barnes, 1967, 1968; Champlin; Hannestad; Carandini; Valera; Baldwin, 1970.

1 First suggested in 1644 by Tristan, 548–9. Le Glay, 355, note 40. The temple contained, according to Arrian, sculptures of Hermes and his obscure descendant or son, Philesius. Pancrates calls Antinous 'son of the Argus-slayer' (i.e. Hermes) so possibly there was a statue of Antinous also as Philesius. Tristan argues learnedly that the name Philesius relates to 'Philesia' or pederastic contests and that Arrian is esoterically referring to the relationship of Hadrian and Antinous (549–550). He was also thought to be shown on the coins of Bithynion as Philesius – Symonds, 1879, 74.
2 Suggested by *IGR*. III, 71, inscription of the Council and Community to Hadrian; Woodward, 162; Magie, 622, note 48; Clairmont, 17; Toynbee, 1967, 267–8.
3 Inscription found by Dörner, 1949, 227; 1952, 40–1.
4 Philostratus, *Sophists*, 533.
5 Oliver, 1970, 131. Perhaps also western cities like Naples, Marseilles and Syracuse were not represented – *ibid.*, 136.
6 Some scholars claim that its functions were merely cultural, e.g. Tod, 1922, 176; Graindor, 1934, 110–1; Weber, 1907, 218; Beaujeu, 180–1; Bengtson, 526. Henderson, 118, 121, is scathing at its futility. Oliver, 1970, 94, 130–7; 1978, 189, stresses its political functions. It is on his evidence that what follows is based.
7 The last mention so far discovered is from 251–2 AD, – Tod, 1922, 177; Oliver, 1970, 137.
8 Dio, 69, 16, 1. Graindor, 1934, 54, 101–2, 154, 246.
9 These are catalogued and discussed in Vermeule, *Berytus*, 1959, 1964 and 1966. They seemed to come from workshops in Corinth and the Piraeus – 1964, 104. Also Vermeule, 1968, 254, 262.
10 Shear, 181. Broneer, 126, contends that the heads on the statue of Corinth are close to a relief of Apollo in the theatre there: the hair, however, clearly bears the wings of Hermes.
11 Compare this profile with that of the Olympia statue in e.g. H. Weber, plate 76. The likeness is astonishing and must help confirm this statue as an idealised portrait of Antinous. This latter has been doubted by Clairmont, 14, note 1, 34; but supported by Vermeule, 1966, *AJA*, LXXIII, 489, and Maza, 167–71, who confuses the two Antinous works from Olympia.
12 *HA. Had*, XIV, 7. The Delphic tripod and designation as 'New Pythios' on the Tarsos coins prompt this supposition. Temple: Blum, 1914, 52; Beaujeu, 249, note 8.
13 Graindor, 1922, 167–8, 173, 186–7. The *agones* contained musical and poetical competitions, a point stressed by Robert, 1952, 191; Graindor, 1922, 167; 1934, 101.
14 Geagan, 148–51; Graindor, 1934, 140–1, 210, note to p. 168.
15 This is Graindor's proposal, 1934, 277–9; Geagan, 148.
16 Weber, 1907, 193; Dittenberger, 1877, 192; Liegle, 44–8; Seltman, 78–80; Toynbee, 1944, 68; Beaujeu, 249; Clairmont, 27 note 1.

17 Fougères, 1896, no. 18. Pausanias, VIII,9,7–8 Guarducci, 1949, 157.

18 Pausanias, *loc. cit.* and VIII,10,1.

19 *Enc. Judaica*, 7, 1055.

20 Only a few coins talk of 'Victory', and although in late 135 Hadrian accepted his second acclamation as *imperator*, he eschewed triumphs and monuments, and refused to gloss over the casualties by sending the usual cheerful greetings to the Senate from the front. Strack, 134–7.

21 Seltman, 84; Toynbee, 1944, 68; Clairmont, 30–1. *Contra:* Follet, 1968, 65, note 6.

22 Blum, 1914, 61. The dating is suggested by the Alexandrian coins which appeared after 29 August 134. *Contra:* Follet, 1968, 58–9.

23 As some inscriptions imply: Mendel, no. 5; Dörner, 1953, no. 84, p. 62. *IGR.* VIII, 72, 75.

24 Follet, 1968, *passim. Contra;* Schwartz, *passim.* Malaise, 422, note 2. Seltman suggests he returned to Olympia in late 135.

25 *HA. Had.,* VII, 3. Dio, 69, 11, 5.

26 Toynbee, 1934, 143, 137; Strack, 125–7, 182–4; Beaujeu, 159.

27 Strack, 139–61; Toynbee, 1934, 1–5, 161, 239–40; Mattingly, CLXXI.

28 *IG.* XIV. 978a. Moretti, 124–5, no. 143.

29 The Lanuvium club was set up on 1 January 133 but its inscription was not placed on the temple there until 9 June 136, implying that the temple was finished nearer the later than the earlier date. It is most unlikely that Hadrian attended the inauguration of a poor men's burial club in 133 as Clairmont suggests (p. 20), though he may have been at the consecration of the civic temple in about 136.

30 Kraus, 1959, 57; 1962, 132, note 24. Those for which there is evidence of finding outside the Villa Adriana but in the vicinity of Rome are Cl. nos 5, 6, 11, 13, 19, 26, 27, 28, 29, 37, 45, 58, 59; Marconi nos 16, 41, 70, 86 (the authenticity of 16 and 86 is in doubt); Uggeri, *Inst. Stud.*, p. 130 (torso in the Mus. delle Terme, Marconi no. 17?). Of these, Cl. nos 19, 26, 27, 28, 37 and 58 either are or come from colossal statues, as are the doubtful 16 and 86. The two Farnese statues in Naples probably came from Rome (Cl. no. 33, Marconi no. 44) and the latter is also a colossal and Roman version of the fine Greek statue of Antinous Dionysos from Aidepsos, now at Chalkis: Holm, 28; Maza, no. 48, 373–4.

31 Accepting the date given in the horoscope discussed in Champlin, 82–4 and Cramer, 175–6.

32 Champlin, 89; *HA. Had.,* VIII, 11.

33 *HA. Had.,* XXIII, 11.

34 What follows is based on the *HA. Ael.,* V. Many authorities consider much in this *Life* to be fictitious – Hohl, 43–8; Birley, HA. (Penguin edit.), 88, note; Barnes, 1967, 77; Syme, 1971, 54–77.

35 E. Clark, 175; Weber, 1937, 225.

36 *HA. Ael.,* V, 2.

37 Especially Pflaum, 1963, *passim.*

38 The Ceionii, Annii, Plautii, Vetuleni and Avidii. Pflaum, 100–7, 110; Syme, 1979, 680–1.

39 Barnes, 1967, 74–9; Champlin, 89; Vermeule, 1968, 109–10; Valera, *passim;* Carcopino, 1949, 313–20; 1965, 76; Pflaum, 105. The view that Hadrian preferred Marcus to the young Lucius was created by the Antonines after Hadrian's death and

accepted by the ancient historians despite contrary evidence embodied in their texts: e.g. Dio, 69, 21, 2; *HA. Marcus*, IV, 5ff.

40 *HA. Ael.*, VII, 2.

41 XXXII, 10, Commodus adopted 'because of his beauty'; *Ael.*, III, 8, the reason Hadrian adopted 'a man he knew as being little fitted to rule was to satisfy his pleasure'; *Ael.*, V, 1, 'he was more acceptable to Hadrian, so the malevolent say, by his beauty than by his character'. Dio, who usually avoids sexual innuendoes, gives no reason for the adoption of Commodus.

42 On the lion hunt tondo and in the foundation of the temple at Socanica he associated Aelius with the memories of Antinous. Though over twenty images of Antinous are known to have been recovered from the Villa Adriana, only one definite image of Aelius has been found there (Gusman, 278) and one claimed to be of him (by Aurigemma, 1961, 110) which has been dismissed – Hannestad, 95; Bieber, 1970, 95.

43 *HA. Had.*, XXIII, 14; *Ael.*, III; IV, 6; VI, 3–6.

44 *HA. Ael.*, VII, 1. The terms used here are similar to those used of Antinous. Aelius was not deified – Hannestad, 69; Hammond, 1959, 207, 226.

45 Traditionally the execution of Fuscus has been put in 136 on the evidence of Dio, 69, 17, 1. The *HA*'s three references to the deaths of Servianus and Fuscus are thoroughly confused, but imply that they were shortly before Hadrian's own (XV, 8; XXIII, 3; especially XXV, 8). The horoscope clearly says that Fuscus died when he was twenty-five, i.e. in 137–8. Perhaps he waited, knowing that Aelius was seriously ill, and made his *coup* after his death, when it was clear that Hadrian was persisting in ignoring his claims. Cramer, 174–8; Champlin, 81–9; Syme, 1979, 681; 1976, 297.

46 Dio, 69, 17, 2.

47 For Carcopino's thesis the date of 136 for her death is crucial as he assumes that Hadrian waited until she was dead before elevating his bastard (1949, 292). Strack says her Roman coins stop in 135–6 (p. 25) and her consecration ones were 137–8 (116, 188). However, she appears as living on the coins of Amisos in 137–8 (Bosch, 32) and as alive on an inscription *with* Aelius Caesar late in 137 (Garzetti, 698). Carandini opts for late 136 or early 137 (p. 97).

48 *HA.*, *loc. cit.* and XXIII, 3–5. See the qualifications of Syme, 1979, 682–4.

49 SAV, XIV.

50 Dio, 69, 204. Cramer, 176.

51 *HA. Had.*, XXV, 7, 'invisusque omnibus' can be translated 'unseen by all', but the true meaning is confirmed by Dio, 69, 23, 2: 'hated by all the people'.

CHAPTER FOURTEEN

Principal sources: Herodotus; Origen; Clem. Alex; Tertullian; Plutarch, *Moralia*; *Pap. Oslo*; *IG*; *IGR*; *ILS*. Symonds, 1879; Dietrichson; Blum, 1913, 1914; Beaujeu; Cumont, 1949; Clairmont; Marconi; Maza; Holm; Lebek; Dusanic; Hermann; Kraus, 1959, 1962; Dörner, 1949, 1952; Bayet; Kambitsis; Graindor, 1934; Weber, 1911; Bianchi; Nilsson; Erman, 1917.

1 Phrases from Origen, *Contra Celsum*, III,38.

2 Calculated from Appendix 1 and sources quoted there: 62 works without attributes out of 115.

3 Pausanias, VIII,9,8, mentions statues of Antinous as such and paintings of him as Dionysos. Dio, 69, 11, talks of portraits and also of sacred images as though they were distinct. Clairmont, 22, note 2.

4 At Nikopolis, Argos, Corinth, Mantineia. The Koinon of Bithynia called him 'Antinous' on some coins and nothing on others. Nikopolis also called him a god. Argos had games to him as a god and Corinth a statue as Hermes and a priest. At Mantineia he was a god and the Koinon of Bithynia shows his temple as that of a god on its coins.

5 E.g. by Pancrates ('beauteous'), by the citharode of Curium ('beautiful', his 'face full of grace'), by the Dionysiac artists of Rome (*ton kalon Antinoon*), by Hadrian on the obelisk ('beautiful countenance' etc.), and by the inscription from the Villa Adriana comparing his beauty with that of Belenus (Dietrichson, 326, no. 3).

6 'A boy of unsurpassed beauty', *Addr. Gr.*, IV, III; also Tertullian, *Ad. Nat.*, 11, 10, 1f; Tatian, *Add. Gr.*, 10; Jerome, *Interpr. Chron. Eus.*, ann. 13.

7 Plutarch, *Moralia: Oracles*, 415A.

8 *IG*. XIV, 978a and 960–1.

9 Blum, 1914, 47; Beaujeu, 167, Phyle list.

10 Plutarch, *loc. cit.* Celsus is quoted in Origen, *Contra Celsum*, V,63; III,37. Significantly, Demeter and Dionysos were also considered daemonic, – Bianchi, 2.

11 E.g. Kraus, 1959, 52, 66; Hermann, 159; Beaujeu, 249; Marconi, 242. *Contra*: Maza, 95, 97.

12 Ganymede, Attis and Agathodaimon. Different historians make different identifications, though the heavy bias in favour of Dionysos comes through all (e.g. Beaujeu, 249; Marconi, 243).

13 Weber, 1911, 25–7, stresses that Hadrian sought to promote Antinous as Hermes and it is true that the principal cult centres (Mantineia, Bithynion and Alexandria), the Dionysiac artists of Rome and other centres (e.g. Nikomedia and Corinth) did so. On the other hand, in places where Hadrian also must have personally promoted the cult (e.g. Athens, Eleusis and Tarsos) Antinous appears as Dionysos and cult images of him as Dionysos certainly existed of him at Mantineia, Bithynion and Antinoopolis (Jomard's torso and the Julius Fidus Aquila bronze). The Villa Adriana had at least four works of Antinous as Dionysos and only one has been found there with attributes of Hermes. Weber may well have over-stressed Hadrian's preference for Hermes. Holm, 46.

14 Herodotus (Penguin edit.), 145, 178, 187; Dietrichson, 59, 96, 159–62; Maza, 292ff., 345ff.; Bianchi, *passim*; Nilsson, 362–6. Apollo was closely linked with Dionysos Zagreus and this may account still more for his identification with Antinous. Holm, 34.

15 Dietrichson, 96; Beaujeu, 172–3, 249, 251 note 2; Carandini, 83; Weber, 1911, 24; Guarducci, 1949, 153, 157; Graindor, 1934, 131–3; Bianchi, 4, 6; Nilsson, 362–3; Geagan, 148. There was a long-standing link of Hermes, the ram and the cult of Eleusis. On the Antinous coins of Smyrna, a ram and a caduceus of Hermes are shown: Blum, 1914, 40, no. 4.

16 Erman, 1917, IIf, 1a.

17 Erman, 1917, IIc; *ILS*. 7212: *collegium salutare*. Carcopino, 1975, 151.

18 *IG*. V (2), 312, Guarducci, 1949, 157.
19 Lebek, line 12; *IG*. XIV, 978a; Blum, 1914, 48; Dietrichson, 350, no. 56.
20 Erman, 1917, IIc and p. 16. Origen, III/36.
21 Kambitsis, *passim*.
22 Reynolds and Ward-Perkins, 89, no. 279.
23 Kraus, 1959, 52, claims that because deities who had no connection with Antinous frequently decorate his coins, his own godly personality suffers in distinctness. In fact, of the 143 issues, 117 have reverse images illustrating his cult or his nature as an oracular deity of fertility, death and renewal assimilated to Dionysos and Hermes and associated with Eleusis. Association with gods like Athena, Herakles, Poseidon, and the Phrygian god Men etc., though striking, are exceptional.
24 *Contra*: Beaujeu, 257; Symonds, 1879, 76–7, 79–80. The myth and culture of Antinous can be too easily overlooked: we know of poems or hymns by Pancrates, Mesomedes, Numenios and the Curium citharode, as well as the prose from Tebtynis and the poem-epitaph on the obelisk; there must have been others. The flower, star and moon occur widely on his coins, the flower on sculptures, and all testify to widespread knowledge of his myth. Antinous clearly had not only a marked human personality but also a defined godly one. Blum, 1914, 70.
25 Weber, 1937, 209–10.

CHAPTER FIFTEEN

Much detailed evidence comes from a close scrutiny of the coins listed in Blum, 1914, and Dietrichson, the sculptures in Marconi, Clairmont and Maza and from inscriptions in *IG, CIG, ILS, CIL*. Other principal sources: *HA*; Eusebius, *Eccl. Hist.*; Origen; Clem. Alex.; Pausanias; Tertullian; Athanasius; Epiphanios, *Ancoratus, De Fide*; Juvenal; Julian; *Pap. Oxyrhyn.*; *Pap. London.* Holm; Beaujeu; Kraus, 1959, 1962; Geagan; Graindor, 1922, 1934; Weber, 1907; Blum, *Theos*, 1913; Seltman; Liegle; Le Glay; Tod, 1951; Robert, 1943, 1952; Majewski; Radnoti; Hermann; Vermeule, 1968; Erman, 1917; Uggeri, 'Antinoo'; Dulière; Poland; Guarducci, 1949; Jomard; Decker; Lippold, 1923; Symonds, 1879; Calza; Toynbee, 1944; Moretti; Dusanic; Kambitsis; Gayet, 1897; Lanciani, 1909; Winckelmann, 1767; Alföldi, 1976.

1 Zayed, 125–9. It is difficult to recognise Antinous, as does Zayed, in the crude and dumpy statuette discovered in a tomb chapel at the oasis of El Kharga.
2 They are: Bithynion, Nikomedia, Trapezus, Chalcedon, Smyrna, Adramyttion, Cyzicus, Hadrianotherai, Tion, Philadelphia, Sardis, Tarsos, Amisos, Sala, Kyme, Mytilene, Ephesos, Kios, Stratoniceia, Amorium, Tmolos, Juliopolis, Ancyra, Thyateira and possibly Eucarpia, Alabanda and Cius – the latter are doubtful because the identity or authenticity of their coins is uncertain. The other 24 are known to have venerated Antinous from coins or sculptures of other evidence.
3 Nikomedia: Blum, 1914, 42, 45; Bosch, 274; Holm, 9, 16; Le Glay, 254. Nikomedia issued coins both as the metropolis of the province of Bithynia and in its own right as a city.
4 At: Bithynion, Nikomedia, Trapezus, Tion, Philadelphia (Blum, 1914, 50, *contra*: Dietrichson, 308, no. 92), Tarsos, Kios – all, except Bithynion and Trapezus, from numismatic evidence.

5 Marconi, no. 73; Maza, 322. Not accepted by H. Weber and Clairmont.

6 Majewski, 1963, *passim*. Of the jars he lists, nos 9, 16a, 34, 38, 42, 103 and 107 are said to be of the Antinous type, though nos 9 and 38 are not very like, whereas nos 34, 36 and 44 also seem to be of the Antinous type. Others from Mainz and Worms (Majewski, 27; Marconi, no. 107), from Sylandos (*Ars Antiqua*, 5, 1964); from Chares, North Portugal (very like Antinous, says Bellido, 455). Discussion of these: Clairmont, 13, note 5; Sieveking, 73, 74; Radnoti, 172–3; Coarelli, *Arch. Classica*, XIII, 1961, 175.

7 Hermann, 151, note 11; Maza, 269, 271.

8 Evidence (inscriptions, coins, literary) of temples in 5 cities in Egypt, 6 on the Greek mainland, 7 in Asia Minor, 7 in Italy and 3 elsewhere.

9 Blum, 1914, 42, Koinon no. 1 and Bithynion no. 1. He, Magie (622), Bosch (174) and Woodward (163) contend that these coins depict the imperial temple at Nikomedia shown on other coins of the Koinon and the city but this is denied by Le Glay, 355; Holm, 9; Beaujeu, 249; Vermeule, 1968, 255. Even if this is not the temple of Antinous, there can be no doubt from the fragment of an architrave found at Bithynion that the temple there was on an impressive scale.

10 Origen, *Contra Celsum*, III,36. Uggeri, *Inst. Stud.*, 131–2.

11 In Rome the priest M. Ulpius Apollonius called himself *prophitis* on his inscription to Antinous (*CIG*. 6007) and this does imply, as is likely, an oracle in Rome. Dietrichson, 93, 96.

12 Clem. Alex., *Protrepticus*, IV.49.

13 Quoted Origen, *Contra Celsum*, V,63.

14 *Loc. cit.* Kishor, 292; Jomard, 40.

15 Satire XV, 47–50. The 'sacred nights' were clearly Bacchanalian in character – Nilsson, 362.

16 *Pap. Lond.* III, no. 1164.

17 Oxyrhynchus and Antinoopolis in Egypt; Athens, Eleusis, Corinth, Argos (*CIG*. 1124; *CIG*. IV, 590), Mantineia and Olympia in Greece; Bithynion in Asia Minor.

18 The figures for the finding places of which we have evidence: Italy 44 (22 from the Villa Adriana, 18 from Rome and environs, 4 elsewhere), Greece 12, Egypt 6, elsewhere 7. Clairmont lists 23 sculptures from his catalogue of 61 as probably being found in Italy, and another 12 with some Italian provenance (p. 21). His lists do not include 8 other sculptures of Antinous in the Egyptian style which were found in the Villa Adriana. He declares that 'over half' those in his catalogue were found in Italy (*ibid.*).

19 This seems to be Clairmont's point on p. 33.

20 Lippold, 1923, 194; Marconi, no. 61.

21 *ILS*. 7212. The club gives its own birthday as that of Diana, the Ides of August. As we know it was formally constituted on 1 January 133 it is fair to assume that it had been in gestation (getting the official permissions noted on the inscription) for some time before. The Ides of August 132 might therefore be in a real sense the day when its founding members decided to go ahead and form their club.

22 Calza, 81, 82, 83.

23 Dietrichson, 94, 137, 320; 211, no. 65. Levezow, 14, note 31; Symonds, 70–1; Beaujeu, 255; Schiff, PW, 1135–6; Hermann, 158, note 28. Garzetti (695) notes that Naples was still profoundly Greek in the second century.

24 Blum, 1913, *Theos*, 74–5. Bust: Marconi, no. 55; Maza, 259; Beaujeu, 253, note 2; Guida, 38–42. Belenus: Pauly-Wissowa, III, 1899, 200.

25 Pozzuoli: Cl. 44. Brindisi: Cl. 53. Both doubted by Heintze, 1971, 398.

26 Symonds, 1979, 70.

27 Blum, 1914, *passim*, adding Olympia (Elis). Olympia issued in 133; Amisos in 133–4; Alexandria in 134–5 and 136–7.

28 E.g. Beaujeu, 255, 'of all the figures of antiquity, Antinous is the one of whom we possess most statues'. Perowne says there are over 500.

29 Calculated from 30 disappeared works listed by Dietrichson, 23 works appearing on the coins, 12 over-restored works still existing, 6 works recorded at Antinoopolis and 12 others deduced from inscriptions or listed in the past and now lost.

30 Jomard, 7, 26, 28.

31 p. 114. Dietrichson lists 70 sculptures of Antinous as genuine, another 18 as doubtful; 348, table 11.

32 *IG*. V(2), 281; Robert, 1943, 184; *IGR*. III, 73.

33 The relief had been carefully repaired in antiquity: Gauckler, 345–6; Rizzo, 14; Clairmont, 20. Bank of Italy: Lanciani, 1909, 184.

34 Blum, *Theos.*, 1913, 69; Cl. no. 45; Dietrichson, nos 73, 93; Cl., no. 32. Bronze of Hermes: Maza, 322.

35 Cl., no. 15; Jucker, *Blätterkelch*, 33, no. 87.

36 Moretti, 143. Lebek, 133–6.

37 *ILS*. 7212; Carcopino, 1975, 151; Maza, 361, claims that there was a prevalent cult of him south of Rome.

38 Blum, *Theos*, 1913, 77; Dietrichson, 332, no. 20; *BCH*, IV, 1880, 108, no. 14; Symonds, 1879, 70.

39 Kambitsis, 217, note 1, seems to doubt if the 'daemon Antinous' was Hadrian's favourite. In favour of this identification is, however: (a) the finding place, Antinoopolis; (b) the invocation of the prematurely dead which Antinous had been; (c) the association with him on this incantation of certain chthonic gods with whom he is linked elsewhere, e.g. Persephone, Hermes, Adonis; (d) the fact that Origen also calls him a daemon at Antinoopolis; (e) the existence of a shrine or cenotaph to him there in which this could have been ritually deposited. The presumption of the daemon being our Antinous is therefore strong.

40 Gayet, 1897, 50–1. Erman, 1934, 424; 1917, IIb.

41 Erman, IId, IIe.

42 E.g. compare Sextus Aurelius Victor's account of the self-sacrifice of *c.* 360 AD with that of Dio of *c.* 210 AD – Symonds, 1879, 56.

43 Pausanias, VIII,2,5; *Orac. Sybill.*, VIII, 57–8. Lucian, *Conv. Gods*, 231. Hermann, 160.

44 *Caesars*, IX.

45 Origen, *Contra Celsum*, V,63; III, 37; Maza, 95.

46 Origen, III,36; VIII,9.

47 I.e. Justin, Hegesippos, Tatian, Theophilos, Athenagoras and also the inter-polation in the *Book of Wisdom*, 14, 1–2, discussed by Dulière, *passim*.

48 Tertullian, *Apol.*, 13, 1f; *Ad. Nat.*, 11, 10, 1f; *Adv. Marc.*, 1, 18; Hermann, 161.

49 *Addr. Gr.*, IV/111; Maza, 31; Dulière, 218; Hermann, 162.

50 *Contra Celsum*, *loc. cit.* Hermann, 160, 164; Dulière, 214–15.

51 *Comm. Isaiah*, 2; Also *De. Vir. Ill.* 22; *Interp. Chr. Eus.* ann. 13; *Adv. Jov.*, 2, 7.
52 Justin, *1st Apol.*, XXIX; Tatian, *Addr. Gr.*, chap. 10; Epiphanios, *Ancoratus*, 106. Charges repeated by Athanasius, *Contra Gent.*, 9, 4; Origen, III,36.
53 *De Corona*, chap. 13.
54 Origen, *Contra Celsum*, III,36–8; V,63; VIII,9. Symonds, 1879, 78, 82.
55 Dulière, 218–20.
56 Weber, 1911, 28; Beaujeu, 257; Marconi, 289; Jucker, 1961–2, 302. Beaujeu 256.
57 Nikomedia, coins to times of Marcus Aurelius (Blum, 1914, 60); and Antoninus Pius (Bosch, 202). Eucarpia, coins to the Antonines (Dietrichson, 248; *contra*: Blum, 50). Bithynion: Blum, 43–5, esp. no. 13.
58 They are Cl. nos 48 (Kansas City), 38 (Leptis Magna), 53 (Brindisi), 45 (Mus. delle Terme diadem head), 66 (Ephesos, Androcles-Antinous: see Hahland, 71, 76), Olympia ephebe statue (H. Weber, 146).
59 9, 4. All in the present tense with respect to worship etc.
60 *Ancoratus*, 106; *De Fid. Cath.*, 12.
61 Winckelmann, *Mont. Ant. Inedit.* 1767, 2, 235; *Anmerkungen*, I, 81. Maza, 357. The bronze wreath and the uraeus or pine-cone have disappeared. The head was found between 1713 and 1729 – Dietrichson, 117.
62 Lanciani, 1909, 184.
63 Maza, 398–401, perceptively disputes if this statue lost its original bronze drapery, which, he thinks, never existed in antiquity. There was some damage to the hair, wreath, left hand, right fingers etc., but it is remarkable that a statue of such size was not more seriously broken or damaged (Marconi, no. 1; Braun, 436; Maza, 114–16, 398ff.).
64 Maza, 114; Symonds, 1879, 82.
65 One contorniate shows a winged victory (Alföldi, 1976, 433) and the legend *Victoria. Aug.* (Blum, 1914, 57, no. 2). There may be alternative explanations to that given in the text, but it does suit the events and the nature of the strange reappearance of Antinous at this juncture.

CHAPTER SIXTEEN

Principal sources; *Antinoopolis Papyri*; Lewis, *Recherches de Pap.*; Wilcken, 1912, 1920; Stocklein (Sigard); Jomard; Dietrichson; Gayet, 1897, 1902, 1903, *Fantômes*; Kübler; Kühn; Johnson; Milne; Bell, 1933, 1936, 1940; Pistorius; Breccia, 1938, 1957; Donadoni, 1938, 1945, 1965–8; Braunert, 1962, 1964; *Inst. Stud. Vic. Or.* (esp. Uggeri); Calderini; Wessell; Hermann; Kraus, 1962; Lewis, 1964; Erman, 1917; Orgeval; Cadell; Lindsay, 1965; Maspero and Wiet; Decker; Blum, *Theos.* 1913; Carpart; Perdrizet.

1 Quoted in Stocklein, vol. 10, 1727, 59–60. Sigard was there on 13–14 November 1715 and his letter is dated 1 June 1716. This letter is better known through its appropriation by a Father Bernat and reproduction as his own report in Montfaucon, vol. III, 1724, 153.
2 Jomard, 7.
3 p. 1.
4 Dietrichson, 104.
5 *Antinoeis Neoi Hellenes*. Kühn, 90, 117–18. Calderini, 104–5.

6 Kühn, 80–3, *contra*: Braunert, 1962, 214–15. Bell, 1940, 138–9; Calderini, 100.

7 Pistorius, 122, denied by Braunert, 1964, 80. Kühn, 119.

8 Kühn, 22; Johnson, 170. The wall was three km long and eighteen metres high (Breccia, 1938, 122). No one is sure if it was part of the Hadrianic design, earlier or later. The city did not seem to extend to its corners or boundaries on the east and south, and, strangely, there seem to be no exits through it to correspond with the south or east gates nearby, though there was an exit on the north.

9 All dimensions from Jomard, 9–34, and Kühn, 22–78.

10 Jomard says they were mediocre in proportions and of the Doric order, pp. 25, 26; but Sigard that they were Corinthian and 'graceful', p. 59; Gayet says Corinthian, 1897, 10.

11 pp. 25–6.

12 Sigard, 59. Lucas of 1714 uses the same phrase – Kühn, 32.

13 p. 38.

14 That seen by Jomard, p. 27; that found by Uggeri, *Ist. Stud.*, 129–32; that proposed by Kraus, 1962, *passim*. The small head, Cl. no. 32, is also sometimes said to come from Antinoopolis.

15 Jomard, 25.

16 Uggeri, *Ist. Stud.*, 125–6; Kühn, 76–8.

17 Pistorius, 112. Calderini, 91.

18 Uggeri, *Inst. Stud.*, 129–32.

19 Braunert contends that women were so entitled, 1962, 346; 1964, 77–8; *contra*: Pistorius, 125.

20 Wessell, 72, 92–3, 127–8.

21 Thompson, 437.

22 Gayet, *Fantômes*, 1904, 22.

23 Maspero and Wiet, 26.

24 Pistorius, 47. Bell, 1933, 518, no. 1905.

25 Gayet, 1903, vol. 30, 31, 122–4; *Fantômes*, 1904, 6. *Antinoopolis Papyri*, 1, 1950, 39, no. 18.

26 Decker, 45, puts forward this view which repeats an old Arab tradition still reflected in local belief. It is difficult to see how the hippodrome, so far from the river and divided from it by the city, could have been so flooded. Kühn, 62–3; Jomard, 24–5; Erman, 1917, IIIa.

27 Sigard, 60. Uggeri, *Ist. Stud.*, 37–63.

28 Maspero and Wiet, 26. Dietrichson, 100.

29 Jomard, 9, 12. He was there as late as 1801 – p. 28.

30 *Ibid., passim*. For example, in two recent and lengthy reports about the excavations of the temple of Rameses II (Donadoni, 1939, *passim*, and 1945, 171–90) no plan of it is given. Jomard gives plans and full dimensions of everything of significance.

31 Jomard, 10, 29, 15, 8, 11–12.

32 Quoted by Carpart, 1938, 335, from the memoirs of Mariette's companion, Vicomte Jacques de Rougé. The statue burnt, as Kraus, 1962, 129, has shown, was not the original bronze of Antinous but the marble Christian replacement of *c.* 390.

33 Quoted in Dietrichson, 104, 105.

CHAPTER SEVENTEEN

The sculptures are also discussed in chaps. 4, pp. 53–5; 14, pp 178, 180; 15, pp 195, 196; and Appendix One.

Principal sources: Dietrichson; Marconi; Clairmont; Maza; Holm; Kraus, 1959, 1962; H. Weber; Hahland; Toynbee, 1934, 1944, 1951, 1967; West; Strong, 1907; D. Strong; Vermeule, 1960, 1968, 1969; Lippold, 1923; Richter, 1951; Jücker, 1961; Squarciapino; Uggeri; Roullet; Heintze, 1971; Blum, 'Delphes', 1913; Winckelmann, 1767; Bülle; Maull; Calza; Gauckler; Rizzo.

1 The numbers given are 46 and 61, but there is an insertion, 8 bis.
2 Various such models have been proposed: the Capitoline 'Antinous', the Sala Rotonda bust, the statues of the Bank of Italy and Naples, the Berlin head and the putative colossus of Antinoopolis (Uggeri, 132). To all of these there are insuperable objections.
3 Clairmont, 21. Over half the works in his catalogue come from Italy, a strange proportion if there was such a moral-religious objection to Antinous there.
4 Cl., nos 1–4, pp. 21–6. Heintze, 1971, 396.
5 E.g. Seltman, 80–5; Toynbee, 1944, 65–73; Squarciapino, 15–17.
6 Clairmont, 30–2.
7 The Peloponnese coins clearly show a bust with an arm stump (Holm, 4; Bl. pl. 1/17, 18, 20), i.e. the artist was copying a bust version of the original, not the statue prototype itself.
8 Toynbee, 1967, 267–8, points out that there is no evidence of a flourishing school of Peloponnese sculptors.
9 Kraus, 1962, 134; Heintze, 1971, 396. Those which diverge are Cl. nos 16, 19, 20, 21, 22, 27, 31, 32, 36, 37, 38, 42, 43, 44, 45 and 46. For example, a close comparison between the hair-style of no. 36 (Aidepsos) and the Naples Farnese on which it is said to be based (Clairmont, 51) does not confirm such dependence.
10 Vermeule, 1960, 4; West, 136; M. no. 61.
11 Clairmont, 32; Toynbee, 1951, 31; 1967, 268; Lippold, 1923, 193; Holm, 24; Marconi, 290–3.
12 Lippold, 1923, 190–1; Holm, 29; Marconi, 232; K. A. Pfeiff, Apollon, pl. 36; Clairmont, 22.
13 Lippold, 1923, 192–3; H. Weber, 134; Holm, 37–8; Marconi, 221.
14 Lippold, 1923, 194; Marconi, 268; Cl., no. 58; E. Strong, 1907, 249.
15 Maza, 128–9, 374, rightly stresses these. Marconi, 214–18, had rigidly excluded the Praxitelean influences overstressed by Dietrichson, 144, 149. Vermeule, 1960, 3; West, 131.
16 Kraus, 1959, 56–7; West, 139.
17 West, 136. Cf. Kraus, 1959, 66–7; Marconi, 268–70; Maza, 357. Not only is the hair-style different from the Athena Lemnia, but the head is less inclined and the masculine traits of Antinous are self-evident.
18 By von Heintze, 1971, 397. She thinks the two Telamones are old but are not of Antinous and briefly dismisses the rest as fakes produced in the period of the 'Egyptian Revival' at the end of the eighteenth century and after and conveniently given the provenance of Hadrian's Villa, from which most are said to come. However, two works, the Dresden and Osborne Osirises, seem to come from Egypt itself: the Dresden head (Clairmont, 16, no. 5) is in an uncompromising archaic style which seems more to suit the cult in Egypt of the 130s than the revived style of

the 1790s. The Osborne work may well have come from Egypt and it is most improbable that fakes of Antinous were being made there in the 1790s. In addition, the Munich Osiris seems to have been recorded by the sixteenth century (Roullet, 86–7) and the Vatican one was discovered in 1740, long before a taste for the Egyptian style infected Europe. Moreover, we know that Antinous was certainly depicted in Italy in the Egyptian format and in Hadrianic times from the reliefs on the obelisk, but the sculptures in a similar style and existing by 1790 cannot be imitating them as the obelisk was only linked with Antinous after 1824. Roullet thinks them all to be genuine Hadrianic creations (82–7). Gavin Hamilton actually records discovering one such bust in the course of his excavation of the Panatello area of the Villa Adriana in 1769 (J. Dallaway, *Anecdotes of the Arts in England*, 1800, 366; E. Fitzmaurice, *Letters of Gavin Hamilton*, 1879, 5–6). There was in fact an 'Egyptian Revival' under Hadrian who filled his villa with authentic archaic works from the Nile and Roman versions of them, of which the Antinous-Osiris group forms a natural part. Until further evidence is produced, we are entitled to presume that most of these works are Hadrianic, though this is not to deny that some may be forgeries or that there were many fakes of Antinous produced from the Renaissance onward.

19 Maza, 122ff.; West, 114.

20 Maza, 228.

21 Winckelmann, *Anmerkungen*, 1767, vol. 2, 123.

22 E.g. Marconi, 268–70, 285, 297; West, 136; Maza, 357. *Contra*: Kraus, 1959, 66–7; E. Strong, 1907, 252; Holm, 22; Lippold, 1923, 194. Heintze, 1971, 397, has challenged the authenticity of this work, as has Charbonneaux, 1963, 165. Kraus, however, confirms after examination its Roman origin (in Heintze, 1974, 424).

23 *Hist. of Anc. Art* (trans. Lodge), vol. 2, 335.

24 See Appendix 1, *passim*. Heintze, 1971, *passim*, has summarily challenged the authenticity of thirty of those works accepted by Clairmont. I have noted her objections in the Appendix – objections which await more sustained evidence and discussion.

25 Androcles, see Hahland, *passim*. Rejected by Clairmont, no. 66, and Maza, 308–9. Despite its late date and departures from the canon, it does bear a close resemblance to the idealised Antinous and does relate to the Ephesos coins. Holm, 18. It is accepted by Inan and Rosenbaum, 1966, no. 37, p. 77. The Olympia statue is rejected by Clairmont, 14, note 1, and by H. Weber, *passim*, accepted by Vermeule, 1969, 489 and Maza, 167. In spite of the uncharacteristic hair-style and thinness of the neck and short stature, there is a remarkably close correspondence in profile and in facial features with the Berlin head (Cl. no. 16). It is difficult to see how Clairmont could claim (14, note 1) that the expression of Antinous is 'fully lacking' in this work. Both the Ephesos and Olympia sculptures are late and may be either idealising and inexact portraits of Antinous or merely of his type, though they are closer than all others. They are certainly closer in facial features and mood than the Vienna, Kansas City and Brindisi busts and the Munich head, all of which Clairmont includes in the canon (Cl. nos 50, 48, 53, 52).

26 E.g. by Gross, 40–4; H. Weber, 146–8; Kraus, 1959, 62 and *passim*; Clairmont, 23.

27 Toynbee, 1951, 18–33, esp. 31. Richter, 1951, 184–91. R. R. Smith, *Jnl. Rmn. St.*, LXXI, 1981, 24–38.

28 Toynbee, 1967, 267–8; 1934, XVIII–XIX, XX, 224, 239–40. Marconi, 288, Clairmont, 33, 47, no. 27; H. Weber, 146.
29 West, 128–30; Kraus, 1959, *passim*. Cf. Marconi, 294; Dietrichson, 154; Maza, 116, 117. Eleanor Clark's assertion that 'his statues announce and glorify sex' (165) is wide of the mark.
30. Kraus, 1959, 66–7, sees the Mondragone as the most successful fusion of the portrait and the godly in the art of Antinous, but this is perhaps to mistake the sort of godhead Antinous assumed in the eyes of his followers, which was far from the Mondragone's impassivity, indifference and remoteness. Antinous was conceived as accessible, benevolently active and compassionate.

APPENDIX 2
Principal sources: Blum, 'Delphes', 1913, 1914; Dietrichson; Holm; Liegle; Seltman; Toynbee, 1934, 1944, 1967; Gross; Kraus, 1959, 1962; Bosch; Vogt; Woodward; Clairmont; Boardman; Furtwängler; Lippold, 1922.

1 Bl. pls. V/2; III/7; II/13; V/8; IV/5.
2 Bl. pls. II/5, 12, 20; III/2, 4, 5, 12; IV/1, 6, 13.
3 Bl. pls. III/5, 10, 17; IV/4.
4 Bl. pls. V/4; I/22; IV/2, 3.
5 Bl. pls. I/1, 11, 15; II/10; III/1, 13.

WORKS REFERRED TO IN THE NOTES

This is a key to those secondary works referred to in the notes by the author's name only. Authors and titles of primary sources (ancient writers, papyri and inscriptions) are given in the notes and are not listed here. Abbreviations are used for academic journals.

Alexander, P. J. 'Letters and speeches of the Emperor Hadrian', *Harv. St. Cl. Philol.*, XLIX, 1938, 141–77.

Alföldi, A. *Die Kontorniaten*, Budapest, 1943.

Alföldi, A. and Alföldi, E. *Die Kontorniat Medallions*, Berlin, 1976.

Arias, P. E. 'Via prenestina – edicola sepolcrale . . .' *Not. d. Scavi*, XV, 1939, fasc., 4, 5, 6; 83–7.

Aufstieg und Niedergang der römischen Welt, ed. H. Temporini, II (2), Berlin, 1975.

Aurigemma, S. *Villa Adriana*, Rome, 1961.

Aymard, J. *Essai sur les chasses romaines*, Paris, 1951.

Baldwin, B. 'Lucian as social satirist', *Cl. Qtly.*, XI, 1961, 198–208.

Baldwin, B. 'Hadrian's farewell to life: some arguments for authenticity', *Cl. Qtly.*, XX, 1970, 372–4.

Bardon, H. *Les Empereurs et les lettres latine*, Paris, 1940.

Barnard, L. W. 'Hadrian and Judaism', *Jnl. Relig. Hist.*, V, 1969, 285–98.

Barnes, T. D. 'Hadrian and Lucius Verus', *JRS*, LVII, 1967, 65–79.

Barnes, T. D. 'Hadrian's farewell to life', *Cl. Qtly.*, XVIII, 1968, 384–6.

Barnes, T. D. 'The sources of the *Historia Augusta*', *Latomus*, LV, 1978.

Baurain, C. 'Suétone et l'inscription d'Hippone', *Et. Cl.*, XLIV, 1976, 124–44.

Bayet, J. *Croyances et rites dans la Rome antique*, Paris, 1971.

Bayle, P. *Dictionnaire historique et critique*, 3rd edit., I, Rotterdam, 1720.

Beaujeu, J. *La religion romaine à l'apogée de l'empire. I. La politique des Antonins*, AD 96–192, Paris, 1955.

Bell, H. I. 'Diplomata Antinoitica', *Aegyptus*, XIII, 1933, 514–28.

Bell, H. I. 'Antinoopolis' in *CAH*, XI, 1936, 650–2.

Bell, H. I. 'Antinoopolis: a Hadrianic foundation in Egypt', *JRS*, XXX, 1940, 133–47.

Bellido, A. G. *Esculturas Romanas de España y Portugal*, Madrid, 1949.

Benario, H. W. 'A commentary on the *Vita Hadriani* in the *Historia Augusta*', *Am. Cl*

St., VII, Scholar's Press, 1980.

Bengtson, H. *Griechische Geschichte*, 3rd edit., Munich, 1965.

Benjamin, A. 'Altars of Hadrian in Athens and Hadrian's pan-hellenic programme', *Hesp.*, XXXII, 1963, 57–86.

Benjamin, A. and Raubitschek, A. 'Arae Augusti', *Hesp.*, XXVIII, 1959, 65–85.

Berghaus, P. 'Zu den Münzbildnissen der Jahre 136–8', in *Festschrift für Max Wegner*, Munster, 1962.

Bernand, A. and E. *Inscriptions du colosse de Memnon*, Paris, 1960.

Bianchi, U. *The Greek mysteries*, Leiden, 1976.

Bieber, M. 'Die Medallions am Konstantinsbogen', *Röm Mitt.*, XXVI, 1911, 214–37.

Bieber, M. Review of Bracker, J., *AJA*, LXXIV, 1970, 94–5.

Birt, T. *Römische Charakterköpfe*, Leipzig, 1913.

Blackman, A. *The temple of Dendur*, London, 1911.

Blum, G. 'Antinoos Theos', *Mel. d'Arch. et d'Hist.*, XXXIII, 1913, 65–80.

Blum, G. 'L'Antinous de Delphes', *BCH*, XXXVII, 1913, 323–8.

Blum, G. 'Numismatique d'Antinoos', *Jnl. Int. d'Arch. Numis.*, XVI, 1914, 33–70.

Blümel, C. 'Ein Porträt des Antoninus Pius . . .' *JDAI*, XLVII, 1932, 90–6.

Boardman, J. *Engraved gems in the Ionides collection*, London, 1968.

Boer, W. den. 'Religion and literature in Hadrian's policy', *Mnemosyne*, VIII, 1955, 123–44.

Boissier, G. *Rome and Pompeii*, London, 1896.

Bonanno, A. 'Portraits and other heads on Roman historical reliefs', *BAR*, Suppl., series VI, 1976.

Bonneau, D. *La crue du Nil*, Paris, 1964.

Bonneau, D. 'Le souverain d'Egypte voyageait-il sur le Nil en crue?', *C d'E*, XXXVI, 1966, 377–85.

Bosch, C. *Die kleinasiatischen Münzen*, II (1), Stuttgart, 1935.

Boucher-Colozier, E. 'Nouveaux visages de Cherchel', *Libya*, II, 1957, 73–87.

Bowersock, G. W. *Greek sophists in the Roman empire*, Oxford, 1969.

Bracker, J. 'Ein Trauerbildnis Hadrians aus Köln', *Ant. Plast.*, VIII, 1968, 75–84.

Braun, E. *The ruins and museums of Rome*, Brunswick, 1854.

Braunert, H. 'Griechische und römische Komponenten im Stadtrecht von Antinoopolis', *Jnl. Jur. Pap.*, XIV, 1962, 73–88.

Braunert, H. *Die Binnenwanderung*, Bonn, 1964.

Breccia, E. *Con sua majesta il re Fuad all'oasi di Amone*, Cairo, 1929.

Breccia, E. 'Note epigrafiche', *Bull. Soc. Arch. d'Alexandrie*, XXIV, 1929, 71–2.

Breccia, E. 'Il viaggio dell'imperatore Adriano in Egitto', *Atti IV Congr. Naz. di Stud. Romani*, I, 1938, 119–23.

Breccia, E. *Egitto greco e romano*, Pisa, 1957.

Broneer, O. 'The Odeum' in *Corinth*, X, excavations of the ASCSA, Cambridge, Mass., 1932.

Brusin, G. 'Il console Tito Cesernio Stazio Quinzio . . . e Aquileia', in *Studi in Onore di A. Calderini e R. Paribeni*, Milan, I, 1956, 259–72.

Budge, E. A. W. *The book of the dead*, London, 1895.

Budge, E. A. W. *Osiris and the Egyptian resurrection*, London, 1911.

Budge, E. A. W. *The mummy*, London, 1925.

Bülle, M. 'Ein Jagddenkmal des Kaisers Hadrian', *JDAI*, XXXIV, 1919, 144–72.

Bulletino della Commissione Archaeologica Communale di Roma, 1893, 248–57.

Buschor, E. 'Die Hadrianischen Jagdbilder', *RM*, XXXVIII–IX, 1923–4, 51–4.

Butler, A. J. *Sport in classic times*, London, 1931.

Cadell, H. 'P. Caire IFAO Inv. 45', *C d'E*, XL, 1965, 357–63.

Calderini, A. *Dizionario dei nomi geografici e topografici dell'Egitto greco-romano*, Madrid, 1966.

Calza, R. *Scavi di Ostia*, V (1), Rittrati, Rome, 1964.

Carandini, A. *Vibia Sabina. Funzione politica, iconografia e il problema del classicismo adrianeo*, Florence, 1959.

Carcopino, J. 'L'hérédité dynastique sous les Antonins', *REA*, LI, 1949, 262–321.

Carcopino, J. 'Encore la succession d'Hadrien', *REA*, LXXVII, 1965, 67–79.

Carcopino, J. *Daily life in ancient Rome*, Penguin edit., London, 1975.

Carney, T. 'How Suetonius's *Lives* reflect on Hadrian', *Pr. Afr. Cl. Assoc.* XI, 1968, 7–24.

Carpart, J. 'Souvenirs du Vicomte Jacques de Rougé, *C d'E*, XIII, 1938, 327–35.

Champlin, E. 'Hadrian's heir', *Z. Pap. Epig.*, XXI, 1976, 79–89.

Chapman, J. J. *Lucian, Plato and Greek morals*, Oxford, 1931.

Chawen, R. 'Problem of Hadrian's visits to North Africa', *Cl. Jnl.*, LXV, 1970, 323–4.

Clairmont, C. W. *Die Bildnisse des Antinous*, Neuchâtel, 1966.

Clark, E. *Rome and a villa*, London, 1953.

Clark, K. *The nude*, Penguin edit., London, 1960.

Colini, A. M. 'Horti spei veteris', *Atti d. Pont. Acc. Rom. d. Arch.*, series III, Memorie, VIII (III), 1955, 137–77.

Condurachi, E. 'La genèse des sujets de chasse des "tondi adrianei" ', *Att. VII Cong. Int. d. Arch. Cl.*, II, Rome, 1961, 451–9.

Cook, A. B. *Zeus. A study in ancient religion*, Cambridge, 1914.

Coste-Mille sière, P. de la. *La sculpture grecque à Delphes*, Paris, 1929.

Coste-Messelière, P. de la. *Delphes*, Paris, 1957.

Cramer, F. H. 'Astrology in Roman law and politics', *Mem. Am. Philos. Soc.*, XXXVII, 1954, 160–84.

Cumont, F. *L'Egypte des astrologues*, Brussels, 1937.

Cumont, F. *Lux perpetua*, Paris, 1949.

Curtius, E. *Alterthum und Gegenwart*, Berlin, 1903.

Dallaway, J. *Anecdotes of the arts in England*, London, 1800.

Dawes, C. R. *A phase of Roman life*, unpubd. MS. Brit. Library, London, 1914.

Decker, W. 'Bemerkungen zum Agon für Antinous in Antinoopolis', *Kölner Beitr. Sportswiss.* II, 1973, 38–56.

Derchain, P. 'A propos de l'obelisque d'Antinous' in *Hommages à Cl. Preaux*, ed. J. Bingen, Brussels, 1975, 808–13.

Dhmitsas, M. G. 'Macedonia Archaeologika', *BCH*, IV, 1880, 108.

Dietrichson, L. H. S. *Antinoos. Eine kunstarchäologische Untersuchung*, Christiania, 1884.

Dittenberger, W. 'Inschriften aus Olympia', *Arch. Z.*, XXXV, 1877, 192.

Domaszewski, A von. *Geschichte der römischen Kaiser*, II, Leipzig, 1909.

Donadoni, S. 'Le prime ricerche italiane ad Antinoë', *Aegyptus*, XVIII, 1938, 285–318 (with E. Breccia).

Donadoni, S. 'Rapporto preliminare degli scavi . . . ad Antinoë, *ASAE*, XXXIX, 1939, 665–77.

Donadoni, S. 'I lavori della missione fiorentina al tempio di Rameses ii', in *Scritti ded. alla mem. Ippolito Rosellini*, Florence, 1945, 171–90.

Donadoni, S. 'Alcune casa est del tempio Rameside', in *Ist. Stud. Vic. Orient.*, XXI, 1974, *Antinoë, 1965–8*, 133–40.

Dörner, F. K. 'Vorbericht über eine Reise in Bithynia', *Anz. österr. Akad. Wiss., phil. hist. class.* LXXXVI, 1949, 224–8.

Dörner, F. K. 'Eine Reise in Bithynia', *Denkschr. österr. Akad. Wiss.*, LXXV, 1952, 32–62.

Dover, K. *Greek homosexuality*, London, 1978.

Dulière, W. L. 'Antinous et le livre de sagesse', *Z. Relig. Geistgesch.*, III, 1959, 201–27.

Dusanic, S. 'Novi Antinojev natpis i metalla municipii Dardanorum', *Ziva Antika*, XXI, 1971, 241–61.

Edwards, I. E. S. *Introduction to Ancient Egypt*, London, 1979.

Eglinton, J. Z. *Greek love*, London, 1971.

Eitrem, S. 'Zwei Grabgedichte auf Isidora aus Hermopolis', *Arch. Religionswiss.*, XXXIV, 1937, 313–22.

El-Amir, M. 'The cult of *hryw* at Thebes in the Ptolemaic period', *JEA*, XXXVII, 1951, 81–5.

Encyclopaedia Judaica, ed. C. Roth and G. Wigoder, VII, Jerusalem, 1971, 'Hadrian', 1054–6.

Erman, A. 'Der Obelisk des Antinous', *RM*, XI, 1896, 113–21.

Erman, A. 'Römische Obelisken', *Abhand. kön. preuss. Acad. Wiss.*, IV, 1917, 10–46.

Erman, A. *Die Religion der Ägypter*, Berlin, 1934.

Farberg, C. F. *The manual of classical erotology*, Paris, 1907.

Ferri, S. *Il 'numen Augusti' di Avallon*, Rome, 1933.

Flacelière, R. (ed.). Plutarch's *Dialogue d'amour*, Annales de l'université de Lyon, XXI, 1952.

Flacelière, R. 'Hadrien et Delphes', *CRAI*, 1971, 168–85.

Follet, S. 'Hadrien en Egypte et en Judée', *Rev. de Philol.*, XLII, 1968, 53–77.

Follet, S. *Athènes au IIe et au IIIe siècle: études chronologiques et prosopographiques*, Paris, 1976.

Fougères, G. 'Fouilles de Mantineia', *BCH*, XIV, 1890, 65–90.

Fougères, G. 'Inscriptions de Mantineia', *BCH*, XX, 1896, 152–4, 164.

Frank, T. (ed.). *Economic survey of ancient Rome*, IV, London, 1938.

Fraser, P. M. 'Hadrian and Cyrene', *JRS*, XL, 1950, 77–90.

Friedländer, L. *Darstellungen aus der Sittengeschichte Roms*, I, III, Leipzig, 1922–3 edit.

Furtwängler. A. *Die antiken Gemmen*, Leipzig, 1900.

Fussell, L. R. *Greek hero cults and ideas of immortality*, Oxford, 1921.

Gaden, A. 'Structure et portée historique de la vie d'Hadrien dans l'Histoire Auguste', *Ktéma*, I, 1976, 139–44.

Gardiner, A. H. 'The ancient military road between Egypt and Palestine', *JEA*, VI, 1920, 99–116.

Garzetti, A. *From Tiberius to the Antonines*, London, 1974 edit.

Gauckler, P. 'L' Antinous du sculpteur Antoninianos d'Aphrodisias', *CRAI*, 1908, 338–56.

Gayet, A. 'L'exploration des ruines d'Antinoë', *Ann. Mus. Guimet*, XXVI (3), 1897, 5–58.

Gayet, A. 'L'exploration des nécropoles d'Antinoë', *Ann. Mus. Guimet*, XXX (2), 1902, 26–46; XXX (3), 1903, 116ff.

Gayet, A. *Fantômes d'Antinoë*, Paris, 1904.

Geagan, D. J. 'Hadrian and the Athenian Dionysiac technitai', *Tr. Am. Philol. Ass.*, CIII, 1972, 133–60.

Getty Museum, *Roman portraits*, 1981.

Gibbon, E. *Decline and fall of the Roman empire*, London, 1777 edit.

Gnecchi, F. *I medaglioni romani*, III, Milan, 1912.

Graindor, P. 'Etudes sur l'ephèbe attique sous l'empire', *Musée belge*, XXVI, 1922, 165–225.

Graindor, P. *Un milliardaire antique: Hérode Atticus et sa famille*, Cairo, 1930.

Graindor, P. 'Inscriptions de la necropole de Touna-el-Chebel (Hermopolis), *Bull. Inst. Fr. Arch. Or.*, XXXII, 1932, 97–110.

Graindor, P. *Athènes sous Hadrien*, Cairo, 1934.

Gregorovius, F. *The Emperor Hadrian*, London, 1898.

Grenade, P. 'Le règlement successoral d'Hadrien', *REA*, LII, 1950, 258–77.

Greppo, J. G. H. *Mémoire sur les voyages de l'Empereur Hadrien*, Paris, 1842.

Gross, W. H. 'Zu den Münzbildnissen des Antinous', *Wiss. Abh. deut. Numis. Gottingen*, 1959, 39–45.

Grosskurth, P. *John Addington Symonds*, London, 1964.

Guarducci, M. 'Adriano e i culti misterica della Grecia', *Bull. Mus. Imp. Rom.*, XII, 1941, in *Bull. Comm. Arch. Gov. Rom.*, LXIX, 1949, 149–58.

Guarducci, M. 'La religione di Adriano', in *Les empereurs romains d'Espagne*, Paris, 1965, 209–19.

Guey, J. 'Encore la pluie miraculeuse', *Rev. de Philol.* XXII, 1948, 27–8.

Guida, P. 'Piastrelle votive del museo di Aquileia', *Aquileia Nostra*, XXXVI, 1965, 38–42.

Gusman, P. *La villa impériale de Tibur*, Paris, 1904.

Hahland, W. 'Ebertöter Antinous-Androcles', *JOAI*, XLI, 1954, 54–77.

Hamilton, G. *Letters*, ed. Lord E. Fitzmaurice, Devizes, 1879.

Hammond, M. 'Composition of the Senate', *JRS*, XLVII, 1957, 74–81.

Hammond, M. *The Antonine monarchy*, Rome, 1959.

Hammond, M. 'The Antonine monarchy', in *Aufstieg*, II (2), 329–53.

Hannestad, N. 'The portraits of Aelius Caesar', *Analecta Romana*, VII, 1974, 67–100.

Harrison, E. B. *The Athenian agora. I; Portrait sculpture*, Princeton, 1953.

Harrison, E. B. 'New sculpture from the Athenian agora', *Hesp.*, XXIX, 1960, 367–92.

Hastings, J. (ed.). *Encyclopaedia of religion and ethics*, New York, 1908.

Heilmeyer, W. D. 'Apollodorus von Damascus, der Architekt des Pantheons', *JDAI*, XC, 1975, 316–41.

Heintze, H. von. *Antike Porträte im Schloss Fasanerie*, Mainz, 1967.

Heintze, H. von. 'Die Bildnisse des Antinous', *Gnomon*, XLIII, 1971, 393–8.

Heintze, H. von. *Römische Porträte*, Darmstadt, 1974.

Hekler, A. 'Beiträge zur Geschichte der antiken Panzerstatuen', *JOAI*, XIX–XX, 1919, 219ff.

Henderson, B. W. *The life and principate of the Emperor Hadrian, 76–138*, London, 1923.

Hermann, A. 'Antinous infelix', in *Mullus, Festschrift für Th. Klauser, Jahrb. Ant. Christ.*, Erganz. 1, 1964, 155–67.

Hoffa, W. 'Die Löwenjagd des Kaiser Hadrian', *Röm. Mitt.* XXVII, 1912, 97–100.

Hohl, E. 'Über die Glaubwürdigkeit der Historia Augusta', *Sitz. deut. Akad. Wiss. Berlin*, II, 1953, 38–48.

Holm, E. *Das Bildnis des Antinous*, Würzburg, 133.

Homolle, T. 'Découvertes de Delphes', *Gaz. Beaux Arts*, Dec. 1894, 441–54.

Hopfner, T. *Fontes historiae religionis Aegyptiacae*, Bonn, 1922.

Hülsen, C. 'Das Grab des Antinous', *Röm. Mitt.* XI, 1896, 122–9.

Hülsen, C. 'Das Grab des Antinous?' *Berliner Philologische Wochenschrift*, XXXIX, 1919, 259–64.

Inan, J. and Rosenbaum, E. *Roman and early Byzantine portrait sculpture in Asia Minor*, London, 1966.

Inan, J. and Alföldi-Rosenbaum, E. *Römische und frühbyzantinische Porträtplastik aus der Turkei*, Mainz, 1979.

Istituto di Studi de Vicino Oriente, Univ. di Roma, *Ser. Arch.*, XXI, 1974, 'Antinoë, 1965–8'.

Iversen, E. *Obelisks in exile*, I, Copenhagen, 1968.

Iwas, W. 'Das Kompositionschema der Gruppe Ildefonso', *Wiss. Zeit. Humboldt Univ. Berlin*, XXV, 1976, 485–8.

Jacobsthal, P. 'Eine Gussform mit dem Bilde des Antinous', *Z. Ägypt. Spr. Alt.*, XLII, 1905, 76–8.

Johnson, J. de M. 'Antinoë and its papyri', *JEA*, I, 1914, 168–81.

Jomard, E. 'Description d'Antinoë', chap. XV, *Description d'Egypte*, II, Paris, 1818.

Jones, A. H. M. *The cities of the eastern Roman provinces*, Oxford, 1937.

Jones, A. H. M. *The Greek city*, Oxford, 1940.

Jones, A. H. M. 'The Greeks under the Roman empire', in *The Roman Economy*, ed. P. A. Brunt, Oxford, 1974.

Jones, C. P. 'Sura and Senecio', *JRS*, LX, 1970, 98–104.

Jordan, H. *Topographie der Stadt Rom in Alterthum*, Berlin, 1907.

Jouguet, P. *La vie municipale dans l'Egypte romaine*, Paris, 1911.

Jouguet, P. 'Notes épigraphiques', *Ann. Inst. de Philol. et d'Hist. Or.*, III, 1931, 227–33.

Jucker, H. *Das Bildnis im Blätterkelch*, Lausanne, 1961.

Jucker, H. 'Aegyptiaca', *Jhrb. Bern. Hist. Mus.*, XLI–II, 1961–2, 289–330.

Kähler, H. *Hadrian und seine Villa bei Tivoli*, Berlin, 1950.

Kähler, H. 'Zur Herkunft des Antinous-Obelisken', *Acta ad Arch. et Art. Hist. Pert.*, VI, 1975, 35–44.

Kambitsis, S. 'Une nouvelle tablette magique d'Egypte', *BIFAO*, LXXVI, 1976, 213–23.

Karageorghis, V. *Sculptures from Salamis*, Nicosia, 1964.

Kiefer, O. *Sexual life in ancient Rome*, London, 1934.

Kienast, D. 'Hadrian, Augustus und die eleusinischen Mysterien', *Jhrb. Numis. Geldgesch.*, X, 1959, 61–9.

Kishor, S. I. *Magnificent Hadrian*, London, 1935.

Kornemann, E. *Kaiser Hadrian und der letzte grosse Historiker von Rom*, Leipzig, 1905.

Kraus, T. 'Das Bildnis des Antinoos', *Heidelberger Jhrb.*, III, 1959, 48–67.

Kraus, T. 'Die Basis des Epistrategen Fidus Aquila aus Antinoopolis', *Röm Mitt.*, LXIX, 1962, 128–35.

Kübler, B. *Antinoopolis*, Leipzig, 1914.

Kühn, E. *Antinoopolis. Ein Beitrag zur Geschichte des Hellenismus im römischen Ägypten*, Göttingen, 1913.

Laban, F. *Der Gemütsausdruck des Antinous*, Berlin, 1891.

Lanciani, R. *Pagan and Christian Rome*, London, 1892.

Lanciani, R. *Ruins and excavations of ancient Rome*, Boston, 1897.

Lanciani, R. *Wanderings in the Roman Campagna*, London, 1909.

Larsen, J. A. O. 'Cyrene and the Panhellenion', *Cl. Philol.*, XLVII, 1952, 7–16.

Lebek, W. D. 'Ein Hymnus auf Antinoos', *Z. Pap. Epigr.*, XII, 1973, 101–37.

Lefranc, G. *Le 'périple du Pont Euxine' d'Arrian*, Paris, 1939.

Le Glay, H. 'Hadrien et l'Asklepion de Pergame', *BCH*, C, 1976, 347–72.

Le Menestrier, J. B. *Médailles illustrées des anciens empereurs et impératrices de Rome*, Dijon, 1642.

Lenormant, F. 'L'Antinous d'Eleusis', *Rev. Arch.*, 1874, 217–19.

Levezow, K. *Über den Antinoos dargestellt in den Kunstdenkmälern des Alterthums*, Berlin, 1808.

Levi, A. 'Hadrian as king of Egypt', *Num. Chr.*, VIII, 1948, 30–8.

Lewis, N. 'Four Cornell Papyri', *Recherches de Papyrologie*, III, 1964, 25–6.

Liegle, J. *Der Zeus des Phidias*, Berlin, 1952.

Lindsay, J. *Daily life in Roman Egypt*, London, 1963.

Lindsay, J. *Leisure and pleasure in Roman Egypt*, London, 1965.

Lindsay, J. *Men and gods on the Roman Nile*, London, 1968.

Lippold, G. *Gemmen und Kameen des Altertums und der Neuzeit*, Stuttgart, 1922.

Lippold, G. *Kopien und Umbildungen griechischer Statuen*, Münich, 1923.

L'Orange, H. P. *Der spätantike Bildschmuck des Konstantinsbogens*, Berlin, 1939.

Lugli, G. *The classical monuments of Rome and its vicinity*, Rome, 1929.

Lugli, G. *I monumenti antichi di Roma*, III, Rome, 1938.

Lugli, G. *Itinerario di Roma antica*, Milan, 1970.

MacKendrick, P. *The mute stones speak*, London, 1962.

Magie, D. *Roman rule in Asia Minor*, Princeton, 1950.

Magnaguti, A. *Hadrianus in nummis*, London, 1934.

Majewski, K. 'Brazowe balsamaria antropomorficzne w cesarstwie rzymskim', *Archaelogia*, XIV, 1963, 95–126.

Malaise, M. *Les conditions de pénétration et de diffusion des cultes égyptiens en Italie*, Leiden, 1972.

Marconi, P. 'Antinoo. Saggio sull'arte dell'età adrianea'. *Mon. Ant. R. Accad. Lincei*, XXIX, 1923, 161–305.

Marrou, H.-I. *Histoire de l'éducation dans l'antiquité*, 6th edit., Paris, 1965.

Marucchi, O. *Gli obelischi egiziani di Roma*, Rome, 1898.

Maspero, J. and Wiet, G. *Matériaux pour servir à la géographie de l'Egypte*, Paris, 1919.

Mattingly, H. *Coins of the Roman empire in the British Museum*, III, London, 1936.

Maull, I. 'Hadrians Jagddenkmal', *JAOI*, XLII, 1955, 53–67.

Maza, F. de la. *Antinoo: el ultimo dios del mundo clasico*, Mexico, 1966.

Méautis, G. *The mysteries of Eleusis*, Madras, 1932.

Meier, M. H. E. *Histoire de l'amour grecque dans l'antiquité*, Paris, 1930.

Mendel, G. 'Inscriptions de Bithynie', *BCH*, XXVII, 1903, 314–33.

Merivale, C. *A history of the Romans under the empire*, VII, London, 1862.

Metcalf, W. E. 'Hadrian, Jovis Olympius', *Mnemosyne*, XXVII, 1974, 59–66.

Millar, F. G. B., 'Epictetus and the imperial court', *JRS*, LV, 1965, 141–8.

Millar, F. G. B. *A study of Cassius Dio*, Oxford, 1964.

Millin, A. L. *Monuments antiques, inédits*, II, Paris, 1806.

Milne, J. G. *History of Egypt under Roman Rule*, 3rd edit., London, 1924.

Moll, A. *Les perversions de l'instinct génital*, Paris, 1897.

Momigliano, A. *Studies in historiography*, London, 1966.

Mommsen, T. *De collegiis et sodaliciis*, Kiliae, 1848.

Mommsen, T. *Römisches Strafrecht*, Leipzig, 1899.

Mommsen, T. *Gesammelte Schriften*, I, Berlin, 1905, 422–8.

Montfaucon, B. de. *Antiquités expliques*, suppl., II, 1719; III, 1724.

Moreau, P. *Des aberrations du sens gérésique*, Paris, 1887.

Morenz, S. 'Zur Vergöttlichung in Ägypten', *Z. Ägyp. Spr. Alt.*, LXXXIV, 1959, 132–43.

Moretti, L. *Inscriptiones graecae urbis Romae*, Rome, 1968.

Müller, W. M. 'Zum Obelisk des Antinous', *Z. Ägyp. Spr. Alt.*, XXVI, 1898, 131–2.

Musurillo, H. A. *Acts of the pagan martyrs*, Oxford, 1954.

Mylonas, G. *Eleusis and the Eleusinian mysteries*, Princeton, 1961.

Nash, E. 'Obelisk und Circus', *Röm Mitt*, LXIV, 1957, 232–54.

Nicosius, C. *De nummio pantheo Hadriani imperatoris*, Lugdunum, 1689.

Nilsson, M. P. *Geschichte der griechischen Religionen*, II, 2nd edit., Munich, 1961.

Oliver, J. H. 'Documents concerning the Emperor Hadrian', *Hesp.*, X, 1941, 61–90, 361–70.

Oliver, J. H. 'Hadrian's precedent, the alleged initiation of Philip II', *AJPh*, LXXI, 1950, 295–9.

Oliver, J. H. 'New evidence on the Attic panhellenion', *Hesp.*, XX, 1951, 31–3. (1951, a.)

Oliver, J. H. 'Athenian citizenship of Roman Emperors', *Hesp.*, XX, 1951, 346–9. (1951, b.)

Oliver, J. H. 'The ruling power: the Roman oration of Aristeides', *Tr. Am. Philos. Soc.*, XCIII (4), 1953.

Oliver, J. H. 'The Athens of Hadrian', in *Les empereurs romains d'Espagne*, Paris, 1965, 123–33.

Oliver, J. H. 'The civilizing power: the Panathenaic discourses of Aristeides', *Tr. Am. Philos. Soc.*, LVIII (I), 1968.

Oliver, J. H. 'Marcus Aurelius: aspects of civic and cultural policy in the east', *Hesp.*, Suppl., XIII, 1970.

Oliver, J. H. 'Panacheans and Panhellenes', *Hesp.*, XLVII, 1978, 185–91.

Orgeval, B. d'. *L'empereur Hadrien. Oeuvre legislative et administrative*, Paris, 1950.

Page, D. L. (ed.). *Select papyri*, III, London, 1970.

Parke, H. W. *The oracles of Zeus*, Oxford, 1967.

Pauly-Wissowa. *Real-encyclopaedie der classischen Altertumswisssenschaft*, 1893–.

Perdrizet, P. *Les terres cuites grecques d'Egypte*, Nancy, 1921.

Perowne, S. *Hadrian*, London, 1960.

Perowne, S. *The Caesars' wives*, London, 1974.

Pflaum, H.-G. 'Le règlement successoral d'Hadrien', *HA Colloq.*, Bonn, 1963, 95–122.

Pickard-Cambridge, A. W. *The theatre of Dionysos in Athens*, Oxford, 1946.

Pistorius, P. V. *Indices Antinoopolitani*, Leiden, 1939.

Platner, S. B. *The topography and monuments of ancient Rome*, Boston, 1911.

Plew, J. *Quellenuntersuchungen zur Geschichte des Kaisers Hadrians*, Strasbourg, 1890.

Poland, F. *Geschichte des griechischen Vereinswesens*, Leipzig, 1909.

Polverini, L. *Le città dell'impero nell'epistolario di Plinio*, Milan, 1963.

Poulsen, F. *Delphi*, London, 1920.

Preisendanz, K. *Papyri graecae magicae*, 1, 2nd edit., Stuttgart, 1973.

Pückler-Muskau, Prince. *Egypt under Mehemet Ali*, I, London, 1845.

Radermacher, L. 'Der Dichter Pancrates', *Berl. Phil. Woch.*, XXXVI, 1916, 883–4.

Radet, G. 'Le pélérinage au sanctuaire d'Amon', *REA*, XXVIII, 1926, 211–40.

Radnoti, A. *Die römischen Bronzegefässe von Pannonien*, Budapest, 1938.

Raffalavin, M.-A. *Uranisme et unisexualisme*, Lyons, 1896.

Raubitschek, A. 'Hadrian as son of Zeus Eleutherios', *AJA*, XLIX, 1945, 128–33.

Reinach, S. Review of Dietrichson, *Rev. Crit. Hist. Lit.*, XIX, 11 May 1885.

Reinach, S. 'Les têtes des médallions de l'arc de Constantin à Rome', *Rev. Arch.*, XV, 1910, 118–31.

Reitzenstein, R. *Hellenistische Wundererzählungen*, Leipzig, 1906.

Reynolds, J. M. and Ward-Perkins, J. B. *The inscriptions of Roman Tripolitania*, London, 1952.

Richter, G. 'Who made the Roman portrait statues?', *Procs. Am. Philos. Soc.*, XCV (2), 1951, 184–91.

Richter, G. 'How were the Roman copies of Greek portraits made?', *Röm Mitt.*, LXIX, 1962, 52–5.

Riencourt, C. *Dissertations sur le culte que les grecs et romains ont rendu à Antinous*, Paris, 1723.

Riis, P. J. 'Two overlooked portraits of Antinous', *Acta Arch.*, XVI, 1945, 175–8.

Rizzo, G. E. 'Antinoo-Silvano', *Ausonia*, III, 1908, 3–16.

Robert, L. 'Notes et discussions', *Rev. Phil.*, XVII, 1943, 176–201.

Robert, L. 'Un médallion d'Asie Mineure', *Hellenica*, VII, 1949, 194–6.

Robert, L. 'Bulletin épigraphique', *REG*, LXV, 1952, 190–3.

Robert, L. 'Deux Inscriptions de l'époque impériale en Attique', *AJPh*, C 1979, 160–5.

Robinson, D. M. and Fluck, E. J. *A study of Greek love names*, Baltimore, 1937.

Roeder, G. *Hermopolis 1929–39*, Hildesheim, 1959.

Roullet, A. *The Egyptian and Egyptianising monuments of imperial Rome*, Leiden, 1972.

Rowe, A. 'Newly identified monuments in the Egyptian museum showing deification of the dead', *ASAE*, XL, 1940, 1–67, 291–9.

Rydberg, V. *Roman days*, New York, 1879.

Salmi, M. 'I dipinti paleocristiani di Antinoe', in *Scrit. Mem. Ipp. Rosellini*, 157–69.

Salmon, E. T. *History of the Roman world 30 BC–138 AD*, London, 1957.

Salzman, E. 'Kaiser Hadrian und das Problem seiner Persönlichkeit', *Neue Jhrb. Wiss. Jug.*, II, 1921, 520–8.

Schefold, K. 'Afrodite von Knidos, Isis und Serapis', *Ant. Kunst*, VII, 1964, 56–9.

Schiller, H. *Geschichte der römischen Kaiserzeit*, I, Gotha, 1883–7.

Schulz, O. T. *Leben des Kaisers Hadrian*, Leipzig, 1904.

Schwartz, J. 'Un prefet d'Egypte frappé de "damnatio memoriae" . . .', *C d'E.*, LIII, 1952, 254–6.

Schwartz, J. Review of Follet, 1968, *C d'E.*, LXXXVII, 1969, 164–8.

Seltman, C. 'Greek sculpture and some festival coins', *Hesp.*, XVII, 1948, 71–85.

Shear, T. L. 'Excavations in the Athenian agora', *Hesp.*, II, 1933, 178–82.

Sherwin-Bailey, D. *Homosexuality in the western Christian tradition*, London, 1955.

Sieveking, J. *Die Bronzen der Sammlung Loeb*, Munich, 1913.

Sigard, J. in Stocklein, *Brief, q.v.* Letter no. 251, 1 June 1716.

Sijpesteijn. P. J. 'A new document concerning Hadrian's visit to Egypt', *Historia*, XVIII, 1969, 107–18.

Smallwood, E. M. *Documents illustrating the principates of Nerva, Trajan and Hadrian*, Cambridge, 1966.

Smallwood, E. M. *The Jews under Roman rule*, Leiden, 1976.

Squarciapino, M. *La scuola di Afrodisia*, Rome, 1943.

Stahr, A. *Torso*, II, Braunschweig, 1855.

Starcky, J. *Palmyre*, Paris, 1952.

Steinmeyer-Schareika, A. *Das Nilmosaik von Palestrina*, Bonn, 1978.

Stinespring, W. F. 'Hadrian in Palestine 129–30', *Jnl. Am. Or. Soc.*, LIX, 1939, 360–5.

Stöcklein, J. *Brief von den Missionariis der Gesellschaft Jesu*, X, 1727.

Strack, P. *Untersuchungen zur römischen Reichspragung des zweiten Jahrhunderts*, II, Stuttgart, 1933.

Strong, Mrs. A. (E). *Roman sculpture*, London, 1907.

Strong, D. E. *Roman imperial sculpture*, London, 1961.

Sweet, C. 'Dedication of the Canopus at Hadrian's villa', *AJA*, LXXVII, 1973, 229.

Syme, Sir R. 'Vibius Maximus, prefect of Egypt', *Historia*, VI, 1957, 480–7.

Syme, Sir R. 'Antonine relatives, Ceionii and Vettuleni', *Athenaeum*, XXXV, 1957, 306–15.

Syme, Sir R. 'The Greeks under Roman rule', *Procs. Mass. Hist. Soc.*, LXXII, 1957–60, 3–20; references to reprint in *Roman papers, q.v.*, 566–81.

Syme, Sir R. *Tacitus*, Oxford, 1958.

Syme, Sir R. 'Hadrian and Italica', *JRS*, LIV, 1964, 142–9.

Syme, Sir R. 'Hadrian the intellectual', in *Les empereurs romains d'Espagne*, Paris, 1965, 243–53.

Syme, Sir R. *Ammianus and the Historia Augusta*, Oxford, 1968.

Syme, Sir R. 'The Ummidii', *Historia*, XVII, 1968, 72–105, references from reprint in *Roman papers*, II, 659–93 (1979).

Syme, Sir R. *Emperors and biography*, Oxford, 1971.

Syme, Sir R. 'Astrology in the *Historia Augusta*', *HA Colloq.*, 1972–4, 291–309.

Syme, Sir R. *Roman Papers*, ed. E. Badian, Oxford, 1979.

Symonds, J. A. *Sketches and studies in Italy*, 1879.

Symonds, J. A. *A problem in Greek ethics*, London, 1908 edit.

Taylor, G. (pseud. for A. Hausrath), *Antinous – an historical romance of the Roman empire*, London, 1884.

Temporini, H. *Die Frauen am Hofe Trajans*, Berlin, 1978.

Thompson, D. L. 'Antinoopolis painter J', *AJA*, LXXVII, 1973, 437–8.

Thornton, M. K. 'Hadrian and his reign', in *Aufstieg*, *q.v.*, 432–76.

de Tillemont, *Histoire des empereurs*, II, 2nd edit., Paris, 1702.

Tod, M. N. 'Greek inscriptions from Macedonia', *JHS*, XLII, 1922, 167–83.

Tod, M. N. 'An ephebic inscription from Memphis', *JEA*, XXXVII, 1951, 86–99.

Tournemine, D. K. 'Explication d'une cornaline du cabinet de Mr Masson', *Mémoires pour l'histoire des sciences et des beaux arts*, Mars, 1713, 427–31.

Toynbee, J. M. C. *The Hadrianic school: a chapter in the history of Greek art*, Cambridge, 1934.

Toynbee, J. M. C. 'Greek imperial medallions', *JRS*, XXXIV, 1944, 65–73.

Toynbee, J. M. C. 'Some notes on artists in the Roman world', *Latomus*, VI, 1951.

Toynbee, J. M. C. Review of Clairmont, *JRS*, LVII, 1967, 267–8.

Travlos, J. *Pictorial dictionary of ancient Athens*, London, 1971.

Tristan, J. *Commentaires historiques*, I, Paris, 1644.

Uggeri, G. 'La chiesa paleocristiana presso la porta orientale', in *Ist. Stud. Vic. Or.*, *q.v.*, 37–63.

Uggeri, G. 'Mosaico con stagione aucupium', *ibid.*, 125–6.

Uggeri, G. 'Antinoo', *ibid.*, 129–32.

Unger, E. de. *To Antinous*, Ilfracombe, 1960.

Valera, G. 'Una tradizione Ceionia nella Historia Augusta', *RAAN*, XL, 1973, 135–94.

Van Groningen, B. A. 'Preparatives for Hadrian's visit to Egypt', in *Studi in Onore di A. Calderini e R. Paribeni*, Milan, II, 1957, 253–6.

Vermeule, C. C. 'Notes on a new edition of Michaelis', *AJA*, LIX, 1955; LX, 1956; with von Bothmer, D., LXIII, 1959.

Vermeule, C. C. 'Hellenistic and Roman cuirassed statues', *Berytus*, XIII, 1959; XV, 1964, supp. I; XVI, 1966.

Vermeule, C. C. 'Antinous, favourite of the Emperor Hadrian', *Nelson Gall. and Atkins Mus. Bull.*, III, 1960, 1–7.

Vermeule, C. C. *Roman imperial art in Greece and Asia Minor*, Harvard, 1968.

Vermeule, C. C. Review of Clairmont, *AJA*, LXXIII, 1969, 488–9.

Vidman, L. *Etude sur la correspondance de Pline le jeune avec Trajan*, Paris, 1960.

Viereck, P. *Griechische Ostraka*, I, Berlin, 1923.

Vogt, J. *Die alexandrinischen Münzen*, I, Stuttgart, 1924.

Wainwright, G. A. *The sky religion in Egypt*, Cambridge, 1938.

Walker, F. G. *Num. Chron.*, VIII, 1908, 375.

Walton, F. R. 'Religious thought in the age of Hadrian', *Numen*, IV, 1957, 165–70.

Waters, K. H. 'The character of Domitian', *Phoenix*, XVIII, 1964, 60–1.

Waters, K. H. 'Trajan's character – the literary tradition', in *Polis and Imperium: studies in honour of E. T. Salmon*, ed. J. A. S. Evans, Toronto, 1974, 233–52.

Waters, K. H. 'Trajan', in *Aufstieg*, *q.v.*, II (2), 381–431.

Weber, H. 'Eine spätgriechische Jünglingsstatue', in *Bericht über die Ausgrabungen in Olympia*, ed. E. Kunze, Berlin, 1956, 128–48.

Weber, I. *Antiquitates Antinoi*, Giessen, 1707.

Weber, W. *Untersuchungen zur Geschichte des Kaisers Hadrianus*, Leipzig, 1907.

Weber, W. *Drei Untersuchungen zur ägyptisch-griechischen Religion*, Heidelberg, 1911.

Weber, W. 'Hadrian', in *CAH*, XI, 1936.

Weber, W. *Herrschertum und Reich*, Stuttgart, 1937.

Wegner, M. *Das römische Herrscherbild: Hadrian* . . . Berlin, 1956.

Wessel, K. *Coptic art*, London, 1965.

West, R. *Römische Porträt-Plastik*, II, Munich, 1941.

Wheeler, G. L. 'The occasion of Arrian's Tactica', *GRBS*, XIX, 1978, 351–65.

Wilcken, U. *Grundzüge und Chrestomathie der Papyruskunde*, Berlin, 1912.

Wilcken, U. *Archiv für Papyrusforschung*, 1920, VI, Berlin and Leipzig; IX, 1930, Berlin and Leipzig.

Williams, G. *Tradition and originality in Roman poetry*, Oxford, 1968.

Winckelmann, J. *Geschichte der Kunst des Alterthums*, Dresden, 1764.

Winckelmann, J. *Anmerkungen über die Geschichte der Kunst des Alterthums*, Dresden, 1767.

Winckelmann, J. *Monumenti antichi inediti*, Rome, 1767.

Woodward, A. M. 'The cistophoric series and its place in the Roman coinage', in *Essays to H. Mattingly*, ed R. A. G. Carson and C. H. V. Sutherland, Oxford, 1956.

Yourcenar, M. *Mémoires d'Hadrien*, Gallimard edit., Paris, 1974.

Zayed, A. 'Some miscellaneous objects found in the neighbourhood of El Kharga oasis', *ASAE*, LVII, 1962, 125–30.

INDEX